FEAR OF THE FALSE

Series editor: Elizabeth S. Anker, Cornell University

CORPUS JURIS: THE HUMANITIES IN POLITICS AND LAW PUBLISHES BOOKS AT THE INTERSECTIONS BETWEEN LAW, POLITICS, AND THE HUMANITIES—INCLUDING HISTORY, LITERARY CRITICISM, ANTHROPOLOGY, PHILOSOPHY, RELIGIOUS STUDIES, AND POLITICAL THEORY. BOOKS IN THIS SERIES TACKLE NEW OR UNDER-ANALYZED ISSUES IN POLITICS AND LAW AND DEVELOP INNOVATIVE METHODS TO UNDERTAKE THOSE INQUIRIES. THE GOAL OF THE SERIES IS TO MULTIPLY THE INTERDISCIPLINARY JUNCTURES AND CONVERSATIONS THAT SHAPE THE STUDY OF LAW.

FEAR OF THE FALSE

Forensic Science and the Law of Crime in Colonial South Asia

Mitra Sharafi

CORNELL UNIVERSITY PRESS ITHACA AND LONDON

Open Access publication of this book was made possible by research funding from the University of Wisconsin Law School.

First published 2026 by Cornell University Press

Librarians: A CIP catalog record for this book is available from the Library of Congress.

ISBN 9781501785979 (hardcover)
ISBN 9781501785986 (paperback)
ISBN 9781501786006 (pdf)
ISBN 9781501785993 (epub)

GPSR EU contact: Sam Thornton, Mare Nostrum Group B.V., Mauritskade 21D, 1091 GC, Amsterdam, NL, gpsr@mare-nostrum.co.uk.

For my nieces,
Sunniva and Stella

CONTENTS

A NOTE ON TERMINOLOGY, CONTENTS, SOURCES, AND ABBREVIATIONS

I have mostly avoided the use of diacriticals for terms in South Asian and Middle Eastern languages, instead using spellings that reflect pronunciation. References to sources in Gujarati and French are based on my own translations. For Bengali sources, I rely on translations by Anwesha Maity.

For the most part, I have used colonial versions and spellings of place names in South Asia (e.g., Madras, not Chennai). When referring to postcolonial cities, however, I use their postcolonial names with reference to these cities after their official name change (e.g., Mumbai, not Bombay, for a book published there post-1995).

This book contains accounts of extreme violence, including against women and girls. I have included them to adhere to the historical sources, although I have avoided the use of graphic visual images.

In this book, I describe stereotypes that were demeaning on a racial, cultural, and gendered basis, namely the concepts of native and female mendacity. I do so to accurately represent the sentiment conveyed by the historical actors described here. For the sake of readability, I do not in all instances put these phrases in quotation marks. I always refer to these concepts as they appear in the historical record, however; I am not endorsing or adopting these ideas myself.

With a few exceptions noted in the introduction, the experts in this study were male.

India Office Records, which are held at the British Library, are identifiable by shelf marks beginning with "IOR/." Although the annual reports of the chemical examiners (and chemical analysers) are printed and available at a number of institutions around the world, I have used the British Library's collection (IOR/V/24), which is the most complete.

ABBREVIATIONS

AAC	Asian and African Collections (British Library)
ABP	*Amrita Bazar Patrika*
AIR All.	*All India Reporter*, Allahabad
AIR Bom.	*All India Reporter*, Bombay
AIR Cal.	*All India Reporter*, Calcutta
AIR Lah.	*All India Reporter*, Lahore
AIR Lower Burma	*All India Reporter*, Lower Burma
AIR Mad.	*All India Reporter*, Madras
AIR Nag.	*All India Reporter*, Nagpur
AIR Oudh	*All India Reporter*, Oudh
AIR Rang.	*All India Reporter*, Rangoon
BHC	Bombay High Court (Mumbai)
BL	British Library (London)
BMJ	*British Medical Journal*
CA	chemical analyser
CE	chemical examiner
CIE	chief inspector of explosives
CrLJ	*Criminal Law Journal of India*
CrPC	Criminal Procedure Code
CWN	*Calcutta Weekly Notes*
DGIMS	director general, Indian Medical Service
FIR	First Information Report
GEQD	government examiner of questioned documents
HC	High Court
ICS	Indian Civil Service
IESHR	*Indian Economic and Social History Review*
ILR All.	*Indian Law Reports*, Allahabad series
ILR Bom.	*Indian Law Reports*, Bombay series
ILR Cal.	*Indian Law Reports*, Calcutta series
ILR Lah.	*Indian Law Reports*, Lahore series
ILR Mad.	*Indian Law Reports*, Madras series

IMCR	*Indian Medico-Chirurgical Review*
IMG	*Indian Medical Gazette*
IMS	Indian Medical Service
IOR	India Office Records (AAC, BL)
IPC	Indian Penal Code
IS	imperial serologist
JCPC	Judicial Committee of the Privy Council (London)
MANU/	Manupatra (case law database)
MAS	*Modern Asian Studies*
Moore NS	*Moore's Privy Council Cases, New Series*
MSS Eur	Private Papers (formerly European Manuscripts) (AAC, BL)
NAI	National Archives of India (Delhi)
PCMC	Parsi Chief Matrimonial Court (Bombay)
TI	*Times of India*
TL	*Times of London*

For a full list of citation abbreviations for colonial South Asian case law see my South Asian Legal History Resources website (last modified on April 19, 2023): https://salh.law.wisc.edu/about-me/citation-abbreviations-explained/.

INTRODUCTION /
Falsity and Forensic Science

Around 1900, the government of British India created a web of new institutions for the scientific detection of crime. An immense stream of body parts and fluids—including human and animal blood, semen, and organs—moved across South Asia for processing in regional hubs. In turn, analysts fanned out across the subcontinent to assess evidence from crime scenes. They examined everything from "poison pen" letters to book bombs.[1] Forensic science was booming worldwide, and what happened in South Asia was part of this global trend.[2] But there was also the fact that India and Burma were colonies: British officials were invested in the "native mendacity" stereotype, the idea that South Asians were constitutionally dishonest.[3] Driven by this deception anxiety, the new forensic analysts focused on uncovering the fake.[4] The idea was to detect or preempt perjury and forgery in the courtroom by relying on scientific tests and experts.[5] But in trying

1. See Frank Brewester, *Contested Documents and Forgeries* (Calcutta: Book, 1932), 109–10; and "Another Bomb Outrage. Machine in a Book," *Times of India* (*TI*), March 16, 1909.

2. For example, the government of Siam invested heavily in forensic infrastructure during this period. See Trais Pearson, *Sovereign Necropolis: The Politics of Death in Semi-Colonial Siam* (Cornell University Press, 2020), 10.

3. Vinay Lal, "Everyday Crime, Native Mendacity and the Cultural Psychology of Justice in Colonial India," *Studies in History* 15 (1999): 145–66.

4. I borrow the phrase "deception anxiety" from Christopher Hamlin, "Forensic Facts, the Guts of Rights," in *Global Forensic Cultures: Making Fact and Justice in the Modern Era*, ed. Christopher Hamlin and Ian Burney (Johns Hopkins University Press, 2019), 20.

5. Radhika Singha, "Settle, Mobilize, Verify: Identification Practices in Colonial India," *Studies in History* 16, no. 2 (2000): 178–79; and Elizabeth Kolsky, *Colonial Justice in British India: White Violence and the Rule of Law* (Cambridge University Press, 2010), 120, 129–35. On common types of forgery

to detect falsity *from without*, including evidence planted by colonized tricksters, these new systems enabled falsity *from within* through their treatment of experts. One group of government lab experts, in particular, was treated as unimpeachable: These figures were not required to appear in court. As fear of false evidence increased with respect to colonized people associated with crime, it decreased with regard to state experts, making wrongful convictions more likely. This structural feature of criminal trials lives on in South Asia today: The colonial-era legacy of unquestioned forensic experts is baked into criminal procedure.

This book sits at the junction of the history of law, science, and medicine, and also draws on historical studies of tricksters, scammers, and fraudsters. I use the theme of falsity to reflect on the question: *What was colonial about colonial forensics?* In other words, what difference did the context of colonialism make to forensic science and the law of crime? "Forensic science," which is broader than the earlier term "medical jurisprudence," means the application of science (presuming expertise) to matters of law, while the "law of crime" covers substantive criminal law, criminal procedure, and the law of evidence as it relates to crime.[6] Through the theme of falsity, I offer several answers. First, although the detection of falsity is a priority of criminal law generally, it loomed especially large in colonial India and Burma. Fear of the false was a deeply colonial anxiety rooted in racial and cultural difference, with gendered dimensions. This belief was not surprising, given the vast power imbalances, mistrust and resentment, and diversity of value systems that permeated colonial life. Fear of the false sprang from a sense of insecurity and a realization (perhaps subliminal) that sabotage was to be expected in a setting where colonizers sustained British rule through force and manipulation.[7] To borrow from James Baldwin in a different context, the fear came from the "guilty white imagination."[8] In South Asia, fear of the false exemplified what

---

involving hospital and birth registers, promissory notes, and land deeds see J. C. Adam, preface to *The Detection of Forgery, or, A Study in Handwriting*, by P. Ramanatha Aiyer and N. S. Ranganatha Aiyer (Trichonopoly: Dodson, 1927).

6. Christopher Hamlin and Ian Burney, "History of Forensic Science," in *Encyclopedia of Forensic Sciences*, ed. Max M. Houck (Elsevier, 2023), 3:169. Hamlin traces the earliest use of the phrase "forensic science" to 1899. Hamlin, "Forensic Facts," 5. Forensic science covered "medical jurisprudence" but extended beyond, including, for instance, the analysis of handwriting, explosives, and firearms. See also E. Claire Cage, *The Science of Proof: Forensic Medicine in Modern France* (Cambridge University Press, 2022), 6, and Katherine D. Watson, *Forensic Medicine in Western Society: A History* (Routledge, 2011), 4–6.

7. Only 0.07 percent of British India's population was European in 1901. Mitra Sharafi, *Law and Identity in Colonial South Asia: Parsi Legal Culture, 1772–1947* (Cambridge University Press, 2014), 104. See generally Harald Fischer-Tiné, ed., *Anxieties, Fear and Panic in Colonial Settings: Empires on the Verge of a Nervous Breakdown* (Palgrave Macmillan, 2016).

8. "James Baldwin Discusses Racism," *The Dick Cavett Show*, May 16, 1969, accessed February 1, 2025, https://www.youtube.com/watch?v=WWwOi17WHpE.

Homi Bhabha calls the paranoia of power—a conviction that the "lying native" with their "sly civility" was covertly breaking the colonizers' rules.[9] It is also worth remembering that fear of the false grew against the backdrop of the 1857 mutiny, the largest anticolonial rebellion in British Indian history, which was brutally crushed and never forgotten on either side. The significant investment in forensic infrastructure circa 1900 was a response to a threat that was both imagined and real, both powered by bias *and* a reaction to subversion of the colonial system.

Of course, fear of the false was not the only force shaping forensic science in colonial South Asia. As the work of legal historian Binyamin Blum reveals, many forensic developments emerged from colonial contexts (including South Asia) because the British empire provided a sense of "necessity, opportunity, and inspiration" for forensic officials. For instance, the use of canine methods of detection and proof were pioneered in mandate Palestine and South Africa to suppress anticolonial activity and because dogs were particularly intimidating to resident populations.[10] While acknowledging the importance of such factors broadly, I focus in this book on the fear of falsity because it was *a* crucial driver of forensic developments in South Asia. In fact, it was a factor that fell within Blum's "necessity" category: The state invested in forensic institutions to root out the deception that was undermining colonial law.

Second, the processes established to bring science and medicine into the courtroom—to cut through mendacity and uncover truth in the service of a neutral vision of justice—looked different in the colonial context than in the imperial metropole. In particular, I focus on the figure of the protected and emboldened government lab expert. In India and Burma (unlike in England), a special class of forensic experts—state toxicologists known as chemical examiners (CEs)—submitted written evidence without having to be cross-examined on their findings under oath. For most of the period covered in this book, this rule was enshrined in s.510 of the Criminal Procedure Code (CrCP) of 1882 and 1898. CEs' written reports, which were occasionally vague or misleading, could exert tremendous influence.[11] This system made it harder for judges and lawyers to identify errors and misconduct by forensic experts themselves. Unlike in modern democracies, where the "rule of expert truth" (including scientific knowledge) normatively stands in productive tension with the "rule of majority

9. Homi K. Bhabha, *The Location of Culture* (Routledge, 1994), 99–100.

10. See, by Binyamin Blum, "From Bedouin Trackers to Doberman Pinschers: The Rise of Dog Tracking as Forensic Evidence in Palestine," in Hamlin and Burney, *Global Forensic Cultures*, 205–34; and "Forensic Empire: How Colonialism Shaped the Forensic Sciences," paper presented at the Global Forensic Histories workshop, virtual, March 26, 2021, 5.

11. For instance see untitled, *Amrita Bazar Patrika* (*ABP*), July 8, 1886.

instincts" (governed by the "common sense" of the voting public), British India and Burma were ruled by colonial authoritarianism.[12] The unusual, unchecked power of CEs was consistent with this larger political reality. In short, this book examines how the colonial context affected the interaction of law and science through the quest to root out falsity. Colonizers' fear of the false accelerated the turn to forensic experts. But this move facilitated a different kind of falsity—by forensic experts themselves.

Relatedly, this book also reflects on criminal trials across South Asia today. Section 329 of India's criminal procedure statute today (formerly s.510 of CrPC, 1882 and 1898) is a vestige of India's colonial-era forensic heyday.[13] According to this rule, the written report (formerly certificate) of an approved scientific expert (formerly CE) constitutes evidence in and of itself. Unlike other experts, these figures do not need to be cross-examined under oath on their written findings.[14] This rule has persisted owing to institutional inertia. It was created for the convenience of colonial experts—to minimize disruption to their lab tests caused by travel—and has continued even when circumstances changed.[15] Such structural features are not examples of legal transplants, but of colonial divergence: The colonial state cut corners in ways that compromised basic procedural safeguards and would not have been tolerated in the imperial metropole. This makeshift, improvised system was *not* a replica of the English legal system. The historical story of how s.329 came to be exposes the flaws in the "railroads and rule of law" argument made by apologists of empire today and in the past. While some downplay the horrors of imperialism by arguing that (at least) British rule brought reliable transportation and law to India, this book shows that an important feature of criminal procedure was, and still is, fundamentally unsound.[16] I am not suggesting that the rule-of-law agenda was not important as a set of values to aspire to (it was, and was used by the nationalist movement to critique British

---

12. On the US today see Sophia Rosenfeld, *Democracy and Truth: A Short History* (University of Pennsylvania Press, 2019).

13. A revised version of India's Criminal Procedure Code (CrPC, 1973) entered into force on July 1, 2024. The new statute is called the Bharatiya Nagarik Suraksha Sanhita (BNSS, no. 46 of 2023). The special rule for experts (now BNSS s.329) was formerly s.370 of CrPC, 1861; s.325 of CrPC, 1872; s.510 of CrPC, 1882 and 1898; and s.293 of CrPC, 1973.

14. See chapter 4 for the full text of CrPC s.510 (1882).

15. See Mitra Sharafi, "Trial by Certificate: Scientific Experts and Bharatiya Nagarik Suraksha Sanhita s.329" (in progress).

16. See Edward Thompson and G. T. Garratt, *Rise and Fulfilment of British Rule in India* (Allahabad: Central Book Depot, 1962), 654; and Peter Mitchell, *Imperial Nostalgia: How the British Conquered Themselves* (University of Manchester Press, 2021).

rule in India).[17] Rather, I argue that one key aspect of criminal procedure in the colony did not conform to rule-of-law requirements as applied in the imperial metropole.

Finally, this book is about testing and wrongful convictions in the colonial context. Fear of the false was a driver for the development of key techniques in forensic science. The precipitin test, which determined the species of origin of a bloodstain, was perfected in colonial South Asia, responding to the suspicion that animal blood was being planted to frame rivals for murder and rape. The CEs pioneered a method of detecting snake venom in rags inserted rectally to poison cattle, guessing that these animals were not simply dying of illness. Fear of the false stimulated forensic development in these ways, but with it came a heightened trust of state lab experts, and this was regressive, particularly when lax legal tests interacted with scientific ones. By allowing CEs not to appear in court, Indian law created a disincentive for lab tests to be done well. This special rule did not exist in England at the time, and it heightened the risk of wrongful convictions in South Asia.

Crimes of Falsity

"Crimes of falsity" included a large and ingenious variety of offenses. A catalog of trickery filled the pages of B. N. Banerjee's *Aids to the Investigation of Professional Crime* (1920), for instance. The author described everything from false coining, impersonation, theft by drugging, and the maiming of livestock to the fraudulent claims of mystic healers and love doctors along with swindles involving railway tickets and telegrams.[18] Crimes of falsity included cons to polish household silver items: Door-to-door swindlers would steal a thin layer of silver by immersing silver items in a nitric acid bath, which they presented to the article's owner as a cleaning solution.[19] It included scams such as boxes with secret, spring-loaded photographic compartments that appeared to double one's paper money but in fact returned photos.[20] Reflecting stereotypes about mendacity held by colonial elites (both British and Indian), Banerjee described many of these crimes as the

17. See Mitra Sharafi, "Indian Constitutionalism, the Rule of Law, and Parsi Legal Culture," *Indian Law Review* 7, no. 3 (2023): 259–80.

18. B. N. Banerjee, *Aids to the Investigation of Professional Crime* (Calcutta: Taraprasanna Das Gupta at the Sanskrit Press, 1920).

19. "Annual Report of the CE to Government for Bengal, 1941," 11 (IOR/V/24/424).

20. "Annual Report of the CE and Bacteriologist to Government and the North-Western Provinces and Oudh, and of the Central Provinces for the Year 1900," 1 (IOR/V/24/414).

specialty of particular tribal, lower-caste, and Muslim "criminal" communities. Crimes of falsity involved seemingly inexhaustible forms of manipulation and exploitation, but also innovation and creativity. They simultaneously inspired disapproval and horror, fascination and respect.

In one transportation scam from Bengal in 1940, tins of ghee (clarified butter) sent by rail were full of nothing but water by the time they arrived at their destination. To try to catch the scammer, samples of water from stations the shipments passed through were tested, but the scammer was a railway worker who was "sufficiently intelligent to foresee the danger of using water from the water supply of his station." He slipped through because he used a different water source from those along his route.[21]

"Shamming" could also involve one's own body. A knocked-out tooth counted as "grievous hurt" under the Indian Penal Code (IPC), and a man was tried for selling his "particularly fine loose tooth" for use in fake grievous hurt cases.[22] In his famous *Textbook of Medical Jurisprudence and Toxicology*, J. P. Modi wrote about self-inflicted wounds and bruises used to falsely accuse others (figures 1 and 2), along with feigned insanity.[23] He described malingerers trying to avoid prison labor or responsibility for their own criminal conduct. In cases like these, feigned disease could look like genuine eye, digestive, reproductive, or nervous conditions. Ulcers, burns, bruises, or injuries of the internal organs could be fake or self-induced.[24]

The Indian Penal Code (IPC) covered an impressive array of crimes of falsity.[25] There were the classic crimes of sneakiness, such as giving false evidence (perjury), forgery, counterfeiting currency, impersonation, false charges, theft, and the use of false weights and measures or false trade and property marks. There was IPC s.420—inducing the delivery of property through cheating—which entered the popular lexicon: In many South Asian languages today, a "420" is a scammer and the inspiration for films, songs, and stories.[26] Several IPC

---

21. "Annual Report of the CE to Government for Bengal, 1940," 18 (IOR/V/24/424).

22. A. A. Irvine, "Some Notes of a Punjab Judge," *English Review*, March 1925, 358.

23. Jaising P. Modi, *A Textbook of Medical Jurisprudence and Toxicology*, 6th ed. (Bombay: Butterworth, 1940), 220–21, 261–63, 412–13.

24. Modi, *Medical Jurisprudence* (1940), 463.

25. For instance see, in Ratanlal Ranchhoddas and Dhirajlal Keshavlal Thakore, *The Indian Penal Code*, 11th ed. (Bombay Law Reporter Office, 1926), IPC ss.170–71, 181–82, 191–211, 229–67, 415–25, 428–40, and 463–89.

26. Radhika Singha, "Punished by Surveillance: Policing 'Dangerousness' in Colonial India, 1872–1918," *Modern Asian Studies* 48, no. 1 (2014): 2. For examples see the film *Shree 420* (dir. Raj Kapoor, 1955) and the song "Charso Bees (420)" by rapper Bohemia (2009). In Nigeria, the IPC s.420 counterpart is s.419, and "419" has also become popular shorthand for fraud. See Sam Fury Childs Daly, *A History of the Republic of Biafra: Law, Crime, and the Nigerian Civil War* (Cambridge University Press, 2020).

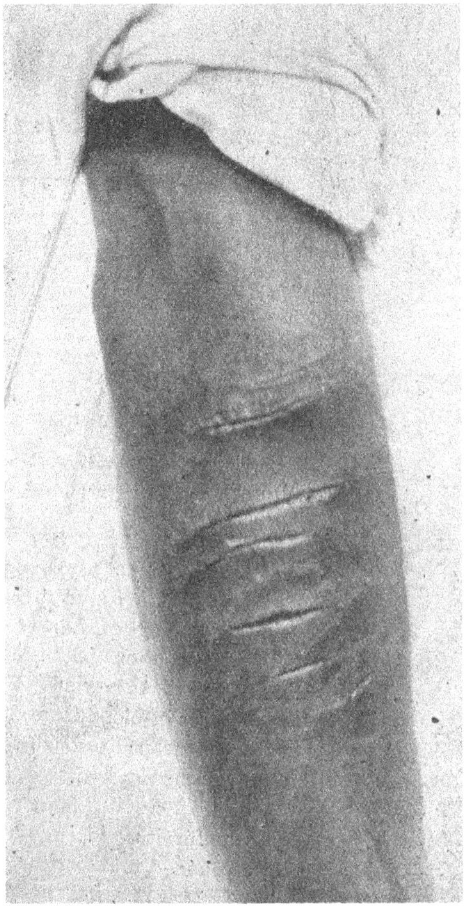

FIGURE 1. / "Self-inflicted wounds on forearm" of a "sweeper who complained that he was struck with a razor by his opponent." J. P. Modi, *A Textbook of Medical Jurisprudence and Toxicology* (Bombay: Butterworth, 1932), 317–18.

sections covered falsity by corrupt public officials. There was mischief, which could be anything from rendering a lighthouse useless to damaging agricultural produce through fire or explosives. Finally, a person who gave false evidence that caused an innocent person to be executed could themselves be sentenced to death.[27] By the early twentieth century, a formidable forensic infrastructure existed to expose crimes of falsity and scams.

27. On the death penalty see, by Alastair McClure, "Killing in the Name Of? Capital Punishment in Colonial and Postcolonial India," *Law and History Review* 41 (2023): 365–85, and *Trials of*

FIGURE 2. / "Feigned strangulation caused by the application to the neck of the juice of a marking nut." J. P. Modi, *A Textbook of Medical Jurisprudence and Toxicology* (Bombay: Butterworth, 1932), 203.

The discovery of such trickery required great skill. In 1940, for example, some insured bags sent by post were tampered with by cutting open their bottoms and then resealing them with wax. The CEs closed in on the culprit; they identified his location by testing the various sealing waxes at the post offices and mail vans that the bags had passed through.[28] To catch malingerers, J. P. Modi recommended that doctors propose "some heroic method of treatment" such as cauterization, major surgery, the application of an electrical current, a procedure called Liston's long splint, or the administration of "some nasty drug" like castor oil. In one case, a man pretending to have lost the ability to speak found his words on the operating table as "a big amputation knife was shown to him to

---

Sovereignty: Mercy, Violence, and the Making of Criminal Law in British India, 1857–1922 (Cambridge University Press, 2024), 145–232.

28. "Annual Report of the CE to Government, Bengal for 1940," 18–19 (IOR/V/24/424).

open his skull to find out the injury on his brain."[29] In short, crimes of falsity and their detection created a cat-and-mouse cycle of innovation, adjustment, and adaptation.

Native Mendacity

Colonial Britons widely believed in the idea of native mendacity, as Elizabeth Kolsky, Bhavani Raman, Wendie Schneider, and Chandak Sengoopta have documented.[30] One leading textbook on medical jurisprudence called false evidence "the great difficulty" of judges in India, devoting a chapter to the topic.[31] Similar to Homi Bhabha's notion of mimicry (whereby Britons were disturbed by South Asian mastery of Western manners), the suspicion that things were not as they seemed in the criminal legal system was part of the psychologically unsettling character of colonial life.[32]

Fear of the false was associated with class and gender in Britain, and in South Asia it was also heavily racialized.[33] Race-based stereotypes about lying existed in Britain too, but in South Asia these ideas were amplified because Europeans felt (and were) so outnumbered.[34] This anxiety was part of what Vinay Lal calls the "Orientalist grammar of India."[35] From forensic treatise authors such as Norman Chevers to High Court judges such as Cecil Walsh, comments were abundant

29. Modi, *Medical Jurisprudence* (1940), 463–64, 516, 640, 779. See also Robert Martin, "The Use of Liston's Long Splint in the Treatment of Fracture of the Femur," *Lancet* 210, no. 5433 (1927): 813–14. On malingering in the Indian military during World War I see Radhika Singha, *The Coolie's Great War: Indian Labor in a Global Conflict, 1914–1932* (Oxford University Press, 2020), 144, 278.

30. Kolsky, *Colonial Justice*, 108–41; Bhavani Raman, *Document Raj: Writing and Scribes in Early Colonial South India* (University of Chicago Press, 2012), 137–60; Wendie Ellen Schneider, *Engines of Truth: Producing Veracity in the Victorian Courtroom* (Yale University Press, 2015), 105–10; and Chandak Sengoopta, *Imprint of the Raj: How Fingerprinting Was Born in Colonial India* (Macmillan, 2003), 48–51.

31. Patrick Hehir and J. D. B. Gribble, eds., *Outlines of Medical Jurisprudence for India*, 5th ed. (Madras: Higginbotham, 1908), 28–35.

32. Bhabha, *Location of Culture*, 85–92.

33. On false claims by women relating to abortion, maternity, and rape in Britain see Alfred Swaine Taylor, *Principles and Practice of Medical Jurisprudence*, 8th ed., ed. Sydney Smith and W. G. H. Cook (London: J. & A. Churchill, 1928), 2:205, 238–42, 435, 450, and 466. On the view that female testimony was unreliable see Schneider, *Engines of Truth*, 206–8; and Hamlin and Burney, "History," 170. On the association of mendacity with lower-class Britons see Schneider, *Engines of Truth*, 5, 10, 18, 21, 29–31, 201–3. On racialized notions of mendacity in India see Lal, "Everyday Crime," 154–66.

34. Only 0.07 percent of the population of British India was European in 1901. Sharafi, *Law and Identity*, 104.

35. Lal, "Everyday Crime," 156.

about South Asians' inability or unwillingness to tell the truth, and the failure to value truth-telling and honesty generally.[36] For instance, the Viceroy Lord Curzon in a speech to Calcutta University students commented that truth as an ideal was "to a large extent a Western conception," as compared to "the East, where craftiness and diplomatic wile have always been held in high repute."[37] British detective fiction, which had deep roots in colonial India, used these same tropes.[38] By Wendie Schneider's account, Britons had "an unprecedented level of agreement among themselves" that perjury was ubiquitous.[39] As popular British writer Beverley Nichols wrote in 1944, after a trip to India: "Courage you must grant to the judges, steering a straight furrow through a jungle of falsehood, trickery, and vituperation."[40] The Calcutta High Court judge Torick Ameer Ali took Nichols to be speaking of British judges alone.[41] Experiments with oath-taking, including having Hindus swear on Ganges water, were examples of colonial attempts to induce truth-telling in the courtroom.[42] Most of all, the belief in native mendacity was driven by colonial racism and bias against South Asian cultures. It was an instance of Partha Chatterjee's "rule of colonial difference," the belief that the colonized population was inherently unlike and inferior to its British colonizers.[43]

In the medico-legal literature, stereotypes about deception were particularly evident in the context of poisoning, a crime deemed cowardly because physical violence was assumed to be nobler and fairer than chemical forms.[44] CEs reported that many South Asian poisoners had crude technique. They used far

36. Norman Chevers, *A Manual of Medical Jurisprudence for Bengal and the North-Western Provinces* (Calcutta, 1856), 7–8; and Cecil Walsh, *Indian Village Crimes with an Introduction on Police Investigation and Confessions* (London: Ernest Benn, 1929), 16–17; and *Crime in India with an Introduction on Forensic Difficulties and Peculiarities* (London: Ernest Benn, 1930), 9.

37. Curzon cited in Torick Ameer Ali, *Echoes of British India* (uncorrected proofs), 116–17, in "Memoirs and Articles by Sir Torick Ameer Ali (1891–1975)" (MSS Eur C336/2). For Ameer Ali's critique see 117–18.

38. Caroline Reitz, *Detecting the Nation: Fictions of Detection and the Imperial Venture* (Ohio State University Press, 2004).

39. Schneider, *Engines of Truth*, 108.

40. Beverley Nichols, *Verdict on India* (London: Jonathan Cape, 1944), 217.

41. Torick Ameer Ali, "On Veracity" (undated), 1, in "Memoirs and Articles by Sir Torick Ameer Ali (1891–1975)" (MSS Eur C336/13).

42. See Justice Mahmood's history of the oath in Indian law in *Queen-Empress v. Maru and Another*, ILR All. 10 (1887–88):207–23; Ameer Ali, "On Veracity," 10–11; and Schneider, *Engines of Truth*, 134–37. Act V of 1840 replaced religiously specific oaths with a religiously neutral affirmation (*QE v. Maru*, 214).

43. Chatterjee focuses on racial bias. See Partha Chatterjee, *The Nation and Its Fragments: Colonial and Postcolonial Histories* (Princeton University Press, 1993), 10, 17–34.

44. On the moralization of physical over chemical methods see Mitra Sharafi, "The History of Poison and Stereotypical Narratives," *Madras Courier*, November 12, 2018.

more poison than necessary, which gave them away.[45] But things were different in "customary" poisoning lineages that transmitted traditional, illicit knowledge over generations. CEs believed that in these groups, knowledge of subtle methods, sources of poison, and dosage had been perfected. By these accounts, Indigenous peoples knew how to use poisoned arrows. Lower-caste leatherworking communities could allegedly poison cattle for their skins, making it look like death by illness.[46] Village midwives (*dais*) could induce abortion without a trace, and Rajput women could commit female infanticide by smearing tiny amounts of opium on a nipple while nursing.[47] In the medico-legal literature, this was colonized deception at its most skilled and threatening.

South Asian thinkers argued against the native mendacity stereotype. In an 1866 speech to the Ethnological Society in London, the early nationalist and future Member of Parliament Dadabhai Naoroji defended South Asian religious traditions against accusations of "Asiatic" mendacity, pointing to Zoroastrian doctrine that required truth-telling "hundreds of years before Christ," along with Hindu scripture.[48] A few decades later, Bombay High Court Justice Badruddin Tyabji put the Scottish star of the bar, J. D. Inverarity, in his place when the latter asserted the superiority of European witnesses: "It is quite true, Mr. Inverarity, there is a great deal of false evidence in Court, but this country has no monopoly of it. Tichborne and his hundreds of false witnesses were not Indians. I think the fact is, that Indian witnesses tell lies less discriminately on facts which it is not necessary for them to deny, whereas the European witnesses are more discreet, denying just what is necessary for them, and therefore it is more difficult to detect where they lie."[49] Like the "princely impostor" who pretended to be a Bengali nobleman gone missing years earlier, Tichborne had tried to convince a court that he was the long-lost claimant to a wealthy estate.[50] A jury in Victorian

45. "Report of the CE to Government, Punjab, for the Year 1879," 4 (IOR/V/24/418); also available in "Papers, compiled in 1960s, relating to the work of the CE, including an extract from the 1879 Report to the Punjab Government" (MSS Eur F161/183).

46. See CE Report for Punjab 1879, 4; and chapter 1.

47. Mitra Sharafi, "Abortion in South Asia, 1860–1947: A Medico-Legal History," *MAS* 55, no. 2 (2021): 378–79, 389; and David Arnold, *Toxic Histories: Poison and Pollution in Modern India* (Cambridge University Press, 2016), 28–29.

48. Dadabhai Naoroji, "The European and Asiatic Races," in *The Grand Little Man of India: Dadabhai Naoroji Speeches and Writings*, ed. A. M. Zaidi (Delhi: S. Chand, 1984), 1:383; see also 375–410.

49. Badruddin Tyabji in Husain B. Tyabji, *Badruddin Tyabji: A Biography* (Bombay: Thacker, 1952), 301.

50. See *The Tichborne Trial: The Summing-Up by the Lord Chief Justice of England, Together with the Addresses to the Judges, the Verdict, and the Sentence; the Whole Accompanied by a History of the Case and Copious Alphabetical Index* (London, 1874); Jaising P. Modi, *A Textbook of Medical Jurisprudence and Toxicology*, 4th ed. (Calcutta: Butterworth, 1932), 72–73; and

England did not believe him, and he received a fourteen-year prison sentence for perjury.

Once South Asians rose to prominence in forensic fields, figures like J. P. Modi and Chunilal Bose replaced theories for crimes of deception grounded in stereotypes about race and culture with new explanations (chapters 1 and 5). Torick Ameer Ali, who sat on the Calcutta High Court bench from 1931 to 1944, proposed that truth-telling was not predominantly about race or culture but about loyalty to one's social circle. Whether they were British or Indian, people lied to the out-group to protect their in-group. "Among all people, but especially in advanced societies, the effective deterrent to untruth is not the oath, or fear of the law, but the commendation or condemnation of the circle to which the deponent belongs." In his court, he had seen "the most worthy and eminent physicians and surgeons" dissemble to protect their colleagues. He had observed seafarers—from captain to cabin boy—lie in court out of loyalty to shipmates. The "abracadabra of the law" was no match for these bonds. It followed that a judge could not assume that a witness was speaking the truth on the basis of his class, education, or race.[51]

It is worth noting that while Indian professionals sympathetic to anticolonial nationalism rejected the concept of native mendacity, they failed to question the idea of female mendacity. In forensic fields, stereotypes about female duplicity persisted even at a time when Indian society was radically remaking itself in other ways. For example, J. P. Modi rejected native mendacity in his medical jurisprudence treatise, but from the 1920s to 1940s his suspicions of women alleging rape (chapter 5) were indistinguishable from the views of a figure like W. D. Sutherland, the first bloodstain analyst known as the imperial serologist, in the 1910s (chapter 3). Nationalist traditionalism on "the women's question" was apparent even in the context of crime and its detection.[52]

Meanwhile, descriptions of *British* deceptiveness were widespread, from the duplicity involved in British diplomacy and the princely states to the trickery associated with Christian proselytization.[53] Many Hindus and Muslims feared

---

Partha Chatterjee, *A Princely Impostor? The Strange and Universal History of the Kumar of Bhawal* (Princeton University Press, 2002). Similarly, see Natalie Zemon Davis, *The Return of Martin Guerre* (Harvard University Press, 1983), and Laurie M. Wood, "Recovering the Debris of Fortunes Between France and Its Colonies in the 18th Century," *Journal of Social History* 51, no. 4 (2018): 812–14. For a fictionalized account of the Tichborne case see Zadie Smith, *The Fraud: A Novel* (Penguin, 2023).

51. Ameer Ali, "On Veracity," 5, 8–9. Ameer Ali was building on a theory in W. H. Sleeman, *Ramblings and Recollections of an Indian Official* (1844; Karachi: Oxford University Press, 1915), 383–411.

52. See Chatterjee, *Nation*, 116–34.

53. Ameer Ali, "On Veracity," 3–4; Michael H. Fisher, *Indirect Rule in India: Residents and the Residency System, 1764–1858* (Oxford University Press, 1991), 257–60; and Mark Knights and Zak

that exposure to ritual pollution was a grooming tactic used by missionaries to prepare South Asians for conversion to Christianity.[54] Similar suspicions had sparked the largest anticolonial rebellion in Indian history. In 1857, South Asian soldiers (sepoys) rose up against the East India Company in response to rumors that their rifle cartridges contained beef and pork grease (offensive to Hindus and Muslims, respectively). When the men tore the packets open with their teeth to load their rifles, they would be ritually polluted and thus primed for Christian conversion.[55] Many South Asians associated colonial vaccination drives—against smallpox, for instance—with similar trickery intended to defile and convert.[56]

Descriptions of British dissimulation permeated the nationalist movement, too. Revolutionary leaders such as S. K. Krishnavarma accused British officials of dishonesty for celebrating press freedom and parliamentary democracy in general while crushing both in India.[57] Indeed, Gandhi's aim through nonviolence was primarily to reveal truth (*satya*), exposing the oppression and violence of British colonial rule.[58] Despite all these efforts, however, the belief in native mendacity, demonstrated in colonial professional writings on law, science, and medicine, overshadowed South Asian critiques or reciprocal accusations of British mendacity in the late colonial period.

The discourse of native mendacity was demeaning and relentless in colonial South Asia and leaves the historian of falsity with the question of what to do with it. In this book, I entertain the possibility of dissimulation *without* accepting the biased explanations for it in the primary sources. In other words, acknowledging the possibility of falsity by colonized individuals does not necessarily or

---

Leonard, "Bribery in Baroda: The Politics of Corruption in Nineteenth-Century India," in *Corruption, Empire, and Colonialism in the Modern Era: A Global Perspective*, ed. Ronald Kroeze, Pol Dalmau, and Frédéric Monier (Palgrave Macmillan, 2021), 142–43.

54. See Mou Banerjee, *The Disinherited: The Politics of Christian Conversion in Colonial India* (Harvard University Press, 2025).

55. Sugata Bose and Ayesha Jalal, *Modern South Asia: History, Culture, Political Economy* (Routledge, 2018), 115–16. For primary-source maps and images of the rebellion see Bernard Cohn Papers (1942–2000), box 5, folder 9–10, and box 7 (oversized), Hannah Holborn Gray Special Collections Research Center, University of Chicago.

56. David Arnold, *Colonizing the Body: State Medicine and Epidemic Disease in Nineteenth-Century India* (University of California Press, 1993), 143.

57. "British Policy of Reform as an Outcome of Nationalist Agitation and Action. Tables Turned—Charge of Dishonesty Brought Home to the Secretary of State for India," *Indian Sociologist* 5, no. 2 (1909), in disciplinary file of S. Krishnavarma (DIS/1/K2), Inner Temple Archives, London. See also Mitra Sharafi, "South Asians at the Inns of Court: Empire, Expulsion, and Redemption Circa 1900," in *In Between and Across: Legal History Without Boundaries*, ed. Kenneth Mack and Jacob Cogan (Oxford University Press, 2024), 193–96.

58. See Shruti Kapila, "Gandhi Before Mahatma: The Foundations of Political Truth," *Public Culture* 23, no. 2 (2011): 431–48.

inherently mean subscribing to the stereotype of native (or female) mendacity.[59] Much of the scholarship on sex crimes in colonial India (chapter 3) resists the possibility of dissimulation by colonized accusers, even in a single case. Implicitly, this approach sets up a chain of credibility assessments between the authors of primary and secondary sources. The primary sources claimed that colonized subjects dissimulated, and attributed that to native (and female) mendacity; the secondary sources claim that the primary source authors, not their subjects, dissimulated, and attribute that to colonial racism (and sexism). This logic essentially mirrors charges of native mendacity with charges of the colonizer's bias, and preempts any further inquiry, since both subjects and sources are judged categorically to be lies and distinctive species of falsity.

It is possible, however, to separate descriptions of mendacity from explanations for it. Using this method, I suggest in this book that not only worry about dissimulation, *but dissimulation itself*, were features of colonial life, and that there are ways of understanding deliberate acts of falsity by colonized people that are not interpretively beholden to colonial racism or sexism. We may regard these acts, for example, as pursuing multiple aims at the same time—not just punishment of a rival, but also subversion, resistance, and resilience in the face of colonial (or gender) hierarchies.[60] We may take our cue from literary scholars who see plagiarism by colonized actors as a form of reverse colonialism.[61] From literature to law, colonized people appropriated colonizers' creations and customized them to meanings and uses not intended by their originators. We may also see false accusations and evidence as reflections of noncolonial modes of disputing, including what I call punitive self-harm (chapter 2 and conclusion): hurting oneself or one's relative to punish an adversary. And falsity may have been the product of coercion, as in some of the rape cases described in chapter 3.

59. For a similar approach see Jonathan Saha's work on corruption in colonial Burma, including "'Uncivilized Practitioners': Medical Subordinates, Medico-Legal Evidence, and Misconduct in Colonial Burma, 1875–1907," *South East Asia Research* 20, no. 3 (2012): 423–43; and "'Devious Documents': Corruption and Paperwork in Colonial Burma, Circa 1900," in *Subverting Empire: Deviance and Disorder in the British Colonial World*, ed. Will Jackson and Emily J. Manktelow (Palgrave Macmillan, 2015), 167–84.

60. See Shelly Chan et al., eds., "Histories of Resilience," *American Historical Review* special issue (2024) 129, no. 4; and Prinisha Badassy, "Stewed Plums, Baked Porridge and Flavoured Tea: Poisoning by Indian Domestic Servants in Colonial Natal," in *Beyond Indenture: Agency and Resistance in the Colonial South Asian Diaspora*, ed. Crispin Bates (Cambridge University Press, 2024), 38–61.

61. See Anwesha Maity, "Imaginary Science and Cultural Signs: Mapping Postcolonial Bangla (Bengali) Science Fiction" (PhD diss., University of Wisconsin–Madison, 2019), 189–90; and Marilynn Randall, "Imperial Plagiarism," in *Perspectives on Plagiarism and Intellectual Property in a Postmodern World*, ed. Lisa Buranen and Alice M. Roy (State University of New York Press, 1999), 136.

Consider the history of dissimulation around the world, which offers diverse motives and explanations for falsity. People have lied to survive. During war, malingerers faked injuries to stay off the battlefield.[62] In volatile contexts of religious change and diversity, people pretended to be what they were not in order to avoid exile or death. Crypto-Muslims (Moriscos) and crypto-Jews (conversos) hid their true religion and pretended to be Christians in early modern Iberia and the Americas.[63] Among Shia Muslims but later among Sunnis too, the doctrine of *taqiyya* required that one dissemble to protect the faith.[64] In early modern Europe, Protestants in Catholic societies and Catholics in newly Protestant ones lied about their religion to stay alive.[65]

Others dissimulated to resist systems of oppression forced upon them. Enslaved and Indigenous populations living under white settler colonialism in the Americas celebrated trickster figures in storytelling and song traditions. Brer Rabbit, Coyote, and Raven subverted the dominant regime with their relentless schemes and ingenious ploys. They faked, dissembled, and sabotaged to undermine the powerful.[66]

There is also a close connection between truth-telling and confrontation that might tacitly encourage dissemblance. Particularly in diverse societies, stark honesty means stark conflict. From early modern courtly cultures to multicultural societies today, etiquette systems have managed difference by compartmentalizing clashing views. But, consequently, what one group deems social graces, another deems dishonesty. The colonial European encounter with ornate traditions of politeness that idealized flowery and indirect language like the Persianate *ta'arof* and Hindi-Urdu concept of *takalluf* probably contributed to Orientalist stereotypes of Middle Easterners and South Asians as inscrutable

62. See Cage, *Science of Proof*, 79–109.

63. See Kevin Ingram, introduction to *The Conversos and Moriscos in Late Medieval Spain and Beyond*, vol. 1, *Departures and Change*, ed. K. Ingram (Brill, 2009), 1–21; and Karoline P. Cook, *Forbidden Passages: Muslims and Moriscos in Colonial Spanish America* (University of Pennsylvania Press, 2016), 80–102.

64. See Etan Kohlberg, "*Taqiyya* in Shi'i Theology and Religion," in *Secrecy and Concealment: Studies in the History of Mediterranean and Near Eastern Religions*, ed. Hans G. Kippenberg and Guy G. Stroumsa (Brill, 1995), 345–80; L. P. Harvey, "The Political, Social and Cultural History of the Moriscos," in *The Legacy of Muslim Spain*, ed. Salma Khadra Jayyusi (Brill, 1992), 211–12; and Shafique N. Virani, "*Taqiyya* and Identity in a South Asian Community," *Journal of Asian Studies* 70, no. 1 (2011): 99–139.

65. Perez Zagorin, *Ways of Lying: Dissimulation, Persecution, and Conformity in Early Modern Europe* (Harvard University Press, 1990).

66. See Barbara Babcock-Abrahams, "'A Tolerated Margin of Mess': The Trickster and His Tales Reconsidered," *Journal of the Folklore Institute* 11, no. 3 (1975): 147–86; John Borrows, *Recovering Canada: The Resurgence of Indigenous Law* (University of Toronto Press, 2002); Richard Erdoes and Alfonso Ortiz, eds., *American Indian Trickster Tales* (Viking, 1998); and Winifred Morgan, *The Trickster Figure in American Literature* (Palgrave Macmillan, 2013).

and insincere.[67] British narratives associating princely states with dishonesty and corruption built on these ideas.[68]

Swindlers, con men, forgers, and counterfeiters dissimulated for financial gain, abetted by others' gullibility.[69] In medieval Europe, forged documents were often inserted into disputes by people trying to secure religious offices and property.[70] In later centuries, refugees and slum dwellers relied on false identity documents to survive (paying a steep price for them, too).[71] At times, con artists first learned their skills out of desperation—to survive the Nigerian Civil War of 1967–70, for instance, when struggling men and women in the secessionist state of Biafra forged military passes and used false identities to persuade foreigners to send them money. But once they had the skills, they continued to use them to earn income, even after wartime conditions ended.[72]

In colonial South Asia, cases of forgery, cheating, counterfeiting, and "false property marks" (using another owner's insignia on one's goods) were often profit-driven.[73] Occasionally, self-protection was the motive for perjury and forgery, particularly when an individual had already engaged in an earlier fraudulent act.[74] Of most interest in this book are cases where falsity was used not as

---

67. See Edward Said, *Orientalism* (Vintage, 2003), 38–39; and Margrit Pernau, *Emotions and Modernity in Colonial India: From Balance to Fervor* (Oxford University Press, 2020), 28. On *ta'arof* generally see Marina Terkourafi, "Lying and Politeness," in *The Oxford Handbook of Lying*, ed. Joerg Meibauer (Oxford University Press, 2019), 387–88; and William Beeman, "*Ta'arof*," in *Encyclopedia Iranica* (online ed., 2017), 1–4. On lying and etiquette see Simone Dietz, "White and Prosocial Lies," in Meibauer, *Oxford Handbook of Lying*, 288–99.

68. See Knights and Leonard, "Bribery in Baroda," 141–70.

69. For example see Stephen Mihm, *A Nation of Counterfeiters: Capitalists, Con Men, and the Making of the United States* (Harvard University Press, 2007); E. J. Balleisen, *Fraud: An American History from Barnum to Madoff* (Princeton University Press, 2017); Susanna Blumenthal, "Humbug: Toward a Legal History," *Buffalo Law Review* 64 (2016): 161–92; Matt Houlbrook, *Prince of Tricksters: The Incredible True Story of Netley Lucas, Gentleman Crook* (University of Chicago Press, 2016); and Mark McNicholas, *Forgery and Impersonation in Imperial China: Popular Deceptions and the High Qing State* (University of Washington Press, 2016).

70. For example see Anthon Grafton, *Forgers and Critics: Creativity and Duplicity in Western Scholarship* (Princeton University Press, 1990); and Levi Roach, *Forgery and Memory at the End of the First Millennium* (Princeton University Press, 2021).

71. For example see Tarangini Sriraman, *In Pursuit of Proof: A History of Identification Documents in India* (Oxford University Press, 2018), 111, 182–91; and Devi Mays, *Forging Ties, Forging Passports: Migration and the Modern Sephardi Diaspora* (Stanford University Press, 2020), 215–37.

72. Daly, *History*.

73. For example see *Queen-Empress v. Tulja and Others*, ILR Bom. 12 (1888): 36–43; *Queen-Empress v. Pera Raju*, ILR Mad. 13 (1890): 27–31; and *Emperor v. Dahyabhai Chakasha*, in *Bombay Law Reporter* 6 (1904): 513–17. On false coining see M. Pauparao Naidu, *The History of Professional Poisoners and Coiners of India* (Madras: Higginbotham, 1912), 84–148.

74. For examples of perjury, forgery, and *benami* transactions (where one person contracted on behalf of an unidentified other) see *Hira Nand Ojha v. King-Emperor*, Cal. Crim. Rulings 10 (1906): 185–88; and *Kamatchinatha Pillai v. Emperor*, ILR Mad. 42 (1919): 558–60.

a shield (defensively), but as a sword (offensively), and not just for monetary but for psychological rewards. False charges of murder could reveal attempts to frame rivals. Prosecutions for false charges of rape could reflect a male adversary's attempt to punish the original female accuser by turning the criminal legal system back on her. The many layers of potential falsity make these cases bewildering, but also analytically rich.

Colonized actors who planted evidence such as poison and animal blood were sometimes advancing noncolonial notions of causation and moral responsibility: they created false evidence to frame true wrongdoers using logics unknown to the colonial legal system. They were pursuing alternative notions of justice by subverting colonial models of truth mechanics—seeking justice not through truth, but lies. In these cases, falsity was a form of agency. In a sinister and ingenious form of play, these tricksters were taking control in a way that could simultaneously subvert the system *and* punish their rivals. Through creative adaptation, they harnessed colonial criminal law for their own ends.[75]

In contrast were cases of falsity produced by coercion. The archives include accounts, for instance, of rape accusations made falsely by a woman or girl under threat of violence. And there were cases where female accusers withdrew or denied their own earlier rape claims because men threatened them with violence if they did not.[76] In these cases, female accusers dissembled to survive. There were also cases of false confessions. Wives told police that they had poisoned their husbands, but testing found no poison in the men's corpses, and analysts doubted the truth of the confessions.[77] Presumably, these women confessed under pressure from police or family. The falsity of a case, then, could reflect agency *or* coercion.

In short, there is more going on in the archive of false cases than some may think. In many cases, these accounts convey a belief in native mendacity by the colonial officials who wrote them down, but this is not the end of the story—or the entire story. These cases also offer a glimpse of the rich, diverse, and complex paths that could motivate alleged falsity. Methodologically, this approach may be useful in interpreting colonizers' primary sources beyond forensics, too, particularly when one can locate a narrator's bias in their *explanation for* a phenomenon. In such situations, the challenge is to separate the colonial author's description

75. I borrow the idea of creative adaptation from Dilip P. Gaonkar's discussion in the context of modernity. Dilip Parameshwar Gaonkar, "On Alternative Modernities," in *Alternative Modernities*, ed. Dilip Parameshwar Gaonkar (Duke University Press, 2001), 18, 22.

76. For example see *Dolabi v. King-Emperor*, Lower Burma Rulings 3 (1905–6): 204–5.

77. For instance see "Report of the Chemical Analyser to Government, Bombay, for the Year 1876–77," 28 (IOR/V/24/405).

of a phenomenon from their explanation for why it happened. What alternative explanations could be possible, including from other sources or comparative contexts? The craft of the historian of the false requires reading against the grain in this way—a version of what Ranajit Guha called reading "an image in a distorting mirror."[78] Using this method, I aspire to do more with and deepen our analysis of false cases.

The Colonial Lab Expert

The first half of this book explores cases believed to be false, particularly murder and rape cases involving South Asians, and the analysis of poison, blood, and sperm cells. But falsity is a broader phenomenon than the products of intentional deception discussed in part 1 of the book. The concept of falsity itself says nothing about intentionality, but only about the truth value of an assertion. Falsity may be the product of deliberate deception, but it may also be the result of a lack of attention or skill, miscommunication, misunderstanding, or poorly designed processes. Many wrongful convictions in our own time are the result of faulty forensic findings that were not necessarily intentionally false.[79] Part 2 of this book takes this wider view, exploring the falsity generated from within the colonial legal system itself, *whether intentional or not*. It contributes to a vibrant conversation about how colonialism shaped forensics among scholars like Chandak Sengoopta, David Arnold, Projit Mukharji, Binyamin Blum, Catherine Evans, Uponita Mukherjee, Chris Hamlin, and Ian Burney.[80] In British India, the new forensics introduced the potential for falsity (and fears of falsity) through careless

78. Ranajit Guha, *Elementary Aspects of Peasant Insurgency in Colonial India* (Duke University Press, 1999), 333.

79. For instance, many US-based experts who testified on bite-mark evidence and shaken baby syndrome in recent decades may have genuinely believed in the reliability of their methods. These methods are now in question. See Deborah Tuerkheimer, *Flawed Convictions: "Shaken Baby Syndrome" and the Inertia of Injustice* (Oxford University Press, 2014); Keith Findley et al., eds., *Shaken Baby Syndrome: Investigating the Abusive Head Trauma Controversy* (Cambridge University Press, 2023); and Adam Deitsch, "An Inconvenient Tooth: Forensic Odontology Is an Inadmissible Junk Science When It Is Used to 'Match' Teeth to Bitemarks in Skin," *Wisconsin Law Review* 2009, no. 5: 1205–36.

80. Sengoopta, *Imprint*; David Arnold, *Toxic Histories: Poison and Pollution in Modern India* (Cambridge University Press, 2016); Projit Bihari Mukharji, "Handwriting Analysis as a Dynamic Artisanal Science: The Hardless Detective Dynasty and the Forensic Cultures of the British Raj," in Hamlin and Burney, *Global Forensic Cultures*, 86–111; Catherine Evans, *Unsound Empire: Civilization and Madness in Late-Victorian Law* (Yale University Press, 2021); Hamlin and Burney, *Global Forensic Cultures*; and Uponita Mukherjee, "Colonial Detection: Crime, Evidence, and Inquiry in British India, 1790–1910" (PhD diss., Columbia University, 2022). By Binyamin Blum see "The Hounds of

or corrupt experts; special concessions for state lab analysts; and conflicts over truth mechanics between men of law and men of science.

Part 2 features the protected colonial lab expert. CrPC s.510 effectively made CEs exempt from cross-examination; most other scientific and medical experts *did* have to be questioned in court.[81] Experts in science, handwriting, or fingerprints were required to give their views, implicitly in court and not simply in writing, under s.45 of the Indian Evidence Act of 1872.[82] Under s.509 of CrPC 1882, the opinions of civil surgeons and other medical witnesses could be taken as depositions "by a magistrate and in the presence of the accused." Alternatively, the evidence of these medical witnesses could be taken on commission, a process used when witnesses in other locations were unable to travel or when many witnesses were in another place.[83] Giving evidence by deposition or on commission included cross-examination under oath.[84] Strikingly, though, these devices were not used for the CEs.

Lab experts in England did not have the protections of CEs in South Asia. In 1879, the Punjab CE described English trials for murder by poison: "All the scientific witnesses, medical and chemical, give their evidence personally as to the facts they have observed, and state the opinions they have formed from them, with their reasons."[85] As another colonial official commented in 1922, "I cannot find that there is in England any corresponding procedure allowing of the exemption from attendance of any kind of expert witness."[86] In 1904, the American legal scholar John Wigmore called cross-examination "the greatest legal engine ever invented for the discovery of truth" in Anglo-American law.[87] In civilian legal systems of continental Europe, judges (more than lawyers) rigorously questioned experts.[88] As explored in chapter 5, Indian criminal procedure mixed elements of common law and civilian legal systems. Yet—and in contrast

---

Empire: Forensic Dog Tracking in Britain and its Colonies, 1888–1953," *Law and History Review* 35, no. 3 (2017): 621–65; "From Bedouin Trackers to Doberman Pinschers"; and "Forensic Empire."

81. On CrPC s.509, for example, see the 1881 case of *K. Venkatroyadu*, Weir Crim. Rulings 2: 659–60.

82. See Cunningham, *Indian Evidence Act* (1908), 121–27.

83. See H. T. Prinsep, *The Code of Criminal Procedure Being Act V of 1898*, 13th ed. (Calcutta: Thacker, Spink, 1901), 497–99.

84. See A. S. Oppé, *Wharton's Law Lexicon . . . with Selected Titles Relating to the Civil, Scots, and Indian Law* (Sweet and Maxwell, 1938), 217, 322–23; and Mitra Sharafi, "Bella's Case: Parsi Identity and the Law in Colonial Rangoon, Bombay and London, 1887–1925" (PhD diss., Princeton University, 2006), 184–86.

85. CE Report for Punjab 1879, 13.

86. L. Graham (September 28, 1922), 3, in "Proposal to amend s.510 of the Criminal Procedure Code so as to include Anatomist, negatived," Home: Judicial, Proc. no. 1336, 1922 (NAI).

87. John Henry Wigmore, *A Treatise on the System of Evidence in Trials at Common Law* (Little, Brown, 1904), 2:1697. Similarly, see Aiyer and Aiyer, *Detection*, 86.

88. See Watson, *Forensic Medicine*, 19–24, 37–39.

with either of these traditions—questioning by lawyers or judges played little role for an important group of expert witnesses in South Asia.

The key feature of s.510 was that it permitted judges at the trial court phase to call these lab experts to court, *but did not require it*. During the colonial period, this decision was a discretionary matter for the judge of first instance, regardless of requests made by the defense or prosecution.[89] The default practice that developed, and that was permitted by statute, was for judges to admit these written findings without cross-examination under oath. This situation has persisted, despite moments of fierce criticism in the case law and treatise literature over the past century and a half. A vague or misleading comment in the written report could be clarified through cross-examination under oath, but the "sanctity" granted to these lab experts' reports by the code means that there is only a brief window of opportunity to do so.[90] If a trial court judge admitted a CE certificate without cross-examination, a High Court judge could not find it inadmissible on appeal.[91] Elsewhere, I discuss how this rule developed over time.[92] Especially relevant here is that the rule developed to spare CEs from having to travel long distances to testify in court, since this would disrupt their other lab work.[93] However, the judicial practice of not calling CEs continued, even after assistant CEs were permitted to testify on behalf of the lab and after advances in transportation shortened travel times. In postcolonial India, Pakistan, and Bangladesh, this concession was extended to an even larger number of experts.[94] And the rule was exported from South Asia to other British colonies across Asia and Africa.[95] Since the story of this unusual exemption began before the bacteriological

---

89. An amendment in 1955 suggested that prior to that date, the choice lay solely with the judge. See Ram Lal Gupta, *Law of Identification* (Lucknow: Eastern Book, 1963), 138. Under the 1955 CrPC (Amendment) Act, CrPC s.510 was revised to read: "The Court may, if it thinks fit, and *shall, on the application of the prosecution or the accused, summon and examine any such person as to the subject-matter of his report*" (italics added). However, under s.293 of CrPC (1973), this change was undone, and the decision to summon the expert reverted to the judge.

90. *Pradeep Ramniklal Bhat v. State of Maharashtra*, MANU/MH/0490/2006, para. 8.

91. Gupta, *Law of Identification*, 149.

92. See Sharafi, "Trial by Certificate" (in progress).

93. *Emperor v. Happu*, ILR All. 56 (1934): 236.

94. See s.510 of CrPC, 1898 in both Pakistan and Bangladesh; and BNSS (2023), s.329(4). See also Sharafi, "Trial by Certificate" (in progress).

95. For colonial or postcolonial versions of this rule see Kenya's Criminal Procedure Ordinance of 1914, s.399; the Uganda Protectorate's Criminal Procedure Code of 1930, s. 150; the Straits Settlements' Criminal Procedure Code of 1935, s.408; and Nigeria's Criminal Procedure Code of 1960, s.250.

revolution, it cannot be attributed to the "star appeal" that lab science acquired from the 1890s on, although this may help explain why the rule persisted.[96]

Today s.510's successor, Bharatiya Nagarik Suraksha Sanhita s.329, expands a rule that began for reasons of colonial experts' convenience and that was contested even before 1947. The rule applied even when a life was at stake in death penalty cases. "And how many men are annually hanged," asked an 1886 *Amrita Bazar Patrika* editorial, "under the authority of these reports of Chemical Examiners!"[97] Although judges must often balance the quest for truth against the need for efficiency, CrPC s.510 and its postcolonial successors go beyond reasonable compromise. In leaning heavily in the direction of efficiency, they sacrifice the basic due process rights of defendants.

Forensic Science for South Asia

The high era of forensic institution-building was the turn of the twentieth century, a period when a wave of new medical institutions was also created in British India.[98] However, two forensic institutions had an earlier start. The first was the coroner's inquest, which came to India with the East India Company in the seventeenth century. The second was the chemical examiners, who were part of the Indian Medical Service (IMS).[99] CE labs were under the control of the inspector general of hospitals, not the police.[100] The first CE was appointed in 1840. By the 1870s, the CEs were well known as a network of military physicians whose

96. See Pratik Chakrabarti, *Bacteriology in British India: Laboratory Medicine and the Tropics* (University of Rochester Press, 2012); and David Arnold, "Colonial Medicine in Transition: Medical Research in India, 1910–47," *South Asia Research* 14, no. 1 (1994): 13, 15, 17.

97. Untitled, *ABP*, July 8, 1886.

98. See appendix 3; and Arnold, "Colonial Medicine," 13–14.

99. On the IMS see D. G. Crawford, *A History of the Indian Medical Service, 1600–1913* (Thacker, 1914); Patrick Hehir, *The Medical Profession in India* (London: Henry Frowde, 1923), 37–64; Arnold, *Colonizing the Body*, 61–63, 114; Mark Harrison, *Public Health in British India: Anglo-Indian Preventive Medicine, 1859–1914* (Cambridge University Press, 1994), 6–35; and, by Pratik Chakrabarti, *Medicine & Empire 1600–1960* (Palgrave Macmillan, 2014), 108–9, 116–17, and "'Signs of the Times': Medicine and Nationhood in British India," *Osiris* 24 (2009): 192.

100. "Plan for the Forensic Science Laboratory, United Provinces, Being the Proposals Formulated by the Forensic Science Laboratory Committee and a Sub-Committee of Specialists, 1945–46," 2, in Papers of Harold Charles Mitchell, Indian Police, United Provinces 1920–47 (MSS Eur F 255/9). On the continuing discussion over the separation of forensic analysts from police see Simon A. Cole, "Afterword: A Tale of Two Cities? Locating the History of Forensic Science and Medicine in Contemporary Forensic Reform Discourse," in Hamlin and Burney, *Global Forensic Cultures*, 329–30.

labs did chemical testing for the state.[101] (In South Asia, as in England, these early forensic analysts were usually trained as physicians, not chemists; forensic toxicology was regarded as a subfield of forensic medicine.)[102] By 1908, there were eight regional labs, some of which used the name "chemical analyser" labs (shown a few decades later in map 1). The medico-legal discussions and case descriptions in their annual reports are key sources for this study.[103]

Most other forensic institutions sprang up in the 1890s–1910s. The world's first fingerprint bureau opened in Calcutta in 1897, and regional fingerprint offices followed. The chief inspector of explosives (CIE), who was called in for bomb cases, was created in 1898. The government examiner of questioned documents (GEQD), a handwriting analyst, was established in 1904. In 1914–16, the office of the imperial serologist (IS) grew out of the Calcutta CE's department and became its own separate office in charge of testing bloodstains. Much of the IS's work involved the detection of planted animal blood through a form of species-of-origin testing called the precipitin test (chapters 2–3).

Alongside the rise of forensic infrastructure was the flowering of a scientific literature on forensic science, initially focused on the narrower field of medical jurisprudence. By the 1850s, it became clear that using British works like Alfred Swaine Taylor's famous treatise would not be good enough for South Asia.[104] Conditions in the subcontinent, including its poison and disease landscapes, were different.[105] India needed its own forensic science. In English, this began with Norman Chevers's treatise, first published in 1856.[106] In its wake came a

---

101. CEs tested the purity of alcohol, ghee, milk, water, kerosene, cocaine, and opium for various state agencies, including Customs and Excise. They dabbled in anesthetics, explosives, chemical warfare, and bacteriology (involving the plague, tuberculosis, typhoid, cholera, syphilis, and leprosy). They also tested for the presence of poisons in food and viscera, both animal and human. See CE Report for Punjab 1879 and Arnold, *Toxic Histories*, 111–17.

102. On England see Alison Adam, *A History of Forensic Science: British Beginnings in the Twentieth Century* (Routledge, 2016), 164–68.

103. For noteworthy discussions in the CE annual reports see Punjab CE reports that included appendices on the quantity of poison found in human viscera (1916), explosives and drug addiction (1930), opium and cremation (1931), as well as a lecture to senior police officers at Phillaur Training School (1936) (IOR/V/24/418–19).

104. Taylor's *Elements of Medical Jurisprudence* was published in 1836. His classic work was *A Manual of Medical Jurisprudence*, first published in 1844 in London. Later called *Principles and Practice of Medical Jurisprudence*, it came out in many British and American editions until the 1980s.

105. On South Asian poisons and the interplay with disease see chapter 1. By the early twentieth century, tropical parasitology also had forensic uses. See Isidore Bernadotte Lyon, *Medical Jurisprudence for India*, 3rd ed., ed. L. A. Waddell (Calcutta: Thacker, Spink, 1904), 96–97; and J. P. Bose, ed., *The Scientific and Other Papers of Rai Chunilal Bose Bahadur* (Calcutta: Forward, 1924), 1:352–56.

106. Chevers, *Manual of Medical Jurisprudence*. See Kolsky, *Colonial Justice*, 129–33. For obituaries see "Obituary: Norman Chevers," *British Medical Journal* (*BMJ*) 2, no. 1355 (1886): 1245; and in

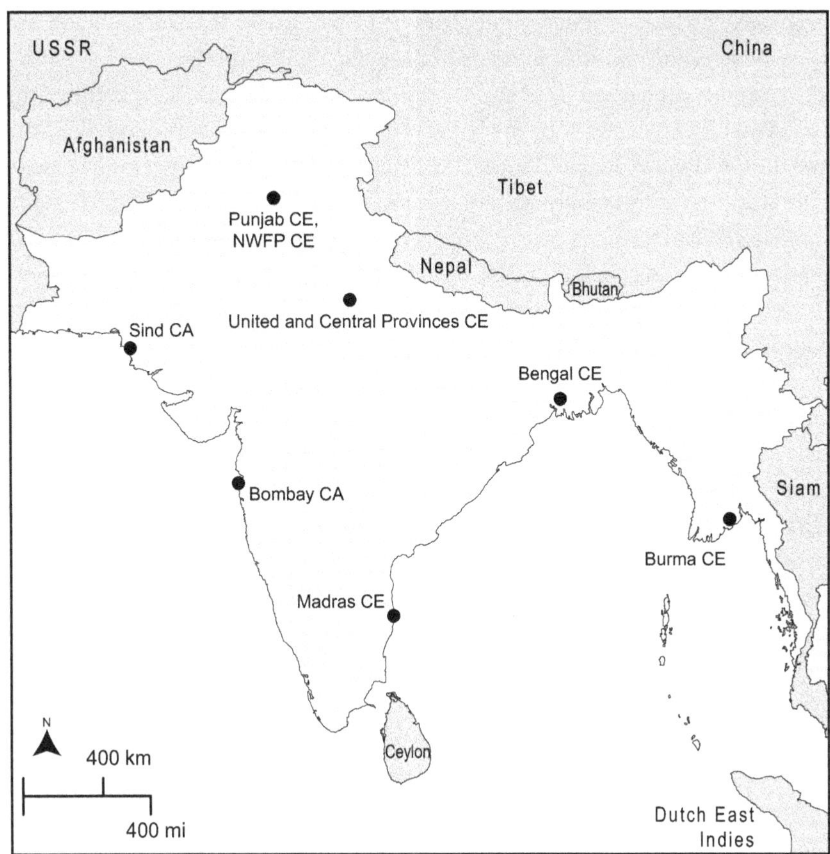

MAP 1. / CE and CA laboratories in the 1930s. CA stands for chemical analyser, CE for chemical examiner. Map designed by Ben Cramer of the University of Wisconsin Cartography Lab.

line of similar works, including many editions of treatises by I. B. Lyon and by Patrick Hehir and J. D. B. Gribble, and the first major South Asian authority in the field, J. P. Modi.[107] There were also forensic treatise literatures in South Asian

Medical Reporter: B. D. Basu, "Indian Medical Celebrities. IX. Norman Chevers" (April 16, 1894) and "The Late Dr. Norman Chevers" (October 16, 1894).

107. I. B. Lyon, *A Text Book of Medical Jurisprudence for India*, 2nd ed. (Calcutta: Thacker, Spink, 1889); J. D. B. Gribble and Patrick Hehir, *Outlines of Medical Jurisprudence for Indian Criminal Courts*, 2nd ed. (Madras: Higginbotham, 1891); and Jaising P. Modi, *A Textbook of Medical Jurisprudence and Toxicology* (Calcutta: Butterworth, 1920). On Hehir see Sharafi, "Abortion," 371–428.

languages, including Bengali and Urdu.[108] In parallel to the treatise literature were medical and scientific journals like the *Indian Medical Gazette*.[109]

The professional worlds of law, science, and medicine converged in the criminal courtroom. Governed by the Indian Penal Code for substantive criminal law and the Criminal Procedure Code (CrPC) and Indian Evidence Act for questions of process and admissibility, men of law and science interacted most of all in the magistrates' and Sessions courts.[110] The written record of their dealings traveled up the pyramid of criminal courts, usually ending in appeals to the High Courts in regional urban hubs across South Asia (map 2).[111] Some of the challenges of coordination and translation between law and science looked similar in colonial South Asia to the story Sheila Jasanoff, Simon Cole, Christopher Hamlin, and others have told about adversarialism and science in British and American courtrooms.[112] In British India (as elsewhere), many men of science regarded their own quest for truth as objective and nonpartisan, and disapproved of the adversarial emphasis on contradiction. In other ways, however, the South Asian story was distinctive: The Indianization of the professions occurred during the last century of colonial rule. The restructuring of the colonial legal system and creation of the High Courts in 1861 opened the way for South Asian lawyers to grow their ranks, to become barristers (trained at London's Inns of Court), and eventually to populate the High Court judiciary across India and Burma.[113] By the late colonial period, the leading criminal law treatise became "Ratanlal and Dhirajlal," as it was known, and law reports and journals came to be dominated

108. For example see Kanai Lal Dey, *Medical Jurisprudence* ([Calcutta]: n.p., [1875]) (Bengali); Raheem Khan, *A Manual of Medical Jurisprudence in Urdu* (Lahore: Anjuman-i-Punjab, 1881); and Srish Chandra Sengupta, *Bhaishajya Bichar or a Handbook of Medical Jurisprudence in Bengali* (Dacca, 1894).

109. The *Indian Medical Gazette* was a publication by IMS members (Chakrabarti, "'Signs of the Times': Medicine and Nationhood in British India," *Osiris* 24 [2009]: 193). It began in 1866 and included articles on forensic topics.

110. See appendix 1.

111. See appendix 2.

112. For example see Sheila Jasanoff, *Science at the Bar: Law, Science, and Technology in America* (Harvard University Press, 1995); Simon A. Cole, "Forensic Culture as Epistemic Culture: The Sociology of Forensic Science," *Studies in History and Philosophy of Biological and Biomedical Sciences* 44 (2013): 36–46; and Chris Hamlin, "Scientific Method and Expert Witnessing: Victorian Perspectives on a Modern Problem," *Social Studies of Science* 16 (1986): 485–513. See also Ian Burney, David A. Kirby, and Neil Pemberton, eds., "Forensic Cultures," special issue, *Studies in History and Philosophy of Biological and Biomedical Sciences* 44 (2013); and Shari Seidman Diamond and Richard O. Lempert, eds., "Science and the Legal System," special issue of *Daedalus*, fall 2018.

113. Sharafi, *Law and Identity*, 105.

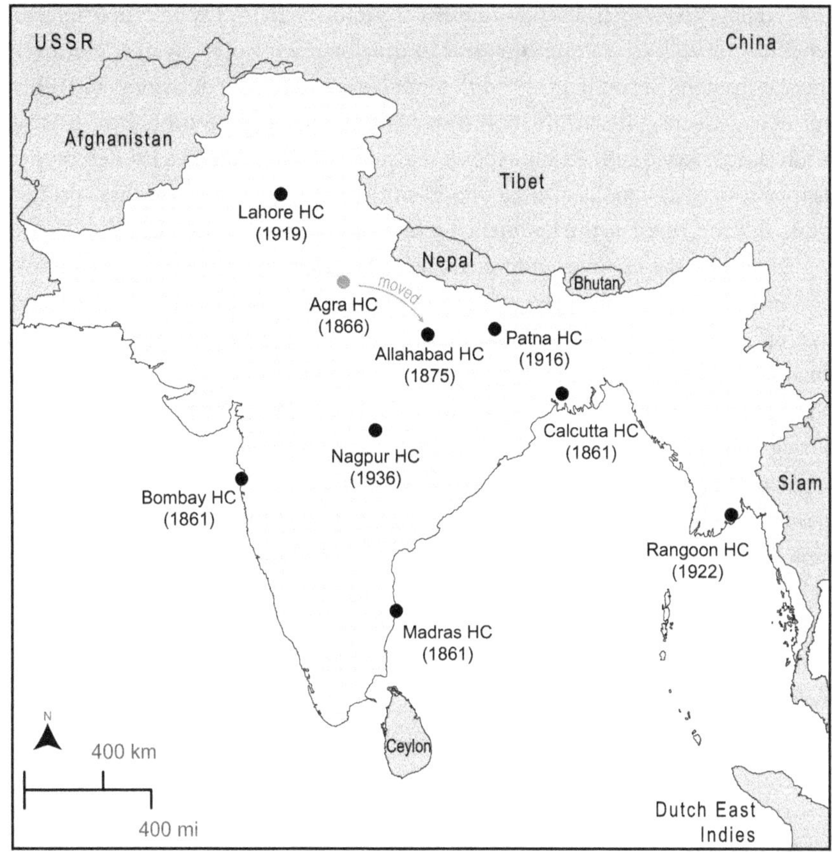

MAP 2. / High Courts (HC) across South Asia in the 1930s, with date of establishment for each. Map designed by Ben Cramer of the University of Wisconsin Cartography Lab.

by Indian law reporters and editors.[114] Similarly, physicians doing the lab science were British during the mid-nineteenth century but largely South Asian by the mid-twentieth, as Indian and Burmese doctors joined the IMS—especially after World War I—and climbed the ranks to become top forensic experts.[115] "Modi's Juris" had become the leading forensic treatise by the late colonial period.[116] Tracing the role of racial identity and racism within these professions is

114. Conversation with Rustom Pheroze Vachha on use of Ranchhoddas and Thakore, *The Indian Penal Code*, in his legal education during the 1940s (Mumbai, February 26, 2004).

115. See Arnold, "Colonial Medicine," 26; and Chakrabarti, "Signs," 192.

116. See Modi, *Medical Jurisprudence* (1940).

challenging, given their discreet cultures of professional loyalty and these figures' tendency to stick to technical matters in the documents they created. However, there were signs in conflicts over differential pay, promotion decisions, and other episodes reflecting discrimination toward South Asian professionals.[117] As this book shows, key South Asian experts rejected racialized mendacity stereotypes as they rose up the ranks. Career opportunities for South Asians in these professions also increased as the nationalist movement gained momentum.[118]

Alongside the creation of forensic infrastructure came the rise of criminology in South Asia. Efforts to stamp out dacoity and thuggee, "systematic and hidden" crimes that involved both deception and violence in highway robbery, emerged in the late eighteenth and nineteenth centuries and culminated in the passage of the Criminal Tribes Act in 1871. As Caroline Reitz has shown, the "Thug Police" became a model for future policing, bridging spy work and modern detection.[119] These developments also laid the groundwork for identification systems that linked ethnology with crime and applied to an estimated four million Indians in the late colonial period.[120] This framework was absorbed into policing through handbooks and criminal history sheets.[121] Criminology as a field of study among scholars emerged in India in the 1920s to 1940s. It included strands focused on South Asian developments (leaning in the direction of social work) and writing informed by European and American criminological theory, including Cesare Lombroso's criminal anthropology.[122]

---

117. See Waltraud Ernst, "The Indianization of Colonial Medicine: The Case of Psychiatry in Early Twentieth-Century British India," *Naturwissenschaften, Technik und Medizin* 20 (2012): 61–89; Arnold, "Colonial Medicine," 27–28, 30 at note 59; and Sharafi, *Law and Identity*, 105–7. On the case of M. G. Deshmukh (assistant chemical analyser in Bombay) see M. G. Deshmukh, *The Evils of the Military Medical Service Monopoly* (Bombay, 1893). I thank Radhika Singha for sharing this source with me.

118. On the legal profession see Sharafi, *Law and Identity*, 103–7. On the medical profession see Chakrabarti, "Signs," 188–211, and Arnold, "Colonial Medicine," 31.

119. Reitz, *Detecting the Nation*, 22–42.

120. Mark Brown, "The Birth of Criminology in Colonial South Asia: 1765–1947," in *Crime, Criminal Justice, and the Evolving Science of Criminology in South Asia: India, Pakistan, and Bangladesh*, ed. Shahid M. Shahidullah (Palgrave Macmillan, 2017), 35–54. See also Radhika Singha, *A Despotism of Law: Crime and Justice in Early Colonial India* (Oxford University Press, 1998), 168–228; Kim A. Wagner, *Thuggee: Banditry and the British in Early Nineteenth-Century India* (Palgrave Macmillan, 2007); and, by Jessica Hinchy, "Conjugality, Colonialism and the 'Criminal Tribes' in North India," *Studies in History* 36, no. 1 (2020): 20–46, and "Gender, Family, and the Policing of the 'Criminal Tribes' in Nineteenth-Century North India," *MAS* 54, no. 5 (2020): 1669–1711.

121. Brown, "Birth of Criminology," 46.

122. Brown, 48–51. See generally Hamlin and Burney, "History," 173. For a Lombroso-inspired early work by a law scholar see the 1920 Tagore Law Lectures: K. Subrahmania Pillai, *Principles of Criminology* (Madras, 1924).

Finally, there is the question of popular awareness. How did average people learn about India's new forensic systems, and how much did they know? Annual CE reports were summarized in professional journals but also occasionally in newspapers.[123] Prominent trials were reported across South Asian newspapers. Poisoners even changed their tactics—turning away from arsenic in the 1930s, for instance—as they learned from newspaper trial accounts that lab testing had improved (chapter 1). Popular "famous trial" books featured cases like the "pinprick" murder case, in which a man at a Calcutta train station was infected with bubonic plague stolen from a lab, and the Alipore bomb case, a high-profile nationalist case involving the attempted assassination of a British magistrate.[124]

There was also a vibrant world of detective fiction in books and magazines, particularly in Hindi, Urdu, Bengali, and English.[125] This genre fulfilled an educational role with regard to forensic science. In the 1910s, for instance, the Hindi-language science monthly *Vigyan* taught readers about science through detective mysteries.[126] In Bengali, detective stories ranged from the thinly veiled memoirs of former police detective Priyanath Mukhopadhyay to the wild adventures of fictional sleuths Kiriti Roy and Byomkesh Bakshi, and featured everything from species-of-origin bloodstain testing to rare poisons.[127] Detectives in these tales often sent items for chemical analysis, particularly to the CE's lab in Calcutta. Bottles and glasses containing alcohol, leftover food from a wedding, and a human stomach were sent for toxicological testing in Mukhopadhyay's

---

123. For instance see "274 Poisoning Cases in 1934. Chemical Analysis in Bombay," and "Poisoning Cases in Madras," both in the *TI*, June 25, 1935.

124. For instance see S. C. Sarkar, *The Notable Indian Trials* (Calcutta: M. C. Sarkar & Sons, [1940–49]); K. L. Gauba, *Famous and Historic Trials* (Lahore: Lion, 1946); and Bejoy Krishna Bose, *The Alipore Bomb Trial* (Calcutta: Butterworth, 1922).

125. On Bengali detective fiction see Shampa Roy, *Gender and Criminality in Bangla Crime Narratives* (Palgrave Macmillan, 2017); and Debayan Deb Barman, ed., *Critical Essays on English and Bengali Detective Fiction* (Lexington Books, 2022). On the genre in Hindi see Francesca Orsini, "Detective Novels: A Commercial Genre in Nineteenth-Century North India," in *India's Literary History: Essays on the Nineteenth Century*, ed. Stuart Blackburn and Vasudha Dalmia (Delhi: Permanent Black, 2004), 435–82.

126. Charu Singh, "The Shastri and the Air-Pump: Experimental Fictions and Fictions of Experiment for Hindi Readers in Colonial North India," *History of Science* 60, no. 2 (2022): 243–46.

127. On bloodstain testing see, by Hemendra Kumar Ray, "Aprilosyo prothum diboshe," in *Jayanta-Manik Samagra (Akhanda Sangskaran)* (n.p., n.d.), 1070, and "Amabosyar raat," in *Bimal-Kumar Adventure Samagra (Akhanda Sangskaran)* (n.p., n.d.), 283. On rare poisons see "Holud Soytan," in Nihar Ranjan Gupta, *Kiriti Omnibus* (Kolkata: Amar, 1972), 2:1–42, also available as Anwesha Maity, trans., "Blood-Faced Dragon," *Metamorphosis* 29, no. 1 (2021): 135–73.

Darogar Daptar stories, for example.[128] Mukhopadhyay's stories were based on real cases, unlike more fantastical accounts like "Blood-Faced Dragon" that combined detective, romance, adventure, and science fiction genres in a novella pitting detective Kiriti Roy against the Chinese toxicologist and serial killer Dr. Wang.[129] Whether these stories came from the author's professional experience or his imagination, though, they raised public awareness of forensic tests and institutions. Some plausible form of colonial infrastructure was usually running in the background.

Detective fiction, newspapers, and "famous trial" books were consumed by far more than literate urban elites. Friends borrowed copies of periodicals from subscribers or had them read out to them, possibly in oral translation, if they were illiterate or did not speak the original language.[130] People gathered at bookshops, hotels, and tea houses and stalls to listen to these texts read aloud.[131] Factories hired "lectors" to read to laborers while they worked.[132] Equally, moviegoers flocked to the talkies by the 1930s to watch detective thrillers and courtroom dramas.[133] People listened to detective stories on the radio, too.[134] In short, South Asian publics—including the nonliterate—learned about forensic infrastructure through news and popular culture with the same appetite as others around the world.[135] As this book shows, however, *what* they absorbed was distinctive to South Asia and the colonial context.

---

128. In Priyanath Mukhopadhyay, *Darogar Daptar* (Kolkata: Punashcha, 2004), vol. 1, see "Motia Bibi" (story no. 133), 42, 47, and "Kaal-Porinoy" (no. 162), 236. In vol. 2 see "Prem Pagalini" (no. 198), 242, 246. In vol. 2 of Gupta, *Kiriti Omnibus*, see "Dainir Banshi," 76, and "Boshonto Rojoni," 409–13.

129. Gupta, "Holud Soytan," or Maity, "Blood-Faced Dragon." Gupta changed his novella's title from its original "Blood-Faced Dragon" (1940) to "Holud Soytan" (Yellow Devil) in 1963 when the work was republished following the Sino-Indian War (1962). I thank Navnidhi Sharma for an illuminating exchange on this topic.

130. On the South Asian diasporic context see Isabel Hofmeyr, *Gandhi's Printing Press: Experiments in Slow Reading* (Harvard University Press, 2013), 44, 132, 141–42.

131. Megan Eaton Robb, *Print and the Urdu Public: Muslims, Newspapers, and Urban Life in Colonial India* (Oxford University Press, 2020), 25.

132. On lectors in South Indian beedi factories see Suramya Thekke Kalathil and Santhosh Abraham, "Regulation and Resistance: Defactorisation in the Beedi Industry of Colonial Malabar, 1937–1942," *Labor History* 61, no. 5–6 (2020): 664.

133. Debashree Mukherjee, *Bombay Hustle: Making Movies in a Colonial City* (Columbia University Press, 2020), 54–55, 170–78.

134. For example see *The Indian Listener* 1, no. 16 (1936). On radio in India before World War II see Isabel Huacuja Alonso, *Radio for the Millions: Hindi-Urdu Broadcasting Across Borders* (Columbia University Press, 2023), 25–32.

135. On the Anglo-American context see Ronald R. Thomas, *Detective Fiction and the Rise of Forensic Science* (Cambridge University Press, 1999).

Plan of the Book

This book consists of two parts. Part 1, "Falsity from Without," focuses on planted poison and animal blood in murder and rape cases. The first chapter, "Planted Poison and Wrongful Convictions," looks at forensic toxicology. It focuses on attempts to interfere with forensic processes, along with lab analysts' concerns over the risk of wrongful convictions. This chapter features mineral poisons like arsenic planted in stomach and liver samples, in cremation ashes, and in unaccompanied forensic samples in transit, as well as snake venom used to poison cows rectally. It tells a history, outside the US context, of concern over wrongful convictions before DNA analysis and the innocence movement. CEs' anxiety over wrongful convictions, this chapter shows, was rooted in their belief in native mendacity. In contrast to the US context today, the concern with wrongful convictions in colonial India was *inspired* by racial bias, rather than envisioned as a corrective to it.

Chapter 2, "Planted Animal Blood and Murder," ties anxiety about this kind of false evidence—planted to punish adversaries—to the creation of the office of the imperial serologist in Calcutta and the precipitin test, which identified the species of origin of bloodstains. Precipitin testing enjoyed a fuller life in India than in Britain, and the reasons for this reveal layers of legal pluralism. The study of legal pluralism examines interactions between coexisting legal orders, including relationships of conflict and competition.[136] This chapter examines in particular a noncolonial mode of dispute resolution that I call "punitive self-harm" (hurting oneself or one's kin to punish an enemy). First, a person might kill their relative to protest against an adversary, and then, as a next step, by planting animal blood, the death could be made to look as if the adversary had committed it. The move reflected the adaptation of a noncolonial mode of disputing to the requirements of colonial law, and an attempt to harness the latter's tools while subverting its larger aims. The precipitin test was so important in British India because it revealed false cases like these, involving punitive self-harm.

The third chapter, "Bloodstains, Spermatozoa, and Rape," tells the story of competitive stain analysis in sexual forensics. During the early twentieth century, a rivalry developed between two kinds of forensic lab work: serology and microscopy. In the 1900s and 1910s, precipitin testing worked in favor of a subset of males accused of rape, namely those who could show that bloodstains in their

136. See William Twining, "Normative and Legal Pluralism: A Global Perspective," *Duke Journal of Comparative and International Law* 20 (2010): 489.

case were in fact animal blood. By the 1930s and 1940s, a new sperm cell staining technique developed in South Asia: Sperm cells suddenly became easier to identify, and this operated in favor of women and girls suspected of making false accusations. The chapter examines the relationship between scientific advances and legal change in the courtroom. As new scientific tools became available, the courts tightened the corroboration rule in rape cases. This rule required independent evidence to confirm the testimony of the female accuser. By the 1930s and 1940s, judges started insisting that this additional evidence be scientific and medical in nature. They also made it harder for a jury to make an exception to the corroboration requirement. Although sperm cell staining could have unraveled older assumptions about female mendacity, the courts instead tightened the corroboration rule and imbued science, not female accusers, with credibility.

Part 2, "Falsity from Within," shifts from individual and largely nonstate examples of planted evidence to state actors. "Expert Misconduct," the fourth chapter, features two disciplinary cases involving British forensic experts. Assistant CE W. S. Newman was dismissed in 1893 for producing a misleading certificate of blood analysis in a Madras murder trial. Civil surgeon C. V. Falvey was investigated in north India in the late 1930s for falsifying medical opinions in sex crime and age determination cases in return for bribes. This chapter describes how CrPC s.510 and internal disciplinary processes provided cover for misconduct, particularly when committed by Britons.

The fifth chapter of the book, "Adversarialism, Inquisitorialism, and Experts," features conflicts between "men of law" and "men of science." (The professionals in this study were almost exclusively male.) It explores a conflict over the best way to discover truth—whether through a competition between opposing narratives (between experts or adversarial lawyers) or a focused quest by a single evaluator (whether expert or inquisitorial judge). This chapter reveals not only conflict between law, on the one hand, and science and medicine, on the other, but also debates *within* each profession. In nineteenth-century England, some men of science embraced the model of a competitive marketplace of ideas for science, while others felt that this adversarialism undermined the scientific quest for truth. Similarly, some legal professionals celebrated a turn to civilian law-based processes that made the courtroom a more inquisitorial and truth-seeking space, using court-appointed experts, than its English-speaking adversarial counterpart, which was often paralyzed by the "battle of the experts." Many men of science and law spoke admiringly of German forensic science (coming out of the civilian tradition); and Scottish forensics (also with civilian roots) disproportionately influenced Indian forensic science because of the many Scots in empire and medicine.[137] The colonial context intensified these debates over truth mechanics. Indian forensic treatise writers like J. P. Modi ultimately removed remnants of the "native mendacity" stereotype from these discussions.

The book's conclusion offers reflections on the relationship between truth and justice in the colonial context. A small number of colonized subjects made false accusations in order to pursue justice (as they saw it) not through truth, but falsity. Their maneuvers revealed a little-known move within legal pluralism: attempts to adapt the colonial legal system for noncolonial and even anticolonial purposes. By contrast, the legal system itself used colonial truth mechanics to try to extract truth through the use of science and medicine in the courtroom. Through the intersection of legal with scientific tests, though, the CrPC (s.510) made CEs less accountable for substandard work. The interaction of systems—punitive self-harm with the criminal legal system, and law with science and medicine—generated special types of falsity in colonial South Asia.

Caveats

It is important to acknowledge the limits of this study. First, police played a key role in creating falsity. They diverted the proper course of justice in return for bribes.[138] They raped women in their custody and lied about it (chapter 3). They falsified records and planted evidence.[139] They framed people for crimes they had not committed.[140] The focus of this study, though, is different, namely fal-

---

137. Medical jurisprudence was a required part of medical training in Scotland (unlike in England), and the earliest university chair in the field in the Anglophone world was created in Scotland. See Clark Bell, "Medical Jurisprudence in America in the Nineteenth Century," *Texas Medical Journal* 16, no. 5 (1900): 203; Douglas Maclagan, "Address in Forensic Medicine, Delivered at the Forty-Sixth Annual Meeting of the British Medical Association, Held in Bath, August 6–9, 1878," *BMJ* 2, no. 920 (1878): 233–39; James C. Mohr, *Doctors and the Law: Medical Jurisprudence in Nineteenth-Century America* (Johns Hopkins University Press, 1993), 5–6; and M. Anne Crowther and Brenda White, *On Soul and Conscience: The Medical Expert and Crime; 150 Years of Forensic Medicine in Glasgow* (Aberdeen University Press, 1988). On Anglophone admiration for German models see Mohr, *Doctors*, 231–32.

138. For a major bribery case resulting in the conviction of Irish detective Charles Ring and nine other police officers in Bombay see *Emp. v. C. E. Ring and Others*, ILR Bom. 53 (1929): 479–508. On Ring see Sharafi, *Law and Identity*, 60.

139. For example see Irvine, "Some Notes," 354; *Amrit Sonar v. King-Emperor*, Patna Law Journal 4 (1919): 525–32; *Queen-Empress v. Muhammad Shah Khan and Another*, ILR All. 20 (1897–98): 307–11; and *Queen-Empress v. Muhammad Saeed Khan*, ILR All. 21 (1898–99): 113–16.

140. A police inspector named Fakir Pakiri was convicted for framing over twenty people in Dedaye, Burma; see Saha, "'Uncivilized Practitioners,'" 435. On the attempted framing of one Malek Chand by police see H. L. Adam, *Oriental Crime* (London: T. Werner Laurie, [1908–9]), 64–101.

sity involving forensic experts. Important new research on policing in modern India by Radha Kumar, Deana Heath, Uponita Mukherjee, Jinee Lokaneeta, and Mayur Suresh documents the mechanics of police falsity, both historically and today.[141] I leave to future researchers the creation of a full portrait of police falsity in the late colonial period, ideally using police archives in India.[142]

Second, there is the matter of gender. Unsurprisingly, women and girls were well represented among the targets of crime in this study, including murder and rape (chapters 1–3). Often, they were the objects of male relatives' violence through punitive "self" harm (chapter 2 and conclusion). A common narrative was that an elderly mother volunteered to be killed by her male relatives in order to falsely incriminate someone as a way to further the family's fight. The logic of punitive self-harm was deeply patriarchal, both because the lives of female relatives were deemed expendable and because of the idea that the good mother should insist on sacrificing herself for the family.

South Asian females were also the subjects of a virulent intersectional version of native mendacity. They were typically viewed with suspicion when accusing men of rape, and when their accounts of physical assault were assessed for the possibility of fabrication. Relatedly, illicit abortions were also blamed on women—not just the pregnant woman, but also the village midwife or *dai,* who was often deemed a secret abortionist, too. Treatise authors vilified *dais* in harsh terms, which was also part of the larger professionalization project of excluding women and Indigenous practitioners from the realm of respectable (allopathic) medicine.[143] Many village midwives were lower caste.[144] More broadly, women in South Asia (as elsewhere) were associated with deviousness and poisoning, particularly when they managed the domestic care and food supply of others.[145]

---

141. Radha Kumar, *Police Matters: The Everyday State and Caste Politics in South India, 1900–1975* (Cornell University Press, 2021); Radha Kumar, "Witnessing Violence, Witnessing as Violence: Police Torture and Power in Twentieth-Century India," *Law & Social Inquiry* 47, no. 3 (2022): 946–70; Deana Heath, *Colonial Terror: Torture and State Violence in Colonial India* (Oxford University Press, 2021); Mukherjee, "Colonial Detection"; Jinee Lokaneeta, *The Truth Machines: Policing, Violence, and Scientific Interrogations in India* (University of Michigan Press, 2020); and Mayur Suresh, *Terror Trials: Life and Law in Delhi's Courts* (Fordham University Press, 2023).

142. See the use of historical records housed at South Indian police stations in Kumar, *Police Matters*; and the archives of police museums in cities like Kolkata and Mumbai.

143. See Sharafi, "Abortion," 378–79, 389.

144. For example, Chamar women were midwives to Thakurs in north India during the early independent period, and probably before. See Bernard Cohn, "Jajman–Parjuniya Relations—Chamars," ethnographic field notes (Senapur, Uttar Pradesh, December 17, 1952), box 4, folder 2, 307, in Bernard Cohn Papers.

145. On the association of women with poisoning see Arnold, *Toxic Histories*, 29–32, and Ian Burney, *Poison, Detection and the Victorian Imagination* (Manchester University Press, 2006), 21–32.

Very few women appear in this study as lawyers, judges, or forensic analysts. There were women who studied law in this period, but they encountered significant barriers when they tried to practice.[146] Women lawyers and doctors in late colonial India got their foot in the door by serving the needs of women, including those who lived in seclusion or *purdah* in the *zenana* (inner quarters of the house reserved for females).[147] However, this did not translate into being active players in state forensic institutions before 1947. There were occasionally female physicians who appeared as experts in civil disputes, including cases in the Parsi Chief Matrimonial Court in Bombay.[148] But women were not allowed into the IMS until World War II.[149] The fact that so many of the forensic analysts in this story were embedded within military hierarchies meant that women were blocked from becoming CEs, for instance. As a result, women and girls appear as dissimulators and targets of crime in this book, but not as the professionals running the system.

---

146. See A. J. C. Mistry, *Forty Years Reminiscences of the High Court of Judicature at Bombay* (Bombay: published by the author, 1925), 43–45; and Sharafi, *Law and Identity*, 108, at note 140.

147. Cornelia Sorabji convinced officials to create the post of lady legal assistant to the Court of Wards for her in 1904. In this role, she gave legal advice to *purdahnashin*, who could not have direct contact with men outside their families. See Cornelia Sorabji, *The Purdahnashin* (Calcutta: Thacker, Spink, 1917); and Mary Jane Mossman, "Gender and Professionalism in Law: The Challenge of (Women's) Biography," *Windsor Yearbook of Access to Justice* 27 (2009): 26. On the importance of *zenana* hospitals for female physicians' education and professional advancement see Sujata Mukherjee, *Gender, Medicine, and Society in Colonial India: Women's Health Care in Nineteenth- and Early Twentieth-Century Bengal* (Oxford University Press, 2017); and Samiksha Sehrawat, "Feminising Empire: The Association of Medical Women in India and the Campaign to Found a Women's Medical Service," *Social Scientist* 41, no. 5–6 (2013): 65–81. On female physicians in colonial India see Geraldine Forbes, *The New Cambridge History of India*, vol. 4, pt. 2, *Women in Modern India* (Cambridge University Press, 1996), 157, 161–67.

148. I have identified three female physicians who testified in the Parsi Chief Matrimonial Court (PCMC) of Bombay: Dr. Edith Pechey-Phipson (case no. 4 of 1893), Dr. Avabai Maneckji Mehta (no. 1 of 1932), and Dr. Myrtle Noronha (no. 12 of 1938). See PCMC notebooks (1893–1947), courtroom 21, BHC. On Pechey-Phipson and/or Mehta see Mridula Ramanna, "Women Physicians as Vital Intermediaries in Colonial Bombay," *Economic and Political Weekly* 43, no. 12–13 (2008): 71–72, 74, 78; and Sharmita Ray, "Women Doctors' Masterful Maneuverings: Colonial Bengal, Late Nineteenth and Early Twentieth Centuries," *Social Scientist* 42, no. 3–4 (2014): 71–72. On the PCMC see Sharafi, *Law and Identity*, 193–236.

149. The Association of Medical Women in India lobbied for the creation of a Women's Medical Service of India (WMSI) that would parallel the all-male IMS. They succeeded, and the WMSI was created in 1913. See Sehrawat, "Feminising Empire." The first women physicians were commissioned into the IMS during World War II. See B. L. Raina, *Official History of the Indian Armed Forces in the Second World War 1939-45: Medical Services. Administration* (Delhi: Combined Inter Services Historical Section, India & Pakistan, 1953), 38. I found neither WMSI nor female wartime IMS members among the ranks of forensic analysts, 1913–47.

Third, this study focuses on crime among South Asians, not on interracial cases. Britons feared poisoning and rape by colonized people in South Asia, as elsewhere in the British empire.[150] However, the number of such interracial cases with a South Asian defendant was small in the reported case law.[151] Britons falsely accused South Asians of crimes including "outraging the modesty" of white women. Some of these were recognized as false by police inquiries.[152] There were a handful of other interracial crimes involving falsity with British defendants. These included everything from rape to forgery in gun purchases and banking.[153] The majority of all types of crimes examined here, though, involved South Asians on both sides.

Although this book is not a study of interracial crime, it is worth addressing the question of whether forensic science was applied differently on a racial basis. Certain crimes were reported to be more prevalent in particular regions, like cattle poisoning in Hindu-majority areas (chapter 1). There were also differences noted in the size and shape of South Asian and European skeletons. For instance, one treatise observed that "different modes of sitting" altered the pelvis, spinal column, and leg bones.[154] Such patterns aside, though, lab-based analysis does not seem to have been conducted differently according to the race of the victim or suspect. Researchers certainly looked for racialized patterns in everything from blood groups to fingerprints.[155] These ventures were largely fruitless for forensic purposes, though.[156] CEs also complained about the lack of contextual information that was forwarded with samples for testing. This made their work more

---

150. For instance see Melanie J. Newton, "The King v. Robert James, a Slave, for Rape: Inequality, Gender, and British Slave Amelioration, 1823–1834," *Comparative Studies in Society and History* 47, no. 3 (2005): 583–610; and Clarence V. H. Maxwell, " 'The Horrid Villainy': Sarah Bassett and the Poisoning Conspiracies in Bermuda, 1727–30," *Slavery and Abolition* 21, no. 3 (2000): 48–74.

151. See chapters 1 and 3.

152. For example see "A Law Point," *Indian Daily News*, July 28, 1904.

153. See chapter 3; *Causley v. Emp*, ILR Cal. 43 (1915): 421–25; *Clifford and Others v. King-Emperor*, CWN 18 (1913): 374–78; and "Accountant Charged with Cheating. Story of False Balance Sheets," *Civil & Military Gazette*, June 14, 1929.

154. Isidore Bernadotte Lyon, *Lyon's Medical Jurisprudence for India*, 7th ed., ed. L. A. Waddell (Calcutta: Thacker, Spink, 1921), 51.

155. For example see Projit Bihari Mukharji, "From Serosocial to Sanguinary Identities: Caste, Transnational Race Science and the Shifting Metonymies of Blood Group B, India c. 1918–1960," *IESHR* 51, no. 2 (2014): 143–76; and Cole, *Suspect Identities*, 97–118.

156. Blood science did, however, provide the foundation for the new discipline of "seroanthropology" in late colonial and early postcolonial India. This field created racialized categories to explain caste and other kinds of demographic difference among South Asians. See Projit Bihari Mukharji, *Brown Skins, White Coats: Race Science in India, 1920–66* (University of Chicago Press, 2022).

time-consuming—but also more independent from police.[157] Non-lab forms of analysis created more opportunities for racial bias, particularly when the expert was British. For instance, death investigation usually involved an awareness of the race of the deceased by the examiner. Autopsies were highly interpretive and were usually not replicable or verifiable: The examination destroyed the thing being analyzed. There was also enlarged-spleen syndrome, which could occur among people infected with malaria. It provided a handy way out for defendants, particularly British employers, who claimed that they had only lightly beaten a South Asian worker who then died unexpectedly.[158] Despite these areas, it was most of all the predominantly white jury (including the "special jury") that slanted criminal case outcomes along racial lines.[159] In other words, it was the adjudication mechanism more than scientific analysis (particularly in the lab) that skewed criminal cases on the basis of race. It is also worth clarifying that the rule in CrPC s.510 did not apply differently to people of different races in India. Rather, it existed in India but not in England, reducing the ability in criminal trials to gain clarity on crucial scientific findings in the colony, which was majority nonwhite. As noted already, the vast majority of criminal cases relating to s.510 involved South Asians on all sides.

Fourth, this study focuses not so much on classic crimes of falsity like forgery, perjury, impersonation, and counterfeiting, nor on the planting of illicit drugs, but on the framing of rivals for serious violent crimes like murder and rape. It was fear of the false in murder and rape cases that led to major forensic developments like the institutionalization of the precipitin test. Other crimes of falsity are prime subjects for future research, building on the work of Bhavani Raman and Jonathan Saha on forgery along with Wendie Schneider on perjury.[160]

Fifth and finally, this study focuses on British India (what is today Pakistan, India, and Bangladesh) and Burma (now Myanmar). I use "South Asia" as shorthand to refer to these regions, while realizing that I am leaving out others

157. For example see CE Report for Bengal 1928, 9, and 1932, 8 (both IOR/V/24/423); and 1942, 7 (IOR/V/24/424).

158. See Jordanna Bailkin, "The Boot and the Spleen: When Was Murder Possible in British India?," *Comparative Studies in Society and History* 48, no. 2 (2006): 462–93; Kolsky, *Colonial Justice*, 135–40; and Sharafi, *Law and Identity*, 53.

159. On the jury see appendix 2.

160. Schneider, *Engines of Truth*, 103–42; Raman, *Document Raj*, 137–60; and, by Jonathan Saha, "Paperwork as Commodity, Corruption as Accumulation: Land Records and Licenses in Colonial Myanmar, c. 1900," in Kroeze et al., *Corruption*, 293–315; and "'Devious Documents.'" For a comparative take on document authentication in the princely state of Hyderabad see Elizabeth Lhost, *Everyday Islamic Law and the Making of Modern South Asia* (University of North Carolina Press, 2022), 155–59.

typically considered part of South Asia: Ceylon (now Sri Lanka), Nepal, Bhutan, the Maldives, and Afghanistan. Ceylon, in particular, was the site of significant forensic developments during the late nineteenth and early twentieth century. As it was a colony governed by the Colonial Office, not the India Office, though, it was administratively quite separate from British India (which included British Burma). Consequently, I leave its forensic histories to other scholars.[161]

Any scholar studying falsity in the past must acknowledge the limits of their own field of vision. An archive of false cases is inherently imperfect, because only the *failed* false cases—the ones where someone messed up—are visible to the historian. Successful acts of dissimulation, whether by colonized tricksters or corrupt lab experts, have passed into history as the genuine thing. If these actors fooled the professionals in this book, then they may fool us, too.[162] Despite these limitations, falsity remains a productive lens (if a cloudy one) through which to see agency in South Asia's past and to press for fair trials in its present. This book moves beyond the assumption that allegations of falsity reflected the rule of colonial difference and nothing else. And it reveals the troubled history of practices that continue to compromise the quality of criminal trials across the postcolonial world today.

Colonial authorities worried about the risk of wrongful convictions because of their belief in native and female mendacity, while failing to recognize the role of legal pluralism and lax criminal procedure in enabling false evidence. Truth and justice did not always travel together, but not for the reasons usually cited by colonial officials. Colonized tricksters knew that justice might flow from their false evidence, which was their intention. Careless and corrupt experts must have realized that injustice would flow from their false evidence, but justice was not their primary concern. According to debates within and between the forensic professions, misinformation and injustice could result from processes that were supposed to generate truth, whether because there was too much competition between ideas (according to some) or not enough (according to others). The relationship between truth and justice, and between legal and scientific forms of knowledge, took on special shape in British India and Burma. Through false cases, this book reconstructs these configurations and the lessons they hold.

---

161. See Blum, "Forensic Empire."

162. On "how-we-know-what-we-know about empire" in light of fabricated primary sources see Saha, "'Devious Documents,'" 169–70, 178–80.

Part I

FALSITY FROM WITHOUT

1

PLANTED POISON AND WRONGFUL CONVICTIONS

In 1880, Dr. William Center described a phenomenon that he encountered regularly as the chemical examiner (CE) of Punjab: planted poison. His lab received stomach and liver specimens from suspected human and cattle poisoning cases. Arsenic would normally be detected in the stomach if it had killed the deceased. But sometimes the liver would also test positive for arsenic, a sign that the poison had been added to that organ *after death*. Not just the location, but also the form of the poison could be wrong in fabricated cases. In a cattle case from the frontier region, chunks of arsenic were crudely inserted into slits made in a liver. The magistrate asked whether arsenic could be deposited in this form by natural causes. A medical officer must have said no.[1]

Center's report showed that CEs had to be on the lookout for double dissimulation. They were watching not only for regular cases of criminal poisoning disguised as illness or accident, but also for situations where one person tried to frame another person by planting poison. Both by dint of numbers and because of colonial stereotypes about deviousness and native mendacity, the actors in false poisoning cases were assumed to be South Asian. In contrast to colonial India's profusion of physical assaults, including torture by police and the kicking and shooting of Indians to death by white men, poisoning was a subtle crime.[2]

1. "Report of the CE to Government, Punjab, for the Year 1879," 12 (IOR/V/24/418).

2. See Deana Heath, *Colonial Terror: Torture and State Violence in Colonial India* (Oxford University Press, 2021); and Elizabeth Kolsky, *Colonial Justice in British India: White Violence and the Rule of Law* (Cambridge University Press, 2010). For a catalog of kicking, shooting, and police torture cases

It was a weapon of the weak, but also of the clever.[3] Planted poison was doubly so—poisoning by one person made to look like poisoning by another—and it fueled colonial stereotypes about South Asian trickery.

Using the annual reports of the CEs from across India and Burma, this chapter examines wrongful convictions and anxiety about them in a colonial context. I join historians Ian Burney and E. Claire Cage in telling a history—but in this case, a non-US and non-European one—of wrongful convictions before the innocence movement.[4] Throughout, the concern with innocence hitched itself to the larger civilizing mission. The prevention of wrongful convictions was part of Britain's rule-of-law agenda, which did important rhetorical work in justifying British rule in India.[5] Racial bias, false evidence, and the desire to avoid wrongful convictions were configured differently in the context of India and planted poison. A heightened awareness of the risk of wrongful convictions was driven not by concern over racial bias in the criminal legal system *but by racial bias itself.* In other words, the CEs' concern with the risk of convicting the innocent was particularly acute because they operated in a colonial setting where they believed "native trickery" was ubiquitous. They worried about wrongful convictions through planted poison because they believed that South Asians dissimulated. Or, at least, this was how the story began at a time when the CEs were British. As South Asians rose through the forensic ranks, they shifted the model away from native mendacity. Chunilal Bose, the first South Asian CE, explained India's high poisoning rates in alternative terms that were not grounded in cultural or racial theories about falsity.

Forensic toxicology and the courts in colonial India were knowledge-producing systems with certain shared goals. Both attempted to identify and punish deliberate poisoning—as a scientific phenomenon detected in the lab and as a legal phenomenon proven in the courtroom. We might think of deliberate poisoning that went undetected in the lab (even though poison was indeed present) and unproven in the courtroom as two forms—scientific and legal "false negatives." CEs and criminal courts alike also tried to avoid "false positives," namely findings in the lab, and in the courtroom, of poisoning where no poisoning had been

---

see *Amrita Bazar Patrika* (*ABP*); and Ram Gopal Sanyal, ed., *The Record of Criminal Cases as Between Europeans and Natives for the Last Hundred Years* (Calcutta, 1896).

3. James C. Scott, *Weapons of the Weak: Everyday Forms of Peasant Resistance* (Yale University Press, 1985).

4. See E. Claire Cage, *The Science of Proof: Forensic Medicine in Modern France* (Cambridge University Press, 2022), 12–13, 42–43, 61–62; and Ian Burney, *Partisans for Justice: Erle Stanley Gardner's Pursuit of Innocence in Postwar America* (in progress).

5. See Mitra Sharafi, "Indian Constitutionalism, the Rule of Law, and Parsi Legal Culture," *Indian Law Review* 7, no. 3 (2023): 263–65.

committed by the person accused. When false positives suggested a deliberate attempt to frame another person for poisoning, they are interesting because they indicate a particularly bold and ambitious form of engagement with colonial institutions. These cases may have been attempts to actively harness colonial science and law to frame rivals for crime.[6] This chapter explores these two parts of the CEs' job—avoiding false negatives and false positives—before focusing on the debate about poison detection rates and the larger aims of justice. Interpretation of a lab's annual poison detection rate was the subject of discussion for decades between the heads of these labs and their military medical superiors. In their own defense, some CEs stressed that a lower poison detection rate did not necessarily mean a less effective lab. Identifying cases where criminal poisoning *had not* occurred was just as important as detecting cases where it *had*. These discussions are especially interesting and relevant here because they reflected a quite striking concern about the conviction of innocent people, especially given that responses to the problem of wrongful convictions in the English-speaking world lagged behind continental Europe at this time, and, in British India, concern over miscarriages of justice was more muted than in England.[7] The CEs' extraordinary attention to the risk of wrongful convictions was closely connected to a belief in native mendacity, manifested in the phenomenon of planted poison.

Avoiding False Negatives: Detecting Poisoning in British India

Forensic toxicologists, who were generally physicians in this period, agreed that known poisoning rates in India were much higher than in England. In 1895, the first Indian CE, Chunilal Bose, and his coauthor J. F. Evans noted that the per capita rate of known murder cases by poison in Bengal was over three times higher than in England.[8] The CE of Punjab, D. R. Thomas, wrote in 1940 that "poisoning, both suicidal and homicidal in India, is very common" compared

---

6. On the quest to identify planted animal blood in similar situations see chapters 2 and 3.

7. See, by Edwin M. Borchard, *Convicting the Innocent: Sixty-Five Actual Errors of Criminal Justice* (Garden City Publishing, 1932), 375, 378, and "European Systems of State Indemnity for Errors of Criminal Justice," in his *State Indemnity for Errors of Criminal Justice* (Washington, DC: Government Printing Office, 1912), 5–33.

8. J. F. Evans and Chunilal Bose, "The Necessity for an Act Restricting the Free Sale of Poisons in Bengal," *Transactions of the First Indian Medical Congress* (1895), in *The Scientific and Other Papers of Rai Chunilal Bose Bahadur*, ed. J. P. Bose (Calcutta: n.p., 1924), 1:211. On Bose see David Arnold, *Toxic Histories: Poison and Pollution in Modern India* (Cambridge University Press, 2017), 114–15.

with its frequency in Western countries, and the number of cases was higher still, he wrote, because "it must be remembered that in India the criminals are not always brought to Justice."[9] In colonial-era writings, poisoning was viewed as an Indian specialty (figure 3). European unfamiliarity with many poisonous plants growing in the Indian countryside amplified the fear of native deception.[10] Unsurprisingly, then, toxicology played an outsize role in Indian forensics. Poisoning often occupied one-third of the pages in textbooks on Indian medical jurisprudence.[11]

A number of patterns emerge from the hundreds of brief case descriptions in the CE reports. There were cases of wives (some with lovers) who fed their husbands arsenic or the crushed glass of their bangles, and of husbands who poisoned their wives with opium.[12] In abortion cases that killed women, the viscera sometimes revealed poison ingested orally or applied to reproductive organs.[13] Many cases of suspected cattle poisoning emerged out of Hindu-majority regions of South Asia. Lower-caste communities such as Chamars were accused of poisoning cows, with the allegation that they made these deaths look like illness to obtain the animals' skins for their leatherwork.[14] Also common were cases of drugged and robbed travelers, particularly religious pilgrims.[15] Poisoning by medical "quacks" (sometimes Ayurvedic and Unani practitioners) who gave patients poisonous pills and powders were another common type of case.[16] There were many suicides involving toxic substances.[17] Equally, there was murder by

9. "Report of the CE to Government, Punjab, for the Year 1940," xii (IOR/V/24/421).

10. On both poisoning and the fear of poisoning (including poison panics) in South Asian history see Arnold, *Toxic Histories*.

11. For instance see Isidore Bernadotte Lyon, *Lyon's Medical Jurisprudence for India*, 7th ed., ed. L. A. Waddell (Calcutta: Thacker, Spink, 1921); and Jaising P. Modi, *A Textbook of Medical Jurisprudence and Toxicology*, 6th ed. (Bombay: Butterworth, 1940).

12. See "Report of the CE to Government, Bengal, for the Year 1915," 6 (IOR/V/24/422); and "The Bombay CA's Report for 1895," *Indian Medico-Chirurgical Review* 4, no. 5 (1896): 236.

13. For example see "Annual Report of the CE to Government, United Provinces and Central Provinces, for the Year 1937," 5 (IOR/V/24/417); and "Report of the CA to Government, Bombay, for the Year 1933," 7 (IOR/V/24/409). See also Evans and Bose, "Necessity," 240–41; and Mitra Sharafi, "Abortion in South Asia, 1860–1947: A Medico-Legal History," *MAS* 55, no. 2 (2021): 371–428.

14. For example see "Annual Report of the CE to Government, Bengal, for the Year 1937," 15–16 (IOR/V/24/424). See also Evans and Bose, "Necessity," 224–25, 256–57.

15. For example see "Annual Report of the CE to Government, Bengal, for the Year 1899," 16 (IOR/V/24/422); and "Annual Report of the CE to Government, Madras, for the Year 1930," 3–4 (G.O. no. 1175, in Annual Reports Government of Madras, box 1144.020000, IOR).

16. For example see "Annual Report of the CE to Government, United Provinces and Central Provinces, for the Year 1937," 6 (IOR/V/24/417). See also Evans and Bose, "Necessity," 267.

17. For example see "Annual Report of the CE to Government, Bengal, for the Year 1914," 7 (IOR/V/24/422); "Annual Report of the CE to Government, Bengal, for the Year 1935," 12

FIGURE 3. / Six poisoners. M. Pauparao Naidu, *The History of Professional Poisoners and Coiners of India* (Madras: Higginbotham, 1912), plate opposite p. 2.

poison made to look like suicide—and less often, suicide by poison made to look like murder.[18] The quintessential colonial fear was that Indian cooks and servants would poison their British employers at home. Only a small number of these cases appear in the archive, dwarfed by anxiety over such cases.[19] There were

(IOR/V/24/424); and "Annual Report of the CE to Government, United Provinces and Central Provinces, for the Year 1940," 5–6 (IOR/V/24/417).

18. On possible poison murders made to look like suicide see "Annual Report of the CE to Government, Bengal, for the Year 1936," 12 (IOR/V/24/424); and "Annual Report of the CE to Government, Bengal, for the Year 1941," 14 (IOR/V/24/424). For a suicide made to look like murder see "Report of the CE to Government, Madras, for the Year 1899," 8, in "Remarks on the Reports of the CEs to Local Governments for the Year 1899" (IOR/P/5878).

19. For the only clear cases I encountered see "Report of the CA to Government, Bombay, for the Year 1891," 5 (IOR/V/24/406); and "Annual Report of the CE and Bacteriologist to the Governments of the United Provinces of Agra and Oudh and of the Central Provinces for the Year 1913," 2 (IOR/V/24/415).

a handful of poisonings motivated by the desire to collect life insurance, but, unlike in England, the numbers were small.[20]

The vast majority of forensic cases CEs received during the late nineteenth century involved arsenic and opium.[21] Arsenic had no taste, color, or smell and was fatal in small doses. It was "the homicidal and cattle poison of India."[22] Opium, with its distinctive smell and taste, was more often used for suicide. Datura, a flowering plant in the nightshade family, stupefied its victims, enabling robbery.[23] Arsenic fell in the poison rankings by the 1930s as its sale became restricted and as potential poisoners learned, through education and newspaper coverage of murder trials, of the effectiveness of testing for arsenic.[24] At this time, opium surpassed arsenic, and oleander became more popular from the 1940s on.[25] Other poisons appeared occasionally in the annual reports, including botanicals such as aconite, croton oil, eucalyptus oil, *Nux vomica*, and plant extracts such as cyanides, morphine, and strychnine.[26] Mineral poisons like copper sulfate, red lead (lead oxide), and mercury appeared regularly in the CEs'

---

20. For example see "Report of the CA to Government Bombay for the Year 1895" (Bombay: Government Central Press, 1896), 9 (IOR/V/24/406); and rapid cremation case from 1931 Punjab in this chapter. On England see Ian Burney, *Poison, Detection, and the Victorian Imagination* (Manchester University Press, 2012), 135–39.

21. "Report of the CA to Government, Bombay, for the Year 1898," 2 (IOR/V/24/406). See also "Poisoning in India," *BMJ* 2, no. 1655 (1892): 642.

22. Evans and Bose, "Necessity," 283 (quoting Dr. Warden, Bengal CE, writing in 1886).

23. For overviews by poison type see appendix to "Report of the CE to Government, Punjab, for the Year 1927," i–ii (IOR/V/24/419); "Poisoning in India," 641–42; Evans and Bose, "Necessity"; and, *Lyon's Medical Jurisprudence*, ed. Waddell (1921), 446, 448. On datura see M. Pauparao Naidu, *The History of Professional Poisoners and Coiners of India* (Madras: Higginbotham, 1912), 1–83. In the late nineteenth and early twentieth centuries, datura usually did not kill its victims, but by the 1930s–40s it had become increasingly fatal (particularly in Punjab and the United and Central Provinces). The case law was divided on whether datura ought to be regarded as a deadly drug. Contrast *Queen-Empress v. Tulsha*, ILR All. 20 (1897): 143–45, and *Emperor v. Bhagwan Din*, ILR All. 30 (1908): 568–71.

24. The Poisons Act (I of 1904) took some years to have an effect, but eventually it seems to have contributed to the fall in criminal arsenic cases. See letter from inspector-general of civil hospitals, Punjab, to the Punjab government, no. 624 (April 14, 1914), 1, in "Report of the CE to Government, Punjab, for the Year 1913" (IOR/V/24/418). On the Act generally see Arnold, *Toxic Histories*, 144–75. On poisoners' awareness of the efficacy of arsenic testing see *Lyon's Medical Jurisprudence* (1921), 483; "Report of the CE to Government, Madras, for the Year 1931," 2 (G.O. no. 1124 in Annual Reports Government of Madras, box 1144.020000, IOR); CA Report for Bombay 1933, 4; and "Annual Report of the CE to Government, United Provinces and Central Provinces, for the Year 1936," 2 (IOR/V/24/417).

25. For instance see CA Report for Bombay 1933, 4; and "Report of the CE to Government, Bengal, for the Year 1942," 12 (IOR/V/24/424).

26. Eucalyptus oil appeared especially in 1930s Madras. See, for example, "Report of the CE to Government, Madras, for the Year 1932," 5 (G.O. no. 1031 in Annual Reports Government of Madras, box 1144.020000, IOR).

work.[27] And substances processed or synthesized in labs around the world also appeared, including chloral hydrate, cocaine, and carbolic acid.[28]

These were the standard cases whose forensic samples were received and tested by state labs, but a much larger universe of forensic materials never reached the CEs in usable form since putrefaction was a major problem.[29] Many forensic packages traveled long distances without refrigeration in hot and humid weather to reach regional labs.[30] Debates over the best kind of preservative to use (alcohol or saline) became entangled with questions of tampering and falsity, and are explored below (and in chapter 4). Another key factor was family and community resistance to granting access to bodies after death.[31]

Relatives and locals sometimes disguised poisoning by attributing it to illness, and CEs were left to grapple with the question: Is it poison or disease?[32] Abortion-related fever was euphemistically called malaria.[33] Strychnine poisoning could be mistaken for epilepsy.[34] The symptoms of oleander poisoning in

---

27. Red lead was used in adulterated versions of vermilion sold to Bengali Hindu wives for the part in their hair. See "Report of the CE to Government, Bengal" for 1938, 6 (IOR/V/24/424) and 1941, 4. It could also be used as an abortifacient. For example see "Report of the CA to Government, Bombay, for the Year 1930," 7–8 (IOR/V/24/409).

28. Most of the cocaine in colonial India was imported from Germany, where it was processed. When this supply became less obtainable during and after World War I, many with a "cocaine habit" replaced it with an "equally deadly 'chloral habit.'" Chloral hydrate was an addictive medication prescribed for insomnia. It was also used to stupefy and rob people. See "Report of the CE to Government, Punjab" for 1920, 2 (IOR/V/24/418) and especially 1930, appendix at ii–iii (IOR/V/24/419); and K. N. Bagchi, "Poisons in Crime," *Indian Police Gazette & Annual* 4, no. 1 (1941): 30.

29. On putrefaction see W. J. Buchanan, "A Chapter on Medical Jurisprudence in India," in Alfred Swaine Taylor, *The Principles and Practice of Medical Jurisprudence*, 5th ed., ed. Fred J. Smith (J. & A. Churchill, 1905), 2:852–53, 855; *Lyon's Medical Jurisprudence* (1921), 19–20; and Arnold, *Toxic Histories*, 110.

30. Indian railways experimented with "insulated vans," which were cooled with ice, from the 1910s. However, this type of train car did not become common until the 1940s. I thank Sanchia deSouza for sharing her research on this point. It is unclear when refrigerated train cars became available for forensic use in India. See also Projit Bihari Mukharji, *Brown Skins, White Coats: Race Science in India, 1920–66* (University of Chicago Press, 2022), 184. For histories of refrigeration in the nineteenth and twentieth centuries see Joanna Radin, *Life on Ice: A History of New Uses for Cold Blood* (University of Chicago Press, 2017), 24–28; and Rebecca J. H. Woods, "Nature and the Refrigerating Machine: The Politics and Production of Cold in the Nineteenth Century," in *Cryopolitics: Frozen Life in a Melting World*, ed. Joanna Radin and Emma Kowal (MIT Press, 2017), 89–116.

31. For example see Mitra Sharafi, *Law and Identity in Colonial South Asia: Parsi Legal Culture, 1772–1947* (Cambridge University Press, 2014), 52.

32. See *Lyon's Medical Jurisprudence* (1921), 453–57; and Evans and Bose, "Necessity," 230–31.

33. W. J. Buchanan, "A Chapter on Medical Jurisprudence in India," in Taylor, *Principles and Practice of Medical Jurisprudence* (1905), 2:861.

34. See "Report of the CE to Government, Madras, for the Year 1934," 5 (G.O. no. 1102 in Annual Reports Government of Madras, box 1144.020000, IOR).

cows closely resembled cattle disease.[35] Most common of all, it was difficult to distinguish arsenic poisoning from cholera.[36] As F. N. Windsor, CE for Bengal, noted in 1911, "The symptoms of arsenic poisoning so closely resemble those of a natural disease (cholera) that instances are not rare in which even experienced medical men have been duped and have certified to cases being cholera, which were proved to be cases of arsenic poisoning by *post mortem* and chemical examinations."[37] Indeed, in an 1894 case, a man died after eating food at a bazaar and then taking a steamer to Calcutta. One physician believed it was arsenic, but three others thought it was cholera. The CE found arsenic.[38] Windsor reported a similar series of cases falsely reported as cholera, including a case of a Muslim woman's body, disinterred after six months. Much of the body had dried up or disintegrated, but the extant fleshy parts tested positive for arsenic.[39] Three years later, the Bengal annual report included a similar case. A man had died after purging and vomiting for four days. His relatives said it was cholera and buried the body. A few days later, a local official received an anonymous letter suggesting murder by poison. The body was exhumed, and although an autopsy could not be performed owing to decomposition, a sample was sent to the CEs. They found arsenic "in marked quantity."[40] One commentator noted in 1905 that during cholera outbreaks, arsenic was used "as a means of getting rid of an enemy," particularly in Bengali land disputes.[41] The cholera-arsenic ruse appears in Bengali detective fiction, too, like Mukhopadhyay's *Darogar Daptar* stories that were based on real cases.[42]

Especially challenging were cases from communities that practiced rapid cremation, usually within twenty-four hours of death.[43] CEs suspected that many murders by poison escaped detection because relatives attributed the death to illness and quickly cremated the body. This phenomenon revealed itself through the occasional intercepted case. In Punjab in 1924, for instance, a woman died

35. CE Report for Bengal 1942, 12.

36. See *Mt. Gajrani and Another v. Emperor*, AIR All. (1933): 396, 399; and *Mt. Gaya Kunwar v. Emperor*, AIR Oudh (1934): 64. For a chart on how to distinguish arsenic poisoning from cholera see Srish Chandra Sengupta, *Bhaishajya Bichar or a Handbook of Medical Jurisprudence in Bengali* (Dacca, 1894), 171–72. On the French context see Cage, *Science of Proof*, 56–68.

37. "Report of the CE to Government, Bengal, for the Year 1911," 5 (IOR/V/24/422).

38. Evans and Bose, "Necessity," 284.

39. "Report of the CE to Government, Bengal, for the Year 1911," 5 (IOR/V/24/422).

40. CE Report for Bengal 1914, 5. For other such cases see *Lyon's Medical Jurisprudence* (1921), 488.

41. Buchanan, "Chapter," 876.

42. See, in Priyanath Mukhopadhyay, *Darogar Daptar* (Kolkata: Punashcha, 2004), "Rokkhok na Bhokhkok" (story no. 167), 1:487, and "Gyati Shotru" (story no. 202), 2:396, 408 (Bengali).

43. See *Mt. Gajrani v. Emp.*, 395–96; and Arnold, *Toxic Histories*, 109–10.

under suspicious circumstances. The body was burning when the police stopped the cremation and sent the viscera for testing. Arsenic was found.[44] When a body was cremated completely, it was impossible to detect a volatile poison like arsenic. But if the cremation was only partial (for instance, if the family could not afford enough wood), then there were forensic opportunities. "Cremation practices help many an Indian poisoner," wrote D. R. Thomas as CE for the North-West Frontier Province in 1926: "Only if some of the spongy tissue of the bones is preserved can testing be done from partially cremated remains—and then only for metallic poisons."[45] By the 1920s, CEs often included a few lines in their reports that cited the number of samples of cremation ashes received, and the number that tested positive for arsenic (or, less commonly, mercury).[46] Between 1924 and 1931, for instance, the CE of Punjab (again D. R. Thomas) received ninety-two cases of ashes and bones from cremations "under suspicious circumstances." Arsenic was detected in ten cases and mercury in five, putting the poison rate at 16 percent.[47]

Thomas wrote more extensively about cremation and forensics than any other CE during the colonial period.[48] He observed that there was probably more cremation in India than in the rest of the world and called it "certainly a very sanitary way of the disposal of the body." But he also noted that it presented obvious challenges for forensic investigators: "There must be some way of preventing murder by poison and obliterating the only possible source of its detection." Rapid cremation was "a most dangerous loop-hole." He attached an appendix on cremation to his 1931 report because of a recent encounter with a troubled police officer. A woman's life had been insured for 30,000 rupees, and she died three months later. A physician produced a death certificate citing natural causes, the cremation took place, and the payout occurred. This officer had "very grave suspicions as to the cause of death, yet he felt he could do nothing." This was just one of many cases that had come to his notice while working for the police. In

44. "Report of the CE to Government, Punjab, for the Year 1924," i (appendix) (IOR/V/24/419). For similar cases involving the bodies of women see "Report of the CA to Government, Bombay, for the Year 1892," 5 (IOR/V/24/406); and "Report of the CE to Government, Bengal, for the Year 1911," 5 (IOR/V/24/422).

45. "Annual Report of the CE to Government, North-West Frontier Province, for the Year 1926," viii (IOR/V/24/429). See also "Annual Report of the CE to Government, Bengal, for the Year 1918," 6 (IOR/V/24/422). On the technique used to test for arsenic in bones see *Lyon's Medical Jurisprudence* (1921), 516.

46. For example see "Annual Report of the CE to Government, Punjab, for the Year 1922," 2 (IOR/V/24/ 419). See generally S. N. Chakravarti, M. Z. Faruqi, and K. R. Ganguly, "Detection of Arsenic in Burnt Human Bones and Ashes," *IMG* 76, no. 12 (1941): 722–24.

47. "Annual Report of the CE to Government, Punjab, for the Year 1931," 11 (IOR/V/24/420).

48. See appendices to CE Report for Punjab 1931, 11–12 and 1940, xiv.

England, the Cremation Act of 1902 created special precautions for cremations. The physician in charge of the case had to issue a special certificate confirming death by natural causes, and then a second certificate had to be issued by a doctor specially empowered to grant such documents. Such a procedure would be impossible for India, where there were few allopathic physicians in the countryside.[49] Although Thomas did not mention the likelihood of social resistance to state intervention in death rites, his superiors probably anticipated it. They declared the time "not yet ripe to propose legislation" on cremation in India.[50]

South Asia's distinctive flora and fauna created further challenges for the CEs, and I will focus here on these unfamiliar poison landscapes. CEs struggled to detect poisons derived from South Asian plants and animals that were little known or poorly understood in Europe. Mineral poisons like arsenic, mercury, and copper had global familiarity. They were mined and sold around the world, having many industrial and commercial uses. Although arsenic did occur naturally in certain parts of South Asia, for instance, most of the arsenic in British India was imported from Europe or China in the second half of the nineteenth century, or later from the Persian Gulf region.[51] Tests developed in Europe for these substances—like the Marsh and Reinsch tests for arsenic—also traveled reasonably well to South Asia.[52] But plants were different.[53] Plant-based poisons were the most elusive and thus the most threatening.[54] The 1879 Punjab report noted that there were plants growing in India and not in Europe that had "powerfully irritant properties" (known as alkaloids), while others were "acro-narcotic," a vague term signifying that "their physiological effects have not been sufficiently studied."[55] Two decades later, the Bombay chemical analyser complained that "the ever recurring tale of unidentified alkaloids" was making his department

---

49. CE Report for Punjab 1931, 11–12.

50. Thomas's military superiors wanted to see stricter regulation of the sale of poisons instead of an attempt to regulate cremation. Cover letter, 2, in CE Report for Punjab 1931.

51. *Mt. Gajrani v. Emp.*, 398; *Lyon's Medical Jurisprudence* (1921), 492–93; and Arnold, *Toxic Histories*, 145.

52. On the Reinsch test see *Mt. Gajrani v. Emp.*, 398–99. On the Marsh test see chapter 5. On both see Ian Burney, "Testing Testimony: Toxicology and the Law of Evidence in Early Nineteenth-Century England," *Studies in History and Philosophy of Science* 33 (2002): 304–5.

53. See Arnold, *Toxic Histories*, 54–71. For leading colonial-era treatises on South Asian botanical poisons see R. N. Chopra, *Indigenous Drugs of India: Their Medicinal and Economic Aspects* (Calcutta: Art, 1933); William Dymock, C. J. H. Warden, and David Hooper, *Pharmacographia Indica: A History of the Principal Drugs of Vegetable Origin, Met with in British India* (Calcutta: Thacker, Spink, 1890); K. R. Kirtikar and B. D. Basu, *Indian Medicinal Plants* (Allahabad: S. N. Basu, 1918), and George Watt, *A Dictionary of the Economic Products of India* (Calcutta, 1889).

54. Arnold, *Toxic Histories*, 56. See also Bagchi, "Poisons in Crime," 28–31, 50.

55. CE Report for Punjab 1879, 4; see also 11.

look bad.[56] And state toxicologists working in the 1930s commented on the continuing need for research on "indigenous vegetable poisons" so that effective tests could be developed.[57]

Botanical poisons were generally harder to detect than mineral ones, disappearing from the body more quickly and leaving few distinctive traces postmortem.[58] In a 1907 case of poisoning by aconite (a flowering plant that grows in mountainous regions), the Bengal lab could not find the poison in the viscera. "This is one of the instances, among many undoubted cases of aconite poisoning, in which the poison could not be detected in the viscera, owing to its rapid elimination." This case, however, was the exception that proved the rule, because some of the victim's stool and vomit had been preserved, and examiners found the poison there.[59]

To a much greater extent than mineral poisons, botanical toxins were also destroyed by the heat of the funeral pyre. CEs struggled to convey this fact to local police and complained regularly that the police were sending in cremation ashes with requests to look for organic poisons such as opium and datura. "Forwarding officers may be again reminded that it is impossible to detect vegetable poisons in ashes, as any such poison present would be entirely destroyed by the heat," wrote the exasperated CE of Punjab, J. A. Black, in 1918. He was making this point in his annual report for the fourth time in eleven years.[60]

Given the challenges of detecting plant poisons, regulation of their sale and possession may have seemed like a plausible solution. But while the Poisons Act (I of 1904) eventually helped diminish the availability of white arsenic, legislation made little sense for botanicals.[61] Many of India's poisonous plants grew wild "in some profusion."[62] The Punjab CE noted in 1893 that it would be impossible

56. "The Bombay Chemical Analyser's Report for 1895," *IMCR*, 236–37.

57. CE Report for Madras 1932, 2; and "Annual Report of the CE to Government, United Provinces and Central Provinces, for the Year 1938," 2 (IOR/V/24/417).

58. CE Report for Punjab 1879, 6, 11; *Lyon's Medical Jurisprudence* (1921), 462–63; and D. P. Lambert, *The Medico-Legal Post-Mortem in India* (London: J. & A. Churchill, 1937), 100.

59. "Report of the CE to Government, Bengal, for the Year 1908," 6 (IOR/V/24/422).

60. "Report of the CE to Government, Punjab, for the Year 1918," 2 (IOR/V/24/418). For similar comments see "Report of the CE to Government, Punjab" for 1907, 2; 1913, 2; and 1914, 2 (all in IOR/V/24/418).

61. On the Poisons Act of 1904 see Arnold, *Toxic Histories*, 144–75; and Shrimoy Roy Chaudhury, "Toxic Matters: Medical Jurisprudence and the Making of the Indian Poisons Act (1904)," *Crime, History & Societies* 22, no. 1 (2018): 97–101.

62. Letter from inspector-general of civil hospitals, Punjab, to the Punjab government, no. 2308 H (April 1, 1910), 1, in "Annual Report of the CE to Government, Punjab for the Year 1909"; and letter from C. J. Bamber, inspector-general of civil hospitals, Punjab, to the revenue secretary to government, Punjab (April 7, 1911), 1, in "Annual Report of the CE to Government, Punjab, for the Year 1910" (both in IOR/V/24/418).

to restrict the use of datura because the shrub grew freely across Punjab. The same was true of aconite, croton, jequirity seeds, madar (also known as *aak*), kaner (*Nerium odorum* or oleander), and many other botanical abortifacients.[63] Several decades later, the CE for the North-West Frontier Province, D. R. Thomas, described his lab's relocation to the hill station of Murree during the hot season. His staff went on an excursion and collected about twenty-five specimens in the hills, which seemed "to abound in poisonous plants." That CEs were locked in a losing battle against vegetal toxins seemed as clear in 1929 as in 1893. Thomas lamented that if only "some of those firms in Northern India, who are at present manufacturing worthless patent medicines with high-fangled names," would redirect their attention to studying indigenous plants, they could meet a pressing public need.[64]

India's forensic toxicologists struggled not only with the plants of South Asia, but also with its animals. Scorpions and insects could be dangerous.[65] And of course there were snakes. Just as they occupied a central place in what Peter Hobbins calls Australia's "ecology of dread," poisonous snakes epitomized the frightfulness of India for colonial Britons.[66] Sneakiness and dissimulation were once again colonial themes: India's poisonous snakes were stealthy and hard to distinguish from harmless ones. They were deadlier than any reptile in the British Isles, reinforcing the stereotypical colonial sense that everything was more dangerous in the empire.[67] India's cobras, vipers, and sea snakes posed a major public health threat in British India. Reported annual death rates due to snakebite around 1869 were 11,000 to 20,000 (out of a human population of 121 million), with a disproportionate number in Bengal.[68] The colonial state offered

63. "Report of the CE to Government, Punjab, for the Year 1893," 5–6 (IOR/V/24/418). On madar see also CE Report for Madras 1932, 3. On botanical abortifacients see Sharafi, "Abortion," 380, 383.

64. "Annual Report of the CE to Government, North-West Frontier Province, for the Year 1929," 6 (appendix) (IOR/V/24/429).

65. See Sengupta, *Bhaishajya Bichar*, 331–32; "Report of the CE to Government, Madras, for the Year 1933," 9–10 (G.O. no. 1202 in Annual Reports Government of Madras, box 1144.020000, IOR); *Lyon's Medical Jurisprudence* (1921), 602–4; and Antoinette Burton, "S is for Scorpion," in *Animalia: An Anti-Imperial Bestiary for Our Times*, ed. Antoinette Burton and Renisa Mawani (Duke University Press, 2020), 164–69.

66. Peter Hobbins, *Venomous Encounters: Snakes, Vivisection and Scientific Medicine in Colonial Australia* (Manchester University Press, 2017), 3. See also Pratik Chakrabarti, *Bacteriology in British India: Laboratory Medicine and the Tropics* (University of Rochester Press, 2012), 116.

67. For a fictional illustration see the India-returned villain Dr. Roylott and his dangerous pets in "The Adventure of the Speckled Band," in *The Adventures of Sherlock Holmes*, by Arthur Conan Doyle (Doubleday, [1930]), 1:257–73.

68. Joseph Fayrer, *The Thanatophidia of India: Being a Description of the Venomous Snakes in the Indian Peninsula, with an Account of the Influence of Their Poison on Life and a Series of Experiments* (London, 1872), 32; and *Lyon's Medical Jurisprudence* (1921), 590.

cash rewards for the bodies of dead snakes and would behead them before burial to prevent disinterment to collect duplicate rewards.[69] Many animals killed under these schemes were probably harmless.[70]

Venomology generated a huge quantity of scientific publishing.[71] There were countless articles in journals like the *Indian Medical Gazette* and *The Indian Lancet*, and monographs on antidotes and explanations for why venomous snakes did not poison themselves.[72] There was Joseph Fayrer's spectacular *Thanatophidia*, a full-color extravaganza on India's poisonous serpents.[73] And an 1874 scientific commission was tasked to decide whether India or Australia had the more dangerous snakes (India won).[74] Most of this literature was oriented toward the development of antidotes to snake venom. There was much less research on forensic venomology.[75] Indeed, no test in the late nineteenth or early twentieth century could detect snake venom in human or animal viscera, a point noted by Sherlock Holmes.[76]

Such a test would have been useful in false snakebite cases. Like cremation, this type of case enabled some poisoning deaths to escape CEs' notice. Snakebite deaths were usually handled by local *panchayats* (caste or village councils), before the bodies were sent for cremation or burial (including water burial).[77] Occasionally, a purported snakebite death was revealed to be another kind of

---

69. Fayrer, *Thanatophidia*, 55; "The Toll of Snake Bite," *TI*, May 16, 1922; "The Cobra Question in India," *Lancet*, February 12, 1870, 242. See also Chakrabarti, *Bacteriology*, 124–27.

70. Fayrer, *Thanatophidia*, 31.

71. For an overview see Vincent Richards, *The Land-Marks of Snake-Poison Literature, Being a Review of the More Important Researches into the Nature of Snake-Poisons* (Calcutta, 1885). On the history of venom research see Hobbins, *Venomous Encounters*; and Jutte Schickore, *About Method: Experimenters, Snake Venom, and the History of Writing Scientifically* (University of Chicago Press, 2017).

72. For example see L. A. Waddell, *Are Venomous Snakes Auto-Toxic? An Inquiry into the Effect of Serpent Venom upon the Serpents Themselves* (Calcutta: Superintendent of Government Printing, India, 1889). See generally Arnold, *Toxic Histories*, 43–49; and Chakrabarti, *Bacteriology*, 113–41.

73. On Fayrer see Chakrabarti, *Bacteriology*, 118; and Hobbins, *Venomous Encounters*, 98–101, 119.

74. Commission for the Investigation of Snake-Poisoning (India), *Report on the Effects of Artificial Respiration, Intravenous Injection of Ammonia, and Administration of Various Drugs, &c. in Indian and Australian Snake-Poisoning, and the Physiological, Chemical, and Microscopical Nature of Snake-Poisons* (Calcutta, 1874). See also Hobbins, *Venomous Encounters*, 100–102.

75. In 1928, the CE of Bengal wrote a piece titled "Questions Relating to the Detection of Snake Venom in Viscera" as an "opinion case." I have been unable to locate this document. Report from T. C. Boyd, CE Bengal, to surgeon-general with government of Bengal, Calcutta (July 4, 1929), in CE Report for Bengal 1928, 6.

76. Fayrer, *Thanatophidia*, 49; CE and Bacteriologist Report for NWP, Oudh, and the Central Provinces, 1895, 48; and Doyle, "Adventure of the Speckled Band," 273.

77. For example see "Indian Intelligence: The Deccan," *Bombay Times and Standard*, January 17, 1861; and "Reports of the CA to Government, Bombay and Sind, for the Year 1927," 4 (IOR/V/24/408).

poisoning. Between 1876 and 1939, chemical analysts in western India detected opium in the viscera of ten people initially believed to have died from snakebite, for instance.[78] These were most likely suicides misrepresented to protect the family name. There were also probable poison murders masquerading as snakebite cases. In 1925, the body of an eighteen-year-old Muslim boy tested positive for arsenic, having been labeled a snakebite case initially.[79] The father of a three-year-old girl who died in 1928 said it was snakebite, but aconite was found in her viscera.[80] In a 1937 case in Benares, body parts of an unknown victim were found to contain datura. This death, too, was initially attributed to snakebite.[81]

Most inventive were cases of murder by poison in which the perpetrator would carve two small holes into the corpse so that the death could be attributed to snakebite. D. P. Lambert warned in his guide to postmortem examination that twin punctures could "be easily imitated," and "the mere presence of punctures should not be accepted as proof conclusive that death was due to snakebite."[82] This was the situation in a 1917 case from Punjab. A man, age forty, had symptoms before death that "resembled those of snake-bite, and the diagnosis appeared to be confirmed by the presence of a double puncture on the man's arm." But the death was in fact due to aconite poisoning.[83] False snakebite cases extended beyond murders by poison. As one treatise writer put it, "Cases of undoubted murder by hanging, strangulation, abortion, etc. have been found to be conveniently reported as 'Death by snake-bite.'"[84] In some of these cases, the punctures were poorly made. The holes could not be made by snake bite, according to a hospital attendant in a 1901 case, because "they were too large for the teeth of a snake."[85] There were also occasions when panicking relatives made

---

On *panchayats* in South Asian legal history see James A. Jaffe, *Ironies of Colonial Governance: Law, Custom and Justice in Colonial India* (Cambridge University Press, 2015).

78. "Report of the CA to Government, Bombay, for the Year 1876–77," 20 (IOR/V/24/405); "Report of the CA to Government, Bombay and Sind" for 1926, 4 (IOR/V/24/408) and 1927, 4; "Report of the CA to Government, Bombay" for 1931, 2 (IOR/V/24/409) and 1933, 4; and "Annual Report of the CA to the Government of Sind for the Year 1938–39," 2 (IOR/V/24/431).

79. "Reports of the CA to Government, Bombay and Sind, for the Year 1925," 4 (IOR/V/24/408).

80. CE Report for Bengal 1928, 13.

81. CE Report for United and Central Provinces 1937, 4.

82. Lambert, *Medico-Legal Post-Mortem*, 94.

83. "Report of the CE to Government, Punjab, for the Year 1917," appendix 2, 1 (IOR/V/24/418).

84. *Lyon's Medical Jurisprudence* (1921), 590. The most high-profile of these was probably the 1880 death of Rajkooverba, the young wife of Prince Chandrasangji. Her death, initially believed to be a snakebite case, was later attributed to her husband, who beat her to death for infidelity. "The Chota Udepur Case," *TI*, January 6, 1881. For another example see Sengupta, *Bhaishajya Bichar*, 325.

85. "Murder in a Paddy Field," *TI*, February 26, 1901 (quoting the newspaper account, not the attendant directly).

a double puncture wound to avoid suspicion—even when the death had been natural or accidental.[86]

In these cases, snakebite was the cover for death by other means.[87] Equally, snake venom itself could be used as a weapon by a human poisoner and made to look like something else. Cattle rags were the classic method: The poisoner would insert a venom-infused rag rectally, and the cow would appear to die of illness. The viscera would not test positive for any of the more commonly used poisons, such as arsenic, and, as noted, there was no direct lab test for venom in human or animal tissue.

The snake-and-banana technique was the most elaborate variation on the cattle rag method. E. H. Hankin, CE and bacteriologist to the United and Central Provinces, first described it in 1893, and his account circulated widely in forensic circles and the press.[88] The poisoner put a cobra and a banana (or plantain) into a small-mouthed earthenware vessel, which was then heated over a flame. "Finding his quarters growing uncomfortable," the snake became agitated and attacked the banana. The handler then removed the vessel from the heat, and the snake and banana from the vessel. This person smeared the venom-infused fruit on a rag and inserted it into a cow's rectum using a piece of split bamboo.[89] For decades, cows with mysterious rectal rags had turned up dead, but no one had figured out the method until Hankin. Norman Chevers, author of the forensic treatise first published in 1856, had dismissed villagers' preoccupation with these rags as "ignorant suspicions of the peasantry." But as Parsi physician N. H. Choksy remarked in 1894, "It seems after all that the ignorant peasantry was in the right" and that Chevers was wrong.[90]

There were many variations on this theme. CEs described cases of cattle, water buffalo, oxen, and goats poisoned rectally or vaginally with rags infused

86. See untitled editorial, *TI*, April 27, 1880; and "An Indian Murder Trial," *TI*, January 31, 1888.

87. A similar phenomenon existed in nineteenth-century South Carolina. See Jeffrey M. Jentzen, *Death Investigation in America: Coroners, Medical Examiners, and the Pursuit of Medical Certainty* (Harvard University Press, 2009), 13.

88. On Hankin's claim to discovering this method first in 1893 see "The Bombay Chemical Analyser's Report for 1895," *IMCR* 4, no. 5 (1896): 237; and "Report of the CE to Government, United Provinces of Agra and Oudh and of the Central Provinces, for the Year 1918," 3 (IOR/V/24/415). On Hankin's work as state bacteriologist (a position apparently created for him) see his annual reports as CE and bacteriologist for the North-Western, United, and Central Provinces, 1894–1921 (excluding 1913) (IOR/V/24/414–15); and "Late Dr. E. H. Hankin," *TI*, April 11, 1939.

89. CA Report for Bombay 1895, 11 (IOR/V/24/406). See also "A Grim Discovery," *TI*, January 25, 1895; and *Lyon's Medical Jurisprudence* (1921), 601–2.

90. [N. H. Choksy], "The Use of Snake Poison for the Destruction of Cattle in India," *IMCR*, July 1894: 515.

with venom or other poisons.[91] Less often, humans were the target, although not by way of their nether regions. One man tried to throw snake venom onto another person's open wound.[92] Another tried to self-inject venom in a suicide attempt.[93] Choksy wondered whether any of "the many mysterious deaths in India" could be explained by "a sharp pointed finger-nail, tipped with the dried venom," scratched onto a victim's skin.[94]

India's botanical and reptilian poisons allowed criminal poisoning to go undetected—false negatives in a sense. Occasionally, the economic botanist to the Botanical Survey of India or the curator of the herbarium at the Royal Botanical Gardens, both in Calcutta, would aid in identifying a plant poison.[95] CEs also conducted their own in-house experiments. Like the chloroform and ganja commissions of the 1880s–90s (which studied the risks of these anesthetic and recreational drugs) and the Indian Pasteur Institutes created in the first decade of the twentieth century, CE labs started experimenting on live animals. Indeed, the passage of antivivisection legislation in England in the 1870s made India a magnet for researchers who wanted to use animals freely.[96] Among CEs, there were two hubs of animal experimentation: the United and Central Provinces lab in Agra in the 1890s, where Hankin devised a system for detecting venom in cattle rags; and the Madras lab in the 1920s and 1930s, where Clive Newcomb oversaw research on plant poisons.

Hankin realized in 1893 that snake venom was being used to poison cattle. Two years later, he corresponded with Albert Calmette, a leading venomologist in Lille, France, and devised a way to harness antidote-focused research for

---

91. See "Annual Report of the CE and Bacteriologist to the Governments of the North-Western Provinces and Oudh and of the Central Provinces, for the Year 1894," 1 (IOR/V/24/414); "Report of the CE to Government, Bengal, for the Year 1905," 8 (IOR/V/24/422); CE Report for Bengal 1918, 7; "Report of the CE to Government of the United Provinces and Central Provinces, for the Year 1929," 5–6 (IOR/V/24/416); and "Report of the CE to Government, Bengal, for the Year 1931," 10 (IOR/V/24/423).

92. "Report of the CE to Government, Madras, for the Year 1929," 6 (G.O. no. 1238 in Annual Reports Government of Madras, box 1144.020000, IOR).

93. CE Report for Madras 1933, 4.

94. [Choksy], "Use of Snake Poison," 516–17.

95. For example see "Annual Report of the CE and Bacteriologist to the Governments of the United Provinces of Agra and Oudh and of the Central Provinces" for 1912, 2, and 1916, 3 (both IOR/V/24/415); CE Report for Bengal 1936, 17; and "Report of the CA to Government, Bombay, for the Year 1940," 11 (IOR/V/24/410).

96. The 1876 Act interrupted the venomological research of Joseph Fayrer and T. Laurer Brunton in London, for example. Vincent Richards and Leonard Rogers continued this research in India, where they could test freely on animals. Chakrabarti, *Bacteriology*, 90–91, and, generally, 86–112. On the history of vivisection regulation in Britain see Shira Shmuely, *The Bureaucracy of Empathy: Law, Vivisection, and Animal Pain in Late Nineteenth-Century Britain* (Cornell University Press, 2023).

forensic needs.[97] Hankin could determine the presence of snake venom by making a watery extract from a rag recovered from a dead cow's digestive or reproductive tract. He injected this extract into an animal (usually a rabbit, guinea pig, or rat) that had been inoculated against the venom of a particular kind of snake with an "anti-venine."[98] He also injected the extract into a second animal, the control animal, who had received no antivenin. If the cattle rag contained the type of snake venom in question, the inoculated animal would survive, while the control animal would die with symptoms of snakebite. Hankin's method worked even with a rag two years old. His discovery was noted in France, where it was communicated to the Académie des Sciences in Paris.[99] Hankin did this work during a decade when he fought against the introduction of antivivisection legislation in India, which was modeled on the English statute of 1876. His efforts at testing and lobbying both succeeded.[100]

Animal testing was useful for unidentifiable botanical poisons, too. It allowed toxicologists simply to say that a particular substance was poisonous (at least to the animal species being tested) without needing to positively identify the plant in question.[101] In the 1920s and 1930s, the Madras CE's lab researched various botanical poisons through animal experimentation. The lab exposed frogs to *oduvan* leaves, areca nuts, and the flowering plant *Gloriosa superba*. These substances were injected subcutaneously and into dorsal lymph sacs. Some were painted on a frog's heart. Some animals survived, but many died in these experiments.[102] For most of the late colonial period, CEs labored under a crushing

---

97. On Calmette see Chakrabarti, *Bacteriology*, 127–31; and Hobbins, *Venomous Encounters*, 142–43, 150–52.

98. The CEs do not seem to have experimented on street dogs, unlike researchers focusing on chloroform, nonforensic venomology, and bacteriology in colonial India. Chakrabarti, *Bacteriology*, 89–94. Researchers in other parts of the British empire used dogs for snakebite studies. See Hobbins, *Venomous Encounters*.

99. CE and Bacteriologist Report for NWP, Oudh, and the Central Provinces 1895, 48. See also "Annual Report of the CE and Bacteriologist to the Governments of the North-Western Provinces and Oudh and of the Central Provinces" for 1896, 2; 1899, 3; and 1902, 1 (all in IOR/V/24/414). By 1918, frogs were being used as test animals. CE Report for Agra, Oudh, and the Central Provinces 1918, 3.

100. Chakrabarti, *Bacteriology*, 104–5, 109. In England, the Cruelty to Animals Act of 1876 created the world's first system for the regulation of animal experimentation. See Hobbins, *Venomous Encounters*, 116–17; and Shira Shmuely, "Law and the Laboratory: The British Vivisection Inspectorate in the 1890s," *Law & Social Inquiry* 46, no. 4 (2021): 933–63.

101. On whether research findings on animals could be applied to human beings see *Lyon's Medical Jurisprudence* (1921), 463–64. I could find no such discussion in the CE reports.

102. See "Report of the CE to Government, Madras" for 1926, 2 (G.O. no. 869); 1930, 3; 1933, 14, in Annual Reports Government of Madras, box 1144.020000, IOR; and 1934, 10–11. Small mammals like rats and cats were also used for poison testing at CE labs across South Asia. For example see CE and Bacteriologist Report for Agra, Oudh, and the Central Provinces 1902, part 1, 1; "Report of

workload that left no time for research, but by the mid-1930s and 1940s the balance of resources tilted in their favor, and they began to publish research findings in leading journals in India.[103] Through animal testing, the Madras lab seemed especially focused on the botanical toxins that had foiled analysts for so long.

Rapid cremation, botanical poisons, snake venom, and the semblance of disease created opportunities for poisoning to go undetected, producing false negatives in the broadest sense. The CEs also grappled with false negatives in the narrower sense, namely situations where they had tested for a poison that was present, but the test results were negative. The absence of a positive test did not necessarily mean that poisoning had not occurred. It could mean that the analyst had not tested for the right poison. CEs complained constantly that forwarding officers (police or local civil surgeons) did not include proper information on symptoms of the victim or other evidence in the case. CEs could not test every forensic sample for every poison, so they had to decide what to look for, based on the information they received.[104] There was also the problem that a botanical poison could decompose before testing was done. A volatile poison could evaporate. Or it could be that there was no chemical test for the poison in question, a frequent problem for the botanical toxins and snake venom already discussed.[105]

Like toxicologists worldwide, CEs faced the challenge of quantity, and determining whether it would have been enough to cause death. A negative test result (or the detection of only trace amounts of poison) did not necessarily mean that no crime had occurred. In fatal poisoning by an "irritant" substance like arsenic, common symptoms were "violent vomiting and purging" (defecation), which could remove most of the poison, followed by further elimination through the kidneys and skin. The CEs knew of cases of fatal poisoning in India and Europe "where death was somewhat delayed and elimination was so complete that no traces of the poison could be detected either in the stomach or in any other organ or tissue examined."[106] The problem also appeared in cases of attempted suicide or murder, where the victim was found alive and attempts were made to save them. In the chaos that ensued, stomach washings could spill. Vomit and excrement might not be properly saved.[107] Children were also especially challenging:

---

the CE to Government, Bengal" for 1903, 6 (IOR/V/24/422) and 1905, 8; and CE Report for Madras 1933, 4.

103. Funding from the Indian Research Fund Association was key. See CE Report for Bengal 1937, 4; and 1938, 6–7.

104. For examples of this frequent complaint see CE Report for Punjab 1879, 8–9, and 1893, 5; and "Report of the CE to Government, Burma, for the Year 1908," 2 (IOR/V/24/425).

105. CE Report for Punjab 1879, 14.

106. "Report of the CE to Government, Punjab, for the Year 1916," appendix 2, 1 (IOR/V/24/418).

107. CE Report for Madras 1933, 8.

A tiny amount of poison could kill them. In a suspected arsenic case from Punjab in 1918, a man and a dog that had eaten some of the man's food both died. Four days later, the man's child also died. No arsenic could be detected in the child's viscera, but the assistant surgeon and a policeman at the scene had collected some clothing stained with the child's vomit and feces. These excreta tested positive for arsenic.[108]

The other key problem was that in poisoning by a narcotic like opium, death was not due to the quantity of poison (or drug) found in the stomach, but to that which had been absorbed through the stomach. Opium detected in the stomach was the excess. In other words, a CE might find only trace amounts or even no poison in the stomach, even though a lethal dose had indeed been taken.[109] Opium infanticides (often of female babies) were particularly difficult with regard to dosage.[110] A tiny amount of opium, smeared on a nursing woman's nipple before breastfeeding, could kill a young infant. These cases usually tested negative for opium, as none was detectable in the baby.[111] The everyday medico-legal work of the chemical examiners was to avoid false negatives. Equally, though, their job was to avoid false positives.

Detecting False Positives: Planted Poison

Planted poison looked almost, but not quite, like a regular poisoning. These cases, which presented some of the most challenging puzzles for state toxicologists, were false positives in the broadest sense: There was poison in the forensic submission, and it was detected through testing, but it had not caused the death or been put there by the accused. In some of these cases, the dangerous substance was in the wrong form or place and thus seemed to have been planted. For instance, it might appear in large chunks in food that the victim would have noticed. In two cases from 1901–2, no arsenic could be found in the victim's vomit, but the bread and flour from the case contained chunks of the poison "visible to the naked eye."[112] Similarly, a 1925 sample of a boy's food in Bombay contained crushed glass, including one large "dark emerald green" piece two-fifths

108. CE Report for Punjab 1918, appendix 2, 1.

109. "Report of the CE to Government, Punjab, for the Year 1916," appendix 2, 1 (IOR/V/24/418). See also CE Report for Punjab 1879, 12–13.

110. See Arnold, *Toxic Histories*, 28–29.

111. CE Report for Punjab 1879, 5–6.

112. "Annual Report of the CE and Bacteriologist to Government of the North-Western Provinces and Oudh, and of the Central Provinces" for 1901, part 1, 1 (IOR/V/24/414) and 1902, part 1, 1.

of an inch in length, from a woman's bangle. The analyst noted that either there was terrible negligence on the perpetrator's part or, as was more likely, the whole story set up by the alleged perpetrator's accuser was fabricated.[113]

Although cremation destroyed botanical poisons, it was possible to fabricate evidence involving mineral poisons in cremation cases. Poisons such as arsenic or mercury could survive a cremation, but only in spongy bone tissue and only if the cremation had been incomplete. In some cases, though, a mineral poison in powdered form was mixed with the ashes of a corpse *after cremation*. "This is a very transparent fraud, but rather a favorite one amongst the natives of this Presidency," wrote the Bombay chemical analyser T. D. Collis Barry about an 1891 case of powdered arsenic found in cremation ashes from Satara. The idea was to "implicate some enemy on a charge of homicide; but as arsenic volatilizes with very moderate heat, it is absolutely impossible that any of it could be present after cremation in the open air," unless the arsenic had been added after cremation.[114] Similarly, in a 1908 Raipur case, mercury was found in cremation ashes, but in never-heated form. A woman had died at 3 a.m. and been cremated within an hour. The CE conducted experiments to show that mercury that had volatilized in one part of the pyre could not have deposited itself on some other part that had cooled, and hence the mercury had probably "been added feloniously" after cremation.[115] And in a 1919 case from the North-West Frontier Province, traces of mercury were found in burnt bones and ashes, "but these appeared to have been added subsequently in order to concoct a false charge."[116]

The preservation and transportation of forensic samples also intersected with the problem of planted poison. Historian Uponita Mukherjee has shown that a debate over whether to preserve samples in alcohol, saline, or a newer chemical called formalin (formaldehyde) was ongoing at the turn of the twentieth century. Mukherjee reveals a caste angle to this debate: Opponents of the salt option argued that using saline enabled lower-caste workers, such as Domes or Chamars (accused of being cattle poisoners), to mix arsenic with the saline preservative in order to frame rivals for poisoning.[117]

---

113. "Reports of the CAs to Government, Bombay and Sind, for the Year 1925," 5 (IOR/V/24/408).

114. CA Report for Bombay 1891, 5.

115. "Annual Report of the CE and Bacteriologist to the Governments of the United Provinces of Agra and Oudh and of the Central Provinces, for the Year 1908," part 1, 2 (IOR/V/24/414).

116. Cover note by E. H. Kealy, secretary to the chief commissioner, North-West Frontier Province (Peshawar, May 7, 1920) to "Report of the CE to Government, North-West Frontier Province, for the Year 1919"; see also 2 (IOR/V/24/428).

117. Uponita Mukherjee, "Colonial Detection: Crime, Evidence, and Inquiry in British India, 1790–1910" (PhD diss., Columbia University, 2022), 169–82.

The poisoning of cows was a crime with complex intercaste valences in the Hindu-majority regions of India.[118] For upper-caste Hindus, it was sacrilegious and ritually polluting to eat beef or kill cows. Among certain lower-caste populations and Dalits, though, leatherwork was the dominant occupation. These communities were permitted to work with carcasses they found but were prohibited from killing cows. Accusations of cattle poisoning (which would make killing look like illness, so that the hide could be used for leather) were common against communities like Chamars, who were often the targets of retaliatory violence.[119]

Whoever the perpetrator, cases with these kinds of associations reached the CE's lab in the following form: The sample would test positive for arsenic because the poison had been mixed into the preservative. A system was devised in response: Local police or civil surgeons were required to collect and send not only the forensic sample soaked in preservative, but also a separate vial of the preservative itself.[120] CE reports routinely noted the test results from the preservative, too.[121] If both the forensic sample and the preservative tested positive for the same poison, the conclusion was that the poison had been planted in the fluid before it was added to the forensic sample—and that the case was false.

The accusation was that lower-caste populations were skilled at mixing arsenic with salt solution as cattle poisoners, and that this skill was transferrable when they were hired for forensic jobs. In Punjab in the 1890s, the job of selecting and packing organs in cattle poisoning cases was often carried out by members of the Chamar community, for instance.[122] There were instances where poison was mixed with the saline due to staff carelessness or error.[123] But the

118. See Ramnarayan S. Rawat, *Reconsidering Untouchability: Chamars and Dalit History in North India* (Indiana University Press, 2011). There were fewer cattle poisoning cases in majority-Muslim and majority-Buddhist regions like northwestern India and Burma, respectively. However, elephant poisoning cases occurred in Burma, where the animals were used for teak logging. For example see "Report of the CE, Burma for the Year 1901," 1 (IOR/V/24/425).

119. On the caste dynamics of suspected cattle poisoning cases see Norman Chevers, *A Manual of Medical Jurisprudence for Bengal and the North-Western Provinces* (Calcutta, 1856), 78–81; Rawat, *Reconsidering Untouchability*, 24–53; and Arnold, *Toxic Histories*, 151–56. Saurabh Mishra describes colonial campaigns associating Chamars with cattle poisoning as witch hunts. Saurabh Mishra, *Beastly Encounters of the Raj: Livelihoods, Livestock, and Veterinary Health in North India, 1790–1920* (University of Manchester Press, 2015), 123–44.

120. Mukherjee, "Colonial Detection," 180–81.

121. For instance see "Report of the CE to Government, Bengal, for the Year 1920," 3 (IOR/V/24/422).

122. Letter from the inspector-general of civil hospitals, Punjab, to the Punjab government, no. 1119 (April 16, 1895), 1, "Report of the CE to Government, Punjab, for the Year 1894" (IOR/V/24/418).

123. For an example of strychnine in saline preservative see "Report of the CE to Government, Madras, for the Year 1897," 6 in "Reports of the CEs to the several Local Governments for the year 1897" (IOR/P/5418, Oct. 1898). For procedures set up to minimize staff error see "Annual Report of

larger anxiety for opponents of saline was that lower-caste workers at the local crime scene might add arsenic to saline solution deliberately—to frame rivals.

And yet poison could be added to alcohol preservative, too.[124] A vial of preservative was supposed to be sent in for testing, whether it was alcohol- or salt-based. In a 1903 case from Jhelum district in Punjab, the CE in Lahore, F. N. Windsor, received four bottles relating to an alleged murder. Three of the vessels contained viscera. The fourth was a sample of the "spirits of wine" in which the body parts were steeped. Arsenic was found in all four, "which of course nullified any analysis." The inspector general of police conducted an inquiry, although its results were not reported in subsequent annual reports from the lab. The 1903 report did complain that forwarding officers only rarely sent a sample of preservative, contrary to protocol.[125] This case showed why the practice of sending a preservative sample mattered and divorced the issue of contamination from the caste-related accusations made in opposition to saline.

Cases of poisoned preservative could be complex. In a 1903 case from the North-West Frontier Province, the stomach of a man reported to have died of arsenic poisoning was sent to the CE, along with a vial of the preservative spirit used. Like his colleague in Punjab in the same year, this analyst noted that the "important rule as to sending such a sample is rarely carried out by forwarding officers." The spirit contained "a large quantity of arsenic in solution." This was presumably white arsenic, the most common form of the poison encountered in India. However, yellow arsenic, in particles, was found in the stomach. This particulate form, which differed from the form of the arsenic in the alcohol, prevented "the nullifying of the whole examination by the presence of arsenic in the sample of spirit."[126] In other words, rather than being a case in which all the incriminating evidence had been fabricated, this may have been a case of genuine evidence (yellow arsenic in particles in the stomach) "bolstered" by the addition of false evidence (nonparticulate white arsenic in the alcohol). This phenomenon was evocative of terms in some South Asian languages for a mixture of truth

---

the CE and Bacteriologist to the Governments of the United Provinces of Agra and Oudh and of the Central Provinces for the Year 1909," part 1, 2–3 (IOR/V/24/414).

124. For an example of mercury detected in an alcohol sample see "Annual Report of the CE to the Governments of the United Provinces of Agra and Oudh and of the Central Provinces for the Year 1919," 2 (IOR/V/24/415).

125. "Report of the CE to Government, Punjab, for the Year 1903," 1, along with accompanying correspondence: letter from inspector-general of hospitals, Punjab, to the Punjab government, no. 1041 (March 15, 1904), 1, and letter from J. McConaghey, inspector-general of civil hospitals, Punjab, to A. B. Kettlewell, judicial and general secretary to government, Punjab (Lahore, March 15, 1904), 1 (IOR/V/24/418).

126. "Report of the CE to Government, NWFP, for the Year 1903," 2 (IOR/V/24/428).

and falsity, like *kharukhotu* in Gujarati and *satyanrta* in Sanskrit.[127] A similar phenomenon existed in bloodstain cases (see chapters 2 and 3), in which animal blood was added to "true" evidence stained with human blood.

Elsewhere in the common law world, the rule was that false evidence tainted the true, making all the evidence from one witness unreliable. As some judges in India asserted, though, the approach in India had to be different, given the frequent mix of the true and the false: A judge should identify and remove the false from consideration, and then decide the case based on the remaining evidence (see chapter 3).

In other cases of poisoned preservative, analysts were able to figure out roughly when the tampering occurred. In a 1937 case from Bengal, the viscera of a man and a woman were received, along with a sample of alcohol preservative. Arsenic was detected in both the biological material and the alcohol. A second sample of the same spirit was obtained from the original medical officer. Again, it contained arsenic. He had received the alcohol from the civil surgeon of Dacca, but a sample of alcohol sent directly from that source tested negative for the poison. In other words, someone had added arsenic to the alcohol *after* the Dacca civil surgeon had sent the forensic material to the medical officer. The form of arsenic in the viscera was the same as in the alcohol. Further examination led to the conclusion that the woman had been throttled, while opium had killed the man.[128] The addition of arsenic to the alcohol may have been intended to divert attention from the true causes of death. The man's death may have been suicide (given the opium), raising the possibility that he strangled the woman before taking an overdose. The report did not suggest that an innocent third party was a suspect.

Some of the most complex cases of falsity and planted poison involved poisoned wells.[129] These involved poison in the right form and location, but with the wrong explanation attached. Similar to claims that Jews had poisoned wells in medieval Europe during plague outbreaks, these cases about shared water supply sometimes combined false accusations and rumors.[130] CEs nevertheless did encounter cases where a well seemed to be deliberately poisoned. In a 1900

127. See George P. Taylor, *The Student's Gujarati Grammar* (Bombay: Thacker, 1908), 111; Bhagu F. Karbhari, *A New Pocket Gujarati-English Dictionary* (Bombay: N. M. Tripathi, 1912), 169; and Standish Grove Grady, ed., *Institutes of Hindu Law; or, The Ordinances of Menu*, trans. William Jones (London, 1869), 70.

128. CE Report for Bengal 1937, 13.

129. On well water types and issues in colonial India see CE Report for Punjab 1879, 32–35.

130. For instance see Samuel K. Cohn Jr., "The Black Death and the Burning of Jews," *Past & Present* 196 (2007): 3–36.

case from the Rampur district in Bengal, they detected aconite in a cloth packet thrown into a well.[131] In a 1916 case from another part of Bengal, a civil surgeon of Pabna submitted "a bundle of cloth containing some dark grey colored pasty substance recovered from a well." The paste contained arsenic.[132] CEs also encountered situations where the intention had been simply to scare people—where the well was not actually poisoned. In 1907 Punjab, "extravagant rumors" circulated that villagers were maliciously throwing dangerous objects into wells. Some suspicious items were seized, but they turned out to be harmless, "their object apparently being only to act on the imagination." In one instance, a dead rat had been thrown into a well. Even if the rat had been infected with the plague, the CE commented (without explanation) that it was unlikely to harm the water supply. But he noted that the act was "calculated to excite disgust and fear."[133]

The CEs came across situations where the rumors were false, and no poison was found. For example, in a 1907 case from the district of Kohat in the North-West Frontier Province, the articles submitted were found to be "quite harmless," consisting of lime and carbonate of lime.[134] And yet it was often hard even for experts to decide what had happened—whether the rumors were true or false. "Many suspected cases of poisoning are totally incapable of proof and suspicion [and] indeed, turn out to be entirely unjustified," wrote the CE of Punjab, D. R. Thomas, in his 1940 report. This was especially true in village cases "where false rumors spread quickly." But that said, many medical practitioners with years of experience could also recall cases where later developments had "not served to abolish their doubts." After declaring a rumor to be false, later events sometimes made them wonder if they had been wrong.[135]

A feature of geography only made things more unclear. In some places, dangerous levels of arsenic occurred naturally in the groundwater. In 1938, the CE of Punjab (again D. R. Thomas) discussed the case of a farm family in Canada. The family had died because of naturally occurring arsenic in their water supply because their well ran through stone with high arsenic content. There was also, he noted, naturally occurring arsenic in Armenia: "The beautiful skins of the Armenians particularly the women have been attributed to the traces of arsenic in the water supply," which could have a "beneficial effect on the skin when taken

131. "Report of the CE to Government, Bengal, for the Year 1900," 14 (IOR/V/24/422).

132. "Report of the CE to Government, Bengal, for the Year 1916," 6 (IOR/V/24/422).

133. CE Report for Punjab 1907, 2. On poison panics and false rumor in the context of communal Indo-Burmese violence see "Report of the CE to Government, Burma, for the Year 1938," 2 (IOR/V/24/427). See generally Arnold, *Toxic Histories*, 78–97.

134. "Report of the CE to Government, NWFP, for the Year 1907," 2 (IOR/V/24/428).

135. CE Report for Punjab 1940, xi–xii.

in medicinal doses." There were arsenic mines in Chitral in India's North-West Frontier Province, but military authorities had tested the water and found no issues.[136] Thomas seemed unaware that parts of eastern India—today known as the "arsenic belt" of West Bengal and Bangladesh—had high levels of naturally occurring arsenic.[137]

The possibility of naturally occurring arsenic made cases from Rangpur district in Bengal particularly confounding. In 1906, well waters were tested for arsenic, and so were some suspicious items recovered from them. One well, belonging to Kali Mohon Ray, was a masonry well (made of bricks). Another was a ring well (made of stacked clay rings) belonging to Mohammad Hossain. Arsenic was found in the water from both wells. But it was only found in one of the recovered items.[138] Could this mean both that there was naturally occurring arsenic in the water *and* that someone had tried to poison one well? Had they also tried to create a scare with the other packet that contained nothing dangerous? Could the harmless items be an attempted setup, with someone knowing that there was already arsenic in the water? The CE did not try to explain this case, but its facts lent themselves to multiple theories. Two decades later, another case from Rangpur revealed arsenic-laden well water. This time, the subdivisional magistrate reported that the *pucca* well of a house had been poisoned. Again, the CE did not confirm or deny by speculating on the cause of the poisoning. But as in the earlier case, the lab found arsenic in the water.[139] Today, Rangpur district (now in northern Bangladesh) has elevated rates of arsenic in the groundwater.[140]

Even more perplexing was a case about a poisoned well in Dinajpur, a district in colonial Bengal (today in Bangladesh). In 1900, two health workers were accused of throwing cholera-infected vomit and excrement into a well to spread the disease. When the CE in Calcutta tested the well water, though, he found not cholera, but arsenic. Was this a false case, where someone planted arsenic to frame the two health workers? Or was it a *false* false case, where naturally occurring arsenic meant there was no fabrication at all?

A parallel discussion of naturally occurring poison existed for cattle deaths in the western part of Bengal Presidency (what is today Bihar in India). Cows

136. "Report of the CE to Government, Punjab, for the Year 1938," xii–xiii (IOR/V/24/420).

137. See Dipankar Chakraborti et al., "Groundwater Arsenic Contamination in Bangladesh—21 Years of Research," *Journal of Trace Elements in Medicine and Biology* 31 (2015): 237–48; and Andrew A. Meharg, *Venomous Earth: How Arsenic Caused the World's Worst Mass Poisoning* (Macmillan, 2005), 170–83.

138. CE Report for Bengal 1905, 8.

139. "Report of the CE to Government, Bengal, for the Year 1925," 8 (IOR/V/24/423).

140. See Chakraborti, "Groundwater Arsenic," 241 (map).

and buffalo grazed without trouble on the mature forms of grasses like *baru* or *kala mucha* (*Sorghum halepense*), *chota jenora*, and linseed plant. These plants were often cultivated specifically as cattle feed. But the immature form of the plants could produce toxic levels of hydrocyanic acid. Sometimes a wave of bovine deaths occurred after cows had grazed on these young plants, and their body parts were sent to the CEs. The labs' explanation of this phenomenon dispelled suspicions of lower-caste groups who were regularly accused of poisoning these ruminants.[141] Like cremation ashes, preservative fluid, and well water, these poisonous-grass scenarios alerted CEs to the hazards of falsity in poisoning cases, and fed into larger discussions of how forensic experts could prevent wrongful convictions.

Wrongful Convictions

In the late twentieth century, a movement to exonerate the wrongfully convicted emerged in the US and spread across the Western world. The innocence revolution was powered by DNA analysis, which revealed the unreliability of evidence such as eyewitness identification and informant ("jailhouse snitch") testimony.[142] Much less well known is the history of wrongful convictions *before* the innocence movement.[143]

During the nineteenth and twentieth centuries, a number of wrongful convictions in Britain were reported across the British empire.[144] The most famous was the case of Adolf Beck, a Norwegian living in England who was found guilty not once but twice of swindling women out of their jewelry while posing as a

141. See CE Report for Bengal for the following years: 1905, 8; 1927, 13 (IOR/V/24/423); and 1937, 15.

142. For histories of the US-based innocence movement see Keith A. Findley, "Innocence Found: The New Revolution in American Criminal Justice," in *Controversies in Innocence Cases in America*, ed. Sarah Lucy Cooper (Ashgate, 2014), 3–20; Brandon Garrett, *Convicting the Innocent: Where Criminal Prosecutions Go Wrong* (Harvard University Press, 2011); Jacqueline McMurtie, "The Innocence Network: From Beginning to Branding," in Cooper, *Controversies*, 21–29; and Daniel S. Medwed, *Wrongful Convictions and the DNA Revolution: Twenty-Five Years of Freeing the Innocent* (Cambridge University Press, 2017).

143. For a US history of these cases, 1960s–80s, see Michael Meltsner, "Innocence Before DNA," in Medwed, *Wrongful Convictions*, 14–36.

144. See Florence Elizabeth Maybrick, *My Fifteen Lost Years* (Funk and Wagnalls, 1905), 150–66. For examples of coverage across the empire see John Sweeney, "My Greatest Cases: A Few Blunders," *Rhodesia Herald*, August 3, 1905; "The Edalji Case," *Eastern Daily Mail and Straits Morning Advertiser*, February 19, 1907; and "The Case of Mr. Adolf Beck," *Kaiser-i-Hind*, December 18, 1904 (Gujarati).

wealthy potential employer of the women (1896–1904). He was convicted on the basis of eyewitness accounts from multiple women and the testimony of a handwriting analyst. He served several years in penal servitude for the first conviction and would have continued for the second, had another man not been discovered to be the true swindler. Beck was pardoned and released.[145] Another highly publicized case involved a young solicitor in Birmingham named George Edalji, who was convicted in 1903 of maiming livestock. He was sentenced to seven years' penal servitude. Edalji was of Parsi descent on his father's side, and his wrongful conviction was attributed by many—including his English mother and a young Jawaharlal Nehru—to racism. A public campaign by Arthur Conan Doyle (the creator of Sherlock Holmes), Adolf Beck, and others led to a pardon for Edalji, who was released after three years in prison.[146] In 1909 in Glasgow, a German Jewish man named Oscar Slater was convicted for the murder, during a home break-in, of an elderly woman named Marion Gilchrist. In what was called the Scottish Dreyfus affair, Slater served eighteen years in prison before his sentence was quashed for a misdirection to the jury. Conan Doyle led the campaign for Slater's release, as he had for Edalji.[147]

Florence Maybrick, an American living in England, was convicted in 1889 of poisoning her husband with arsenic. Over time, her case came to be regarded as a wrongful conviction. The small amount of poison in the husband's body could be explained in ways that did not implicate his wife: He may have been a habitual

145. For detailed accounts of the case see George R. Sims, *Two King's Pardons: The Martyrdom of Adolf Beck* (London: Daily Mail, [1905]); and Eric R. Watson, *Adolf Beck (1877–1904)* (Edinburgh: William Hodge, [1924]). For an overview see "The Adolf Beck Case," *Canadian Law Review* 4, no. 1 (1905): 60–64.

146. In *TI* see "Defense of Edalji. Sir C. Doyle's Powerful Letters," January 26, 1907; "West and East," February 11, 1904; "The Edalji Case. A Legal View," February 16, 1907; "The Edalji Conviction. Speech by Mr. Adolf Beck," February 28, 1905. See also Arthur Conan Doyle, *The Story of Mr. George Edalji*, ed. Richard Whittington-Egan and Molly Whittington-Egan (Grey House Books, 1985); and the *Pearson's Weekly* series: George Edalji, "My Own Story. The Narrative of Eighteen Years' Persecution," February 7, 1907, 525–26; February 14, 1907, 541–42; February 28, 1907, 578–79; March 7, 1907, 594–95; March 14, 1907, 610–11; March 21, 1907, 630–31; March 28, 1907, 646–47; April 4, 1907, 666; April 11, 1907, 682; April 18, 1907, 698; April 25, 1907, 720; May 2, 1907, 740; May 9, 1907, 756; May 16, 1907, 784; May 23, 1907, 802; May 30, 1907, 836; and June 6, 1907, 845. For overviews of the case see Jairam N. Menon, "Conan Doyle and the Edalji Case," *TI*, January 13, 1980; and Ullattil Manmadhan, "Doyle and the Edalji Case," *National Medical Journal of India* 29, no. 5 (2016): n.p.

147. Arthur Conan Doyle, *The Case of Oscar Slater* (Hodder & Stoughton, 1912); William Park, *The Truth About Oscar Slater* (London: Psychic, [1927]); and William Roughead, *Trial of Oscar Slater* (Edinburgh: William Hodge, 1915). See also M. Anne Crowther and Brenda White, *On Soul and Conscience: The Medical Expert and Crime; 150 Years of Forensic Medicine in Glasgow* (Aberdeen University Press, 1988), 45–47. For a popular history see Margalit Fox, *Conan Doyle for the Defense: The True Story of a Sensational British Murder, a Quest for Justice, and the World's Most Famous Detective Writer* (Random House, 2018).

"arsenic eater."[148] Florence Maybrick was released after fifteen years' imprisonment.[149] The Beck, Edalji, and Maybrick cases led to the creation of the Court of Criminal Appeal in England in 1907.[150] Previously, one could only appeal to the monarch for a pardon.[151] The Slater case contributed to the establishment of a similar criminal appellate court in Scotland in 1926.[152] These cases also figured prominently in debates over the abolition of the death penalty in England and elsewhere.[153] Slater and Maybrick had been condemned to death before their sentences were commuted to prison terms.

Readers in India knew all about these cases, thanks to reprinted and original stories in South Asian newspapers.[154] Three of the four cases had an Indian connection. George Edalji was of South Asian descent. The judge presiding over Florence Maybrick's trial was James Fitzjames Stephen, the draftsman of key Indian statutes who by then had moved back to England.[155] He was already struggling with the illness that would end his judicial career. One newspaper blamed Maybrick's conviction on "an insane Judge" who was soon after dismissed from the bench for incompetence and then died in an insane asylum.[156] John Edge, a former chief justice of the Allahabad High Court, was one of three members of the Committee of Enquiry that investigated the Beck case after his release.[157] Gaumont, one of Europe's leading film studios, produced a popular silent film about Beck's case in 1909 that featured Beck himself reenacting scenes from his

---

148. Note, however, that the forensic treatise author J. P. Modi did not consider Maybrick to have been wrongfully convicted. Modi, *Medical Jurisprudence* (1940), 546.

149. For detailed accounts of the case see Maybrick, *My Fifteen Lost Years*; and H. B. Irving, *Trial of Mrs. Maybrick* (John Day, 1927). For an overview see untitled, *TI*, February 2, 1904.

150. See Pendleton Howard, "The English Court of Criminal Appeal," *American Bar Association Journal* 17, no. 3 (1931): 149–52.

151. D. Michael Risinger, "Boxes in Boxes: Julian Barnes, Conan Doyle, Sherlock Holmes, and the Edalji Case," *International Commentary on Evidence* 4, no. 2 (2006): 88–89.

152. Edwin R. Keedy, "Criminal Procedure in Scotland. A Report Presented to the American Institute of Criminal Law and Criminology," *Journal of Criminal Law and Criminology* 11 (January 1913): 38–39; and Lindsay Farmer, "Arthur and Oscar (and Sherlock): The Reconstructive Trial and the 'Hermeneutics of Suspicion,'" *International Commentary on Evidence* 5, no. 1 (2007): 3, 15–16.

153. "Death Sentence. Lord Buckmaster Argues Against It," *TI*, April 23, 1930; and "No Innocent Man Hanged," *Madras Law Journal* 59 (1930): 77. From early independent India see "Capital Punishment. The Case for and Against," *TI*, July 18, 1951; and "Capital Punishment," *TI*, May 10, 1962.

154. The *Pearson's Weekly* series noted above was reprinted for Calcutta readers in *ABP*. See, for example, "My Own Story," *ABP*, February 23, 1907, and February 28, 1907.

155. While in India as law member of the Viceroy's Legislative Council (1869–72), Stephen oversaw the passage of the Indian Evidence Act, Contract Act, and a revised version of the CrPC.

156. "Mrs. Maybrick," *ABP*, July 8, 1899; and Irving, *Trial*, 11.

157. "Adolf Beck Case," 62.

case. Viewed by packed audiences in British cinemas, the film was also screened in India.[158]

These cases invited comparisons in, and to, India. In its coverage of the Beck case, the nationalist *Amrita Bazar Patrika* (*ABP*) observed that if innocent people could be convicted in Britain, they were even more at risk in India.[159] Police acted with greater impunity in India, and magistrates were more beholden to them there.[160] There was little press coverage (in any language) or public outrage over "so many cases of gross miscarriage of justice" that "occur in this country almost daily." Indians were becoming "utterly apathetic, and see nothing extraordinary in the spectacle of an innocent fellow-being having been sought to be sent to the gallows."[161]

One wrongful conviction unearthed by legal historian Alastair McClure at the Allahabad High Court involved a widow named Goshain Thakurani in the early 1890s.[162] Under police coercion, the woman falsely confessed to the illegal concealment of her newborn baby's corpse.[163] Thakurani was convicted, but in the early days of her prison sentence, a medical exam revealed that she was seven months pregnant. It was therefore impossible for her to have given birth to the infant in question just a few months before. She had told police early on, but they had not listened. The widow was presumably granted a pardon. Other than appeals, pardons were "the last safe-guard against the miscarriage of justice" post-conviction (although they did not reverse the conviction).[164] A policeman

158. In *The Bioscope* see "Another Big Gaumont Success," January 20, 1910, 9; and "The Life Story of the English Dreyfus," December 23, 1909, 15. The film was shown at Calcutta's Elphinstone Bioscope cinema on March 8, 1911. Untitled article, *ABP*, March 9, 1911. It was directed and its script written by George R. Sims, the author of *Two King's Pardons*. No copy of the film seems to have survived.

159. In *ABP* see untitled, September 22, 1904; September 25, 1904; and April 14, 1910.

160. For instance see untitled article (on police), *ABP*, June 18, 1893; and "The Hon'ble Mr. Fraser," *ABP*, September 3, 1902.

161. Untitled article, *ABP*, July 8, 1895.

162. Alastair McClure, "Violence, Sovereignty, and the Making of Colonial Criminal Law in India, 1857–1914" (PhD diss., University of Cambridge, 2017), 105–6.

163. For other examples of women making false confessions see CA Report for Bombay, 1876–77, 28; and "Annual Report of the CE and Bacteriologist to the Governments of the United Provinces of Agra and Oudh and of the Central Provinces for the Year 1907," part 1, 2 (IOR/V/24/414).

164. Untitled article, *ABP*, June 25, 1896. See also untitled article, *ABP*, December 24, 1900; Edward Albert Wurtzburg, ed., *Wharton's Law Lexicon* (London: Steven & Sons, 1916), 633–34; and McClure, *Trials of Sovereignty*. The right of appeal was much more limited in criminal cases than in civil ones. "Criminal Appeals," *TI*, October 8, 1940. In addition, the grounds for appeal of a criminal case to the JCPC were extremely narrow. See appendix 2.

was convicted for his role in her case, although his sentence was comparatively light.[165]

In other cases, wrongful convictions were narrowly averted because the murder victim turned up alive. In a pre-1911 case from Rangpur (again from the Bangladesh arsenic belt today), a dead body was produced, and five people confessed. While the trial was happening, however, the deceased appeared in court.[166] In other cases, the alleged murder victim appeared alive only when it was too late—that is, after the execution. In an undated case reported in the Calcutta law reports, an old man was convicted of murdering a young girl and "doing away with" her body. He protested his innocence but was convicted and executed. Two years later, the girl appeared in her home village, having run away earlier.[167]

Sometimes the wrongful conviction was discovered in time, but the accused died anyway. In a notorious case from Howrah (outside of Calcutta) in the early 1870s, Iswar Napit was put on trial for the murder of his daughter. A skull and bones were produced in court and were believed to belong to the young woman. They were considered "a strong piece of evidence against the accused." The father was "on the point of being convicted, when, to the utter surprise of all in court," the daughter appeared "in flesh and blood."[168] She had eloped and was living in Benares, by one account.[169] By another, she had disappeared into the sex trade.[170] For decades to come, this case was noted for its lesson for similar cases: It was dangerous to convict in capital cases where no body—or the wrong bones—had been found.[171] Iswar Napit avoided wrongful conviction and the death penalty because his daughter appeared in time. In a terrible twist, though, he still died—after being tortured by the police. A police officer was convicted for causing this

---

165. The police officer was sentenced to two concurrent sentences of nine months' rigorous imprisonment. The Allahabad High Court refused to enhance his sentence. *Shere Ali v. Queen-Empress*, Criminal Revision 260 of 1891 (unpublished case records, Allahabad High Court Criminal Records Room, India), in McClure, "Violence," 105–6.

166. "Mymensing Murder Case," *ABP*, September 26, 1911.

167. 35th Indian Law Commission Report, 1:79, cited in McClure, "Killing," 377. Similarly, see Thomas Overbury and Joseph Strutt, *An Account of Two Remarkable Trials for Murder, in the Counties of Gloucester and Essex* (London, 1806), 5–27.

168. "A Rajshahye Murder Case," *ABP*, March 4, 1899. See also "Mymensing Murder Case," *ABP*, September 26, 1911.

169. "Mymensing Murder Case."

170. "The Howrah Police Case," *ABP*, May 22, 1873.

171. For reference to the Iswar Napit case in subsequent cases see "A Rajshahye Murder Case," *ABP*, March 4, 1899; and untitled, *ABP*, August 29, 1914. In a comparative context see similarly Daniel Asen, *Death in Beijing: Murder and Forensic Science in Republican China* (Cambridge University Press, 2016), 22–23.

death but was later pardoned and reinstated by George Campbell, the lieutenant governor of Bengal, who claimed that "if Police officers were too closely judged, there would be no detection of crime" and that the inspector's colleagues would be "disheartened" if he was not released.[172]

Iswar Napit's case was well publicized in India because it was so shocking: It combined a narrowly averted wrongful conviction with death by police brutality. It also came to light because Napit was a barber of Bengal's lieutenant governor (the same man who would pardon Napit's torturer) and because Napit was "aided by educated and public spirited men" before his death. But the *ABP* wondered how many similar cases were never exposed. In fact, it was a "custom" among some police in the *mofussil* or countryside to dig up cases and send them to magistrates who were "too willing to convict." "In this way," the *ABP* exclaimed, "how many innocent people have been unnecessarily dragged into the Court and put on their trial and sentenced to various terms of imprisonment!"[173]

Like the *Amrita Bazar Patrika*, there were also judges who worried about wrongful convictions in India. A string of poisoning cases stretching from the 1880s until the 1930s turned on the status of CE certificates. Many of these judges acquitted, expressing concern for the due process rights of criminal defendants. In 1884, for instance, Justices Tottenham and Norris of the Calcutta High Court acquitted Autal Muchi, a man accused of attempting to poison cattle. A group of villagers claimed they had seen him offering bamboo leaves to some cows, and when they searched him, they found a small packet containing some white powder. This substance was apparently sent from this rural area to the CE for testing in Calcutta; however, there were chain-of-custody issues. There was no evidence to show that the packet found on the man was the same one sent to the CE. The civil surgeon from the area, who had supposedly received the packet and sent it on to the lab, was not called to court. And the judges had doubts about the certificate they received, which did not conform to the standard format. "Serious miscarriage of justice may result from the production of certificates such as the one under discussion," they warned, finding the certificate inadmissible.[174]

CEs also talked about wrongful convictions, a theme that emerged with reference to the poison detection rate. Every year in their annual reports, these analysts noted the percentage of cases in which their lab had detected poison,

---

172. Quoting *ABP* (not Campbell) in untitled, *ABP*, January 8, 1885; and in "Two-Thirds Pay for Natives," *ABP*, December 16, 1886. The timing of Iswar Napit's torture is unclear in relation to the appearance of his daughter. He may have been tortured before she appeared but then died afterward. See "The Howrah Police Case."

173. "The Howrah Police Case."

174. *Queen-Empress v. Autal Muchi*, ILR Cal. 10 (1884): 1027.

for both human and animal poisoning cases, and the figures ranged widely from year to year. For instance, the CE of Madras, C. Newcomb, noted in 1926 that the average poison detection rate for his lab over the previous twenty years had been 50.1 percent, with variations from 33.2 percent to 73.8.[175] Some CEs manipulated the method of calculation to boost their figures. For example, the Punjab CEs in 1915–17 could report poison detection rates of 90 percent because they moved cases involving "another cause of death" into an appendix, excluding them from the count.[176] From 1890s Punjab to 1940s Bombay, unnecessary submissions were a source of complaint for CEs when their poison detection rates fell. They blamed the drop on local officials who were careless or lacking in judgment.[177] In 1936, the United and Central Provinces CE, S. N. Chakravarti, requested that forwarding officers be "a little more careful" and stop sending "bogus and trivial cases" for chemical examination. They should only send cases where there was "reasonable ground for suspecting that poisoning may have been the cause of death."[178] The 1941 Bengal CE, K. N. Bagchi, lamented the inflow of cases that could not "by any stretch of imagination, be connected with any form of poisoning." In these cases, local medical officers had concluded from the postmortem exams that death was due to shock, hemorrhage, hanging, drowning, infectious disease, or heart failure. If only local officers would exercise more discretion, "considerable waste of time and energy by the analysts and of expensive chemicals of the department" could be avoided.[179]

Panics could also decrease the poison detection rate. For instance, the Madras lab's detection rate fell by 18 percent in 1899 because of "a number of packets of harmless powder" found on the street after the anti-Shanar riots in Madura and Tinnevelly (intercaste conflicts over temple access). False rumors swirled, and local officials were on edge. But no poison was found in the packets. To prevent the panic from dragging down his numbers, the CE removed these cases from the tally. The lab could then report a respectable 64 percent poison detection rate that year.[180]

---

175. CE Report for Madras 1926, 2. This average and range of rates was representative of other CE labs in South Asia.

176. CE Report for Punjab 1915, 1; 1916, 1; and 1917, 2.

177. Letter from inspector-general of civil hospitals, Punjab, to the Punjab government, no. 1119 (April 16, 1895), 1, in CE Report for Punjab 1894; and "Report of the CA to Government, Bombay" for 1946, 2, and 1947, 2 (both IOR/V/24/410).

178. "Report of the CE to Government, United Provinces and Central Provinces, for the Year 1936," 2 (IOR/V/24/417).

179. CE Report for Bengal 1941, 8. Similarly, see "Report of the CE to Government, Bengal, for the Year 1940," 11 (IOR/V/24/424).

180. CE Report for Madras 1899, 6 and 16. On the riots see Edgar Thurston and K. Rangachari, *Castes and Tribes of Southern India* (Madras: Government Press, 1909), 6:364; and Arun Bandopadhyay,

The poison detection rate was the metric that best captured the lab's annual performance. A rising poison detection rate meant that the lab was becoming more effective, that local officials were becoming more selective in what they sent in, or both. In 1891, the assistant surgeon Lala Guranditta Mal was commended for his good work at the Punjab lab, for instance, because of "the high percentage of detection in cattle cases."[181] The rising rates at the same lab two years later were called "satisfactory" by military superiors, "whether due to greater care in submitting cases to the CE or to more careful treatment in the laboratory."[182] The general assumption was: the higher, the better.

But not everyone agreed. Some CEs cautioned that a higher poison detection rate did not mean a more successful lab. In the flagship Bengal lab, the 1903 poison detection rate of 45–46 percent was criticized for being rather low. The CE, D. St. J. D. Grant, objected: His job was not simply to try to find poison in as many samples as possible. Sometimes it was just as important to find *no* poison. "As much assistance may be rendered to justice by proof that a charge of poisoning is false as by proof that such a charge is true."[183] This dialogue recurred time and again, as CEs defended their work through a more nuanced interpretation of the poison detection rate and a tacit concern for wrongful conviction. The CE pointed out that this rate did not necessarily "reflect on the usefulness of his work, as in some cases the fact that a substance contains no poison reveals the mistaken or false nature of a charge of murder."[184] Many so-called unnecessary submissions were not, in fact, careless but care*ful:* "It is better that such cases should be submitted to the definite test of analysis than that crime should remain untraced or innocent persons remain under an unjust suspicion."[185] A finding of no poison could help vindicate the wrongly accused.[186] The CE for the United and Central Provinces in 1907, E. H. Hankin, noted that some cases submitted to his lab would inevitably be "trivial," but that was because an important part

"The Origin of a Social Conflict in South India: The Sivakasi Riots of 1899," *Studies in People's History* 1, no. 1 (2014): 69–80.

181. "Report of the CE to Government, Punjab, for the Year 1891," 12 (IOR/V/24/418).

182. Letter from the inspector-general of civil hospitals, Punjab, to the Punjab government, no. 822 (March 28, 1894) in CE Report for Punjab 1893.

183. Letter from the inspector-general of civil hospitals, Bengal (February 22, 1904) in CE Report for Bengal 1903.

184. Letter from the secretary to the government, N.-W. Provinces and Oudh to the inspector-general of civil hospitals, N.-W. Provinces and Oudh (Naini Tal, April 27, 1900), 1, in CE and Bacteriologist Report for NWP, Oudh, and the Central Provinces 1899, part 1.

185. Letter from the inspector-general of civil hospitals, Punjab, to the Punjab government, no. 2524 (April 15, 1907), 1, in "Report of the CE to Government, Punjab, for the Year 1906" (IOR/V/24/418).

186. CE Report for Punjab 1906, 2.

of his work was "to assist in clearing the character of persons unjustly suspected by showing that substances supposed to contain poison are really harmless."[187]

Some CEs gave specific examples. In a 1907 case from Gorakhpur, a man complained that he had bought ten annas' worth of flour, which was "mixed with such things that when he took the bread it caused the stomach to swell." The chapati tested negative for poison, however, which cleared the seller's name.[188] Similarly, the same lab tested a man's vomit a few years later. He had accused his wife of putting in his food the toxic leaves of the *Gloriosa superba* plant, which was "supposed by natives to be poisonous." There were leaves in the vomit, but not of *Gloriosa superba*, and no poison was detected. The wife had been wrongly accused.[189] A decade earlier, D. St. J. D. Grant (then CE of Punjab) pointed to four cases in which death was due to drowning. The initial worry was that these bodies had been poisoned, then "thrown into water to give color to the theory of drowning." The absence of poison did not mean that these bodies should not have been sent to the lab.[190] Even though they would have diminished the lab's poison detection rate for 1896, in other words, these submissions were not wasteful or careless. Most impressive were reminders by CEs of these subtleties *even when* their annual detection rate had risen, as in Punjab in the late 1890s.[191]

The concern with innocence and wrongful conviction threaded its way through CE reports. It appeared not only under the medico-legal heading, but in other sections such as testing done for Customs and Excise. The CE of Punjab, D. R. Thomas, noted in 1930 that some of the samples of alcoholic spirits he had tested for Customs and Excise were "very suspicious." However, they had produced unclear results. Like a judge in court, analysts in the lab had to err in favor of the accused when the evidence was ambiguous: "This is the price that any civilized country has got to pay in order to make sure that an innocent person is not wrongly convicted."[192] Fifteen years later, the same analyst offered

187. CE and Bacteriologist Report for United and Central Provinces 1907, part 1, 2.

188. CE and Bacteriologist Report for United and Central Provinces 1907, part 1, 2.

189. "Annual Report of the CE and Bacteriologist to the Governments of the United Provinces of Agra and Oudh and of the Central Provinces for the Year 1911," 3 (IOR/V/24/415).

190. Letter from the inspector-general of civil hospitals, Punjab, to the Punjab government, no. 1533 (April 15, 1897), 1, in "Report of the CE to Government, Punjab, for the Year 1896" (IOR/V/24/418).

191. For example see letter from the inspector-general of civil hospitals, Punjab, to the Punjab government, no. 1533 (April 15, 1897), 1, in "Report of the CE to Government, Punjab, for the Year 1896" (IOR/V/24/418); and letter from the officiating inspector-general of civil hospitals, Punjab, to the Punjab government, no. 1377 (April 1, 1899), 2, in "Report of the CE to Government, Punjab, for the Year 1898" (IOR/V/24/418).

192. "Report of the CE to Government, Punjab, for the Year 1930," iv (appendix) (IOR/V/24/419). For a famous case involving chemical testing and the evasion of taxation for alcohol see Projit Bihari

an almost identical "Word of Advice": When lab results for a certain drug were inconclusive, the analyst had to give a negative report to avoid a wrongful conviction.[193]

When those who favored higher poison detection rates complained of "fictitious" poisoning cases, they meant cases that they thought never should have been submitted in the first place.[194] Analysts with a more complex view of the poison detection rate had a different kind of fiction in mind. They were concerned with cases in which an innocent person was wrongly suspected of poisoning and was vindicated through test results. The phenomenon of false poisoning added one more layer of complexity: Here, the lab test did find poison, but in an impossible location or form that meant that someone had been wrongly suspected of poisoning earlier. Debates over how to interpret the poison detection rate did not address planted poison specifically. Nonetheless, their concern with wrongful convictions in the simpler type of false case—accusations of poisoning where no poison was found—must have extended to the more subtle and challenging phenomenon of planted poison, too.

There was a distinctly colonial aspect to the concern with innocence. Forensic analysts were especially concerned with false cases because they believed that colonized people dissembled. In this, their position resembled that of J. Douglas Young, the High Court judge who worried about "the protection of accused persons" because "it is notorious in this country that any document may be forged or substituted by a forged document."[195] CE reports, like so many other professionals' records, were dry and terse, not prone to speculation or elaboration, and only rarely gave voice to broader ideas about falsity, race, and culture. However, the treatises of medical jurisprudence that must have lined their lab library bookshelves were explicit about these connections.[196] From Chevers to Greval, works of this genre typically included an early section about Indian untruthfulness and its manifestation in crime.

Mukharji, "Gariahat Whisky: Bootlegged Cosmopolitanism and the Making of the Nationalistic State, Calcutta, c. 1923–1935," 197–99, in *Alcohol Flows Across Cultures: Drinking Cultures in Transnational and Comparative Perspective*, ed. Waltraud Ernst (Routledge, 2020).

193. "Report of the CE to Government, Punjab, for the Year 1945," 10 (IOR/V/24/421).

194. For example see Order no. 489, Public (April 30, 1897), "Report of the CE to Government, Madras, for the Year 1896," 18, in "Reports of the CEs to the Governments of Madras, Bombay, Bengal, the North-Western Provinces and Oudh, the Central Provinces, the Punjab, and Burma, and the Resolutions of the Respective Governments Recorded Thereon" (IOR/P/5185, December 1897).

195. *Emp. v. Happu*, ILR All. 56 (1934): 233–34. On this case see also chapters 4 and 5.

196. On the CEs' libraries see Stanley Kemp, *Catalogue of the Scientific Serial Publications in the Principal Libraries of Calcutta* (Calcutta: Asiatic Society of Bengal, 1918), vi; "Report of the CE to Government, Bengal, for the Year 1935," 5 (IOR/V/24/424); and CA Report for Bombay 1946, 9.

One leading treatise author was himself a chemical examiner. L. A. Waddell (figure 4) significantly expanded *Lyon's Medical Jurisprudence for India* in its third edition (1904) and oversaw the publication of six editions over twenty-five years (1904–28).[197] In 1935, Waddell's successor, T. F. Owens, called the treatise the leading work of Indian medical jurisprudence for the past half century (its first edition, by I. B. Lyon, appeared in 1888).[198] Waddell was a Scottish military physician in the IMS who was CE of Bengal in the 1880s and '90s.[199] Not only did Waddell's treatise offer the clearest example of how a British CE thought about native mendacity; it was also a key reference work—with one-third of its pages devoted to poisoning—for CEs across India and Burma, who cited it in their reports.[200] Waddell inherited the treatise from another state toxicologist: Lyon had been the chemical analyser of Bombay for over twenty-six years, retiring in 1892.[201]

The introduction to Waddell's treatise included a section titled "Falseness of much of the evidence given by natives of India." The "untrustworthiness of native evidence" in India was notorious, according to Waddell. He claimed that nearly every case included some false evidence, whether caused by "fear, stupidity, apathy, malice, or innate deceit." Even the imperial apex court, the Privy Council, had described the phenomenon, complaining of "the lamentable disregard of truth prevailing amongst the natives of India." Waddell then described cases in which Indians tried to frame their enemies for murder. In one "very common form of conspiracy," one person would cause a second person to disappear and

197. See S. D. S. Greval, "Preface to the Tenth Edition," in *Lyon's Medical Jurisprudence for India*, 10th ed., ed. S. D. S. Greval (Calcutta: Thacker, Spink, 1953).

198. T. F. Owens, "Preface to the Ninth Edition," in *Lyon's Medical Jurisprudence for India* (1953), xi.

199. Waddell was also professor of chemistry and pathology at Calcutta Medical College and examiner in medical jurisprudence at Calcutta University. In the late 1890s he was editor of the *Indian Medical Gazette*, a leading medical journal. Waddell's private papers are at the University of Glasgow Special Collections (MS Gen 1691), but they pertain almost exclusively to his interests in Eurasian archaeology and mythology. The only signs of his forensic work are on the back of scrap paper. The collection also reflects his antisemitism. Waddell wrote book reviews for the Imperial Fascist League (IFL) and corresponded with its head, Arnold Leese. See letter from A. Leese to L. A. Waddell of September 5, 1935 (MS Gen 1691/3/78) and (on IFL stationery) April 14, 1937 (MS Gen 1691/3/79), along with draft "Dear Leese" letters by Waddell of April 24, 1939 (MS Gen 161/3/80), and undated (MS Gen 1691/5/3). The IFL was the most extreme Nazi organization operating in interwar Britain. Graham Macklin, "The Two Lives of John Hooper Harvey," *Patterns of Prejudice* 42, no. 2 (2008): 167–68, 171–72.

200. For instance see "Report of the CE and Bacteriologist to the Government of Burma for the Year 1906," 2 (IOR/V/24/425), and "Annual Report of the CE and Bacteriologist to the Government of the United Provinces of Agra and Oudh and of the Central Provinces, for the Year 1916," 3 (IOR/V/24/415).

201. CA Report for Bombay 1892, 22.

FIGURE 4. / L. A. Waddell with unidentified woman, probably in Scotland during the 1930s. Courtesy of the University of Glasgow Archives & Special Collections, Papers of Laurence Austine Waddell collection, MS Gen 1691, Photo/50, undated.

then have a third person charged with their murder. A "putrid corpse" would be pulled out of a river and gashed, then given to the authorities as the alleged victim. Eyewitnesses might give detailed testimony about the facts of the killing or disposal of the body, and a murder conviction would result. It was only when the murder victim showed up alive that the "falsity of the whole proceedings" was discovered. Waddell provided examples, including cases of false confessions and evidence fabricated by Indian police.[202]

202. *Lyon's Medical Jurisprudence* (1921), 22–24.

The larger point was that Waddell understood false cases to be products of a South Asian propensity for dissimulation. And he noted that poisoning, "with its secret treachery," was a specialty of "the East" and far more common in India than in Europe.[203] Waddell's concerns about false accusations, including through planted poison, were annealed to racial or cultural stereotypes about dissimulation. A century later, concern over racial bias in the American criminal legal system would be a key driver of the innocence movement. In colonial India, however, concern with innocence was powered *by racial bias itself.* CEs like Waddell were so alert to the possibility of planted poison and miscarriages of justice because they believed so deeply in native mendacity.

Admittedly, CEs did identify many planted poison cases. It is impossible to determine whether the rate of detected planted poison was greater among South Asians than among Europeans in British India, given the tiny proportion of Europeans both in British India (0.07 percent of the population in 1901) and in the annual reports.[204] Furthermore, analysts' test results provided evidence that poison had been planted, but not by whom. Nonetheless, it is plausible that authorities may have found more crime of this type in India because they were so focused on looking for it.[205] In other words, suspicion may have sharpened detection, and detection in turn reinforced suspicion. And the CEs' focus on innocence and wrongful conviction was animated by beliefs that South Asians dissembled. Planted poison cases fed anxieties about native mendacity and analysts' appetite to find more cases.

South Asian Forensic Professionals and the Rejection of Native Mendacity

Over the period covered by this book, Western science and allopathic medicine were adapted to South Asian contexts and reconfigured as blended traditions. This meant the rise of "braided sciences" like the incorporation of tiny technologies—the pocket watch and thermometer, for instance—into Ayurvedic

203. *Lyon's Medical Jurisprudence* (1921), 440; see also 461.

204. *Statistical Abstract Relating to British India from 1894–95 to 1903–4* (London: HMSO, 1905), tables 1 and 9.

205. For a similar argument made in other contexts see Mishra, *Beastly Encounters*, 129–30; and Angela J. Davis, ed., *Policing the Black Man: Arrest, Prosecution, and Imprisonment* (Pantheon Books, 2017).

medicine, the South Asian healing tradition grounded in Sanskrit texts.[206] It involved the emergence of vernacularized scientific publications for popular, non-Anglo audiences, and a new quest to rediscover Hindu science and uncover its ancient roots.[207] Most important for this study was the Indianization of the forensic professions.[208] When Chevers published his treatise in 1856, the lawyers, judges, physicians, and other analysts involved in forensic work at the upper levels were British. Staff at state toxicology labs and key contributors to forensic publications were South Asian, but the CE himself was British.[209] This started to change in the 1910s and 1920s.[210] Chunilal Bose was the officiating CE of Bengal from 1915 to 1920, having served in this role for shorter periods between 1889 and 1915.[211] N. J. Vazifdar was chemical analyser at the new Sind lab in Karachi (an offshoot of the Bombay lab) in 1914 and 1916. Others followed, including Devendra Nath Chatterji (1922–36) and S. N. Chakravarti (1936–45) at the United and Central Provinces' lab; Bhujangrao S. Beltangady in Sind (for much of 1917–27) and Bombay (1936–39); H. C. Hiranandani in Sind (1936–41); Muhammad Aziz-ul-lah in Madras (1927–29); Chit Thoung in Rangoon (for much of 1930–40); and Udho Ram (for much of 1933–42) and

---

206. Projit Bihari Mukharji, *Doctoring Traditions: Ayurveda, Small Technologies, and Braided Sciences* (University of Chicago Press, 2016).

207. By Charu Singh see "The Shastri and the Air-Pump," 232–54, and "Science in the Vernacular? Translation, Terminology and Lexicography in the *Hindi Scientific Glossary* (1906)," *South Asian History and Culture* 13, no. 1 (2022): 63–86. See also Pratik Chakraborty, "Science, Nationalism, and Colonial Contestations: P. C. Ray and His *Hindu Chemistry*," *IESHR* 37, no. 2 (2000): 185–213; and Gyan Prakash, *Another Reason: Science and the Imagination of Modern India* (Princeton University Press, 1999), 8–9, 86–120.

208. On the Indianization of the medical services specifically see Waltraud Ernst, "Indianization of Colonial Medicine: The Case of Psychiatry in Early Twentieth-Century British India," *Naturwissenschaften, Technik und Medizin* 20 (2012): 63–64.

209. For instance, Kanai Lal Dey (or Kanny Loll Dey) of the Calcutta CE lab contributed to Chevers's treatise. He also published his own important treatises (in Bengali and English) on medical jurisprudence and indigenous drugs, particularly *The Indigenous Drugs of India* (Calcutta, 1867); and *Medical Jurisprudence* [Calcutta, 1876] (Bengali). See Chunilal Bose, "A Brief Summary of Research-Work in Chemistry in Bengal," in *Scientific and Other Papers*, 105–6; Arnold, *Toxic Histories*, 74, 114; and Roy Chaudhury, "Toxic Matters," 90–96.

210. Patrick Hehir, *The Medical Profession in India* (London: Henry Frowde, 1923), 1. For earlier allegations of racial discrimination at the Bombay CA lab see Moreshvar Gopal Deshmukh, *The Evils of the Military Medical Service Monopoly* (Bombay, 1893); and, less directly, "Dr. Deshmukh Explains," *TI*, January 31, 1893.

211. See Satyendra Nath Sen, "Rai Chunilal Bose Bahadur," *Indian Journal of Medicine* 1, no. 3 (1920): 209–25; J. P. Bose, "A Brief Record of the Life and Career of Rai Chunilal Bose Bahadur," in *The Scientific and Other Papers of Rai Chunilal Bose Bahadur*, ed. J. P. Bose (Calcutta, 1924), 1:xiii–xxiv; and Indranil Sanyal, "Dr. Chunilal Bose: A Forgotten Scientist and a Science Communicator," *Indian Journal of History of Science* 57 (2022): 154–55.

B. H. Syed (1947–48) in Lahore.[212] In the 1920s, G. C. Mitra was the first South Asian to occupy the post of imperial serologist, the bloodstain expert (and the focus of chapter 2).[213] S. D. S. Greval occupied the post from the mid-1930s on.[214]

Parallel to this transformation, and following the 1861 reorganization of the legal profession through the creation of the High Courts, Indians rose through the ranks of lawyers and then judges.[215] By 1908, managing clerk and memoirist A. J. C. Mistry observed that South Asian lawyers and law firms were taking over in Bombay.[216] During the 1920s and 1930s, in Partha Chatterjee's words, the Indianization of the legal profession reflected "the secret story of the transfer of power in late colonial India." This transformation was carried out not in "street demonstrations, prisons, and conference tables but within the interstices of the governmental apparatus itself."[217] I disagree that lawyers were necessarily part of the state—often, they were fighting *against* it.[218] But for the forensic professions in particular, Chatterjee's observation holds true. By 1947, forensics in India and Burma were not just South Asian in subject matter and tools, including a vast body of treatises, annual reports, scientific articles, and case law, but also South Asian in personnel.

With the Indianization of the forensic professions came a shift in explanations for India's high rates of poisoning. The best example was Chunilal Bose (figure 5). He gave a famous lecture and coauthored an article with J. F. Evans in

212. See annual reports for the relevant CE or CA lab and year; and Arnold, *Toxic Histories*, 115.

213. Notification no. 233 from the government of India, Department of Education and Health (Medical) (Delhi, April 4, 1922), in "Pay of Ravi Gopal Chandra Mitra Bahadur while officiating as Imperial Serologist to Government Bengal," Education and Health: Medical B, September 1922, file no. 92–93 (NAI). I also thank Projit B. Mukharji for sharing a blood sugar report form dated May 13, 1967, which fell out of a used book he purchased in Kolkata. Beneath "Calcutta Serological Institute Laboratory" appears the line: "Founder: Late Rai Dr. G. C. Mitra Bahadur, 1st Indian Imperial Serologist" (image on file with author).

214. S. D. S. Greval was a Punjabi IMS officer with medical, surgical, and public health degrees from the University of Liverpool. See "Question of the Selection of an Officer for Appointment as Chemical Examiner . . . Appointment of Major S. D. S. Greval, IMS, as Officiating Imperial Serologist," Education, Health and Lands: Health, 1934, file no. 11–2/34-H (NAI). See also annual confidential reports on Greval (1934–35 to 1939–40) in personal file, "Shiva Deva Singh Greval" (IOR/L/MIL/14/68739: 1919–48).

215. See Cynthia Farid, "Imperial Constitutionalism: Judicial Politics and Separation of Powers in Colonial India (1861–1935)" (SJD diss., University of Wisconsin–Madison, 2020), chap. 2.

216. A. J. C. Mistry, *Reminiscences of the Office of Messrs Wadia Ghandy & Co.* (Bombay: published by the author, [1911]), 73–76; discussed in Sharafi, *Law and Identity*, 107. I thank Wadia Ghandy & Co. (Mumbai) for allowing me to consult the firm's copy of this rare work.

217. Partha Chatterjee, *A Princely Impostor? The Strange and Universal History of the Kumar of Bhawal* (Princeton University Press, 2002), 378.

218. For example see Sharafi, *Law and Identity*, 103.

FIGURE 5. / Portrait of Chunilal Bose. From Chunilal Bose, *Food* (University of Calcutta, 1930), frontispiece.

the *Transactions of the First Indian Medical Congress* in 1895.[219] Bose and Evans, who were CEs in Bengal, addressed the problem of high poisoning rates in India. This piece was famous because it led to the passage of the Poisons Act of 1904, a statute that eventually helped curtail the criminal use of arsenic.[220] Bose and Evans detailed India's long historical and literary poison trail, from the classical *Shastras* and Sushruta's Ayurvedic medical texts to harem intrigue and the poisoning of Burmese and Nepali wells by locals as British armies approached.[221] This line of reasoning would have landed most British authors in a place akin to Waddell's opening chapter: South Asian dissimulation. But Bose and Evans had a different explanation for India's problem with poison: availability.

Poisons were much more regulated by the state in England than in India. The motives for poisoning in India, they wrote, "are the same [as] everywhere": revenge,

219. David Arnold asserts that Bose was the lead author. Arnold, *Toxic Histories*, 157.

220. See Sanyal, "Dr. Chunilal Bose," 157–60.

221. Evans and Bose, "Necessity," 225–27. Similarly, see *Lyon's Medical Jurisprudence* (1921), 440–41.

jealousy, lust, greed, and avarice. Bose and Evans assumed a certain universality to human nature. Implicitly, they were rejecting cultural and racial stereotypes about the dissimulating colonized subject. If imported mineral poisons like arsenic could be better controlled by legislation, perhaps India's poisoning rates and England's would look similar. Granted, botanical (and animal) poisons were harder to control, as they grew "in every hedge and garden" in India.[222] But still, the problem was not rooted in any cultural or racial propensities. It was simply much easier to obtain poisons in India than in England. In the centuries-long debate over whether perpetrators' inner workings or the ready availability of weapons causes higher crime rates, Bose and Evans chose the latter.[223]

Not all British forensic experts subscribed to cultural or racialized explanations for poisoning. Chunilal Bose's coauthor Evans did not, for instance. And not all South Asians rejected it. S. D. S. Greval took over the publication of Lyon's treatise in 1953, inheriting it from Waddell and then Owens. Greval retained the opening section on Indian mendacity. He defended Europeans as not "ignorant by nature" but simply "misinformed" by "local Eastern informants in their zeal to adopt Western sentiments."[224] The move suggested "white coats" alienated from their own "brown skins."[225] Figures like Greval aside (whose volume was a blip against the trend), the rise of South Asians in the forensic professions opened the way for different ideas about crimes of stealth, including poisoning. The author of the forensic treatise that pulled ahead of Greval's in the 1950s—J. P. Modi—continued in Chunilal Bose's path. Although he discussed false injuries at length, Modi (see chapter 5) rejected native mendacity as the structuring concept of his forensic treatise.[226] Poisoning and other crimes of deception happened in India for the same tragic motives as anywhere else.

---

222. Evans and Bose, "Necessity," 261.

223. For a version of this argument on gun violence in the US today see Jennifer Carlson, "Gun Studies and the Politics of Evidence," *Annual Review of Law and Social Science* 16 (2020): 186.

224. See S. D. S. Greval in *Lyon's Medical Jurisprudence* (1953), 24–26. Greval's "misinformed" comment was in the context of European pity for opium users in India: *Lyon's Medical Jurisprudence* (1953), vi. Greval and his British wife Dorothy remained in India after independence. In the *IMG* during the 1940s–50s he published on serology and toxicology (among other medical themes), and she published on how to run a household. For an *IMG* sample see S. D. S. Greval, "The Use of Blood Tests in Excluding Paternity and Maternity," April 1946, 204–7, and "Mushroom Poisoning in India," November 1950, 513–14; and Dorothy Greval, "Pantry, Kitchen and Servants' Quarters," December 1954, 749–50, and "Furniture in the Tropics," February 1955, 71–72.

225. See Mukharji, *Brown Skins*, 263.

226. It is no surprise that Modi's treatise appeared most recently in its twenty-sixth edition in 2018, while Greval's 1953 edition was the final edition of Lyon's treatise.

The earlier logic that explained fabricated evidence as the product of native mendacity faded out when the British left in 1947. But the colonial character of a heightened concern with wrongful convictions was clear in earlier reports of the CEs, who sought to detect not only false negatives but also false positives. Planted poison was the ultimate puzzle and challenge. It reveals an alternative history of concern over wrongful convictions, and one that contrasts starkly with the innocence movement of our own time. In British India, the desire to prevent miscarriages of justice in poisoning cases was not a counterweight to the rule of colonial difference, but a product of it.

2

PLANTED ANIMAL BLOOD AND MURDER

In 1916, news of a conflict between South Indian caste communities reached the pages of the *British Medical Journal*.[1] Naikers had planned to build a wedding canopy in front of a temple. Nadars objected because the structure would interfere with the carrying of palanquins in their own processions nearby. A magistrate held an inquiry to resolve the dispute, but the Nadars remained dissatisfied. They decided to further the dispute by framing their adversaries for murder. Determined to kill one of their own and blame it on the Naikers, the Nadars selected the mistress of one of their members as the victim. She was childless and had no relatives to avenge her death. This unfortunate woman was beaten to death, and her body was left at the temple, with sheep's blood poured on the ground surrounding her and on some clothing belonging to a Naiker. The Nadars sent a telegram to the district authorities, reporting that the woman had been murdered at the temple by Naikers.[2]

This chain of events could have resulted in the conviction of a hapless Naiker for murder. But colonial authorities applied a new form of forensic analysis to the bloodstains in the case. Precipitin testing had been institutionalized in

1. "Blood Stains," *BMJ* 1, no. 2877 (1916): 283–84. See also "Note by Lieut.-Col. W. D. Sutherland, IMS, on the legal serological work carried out by him," May 29, 1915, 8, in "Appointment of an imperial serologist for the whole of India," Bhopal Agency: General, Proc. no. 5, 1914 (NAI).

2. On false cases between Nadar and Naiker communities in the 1930s see Radha Kumar, *Police Matters: The Everyday State and Caste Politics in South India, 1900–1975* (Cornell University Press, 2021), 68–69.

India in 1914–16 through the creation of an official post known as the imperial serologist, who ran a laboratory in Calcutta. This official, who had no equivalent in Britain, tested stains for the courts.[3] For bloodstains, his task was to use precipitin testing to assess whether blood was human or from some other kind of animal.[4] Precipitin testing determined the species (or species group) of origin for a bloodstain.[5] In the South Indian case, the imperial serologist determined that the stains at the temple were sheep's blood. Equally, both human and ovine blood were found on the bloodstained loincloth belonging to the accused Naiker.[6] Because of the odd presence of sheep's blood both at the temple and on the Naiker's clothing, the judge concluded that all the blood had been planted, and that this man was being framed for murder. He acquitted the Naiker defendant for lack of evidence. The *British Medical Journal* published the account so that the empire could learn of precipitin testing success in India. When animal blood was planted "to obscure or divert the path of avenging justice," the imperial serologist could now spot the falsity.[7]

Although precipitin testing appeared periodically in criminal trials in Britain in the early twentieth century, it enjoyed a much fuller life in British India.[8] This chapter explores why this was so and suggests that the technique took hold in India because it spoke to a priority of the colonial state: the detection of fabricated evidence and mendacity in cases involving South Asians. Detecting

---

3. There were experts who used forensic serology in English and Scottish criminal trials during the early twentieth century, but there was no official dedicated exclusively to this field. The senior official analyst to the Home Office, county analysts in England, and university professors of medical jurisprudence in Scotland covered both forensic serology and toxicology. See, e.g., "Doctor's Death from Drugs," *Times of London* (*TL*), September 21, 1921; "Double Murder Charge," *TL*, November 1, 1928; "Doctor's Suspicions of Arsenic," *TL*, August 20, 1929; "Trunk Murder Charge," *TL*, August 8, 1934; Alison Adam, *A History of Forensic Science: British Beginnings in the Twentieth Century* (Routledge, 2016), 132–42; and M. Anne Crowther and Brenda White, *On Soul and Conscience: The Medical Expert and Crime; 150 Years of Forensic Medicine in Glasgow* (Aberdeen University Press, 1988).

4. "Chemistry and Crime: The Detective in the Laboratory," *Leader*, April 8, 1914. When distinguishing between human and animal blood in this book, I use "animal" as shorthand for nonhuman animal.

5. Strictly speaking, precipitin testing was not a blood test but a serum-based "specific protein" test that could be used on blood, bone, skin, muscle, semen, or "albuminous urine." R. B. Lloyd, "The Serological Analysis of Bloodstains in Criminal Cases (Illustrative Cases)," *IMG* 61, no. 5 (1926): 220; Alfred Swaine Taylor, *Principles and Practice of Medical Jurisprudence*, 8th ed., ed. Sydney Smith and W. G. H. Cook (London: J. & A. Churchill, 1928), 1:499. Nonetheless, I refer to it as a blood test because bloodstains were the usual objects of analysis. In this book, references to Taylor pertain to editions of the treatise revised and issued after the original author's death in 1880.

6. "Note by Lieut.-Col. W. D. Sutherland," 33–34.

7. "Blood Stains," 183.

8. For example see "Bungalow Crime," *TL*, June 7, 1924; and Donald Carswell, *Trial of Ronald True* (Edinburgh: William Hodge, 1925), 71.

dissimulation was a special focus of the criminal legal system in British India. Furthering Projit Mukharji's characterization of the early twentieth century as the age of "serotropicality" in the British empire—when blood science became a prime focus of tropical medicine—this chapter explores how precipitin testing emerged out of, and then reinforced, anxieties about truth and trust in empire.[9]

Typically, scholars have attributed the "native mendacity" stereotype to colonial administrators' racism and invention, and have ended their analysis with this explanation. By contrast, this chapter entertains the possibility of actual instances of dissimulation but without accepting the racist explanations for it provided by colonial sources. In examining precipitin testing, I explore beyond the racialized stereotype of the dissimulating native to propose an alternative explanation for potentially false evidence. The imperial serologist's records concerning precipitin testing allow us to read primary sources against the grain and to catch a glimpse of how certain noncolonial notions of identity, punishment, and causation were remade and refashioned by nonstate actors. In this way, the history of precipitin testing is a story about legal pluralism, revealing how state and nonstate normative orders interacted.[10] In one important subset of cases, fabricated evidence was the product of what we might call punitive self-harm. Specifically, precipitin cases show that a noncolonial mode of disputing (hurting oneself or one's relative to punish an adversary) morphed into something else (framing an opponent for murder by planting animal blood) to harness the punitive powers of colonial criminal law and customize them to alternative notions of justice. This chapter reveals how colonized tricksters pursued justice (as they saw it) not through truth but falsity.

In the story told here of the interplay between two forms of disputing, punitive self-harm adapted and contorted itself to meet the requirements of colonial criminal law, while in the process subverting the larger aims of the criminal legal system. The first section of this chapter focuses on the history of science and institutions, and it examines the rise of precipitin testing and the creation of the imperial serologist in British India during the 1910s. The second section brings legal history into the discussion and examines the problem of fabricated evidence, which was considered a leading challenge for the criminal legal system in late colonial India. The third section uses the concept of legal pluralism to elaborate punitive self-harm as a set of noncolonial disputing practices. Precipitin testing revealed planted animal

9. Projit Bihari Mukharji, "Sero-Tropicality: Blood and the Reinvention of Tropical Medicine, 1930–50," talk presented at the University of Wisconsin–Madison, March 20, 2015. This chapter focuses on a slightly earlier period than Mukharji, tracing the age of serotropicality in forensics back to the first decade of the twentieth century.

10. See Sally Engle Merry, "Legal Pluralism," *Law & Society Review* 22, no. 5 (1988): 869–96, and Paul Schiff Berman, *Global Legal Pluralism: A Jurisprudence of Law Beyond Borders* (Cambridge University Press, 2012).

blood in some cases. For us, more significant than the evidence's falsity—the prime concern of the colonial legal system—is the alternative logic at play in these cases, particularly around notions of causation and responsibility. Even if a person had been framed, he could still be deemed morally responsible and punishable for a death because he "caused" the death with his original wrong. This noncolonial reasoning of punitive self-harm made the fabrication of evidence legitimate for its proponents. The colonial state saw its serological expertise as exposing native mendacity rather than alterity, but its own sources reveal interactions between two dispute-resolution systems—and two different ways of punishing wrongs. Colonial sources referred to the Nadar-Naiker dispute as a feud.[11] Across the British empire, colonial authorities found themselves pulled into group disputes whose longer histories remained largely illegible to them. In such cases, the colonial state in India failed to recognize the process of adaptation and the alternative concept of justice that motivated and legitimated the planting of animal blood.

Precipitin Testing and the Imperial Serologist

For most of the twentieth century, blood group testing and blood spatter analysis were the best known methods of forensic blood testing. Karl Landsteiner proposed the ABO blood grouping system in 1901, which enabled the expansion of blood transfusion worldwide during the first four decades of the twentieth century.[12] By the late 1930s, it rose to prominence as a method of excluding paternity and maternity in English and Indian courts.[13] It was also used to determine whether bloodstains could have belonged to the victim or perpetrator of violent crime.[14] Blood spatter analysis developed in the 1950s, emerging as a forensic technique after Indian independence.[15]

---

11. See letter in support of the creation of the imperial serologist (amid feuding behavior in the province) from chief commissioner, North-West Frontier Province, to secretary to government of India, Home department, January 6, 1914, Proceedings of the Home dept. September 1914, no. 7 (IOR/P/9457).

12. On aspects of ABO blood-group testing in India during the first half of the twentieth century see Projit Bihari Mukharji, "From Serosocial to Sanguinary Identities: Caste, Transnational Race Science and the Shifting Metonymies of Blood Group B, India c. 1918–1960," *IESHR* 51 (2014): 143–76.

13. See the articles by S. D. S. Greval: "The Use of Blood Tests in Excluding Paternity and Maternity," *IMG* 74, no. 7 (1939): 388–91; and 80, no. 4 (1945): 204–7.

14. See D. P. Lambert, "A Preliminary Report on the Medico-Legal Value of the Finding of Blood on Nail Parings," *IMG* 74, no. 12 (1939): 745; and Jaising P. Modi, *A Textbook of Medical Jurisprudence and Toxicology*, 6th ed. (Bombay: Butterworth, 1940), 106–7.

15. Eduard Piotrowski published a book proposing blood spatter analysis in 1895, but the forensic study of the physics of blood patterns emerged as a distinct field only in the 1950s with the Sam Sheppard case in the United States. See Ian Burney, "Spatters and Lies: Contrasting Forensic Cultures

Since the mid-nineteenth century, forensic experts had attempted to determine the species of origin of a blood sample by comparing under the microscope the size of red blood cells. However, the overlap between species' size ranges limited this method's use in court. Often, one could only say that a bloodstain could be human or from another species. The blood sample also had to be relatively fresh.[16] However, around the same time as Landsteiner's work on ABO blood grouping, immunological researchers developed a new form of testing whereby the production of antibodies in blood could be used to determine the species (or species group) of origin.[17] Paul Uhlenhuth proposed in 1901 that precipitin testing (as it was called) could be put to forensic use. Historian of science Tal Golan has traced how precipitin testing overtook microscopy in the early twentieth century in the United States.[18] Precipitin testing could produce clearer results even on an old or small sample, or on a sample that had been exposed to heat up to 50° to 60°C (122° to 140°F)—relevant in the South Asian context especially.[19] An animal (typically a rabbit or bird) would be injected with blood or serum of another species (e.g., human blood).[20] Over several days, this animal's blood developed antibodies in response to its exposure to human blood. This blood would be extracted from the animal, and from it, antihuman serum was preserved. Next, an extract would be created from the suspected stain (known

---

in the Trials of Sam Sheppard, 1954–66," in *Global Forensic Cultures: Making Fact and Justice in the Modern Era*, ed. Ian Burney and Chris Hamlin (Johns Hopkins University Press, 2019), 112–46.

16. "Report of the CE to Government, Punjab, for the Year 1879," 17–18 (IOR/V/24/418); Alfred Swain Taylor, *Principles and Practice of Medical Jurisprudence*, 4th ed., ed. Thomas Stevenson (London, 1894), 1:594–600; W. D. Sutherland, *Blood-Stains: Their Detection, and the Determination of Their Source* (London: Ballière, Tindall and Cox, 1907), 48–68; P. C. Gane, "The Serum or Precipitin Test for Blood: Its Forensic Aspect," *Criminal Law Journal of India* 5, no. 8 (1907): 89; and Isidore Bernadotte Lyon, *Lyon's Medical Jurisprudence for India*, 7th ed., ed. L. A. Waddell (Calcutta: Thacker, Spink, 1921), 176–79.

17. See "Annual Report of the CE and Bacteriologist to the Government of the North-Western Provinces and Oudh and of the Central Provinces for the Year 1901," 2–3 (IOR/V/24/414).

18. Tal Golan, *Laws of Men and Laws of Nature: The History of Scientific Expert Testimony in England and America* (Harvard University Press, 2004), 174–75. For the earlier nineteenth-century history, including the struggle between the "smell test" and microscopy to establish species of origin, see José Ramón Bertomeu-Sánchez, "Chemistry, Microscopy and Smell: Bloodstains and Nineteenth-Century Legal Medicine," *Annals of Science* 72, no. 4 (2015): 490–516.

19. G. S. Graham-Smith and F. Sanger, "The Biological or Precipitin Test for Blood Considered Mainly from Its Medico-Legal Aspect," *Journal of Hygiene* 3, no. 2 (1903): 268–71, and no. 3 (1903): 354–56; George H. F. Nuttall, *Blood Immunity and Blood Relationship* (Cambridge University Press, 1904), 117–18; Gane, "Serum or Precipitin," 93; and *Lyon's Medical Jurisprudence* (1921), 185.

20. By the late 1930s, rabbits were used to make bird antiserum, while birds were used to make the antisera of humans and other mammals. "Annual Report on the Working of the Imperial Serologist's Department, Calcutta for the Year 1938–39," in "Report: Imperial Serologist's Department, Calcutta, 1938–39," Education, Health and Lands: Health, file no. 33–5/39-H, 26, 1939 (NAI).

to be blood through other prior testing).[21] This mystery extract would be mixed with the antihuman serum. If the stain was also of human origin, a precipitate ("precipitin") would form within twenty minutes.[22] If no precipitate formed, the stain extract would then be mixed with a series of antisera for other species, one by one, until a precipitate formed, and a match could be declared (figure 6).[23]

In the first two decades of precipitin testing (from 1901 until the 1920s), stakeholders debated its ability to distinguish between related species.[24] Could goat's blood be distinguished from sheep's blood?[25] Could the test tell the difference between human and ape blood?[26] Alfred Swaine Taylor's posthumously edited treatise on medical jurisprudence (the leading work in the imperial metropole) oscillated between declarations like "the anti-serum is very definitely specific" (in 1920) and an acknowledgment (in 1928) that in some cases the test produced inconclusive results between similar species.[27] Notwithstanding the allied species problem, the test established itself in the early twentieth-century criminal courtroom.[28]

---

21. G. Roche Lynch, "The Technique of the Precipitin Test and Its Forensic Value," *Analyst* 53 (1928): 8. On the use of chemical and spectroscopic analysis to determine whether a stain was blood at all see Sutherland, *Blood-Stains*, 11–47.

22. According to Sutherland, a precipitate would form between mammalian serum and antiserum after twenty minutes (what Nuttall called the "mammalian reaction"). Only test results obtained within the first twenty minutes could thus be of use for forensic purposes. Sutherland, *Blood-Stains*, 117.

23. For detailed descriptions of precipitin testing see Sutherland, *Blood-Stains*, 116–17; Taylor, *Principles and Practice of Medical Jurisprudence* (1928), 1:499–500; and "Annual Report on the Working of the Imperial Serologist's Department," 27.

24. See "Blood Relationship and the Precipitin Test," *BMJ* 2, no. 2341 (1905): 1304–5. A subsequent study asked whether precipitin (or blood group) testing could distinguish between human races. Among most populations, neither test could do so. "The British Association: Races of Mankind," *TL*, September 6, 1932.

25. See *Lyon's Medical Jurisprudence* (1921), 187. Distinguishing between ruminants became important in cases involving the killing and maiming of domesticated animals and in Hindu-Muslim violence involving the blood of cows.

26. Albert S. F. Grünbaum, "Note on the 'Blood Relationship' of Man and the Anthropod Apes," *Lancet*, January 18, 1902, 143; Sutherland, *Blood-Stains*, 109–14; Gane, "Serum or Precipitin," 92, 95–96; "Blood Stains," 283; *Lyon's Medical Jurisprudence* (1921), 183; and K. Landsteiner and C. Philip Miller, "Serological Studies on the Blood of the Primates," *Journal of Experimental Medicine* 42, no. 6 (1925): 841–52. See also C. P. Lukis, "Explanatory Note on Major W. D. Sutherland's Investigations into the Applicability to Medico-Legal Work in India of Bio-Chemical Methods for the·Detection of Blood Stains," 10, in "Report by Major W. D. Sutherland on His Investigation in Connection with Blood Stains: Proposed Appointment of a Government Serologist," Home: Medical, Proc. no. 149–52, March 1910, part A (NAI).

27. Compare Alfred Swain Taylor, *Principles and Practice of Medical Jurisprudence*, 7th ed., ed. Fred J. Smith (London: J. & A. Churchill, 1920), 2:155; and (1928), 1:500–501.

28. See Roche Lynch, "Technique of the Precipitin Test," 12–13.

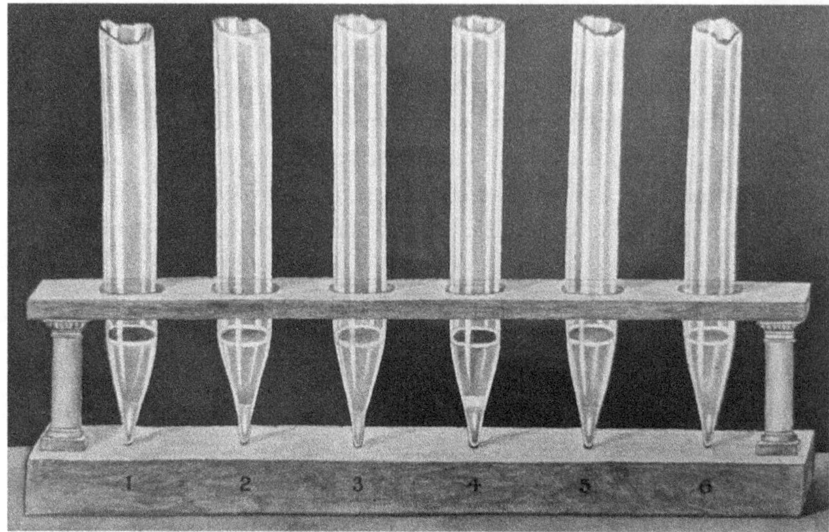

FIGURE 6. / The precipitin test to determine the species of origin of a bloodstain. Test tube number four shows the formation of a white precipitin or precipitate, indicating a species match between the antiserum of a known species and the bloodstain of an unknown species. *Lyon's Medical Jurisprudence for India*, ed. L. A. Waddell (Calcutta: Thacker, Spink, 1914), frontispiece.

The empire played a special role in the development of precipitin testing in these early years. Cambridge biologist and physician George H. F. Nuttall, who carried out sixteen thousand experiments on 586 different animal species, wrote one of the leading works in the field. In the acknowledgments to his *Blood Immunity and Blood Relationship: The Precipitin Test for Blood* (1904), he thanked "some seventy gentlemen" who had helped him procure a Noah's ark of animal blood from around the world. Nuttall could not have created his antiserum reference library without the British empire: In a distinctive form of colonial extraction, he received animal blood from British central Africa, Canada, the Cape and Lagos colonies, Egypt, Ireland, and Uganda. The largest number of samples came from South Asia. Nuttall thanked colleagues (including many military men) in Bombay, Calcutta, Ceylon, Chitral, Kashmir, Khandesh, South Sylhet, and elsewhere.[29]

British India also played an outsize role in the field of precipitin testing through the figure of William Dunbar Sutherland. Like so many Britons in medicine and

29. Nuttall, *Blood Immunity*, 411–13.

the empire, he was Scottish.[30] He obtained his medical education in Edinburgh and then at the army medical school in Netley on England's south coast. By the 1890s Sutherland had proceeded to India as a member of the Indian Medical Service, which rotated him through South Asia on posts in Burma, Madras, and the Central Provinces. He was chief medical official in charge of a jail and a "lunatic asylum." Just before the creation of the imperial serologist position, Sutherland was stationed in the CE's office in Calcutta. Around 1908, the CE of Calcutta (at the flagship department) began exploring the potential of precipitin testing for bloodstains, which were then sent to his lab for analysis. Sutherland had published *Blood-Stains* in 1907, and spent 1908–9 working exclusively on the technique at Calcutta's Medical College.[31] In 1910, he published a work on forensic uses of precipitin testing in the series "Scientific Memoirs by Officers of the Medical and Sanitary Departments of the Government of India."[32] By 1912, he was offering classes in serology to medical officers from across India at the college.[33] The Calcutta CE begrudgingly shared his lab space with Sutherland and his growing traffic of incoming bloodstains until 1916, when Sutherland established his permanent serological lab (under orders from the central Indian government) in the new Calcutta School of Tropical Medicine, founded in 1914.[34]

In writing *Blood-Stains* (his most extensive work on precipitin testing), Sutherland drew on his own earlier Edinburgh dissertation on blood testing (although not precipitin testing) and methods used in Frankfurt.[35] The short book was aimed at a metropolitan and imperial audience. It included mainly European case studies and issues (it predated the establishment of the

30. On Scots in the IMS see Mark Harrison, *Public Health in British India: Anglo-Indian Preventive Medicine, 1859–1914* (Cambridge University Press, 1994), 26, 30–31, 35. On Scots in British India see Raymond Cocks, "'The Bengal Boiler': Legal Networks in Colonial Calcutta," in *Networks and Connections in Legal History*, ed. Michael Lobban and Ian Williams (Cambridge University Press, 2020), 142–47; T. M. Devine, *Scotland's Empire 1600–1815* (Allen Lane, 2003); and John M. MacKenzie and T. M. Devine, eds., *Scotland and the British Empire* (Oxford University Press, 2011).

31. "Annual Report of the CE's Department, Bengal, for 1908," 2 (IOR/V/24/422).

32. W. D. Sutherland, *The Applicability to Medico-Legal Practice in India of the Biochemical Tests for the Origin of Blood-Stains* (Calcutta: Superintendent Government Printing, India, 1910).

33. Letter from G. F. A. Harris, inspector-general of civil hospitals, Bengal, to secretary, government of Bengal, Municipal dept., no. 4455 (Calcutta, April 4, 1912), in "Annual Report of the CE's Department, Bengal, for 1912," and "Annual Report of the CE's Department, Bengal, for 1913," 1 (both IOR/V/24/422).

34. CE Report for Bengal 1912, 1; and letter from W. R. Edwards, surgeon-general with government of Bengal, to secretary, government of Bengal, Financial (medical) department, no. 2827 (Calcutta, February 23, 1917), in "Annual Report of the CE's Department, Bengal, for 1916" (both IOR/V/24/422).

35. Untitled obituary for W. D. Sutherland, *BMJ* 2, no. 3109 (1920): 189; and Sutherland, *Blood-Stains*, 129.

imperial serologist in India) but with the occasional reference to tropical settings. Sutherland was in fact presenting German research to an English-speaking audience, noting that little appeared on the precipitin test in Anglo-American textbooks of legal medicine.[36] He was also trying to create a useful resource for "workers in the tropics and in the colonies, where libraries are few and but poorly filled with works of reference."[37]

Sutherland made his mark on Indian institutions. His pursuit of precipitin testing led to the creation of the office of the imperial serologist, a figure with no equivalent elsewhere in the empire until the 1930s (figure 7).[38] Sutherland was taking his cue from the German-language research. He noted in *Blood-Stains* Paul Uhlenhuth's recommendation that the state take control of precipitin testing in order to guarantee the quality of various animals' antisera; the department of the imperial serologist did just that.[39]

Sutherland succeeded in institutionalizing precipitin testing in India where others had earlier failed. In 1903, E. H. Hankin had unsuccessfully proposed the idea to the central government of British India. Hankin was CE in India's United and Central Provinces, and he had been conducting his own experiments with precipitin testing. Following Hankin, F. N. Windsor (another CE) had tried unsuccessfully to perfect his technique in Burma.[40] (Antiserum could take a month or two to prepare, required special refrigeration, and by Sutherland's account had

36. Sutherland, *Blood-Stains*, ix–x. Sutherland's fluency in German was important not only for his serological work but also his lifelong interest in psychoanalysis. He was a founding member of the British Psycho-Analytical Society and visited Sigmund Freud in Vienna. Sutherland had "a remarkable knowledge of Indian Folk-Lore" and occasionally published articles in the racy German-language journal *Anthropophyteia*, a publication on erotic ethnology from which Freud drew material. "Obituary," *International Journal of Psycho-Analysis* 1 (1920): 341.

37. Sutherland, *Blood-Stains*, x–xi.

38. In Ceylon, Egypt, southern Nigeria, and Palestine, officials like government analysts and official chemists oversaw the testing of both poisons and bloodstains during the first few decades of the twentieth century. Richard B. Pilcher, "A List of Official Chemical Appointments, p. 166," *Proceedings of the Institute of Chemistry of Great Britain and Ireland* 36 (1912): H001–H246; "Government Analyst's Report for 1918," *Ceylon Observer*, May 13, 1919, 699; "Analytical: Local Administration Report," *Ceylon Observer*, May 18, 1921, 15; "Government of Palestine: Annual Report of the Government Analyst for the Year 1928," *Analyst* 55 (1930): 48–49; "Egypt: Report on the Work of the Chemical Laboratory, Ministry of Justice, for the Years 1929–34," *Analyst* 64 (1939): 353–54. Outside of India, state serologists began to appear by the 1930s. On South Africa see "Public Appointments," *TL*, December 28, 1933, 3. On the Federated Malay States see "The Work Done by the Institute of Medical Research," *Straits Times*, September 26, 1937, 13. See also note 3 above.

39. Sutherland, *Blood-Stains*, 133.

40. Letter from F. N. Windsor to inspector-general of civil hospitals, Burma, Rangoon, April 22, 1910, "Proposed Appointment of a Serologist for India," in "Proceedings of the Home Department, August 1910," nos. 966–75 (August 29, 1910) (IOR/P/8443).

FIGURE 7. / "In the Imperial Serologist's Laboratory—Medico Legal Blood Test Day." From the British Library Collection: Bengal Medical Department, "Report of the Calcutta School of Tropical Medicine and Hygiene" [1923/24–1931/32] (IOR/V/24/754.2).

to be used on site.)[41] Again in 1910, the government of India revisited the question. Some officials recommended the creation of an imperial serologist, while others protested that India was "a poor country" that could not afford "fancy" appointments.[42] Most persuasive was correspondence from Thomas Stevenson and W. H. Willcox, two physicians in London who had given precipitin-based

41. Letter from F. N. Windsor to inspector-general of civil hospitals, Burma; letter from W. H. Willcox, MD, St. Mary's Hospital, to under secretary of state, Home Office (London, February 15, 1910); and letter from H. Wheeler, secretary to the government of Bengal, municipal government, to secretary to the government of India, Home department (Darjeeling, June 20, 1910), no. 566-T.-Med., in "Proposed Appointment of a Serologist for India," 39 (IOR/P/8443). On Willcox see Adam, *History*, 98–100, 145, 157, 204. On antiserum production in India in the 1930s–60s see Projit Bihari Mukharji, *Brown Skins, White Coats: Race Science in India, 1920–66* (University of Chicago Press, 2022), 168–76.

42. L. Jenkins (August 15, 1910) in a letter from the government of Bombay, no. 3290 (July 14, 1910), 4, in "Proposed Appointment of a Serologist for India," Home: Medical, Proc. no. 145, August 1910, part A (NAI).

expert witness testimony in the English courts. They suggested that precipitin testing fell short of the criminal "beyond a reasonable doubt" standard of proof.[43]

Yet just a few years later, in 1914–16, Sutherland's efforts succeeded. His own research claimed to fine-tune the test such that it produced clearer results in a larger number of cases. And yet if India could not afford the "luxury" of a state serologist in 1910, it surely could not afford one in the midst of World War I. Then again, the war gave license for state action in a number of domains. Many new industrial and scientific enterprises were created around World War I in India, particularly in areas where India had previously been dependent on German-supplied chemicals.[44] Although antiserum could be purchased in Britain, analysts considered it risky to use antiserum that one had not made oneself.[45]

No matter the factors that led to its ultimate creation in 1914–16, the imperial serologist's department was wildly successful in the economic terms that the state understood best. In its first decade, authorities made occasional threats to close the department if it was not self-supporting.[46] Not only did the imperial serologist's office support itself—it also made a sizable profit for the central government of India through the fees charged to provincial governments and princely states.[47] By the 1920s and 1930s the imperial serologist's lab was processing over ten thousand bloodstained articles annually, on cloth, soil, metal, wood, leather, and other materials. It did blood group testing for blood transfusions and

43. Letter from Thomas Stevenson to the under secretary of state, Home Office (London, January 12, 1907), in "Proposed Appointment of a Serologist for India," no. 135, 30 (IOR/P/8443). In the same file see further correspondence from Stevenson and Willcox (September 12, 1904, to February 15, 1910), 29–32.

44. See, e.g., the history of the Pioneer Magnesia Works, in Mitra Sharafi, "Parsi Life Writing: Memoirs and Family Histories of Modern Zoroastrians," in *Holy Wealth: Accounting for This World and the Next in Religious Belief and Practice: Festschrift for John R. Hinnells*, ed. Almut Hintze and Alan Williams (Wiesbaden: Harrassowitz, 2017), 265. I also thank Radhika Singha for her observation that government laboratories proliferated in British India circa World War I.

45. On the sale of antiserum in Britain see letter from Willcox (February 15, 1910). I have found no references to antiserum being available for purchase in India. Roche Lynch advised against the use of commercial antiserum even two decades later: "Note: The Precipitin Test for Blood," *Analyst* 53 (1928): 435a.

46. For example see "Recommendation by the Indian Retrenchment Committee," 23, in "Blood Stained Cases: Creation of the Post of Imperial Serologist for the Examination of Blood Stained Cases for the Whole of India (Baghelkhand Agency), 1914," Baghelkhand Political Agency: English Files, Proc. no. 304, 1914 (NAI).

47. See, e.g., "Transfer of the Imperial Serologist's Department to the Direct Control of the Government of India and Revision of Emoluments of the Imperial Serologist," Finance: Expenditure-I, 1933, Proc. nos. 83–Exl, 1933 (NAI); and cover letter from Education, Health and Lands department to director-general, Indian Medical Service, u.o. no. 29–13/39/9 (February 12, 1940), 2, in Annual Report of the Imperial Serologist 1938–39 (NAI).

ran a blood bank.[48] The imperial serologist and his assistants also had a lucrative side business in Wassermann testing for syphilis, retaining most of these fees privately.[49] The Calcutta Veterinary College and the municipal government's slaughterhouses provided a steady supply of animal blood.[50] Human blood (which could not be purchased) came from a nearby maternity hospital and the lab's own Wassermann test samples.[51] The imperial serologist taught courses on serology and immunology at the Calcutta School of Tropical Medicine and the All-India Institute of Hygiene and Public Health.[52] By the early 1940s, the department consisted of ten people: the imperial serologist (who was European until G. C. Mitra's appointment in the 1920s) and eight others, who over time were increasingly South Asian and consisted of assistant imperial serologists, clerks, and lab assistants.[53]

Early characterizations of the imperial serologist as a "fancy" luxury quickly faded. In 1918, officials complained that authorities in the Andaman Islands' penal colony had failed to send the bloody clothing of a man being tried for murder to Calcutta for analysis by the imperial serologist. Blood examination was a "very highly specialized and extremely technical proceeding," and because "the life of the accused person frequently depends on its result," it was imperative that bloodstains be sent from Port Blair to Calcutta in the future (the man in question was convicted and executed without bloodstain analysis).[54] Other officials echoed

48. Annual Report of the Imperial Serologist 1938–39, 3, 3a, 27–28; R. B. Lloyd, "Report of the Professor of Serology and Immunology," in "Annual Report of the Calcutta School of Tropical Medicine Institute of Hygiene and the Carmichael Hospital for Tropical Diseases for the Year 1924" (IOR/V24/754). See also Projit Mukharji, "Between Empire and Nation: War, Competitive Philanthropy and the Birth of Blood Banking in British India," talk presented at the American Association for the History of Medicine annual meeting, Minneapolis, April 29, 2016.

49. The Wassermann test for syphilis was much in demand in the early twentieth century. For example see the judgment notebooks of the Parsi Chief Matrimonial Court, 1893–1947 (courtroom 21, Bombay High Court).

50. Annual Report of the Imperial Serologist 1938–39, 5; untitled statement by J. W. D. Megaw, April 1, 1933, Education, Health and Lands dept., 13, in "Transfer of the Imperial Serologist's Department to the Direct Control of the Government of India and Revision of the Emoluments of the Imperial Serologist," Finance: Expenditure-I, Proc. nos. 83–Exl, 1933 (NAI).

51. "Question Asked by the General Purposes Sub-Committee of the Retrenchment Advisory Committee Regarding the Imperial Serologist's Dept.," 14 in Education, Health and Lands: Health, file no. 103–4/32-H, 1932 (NAI).

52. See Lloyd, "Report of the Professor of Serology and Immunology," and Annual Report of the Imperial Serologist 1938–39.

53. On G. C. Mitra see chapter 1.

54. Letter from secretary to government of India, Home department, to superintendent, Port Blair (no. 726-C, February 5, 1918), 15, in "Confirmation of the conviction of the sentence of death passed by the Additional Sessions Judge, Port Blair, upon life-convict Johir Ghazi, no. 21374. Decision that blood stains requiring expert examination in connection with criminal cases in the Andamans

these positive, even imperative, views of bloodstain analysis in the decades that followed. Writing in 1932, one official commented that the position was more important than that of a High Court judge, routinely involving "questions of life and death as well as matters which affect the efficiency of justice."[55] The director-general of the Indian Medical Service agreed, calling the imperial serologist's work "an essential wheel in the machinery of the administration of justice."[56] This quick and enthusiastic endorsement of the imperial serologist's laboratory, once created, made sense in light of colonial anxieties over dissimulation. As the next section will show, the colonial context shaped this branch of forensic science not only through the practical matters of research samples and institutionalization but also because the concern about native mendacity sharpened the desire to have forensic tests that were putatively beyond suspicion.

Fabricated Evidence

Precipitin testing took hold in India earlier and in a more institutionalized form than in Britain, where the courts did not consistently accept test results until the early 1930s.[57] This was the case because precipitin testing helped to allay officials' anxieties over the manipulation of the criminal legal system by South Asians. Forensic science promised relief generally: By privileging scientific experts and tests, courts did not have to depend as much on Indian witnesses. The colonial stereotype of native mendacity portrayed Indians as unreliable, and perjury and forgery as rife.[58] More specifically, precipitin testing helped officials detect

---

should be sent to the Imperial Serologist in Calcutta," Home: Port Blair, Proc. no. 10–14, February 1918, part A (NAI).

55. Untitled statement by J. W. D. Megaw, October 13, 1932, in "Transfer of the Imperial Serologist's Department," 6.

56. Director-general of the Indian Medical Service, quoted in statement by Ram Chandra, November 17, 1932, in "Transfer of the Imperial Serologist's Department," 9.

57. The first prominent English murder trial to use precipitin testing was the 1911 Clapham murder case. "The Clapham Murder," *TL*, February 9, 1911; "The Detection of Human Bloodstains," *TL*, February 14, 1911. But the test was not generally accepted as reliable in the English or Scottish courts until the early 1930s. See Crowther and White, *On Soul and Conscience*, 61; Roche Lynch, "Technique of the Precipitin Test," 13; and "Body in Blazing Car," *TL*, January 28, 1931. By the time of the high-profile Buck Ruxton case of 1935–36, in which John Glaister Jr. analyzed the bloodstains, precipitin testing had become generally accepted or "blackboxed." See "Ruxton Case," *TL*, December 12, 1935; John Glaister and James Couper Brash, *Medico-Legal Aspects of the Ruxton Case* (Baltimore: William Wood, 1937), 199–225, 264–72.

58. Catherine L. Evans, *Unsound Empire: Civilization & Madness in Late Victorian Law* (Yale University Press, 2021), 58–61; Elizabeth Kolsky, *Colonial Justice in British India: White Violence and the Rule of Law* (Cambridge University Press, 2010), 108–19, 217–18; Bhavani Raman, *Document*

attempts to frame innocent parties through the planting of fabricated evidence. "In some cases," declared Sutherland in 1915, a "fantastic web of lies" could be "torn to pieces by the determination of the true origin of the blood. And above all, in some cases the innocence of a suspected person was established."[59]

Writings for different audiences indicate that the fear of false evidence was particularly acute in India. Sutherland's *Blood-Stains*—written for a metropolitan and imperial audience—did not include a single case where an item stained with animal blood was planted in an attempt to frame an innocent person for murder.[60] Alfred Swaine Taylor's canonical work (also written for a Britain-based audience) similarly offered no such case studies in his section on the precipitin test.[61] By contrast, Sutherland's chapter on bloodstains in Lyon and Waddell's treatise for India included numerous cases—almost one-third, in fact—involving fabricated evidence in murder, rape, and sodomy cases.[62] In a 1915 printed report by Sutherland that circulated widely among government officials, precipitin testing suggested that fabricated evidence appeared in half of forty-two case studies.[63] In an article published by Sutherland's successor R. B. Lloyd in 1926, twenty-four of twenty-seven bloodstains submitted in murder or culpable homicide cases tested positive for animal blood, which suggested fabricated evidence.[64]

In the treatise literature on precipitin testing outside of India, the typical case scenario involved a person accused of murder who was found with a bloodstained item of clothing or a weapon. The accused accounted for the blood by telling authorities that he had recently slaughtered an animal. If precipitin testing revealed that the blood was in fact human, the accused would usually be convicted. But the cases that occasionally appeared in the Indian literature were different. In these cases, a murder suspect was found with alleged human blood on his clothing, on a weapon, or at his home. Here the suspect made no claim

---

Raj: Writing and Scribes in Early Colonial South India (University of Chicago Press, 2012), 137–60; and Wendie Ellen Schneider, *Engines of Truth: Producing Veracity in the Victorian Classroom* (Yale University Press, 2015), 103–42. See also Projit Bihari Mukharji, "Handwriting Analysis as a Dynamic Artisanal Science: The Hardless Detective Dynasty and the Forensic Cultures of the British Raj," in Burney and Hamlin, *Global Forensic Cultures*.

59. "Note by Lieut.-Col. W. D. Sutherland."

60. In *Blood-Stains*, Sutherland included two cases in which a person fraudulently claimed to be suffering from an illness or injury. Both involved benefit fraud rather than false murder charges, however (136, 138).

61. See Taylor, *Principles and Practice of Medical Jurisprudence* (1920), 1:153–55.

62. Sutherland in *Lyon's Medical Jurisprudence* (1921), 200–212.

63. "Note by Lieut.-Col. W. D. Sutherland," 8–13.

64. Lloyd, "Serological Analysis," 220–22.

to have recently killed an animal.[65] Precipitin testing revealed animal blood, and forensic authorities assumed that it had been planted to frame the innocent suspect.

In a less common scenario in India, an individual tried to frame others for her own presumed death. In 1945, an old woman disappeared from her house in South India. Bloodstains were found under her bed and elsewhere in her home, but precipitin testing revealed that the blood was avian. After the woman was caught by the police, the local submagistrate reported that she had planted the bird blood to try to "foist a case of murder" on her relatives after she "made herself scarce in a mysterious manner."[66]

Other cases of fabricated evidence involved communal violence. In a 1944 case from a village in Bihar, a group of a hundred Hindus raided Muslim homes, claiming that a Muslim had offended them religiously by slaughtering a cow. Soil and pieces of cow dung were sent to Calcutta for analysis. The soil was stained with sheep or goat blood, not the blood of a cow. The cow dung, in turn, was stained with human blood, presumably from the communal violence. The claim of cow killing was regarded as a false pretext, and thirty-two Hindu rioters were prosecuted.[67]

A final category of cases also involved mixed blood. In these scenarios, both human and animal blood were identified through precipitin testing, suggesting that the alleged crime of murder had occurred but that there was also some "bolstering" or enhancement of the evidence through the planting of animal blood. Hehir and Gribble's treatise chapter on false evidence addressed this pattern. "Even in cases which are substantially true, there is generally a certain amount of concocted evidence." The job of the judge in India was not to decide which side was true and which was false. Rather, it was to identify the false evidence on each side, and then to decide the case based on what remained.[68] Put another way, false evidence did not necessarily mean a false case. In a murder case from Bengal, for instance, a rope and two specimens of soil were submitted to the

---

65. It is worth noting that many Indians were not vegetarian. Meat eating and thus animal slaughter were particularly common among those who were not upper-caste or Hindu.

66. Isidore Bernadotte Lyon, *Lyon's Medical Jurisprudence for India*, 10th ed., ed. S. D. S. Greval (Calcutta: Thacker, Spink, 1953), 323.

67. *Lyon's Medical Jurisprudence* (1953), 323. On cows in Indian legal history see Matthew Groves, "Law, Religion and Public Order in Colonial India: Contextualising the 1887 Allahabad High Court Case on 'Sacred' Cows," *South Asia: Journal of South Asian Studies* 33, no. 1 (2010): 87–121; and Rohit De, *A People's Constitution: The Everyday Life of Law in the Indian Republic* (Princeton University Press, 2018), 123–68.

68. Patrick Hehir and J. D. B. Gribble, *Outlines of Medical Jurisprudence in India* (Madras: Higginbotham, 1908), 28.

imperial serologist. Testing revealed bird blood on the rope and one soil sample. The other piece of earth, however, tested positive for human blood.[69] There was also mixed blood (human and animal) in the Nadar-Naiker and communal cases just noted, but for some reason these were not interpreted as true cases supplemented by false evidence, but as fundamentally false cases.

How did colonial officials make sense of these cases? From its fifth edition in 1905 onward, editions of Taylor's medico-legal treatise included a chapter on India. The author of this contribution was a member of the Indian Medical Service, W. J. Buchanan. Like Sutherland, he was a Scot. He was also editor of the *Indian Medical Gazette* and inspector general of prisons in Bengal. Buchanan spent two pages discussing the "falseness of much of the evidence given by natives of India." He considered whether fabricated cases were the consequence of "inherent Oriental deceit" or "fear, stupidity, apathy, or malice, or to the fact that the witnesses have been 'tutored' by police."[70] This line recurred in the era's treatises (see chapter 1), reflecting the common impulse among British experts to fall into cultural and racialized stereotypes.

Historians of colonial South Asia usually attribute such characterizations of native dissimulation to the "the rule of colonial difference" or racial prejudice.[71] Without downplaying the depth of racism in colonial officialdom, however, there is more to be gleaned from acts of dissemblance—and primary sources that comment on dissemblance—beyond the analytically preemptive move of identifying their racist bias. Racial bias prevented officials from seeing particular patterns in their own sources, and it is critical that scholars not replicate the logical fallacy (albeit for different reasons) by also stopping short when interpreting these sources. We turn in the last section to an alternative explanation for the phenomenon of fabricated evidence that emerges out of the precipitin archive.

Punitive Self-Harm

Colonial reports of South Asian mendacity could have been referring to several things. When dissimulation by an Indian witness or accuser was voluntary and

69. Lloyd, "Serological Analysis," 222 (case no. 24).

70. W. J. Buchanan, "A Chapter on Medical Jurisprudence in India," in Alfred Swain Taylor, *Principles and Practice of Medical Jurisprudence*, 5th ed., ed. Fred J. Smith (London: J. & A. Churchill, 1905), 2:853–54.

71. Partha Chatterjee, *The Nation and Its Fragments: Colonial and Postcolonial Histories* (Princeton University Press, 1993); and Kolsky, *Colonial Justice*.

intentional, it may have been a form of resistance.[72] Dissimulation by an Indian police officer could have been labeled as corruption. Complaints in the medico-legal literature about native mendacity extended to Indian police.[73] Perhaps, for example, an Indian police officer engaged in foot-dragging or petty disruptions of everyday processes, or something more significant, such as bribery, to sabotage colonial rule from within.[74]

At times, though, what colonial sources labeled "native mendacity" was something quite different. In an important subset of false charge cases like the Nadar-Naiker conflict, colonized people adapted and customized noncolonial modes of disputing to meet the new requirements of the colonial legal system. CEs and imperial serologists regarded these cases as duplicitous perversions of justice. But South Asian accusers in these cases probably saw their own actions as consistent with noncolonial understandings of justice: They were harnessing the colonial system to arrive at the same destination they would have reached otherwise. For example, Buchanan's chapter in Taylor's textbook included these incidents of South Asian "moral insensibility": "A master murdered his servant and dragged the body to the door of his enemy solely in order that a charge of murder might be brought against the latter; a father murdered his daughter, because his neighbor had slandered her, in order that her blood might be upon the neighbor's head."[75]

These cases were animated by a model of identity, responsibility, causation, and punishment that was so far from Buchanan's own worldview that he failed to understand what he was observing. Presumably, notions of family identity and honor made the father's killing of his daughter an act of "self"-sacrifice rather than the murder of a disempowered, putatively less valuable female relative to protect the self-interest of the senior male. As I explain shortly, such self-harm practices were premised on an extended view of the "self" that was deeply gendered. Similarly, the master who murdered his servant may have regarded the household as the crucial social unit, and the killing of the servant as the master's own prerogative. By the logic of punitive self-harm, the original wrongdoer (the enemy in the first case and the neighbor in the second) was directly responsible and punishable for the death of the servant or the daughter. It was *he*, and

---

72. I am using "accuser" to mean a person who accused another of a crime, rather than an informant cooperating with the prosecution.

73. See, e.g., Sutherland in *Lyon's Medical Jurisprudence* (1921), 208; and Kumar, *Police Matters*, 57.

74. See Jonathan Saha, *Law, Disorder and the Colonial State: Corruption in Burma c. 1900* (Palgrave Macmillan, 2013).

75. Buchanan, "Chapter on Medical Jurisprudence in India," 853.

not the master or father, who had caused the death. Otherwise put, his original wrong set in motion a chain of foreseeable events that culminated in the death of the servant or daughter. The East India Company had made efforts in the late eighteenth century to prohibit punitive self-harm.[76] Curiously, though, early twentieth-century figures like Buchanan seemed to have lost any awareness that this mode of disputing existed, and that it underpinned the two cases described. Buchanan attributed these examples to simple cruelty and barbarism, missing the phenomenon of legal pluralism.

Punitive self-harm had a long and varied history in South Asia, including Gandhian modes of nonviolent resistance (like the hunger strike), political protest suicides, and even some cases of *sati* or ritual widow immolation.[77] At its core was the idea that a person would hurt himself or herself to protest a wrong done by another. Although Hindu law considered such acts legitimate only if inflicted upon oneself, the practice of punitive self-harm was at times extended.[78] In this version, the "self" in self-harm referred not only to the individual wronged but also to members of the person's family or even caste community.[79] These were typically elderly women or little girls—vulnerable females deemed expendable by this patriarchal worldview.[80]

Conducting *dharna* was the most common practice associated with this mode of disputing.[81] It shaded into the fast-unto-death, known in Sanskrit as *prayopavesha*.[82] To protest a wrong, a person sitting in *dharna* would wait at the doorstep of the wrongdoer, refusing to eat or leave until the wrong was redressed.

---

76. See Jörg Fisch, *Cheap Lives and Dear Limbs: The British Transformation of the Bengal Criminal Law, 1769–1817* (Wiesbaden: F. Steiner 1983), 50–51, and Radhika Singha, *A Despotism of Law: Crime and Justice in Early Colonial India* (Oxford University Press, 1998), 97–100.

77. For a case of *sati* committed in protest during a feud see Singha, *Despotism*, 93 at note 54. On Gandhian modes of protest see Ranajit Guha, *Dominance Without Hegemony: History and Power in Colonial India* (Harvard University Press, 1997), 57; Ishita Banerjee-Dube, *A History of Modern India* (Cambridge University Press, 2015), 262–63, 278–79; and Durba Ghosh, "Gandhi and the Terrorists: Revolutionary Challenges from Bengal and Engagements with Non-Violent Political Protest," *South Asia: Journal of South Asian Studies* 39, no. 3 (2016): 564, 571. On suicide protest in South Asia today see Simanti Lahiri, *Suicide Protest in South Asia: Consumed by Commitment* (Routledge, 2014).

78. On Hindu law's prohibition on killing one's mother in protest see Singha, *Despotism*, 100.

79. On relatives as targets see *Lyon's Medical Jurisprudence* (1921), 26–29, 142. For a company-era example of fellow caste members being killed in protest in western India see Singha, *Despotism*, 96.

80. See Singha, *Despotism*, 98–100.

81. See *Lyon's Medical Jurisprudence* (1921), 29; and J. Duncan M. Derrett, *Religion, Law, and the State in India* (Oxford University Press, 1999), 216–17.

82. See Washburn Hopkins, "On the Hindu Custom of Dying to Redress a Grievance," *Journal of the American Oriental Society* 21 (1900): 146–59. In South Indian languages like Tamil and Malayalam, the term for the fast-unto-death was *pattini*. I thank Donald R. Davis Jr. for sharing his knowledge on this point.

If the protester died in the process, the wrongdoer was responsible and would be cursed, even haunted, by the protester's ghost.[83] In the classic scenario, a creditor would sit in *dharna* at the doorstep of a debtor who had not repaid a loan.[84] But these practices also had broader applications, including protest against state legal processes that were misguided, impotent, or absent.[85] *Dharna* was particularly powerful when carried out by Brahmins, who might increase the pressure by threatening to stab themselves or drink poison. Nothing could expiate the sin of causing a Brahmin's death.[86]

Traga was defined by the *Hobson Jobson* as "the extreme form" of *dharna*, in which a person tortured or killed himself or a relative as a means "for bringing vengeance on the oppressor."[87] In late eighteenth-century Bengal, Beechuk Brahmin beheaded his own mother in protest during a conflict over revenue-collection rights, while a lower-caste man named Dhunoo Chamar killed his four-year-old daughter at the house of a village headman after being criticized for drinking and abusing his superiors. Government officials commented that the latter had acted "in conformity with the usage established in Benares with regard to such cases."[88] Establishing a *kurh* was another expanded version of punitive self-harm. A person resisting arrest or some other action he considered wrongful (like the payment of a tax) would construct a circular enclosure, usually of wood. Inside, he placed an elderly female relative or a cow. In this extreme version of patriarchal logic and bovine-centric cosmology, these were lives imbued with sufficient honor to make a statement but also expendable enough to sacrifice. The protester would then threaten to set fire to the wood if touched or forced to undertake the action he was resisting.[89]

---

83. In late eighteenth-century Bengal, death rites were not performed for such a protester, making the person's spirit restless. Rather than being cremated or placed in a river, the corpse was buried at the disputed site (for land or temple disputes) or buried outside the wrongdoer's house. The ghost or *bhut* would later be summoned by the beating of a drum. If the dispute was resolved between the wrongdoer and the deceased's heirs, the body would be removed and given proper death rites to put the spirit at rest. Singha, *Despotism*, 91–92, 95–96.

84. See H. R. Fink, "The Hindu Custom of 'Sitting Dharna,'" *Calcutta Review* 62 (1876): 37–52.

85. See Donald R. Davis Jr., *The Boundaries of Hindu Law: Tradition, Custom and Politics in Medieval Kerala* (Turin: CESMEO, 2004), 115–17; Donald R. Davis Jr. and John Nemec, "Legal Consciousness in Medieval Indian Narratives," *Law, Culture and the Humanities* 12, no. 1 (2016): 106–31; and Neil Rabitoy, "Sovereignty, Profits, and Social Change: The Development of British Administration in Western India, 1800–1820" (PhD diss., University of Pennsylvania, 1972), 315–45.

86. Singha, *Despotism*, 88.

87. Henry Yule, *Hobson-Jobson: A Glossary of Colloquial Anglo-Indian Words and Phrases*, ed. William Crooke (London: J. Murray, 1903), 937.

88. Singha, *Despotism*, 92, 99.

89. See Fink, "Custom," 48; Fisch, *Cheap Lives*, 50; and Singha, *Despotism*, 87.

Similarly, some communities guaranteed contracts by using this extended version of punitive self-harm.[90] The Bhats and Charans of western India were known for making themselves—and their relatives—available for hire as human collateral for contracts.[91] Written contracts that were Bhat-guaranteed bore the sign of a dagger.[92] When the relative of a Bhat or Charan was killed to punish another person's breach of contract, the violence was sometimes processed by the state as a prosecution for murder. Bombay High Court judge F. C. O. Beaman offered one remarkably detailed description of such a case, an 1892 murder trial in his *mofussil* or countryside court in western India.[93] Two parties had made a contract and guaranteed it by engaging a third person, a member of the Charan caste. "If the debtor whose [debt] the Charan had guaranteed, refused to pay, in the last resort his obligation would be enforced by the Charan spilling his sacred blood on the lintel of the offender's house."[94] The debt was not repaid. The debtor laughed at the idea of having the contract enforced "the ancient, grim, terrible way" through the spilling of Charan blood: "You and your curses, he said, no longer have any terrors for me. Are there not the Courts of the Sirkar [colonial state]? If my friend thinks that I owe him money, they are open to him. Let him sue in due form. I am rich. I can engage the best Vakil [lawyer]. Let us see then."[95] The Charan went home to his family, where he, his mother, son, and daughter "each in turn prayed that he or she might be used as the divine scourge." "Charan honor must be maintained," wrote Beaman.

The Charan's elderly mother prevailed. By Beaman's account, she claimed that she had already lived a long life and thus should be the sacrificial martyr. The case reproduced the strongly gendered pattern in punitive self-harm cases: Young, elderly, or otherwise marginal female relatives were selected. On the debtor's front doorstep, the Charan stabbed his mother in the heart and "smeared the lintels of the house with her blood, calling down the curses of the angry Gods on this hardened sinner." Beaman was the judge who had to try the Charan

---

90. For example see Hopkins, "Hindu Custom of Dying to Redress a Grievance," 157.

91. On Bhat contracts see Alexander Kinloch Forbes, *Ras-Mala: Hindu Annals of Western India with Particular Reference to Gujarat* (1878; Delhi: Heritage, 1973), 558; Rabitoy, "Sovereignty," 305–55; and Howard Spodek, "On the Origins of Gandhi's Political Methodology: The Heritage of Kathiawad and Gujarat," *Journal of Asian Studies* 30, no. 2 (1971): 363. Relatedly, see R. K. Saxena, *Social Reforms: Infanticide and Sati* (Delhi: Trimurti, 1975), 19–56.

92. Rabitoy, "Sovereignty," 308; and Forbes, *Ras-Mala*, xii, 559–60.

93. F. C. O. Beaman, "Eheu Fugaces," *Bombay Law Journal* 3, no. 6 (1925): 211–12. For a similar case see Mary Frances Billington, *Woman in India* (London, 1895), 248–50.

94. Beaman, "Eheu Fugaces," 211.

95. Beaman, 211.

(and his son) for murder, but he was also a defender of tradition and caste.[96] "Of course they were not hanged." In the judge's words, "It is ill to set up new Gods in place of the Old, too hastily, to flout immemorial usage, and incur the stain of Charan blood."[97] Beaman's sympathies were unusual for a British judge at the turn of the twentieth century. As a judge who came up through the Indian Civil Service, however, Beaman spent more time in the *mofussil* (and from an earlier age) than did his judicial colleagues who had been trained as barristers in London.[98] In any case, the extended version of punitive self-harm revealed itself through this murder trial.

Where colonial criminal law operated on the basic assumption of individual responsibility and punishment, some punitive self-harm practices worked through a different—more expansive—notion of identity, responsibility, and punishment. Colonial officials (Beaman aside) considered it murder when a man killed his own daughter to punish a person who had slandered her or when the Charan stabbed his own mother because another person had breached a contract. Within the logic of extended punitive self-harm, however, both men would have seen their actions as legitimate forms of self-harm.[99]

Furthermore, it was not just the human unit—individual or collective—that distinguished these modes of dispute resolution. Conceptions of causation also differed. In the extended self-harm tradition, the man who had wronged the father (in the Buchanan case) *caused* the daughter's death; the father who most directly committed the killing had not. This initial offender would suffer cosmically for the death. In the colonial criminal legal system, though, it was the *father*, not the man who wronged him, who was solely responsible for the daughter's death. Any attempt to attribute the death to the initial wrongdoer would be superseded by the father's actions, which broke the chain of causation: The father had directly and physically killed his daughter. Unusually (among Britons), Beaman sympathized with the logic of Charan contracts, noting that "notwithstanding his western veneer, the real offender" almost instantly fell ill and died. He was "looked on askance by his former friends, pitied by none."[100]

---

96. For the similar case of Thomas Keate, a judge who was sympathetic to customary Bhat contracts, see Rabitoy, "Sovereignty," 328–32. On Beaman see Mitra Sharafi, "Judging Conversion to Zoroastrianism: Behind the Scenes of the Parsi Panchayat Case (1908)," in *Parsis in India and the Diaspora*, ed. John R. Hinnells and Alan Williams (Routledge, 2007), 162–63.

97. Beaman, "Eheu Fugaces," 212.

98. See Sharafi, "Judging Conversion," 162.

99. For example see Rabitoy, "Sovereignty," 311.

100. Beaman, "Eheu Fugaces," 212.

By this logic, responsibility for the elderly woman's death lay with the debtor, not her son who had killed her.

It was only one step from killing another person in protest to making that death look like it had been committed by the original wrongdoer through the planting of animal blood, and this is where the system of punitive self-harm became especially relevant to the imperial serologist.[101] The Nadar-Naiker conflict is an example, and the master who killed his servant and left the body at his enemy's doorstep could have been another—had animal blood been planted on the enemy's doorstep or clothing. The fabrication of evidence, in other words, furthered the logic of noncolonial practices of private disputing and punishment.

To be sure, these practices changed as colonized people adapted to the colonial legal system. One would no longer receive the publicity or perceived social credit for committing extended self-harm if one framed the original wrongdoer for murder. The dividends, such as they were, of successfully framing an enemy were also more earthly than otherworldly. Cases that went undetected as a setup would no longer produce just a good haunting but also perhaps an execution. Actors planting animal blood were tacitly rejecting the colonial state's attempt to monopolize dispute resolution and punishment and must also have derived satisfaction from using criminal law for their own ends. Whatever the case, planting bloodstained evidence, when successful, would achieve the same goal as punitive self-harm: It punished the original wrongdoer. And precipitin testing enabled officials to identify these cases.

Over time, as news of the test's power spread, did fabricators of evidence simply start planting human blood at crime scenes, instead of animal blood? In one suggestive 1938 murder case, the Lahore High Court ruled that a bloody spearhead had no value as evidence. Although the blood was human, other aspects of the murder made the item suspect. Crucially, all twenty-eight of the victim's wounds were cuts or incisions, not puncture wounds. The court held that no spear could have been used in the murder. The bloody spearhead was probably false evidence.[102]

With cases like this in mind, the historian must acknowledge the limits not only of the test but also the archive. The historian of deception works with an archive of imperfect trickery: It is only when ruses failed that they became visible in the primary sources. There may have been successful countermoves to the powerful new test, but such instances remain almost by definition hidden from the historian. It is possible that the imperial serologist's usefulness diminished

101. See similarly Kumar, *Police Matters*, 72.

102. *Ujagar Singh and Others vs. Crown*, ILR Lah. 20 (1939): 211–12. See chapter 5.

as popular awareness of the precipitin test grew. Equally, precipitin testing may have come to play a secondary role in court over time. Clearly, however, the imperial serologist's heyday lasted for several decades at least—from the 1910s until the 1930s. The fact that other colonies started appointing state serologists from the 1930s suggests the continuing utility of precipitin testing.

In 1914, the fifth edition of *Lyon's Medical Jurisprudence for India* was published. Its editor, L. A. Waddell, celebrated the addition of an important new chapter on precipitin testing. The chapter's author, W. D. Sutherland, had perfected the technique such that the "great climatic difficulties hitherto experienced" in carrying out this test in India had now been overcome. The test could now be used "with as absolutely certain and trustworthy results as in Europe," and Waddell predicted that the test would now be used in all murder cases in India.[103] For Waddell, precipitin testing in India was now on an equal footing with precipitin testing in Britain. As we have seen, though, the technique played a larger role in the colony than in the metropole, as indicated by, among other things, the creation of the imperial serologist position.

The explanation for this difference between colony and metropole brings us back to the concept of native mendacity. Why did precipitin testing take hold in India in special ways—like the creation of the imperial serologist? This form of forensic testing gave colonial officials a tool to respond to a central obsession of the colonial criminal legal system: fear of dissimulation, particularly the creation of fabricated evidence by colonized subjects. Reading colonial sources against the grain reveals that both stereotypes of native mendacity and scholarly explanations based on the "rule of colonial difference" overlook practices like punitive self-harm that cannot be reduced to, contained in, or explained by either. In other words, these practices are neither examples of native mendacity as colonial racists would have it nor easily disregarded as contrived examples of colonial racism in the documents as scholars would have it. This is not, or not exclusively, a story of racial difference and bias but a story of noncolonial modes of disputing as colonized people adapted them to new colonial rules. The story is about legal pluralism: how layers of disputing norms interacted, with parties adapting one norm to fit into the other in order to use new tools, or interpreting one illegible system according to the legible rules of their own. When bloodstained evidence was planted near an enemy, colonial officials interpreted it as an attempt to frame an innocent party. But if the concerned parties saw the group, not the individual,

103. Isidore Bernadotte Lyon, *Lyon's Medical Jurisprudence*, 5th ed., ed. L. A. Waddell (Calcutta: Thacker, Spink, 1914), v.

as the key unit, and if they interpreted causation broadly, was the framed party—even if framed—undeserving of punishment? Planting animal blood made the killing of one's own relative punitive in a new dimension. When it succeeded, it produced a criminal conviction, in addition to punishing the adversary socially and psychologically by the noncolonial logic of punitive self-harm. The work of the imperial serologist and precipitin testing exposed not so much schemes to sabotage colonial law as attempts to make it work for what Beaman would have called the "old gods" of punitive self-harm. Through the planting of animal blood to make punitive self-harm look like murder by a rival, this noncolonial mode of disputing was adapted to produce punishment in the colonial mode. Neither colonial analysts nor later scholars may have recognized it, but precipitin testing exposed the interaction between two normative systems. Beyond colonial attributions of fabricated evidence to native mendacity lay a world of noncolonial disputing.

Serology overtook microscopy by the early twentieth century in forensic species-of-origin analysis. And yet even at its heyday, serology was entering into a new rivalry with microscopy in the broader field of stain analysis, particularly in rape cases involving blood and semen stains. In the next chapter, we will see how these two fields functioned as competitors because one (serology for blood stains) aided males falsely accused of rape, while the other (microscopy for sperm cells) worked in favor of females suspected of making false accusations. And yet, at just the moment in the 1930s when the new sperm cell staining could have demolished assumptions of female mendacity in rape cases, the courts tightened the corroboration rule, elevating scientific evidence and demoting witness testimony (including the female survivor's own account). Science and law were once again linked in a dynamic relationship that was woven through with notions of mendacity—not just native but also female.

3

BLOODSTAINS, SPERMATOZOA, AND RAPE

After crimes of dissimulation like perjury, forgery, and counterfeiting, colonial officials associated falsity with the crime of rape. Forensic treatises were full of tips on how to identify false rape claims.[1] Few experts were more suspicious than the first imperial serologist, W. D. Sutherland. In a 1917 lecture for the new detective training school at Howrah, Sutherland declared that 99 percent of rape charges were false. "When you have a case of rape always think of blackmail," he told his audience. If his listeners found bruises on the arms of the accuser, they should not believe that these were genuine. False injuries could be made by rubbing marking nut (*Semecarpus anacardium*) on the skin (figure 2). Sutherland warned his listeners not to be fooled by bleeding from a young girl's genitals: It could be due to "her mother having scratched her vagina with her finger nail." The accuser's account could also be tested verbally—an early form of forensic linguistics. Sutherland recommended interrupting the accuser in the middle of a sentence. "If the case is a concocted one, she must begin again from the very beginning." He advised caution when an accuser claimed that her attacker had ejaculated outside of her body as he withdrew. In Sutherland's

1. See Pratiksha Baxi, *Public Secrets of Law: Rape Trials in India* (Oxford University Press, 2014), 61–116; Elizabeth Kolsky, "'The Body Evidencing the Crime': Rape on Trial in Colonial India, 1860–1947," *Gender & History* 22, no. 1 (2010): 112–15; Mitra, *Indian Sex Life*, 123–24; and Durba Mitra and Mrinal Satish, "Testing Chastity, Evidencing Rape: Impact of Medical Jurisprudence on Rape Adjudication in India," *Economic & Political Weekly* 49, no. 41 (2014): 51–55.

view, this was usually an attempt to explain away the absence of semen or sperm in a false case.[2]

Unsurprisingly, Sutherland recommended precipitin testing (chapter 2) for rape cases. When animal blood was planted, precipitin testing was a powerful exculpatory tool for those accused of sexual assault. (I use "rape" and "sexual assault" synonymously in this book.) But in the 1920s to the 1940s, with advances in cell staining techniques, a rivalry developed in South Asia between bloodstain and sperm analysis. The precipitin test favored a subset of men and boys accused of rape, to show that evidence had been planted against them, while sperm cell staining favored a subset of women and girls who reported rape, corroborating their accusations.

This distinction between forensic techniques complicates the scholarly view that forensic science and medicine consistently reinforced the idea of the mendacious rape complainant.[3] Many forensic techniques did, but others did not, producing results that were at odds with the value systems of their most biased practitioners. This chapter focuses on the dynamics within lab science during a period of notable advances: the 1900s to the 1940s. Scholars of rape have focused on physicians' examinations of accuser and accused, for instance, through hymen analysis and the search for injuries from violent struggle.[4] There was also important work being done in the forensic laboratories of British India and Burma, and some of it benefited women and girls.

Despite the work done by sperm cell staining for many female accusers, however, developments in competitive stain analysis did not prompt a reassessment of stereotypical notions of female mendacity. The last part of this chapter steps back from the contest between forensic techniques to consider the broader view, and relationship, between sexual forensic science and criminal law. New types of sperm analysis had the potential to vindicate accusers otherwise dismissed as mendacious (native) females, and scientific advances were observed closely by

2. "Notes of a lecture delivered at the Detective Training School, Howrah by Colonel Sutherland, Government Serologist" [1918], no. 1, 3 (unpaginated) in Papers of Ormandy Ballantine Fane Sewell (MSS Eur F419). For similar references to blackmail and scratching mothers in nineteenth-century France see E. Claire Cage, *Science of Proof: Forensic Medicine in Modern France* (Cambridge University Press, 2022), 145–46, 164–65.

3. For example see Kolsky, "'Body Evidencing the Crime,'" 112, 115; and Gagan Preet Singh, "Forensics, Body and State Power in South Asia: Recent Interventions and Their Importance," *History Compass* 19, no. 11 (2021): 3–4, 7.

4. See for instance Stephen Robertson, "Signs, Marks, and Private Parts: Doctors, Legal Discourses, and Evidence of Rape in the United States, 1823–1930," *Journal of the History of Sexuality* 8, no. 3 (1998): 345–88; and Victoria Bates, *Sexual Forensics in Victorian and Edwardian England: Age, Crime and Consent in the Courts* (Palgrave Macmillan, 2016).

the legal professionals who ran the criminal legal system. But during the 1930s and 1940s, the law of rape actually shifted in a direction adverse to female accusers: Around the time that scientific sperm analysis tests improved, the corroboration rule itself became more restrictive. This chapter examines the dynamic interplay of legal and scientific developments. As forensic labs offered a growing array of useful tools, the legal system insisted more adamantly on corroborating evidence that was independent of the accuser's testimony. The ideal type of corroborative evidence was medical or scientific, deemed neutral and objective. As the science developed, the legal system became increasingly dependent on it. Put another way: Sperm cell staining strengthened the authority of science more than the credibility of female testimony. As forensic labs' capabilities expanded, instructions enabling jurors to convict solely based on the accuser's testimony were revised apace. In this chapter we see how the turn to forensic science could both subvert and then reinforce presumptions of native female mendacity. As lab analysis improved, so too did the legal test for corroboration close in around it, leaving female accusers' testimony to be deemed as inadequate as before.

As in other times and places, it is most likely that only a tiny number of rape cases were reported to the police, and only a small number of those cases advanced to judgment in a form visible to historians. This chapter draws from that visible, narrow sliver of rape cases, namely sixty-nine rape cases from law reports, newspapers, and treatises of the period. It is also based on the records of forensic testing contained in the chemical examiners' annual reports, articles in scientific and medical journals in India, and archival sources relating to the imperial serologist. My focus is on rape cases with live survivors, as only a handful of the cases surveyed were fatal ones.[5] I focus on live cases because many involved both accusers' testimony and scientific evidence, revealing how judges regarded these kinds of evidence in relation to each other.

This chapter begins with an overview of the law, evidence, and life cycle of rape cases, followed by a discussion of what judges considered signs of falsity, and their explanation for it. I then move into competitive sexual forensics, exploring the history of bloodstain analysis in the 1900s–20s and seminal stain testing, particularly in the 1930s–40s. Finally, the chapter steps back to trace a key development in the case law on rape, the tightening of the corroboration rule in the 1930s–40s, before considering the relationship between these legal and scientific

5. For fatal rape cases see *Queen-Emp. v. Hurree Mohun Mythee*, ILR Cal. 18 (1891): 49–68; *Nga San Pu v. Emp.*, AIR Lower Burma (1918): 81–83; and *Ram Kala v. Emp.*, AIR All. 33 (1946): 191–95. On Phulmoni Dasi's case see Baxi, *Public Secrets*, 21–23; and Ishita Pande, *Sex, Law, and the Politics of Age: Child Marriage in India, 1891–1937* (Cambridge University Press, 2020), 31–71.

developments. This chapter uses the concept of falsity to reveal what happened in the lab and in court, exploring dynamics within forensic science and between forensic science and law.

It is important to be clear at the outset: We cannot know if cases labeled false were in fact so. A theme throughout this book has been the trickiness not only of falsity itself but of *studying* falsity. In the rest of this book, the danger for the scholar is that cases of skillfully executed falsity are invisible in the records, but in this chapter, the danger is the opposite: Genuine cases of rape might have been visible but deemed false by the criminal legal system. In recognition of this unique danger, this chapter hones the discussion to judicial narratives around falsity and the interplay of forensic stain analysis and these narratives.

It is also worth stating the obvious: Rape may have occurred without the production of blood or seminal stains. Under Indian criminal law, it was the start of penetration, not emission, that mattered, and rape need not have drawn blood. But in the late colonial world of rape that often involved violent struggle and young girls, blood and seminal stains were taken as evidence that rape clearly had occurred. Stain analysis was a shortcut that identified the "easy" or obvious cases. Their negative findings—an absence of blood, semen, or sperm—worked against the harder cases, such as those not involving violence that left physical marks or those that turned on the question of consent.[6] These hard cases were sometimes labeled false and ended in acquittals. This chapter acknowledges this phenomenon, while focusing on the cases that did involve stains.

The Law, Evidence, and Life Cycle of a Rape Case

Under the Indian Penal Code (IPC), rape occurred if a male had sexual intercourse with a female who was not his wife and that was against her will or without her consent (including by fraud or fear of death or hurt) or if she was under the age of fourteen. Penetration, not emission, was sufficient.[7] A husband who forced his wife to have sex committed rape only if she was underage. Otherwise,

6. For cases in which the question of consent was central see *P. F. Conroy v. Emperor*, MANU/NA/0019/1943; and Jonathan Saha, "'Uncivilized Practitioners': Medical Subordinates, Medico-Legal Evidence, and Misconduct in Colonial Burma, 1875–1907," *South East Asia Research* 20, no. 3 (2012): 438.

7. IPC s.375, in Ratanlal Ranchhoddas and Dhirajlal Keshavlal Thakore, *The Indian Penal Code*, 11th ed. (Bombay Law Reporter Officer, 1926), 320–21. On the shift from "against her will" to "without her consent" in nineteenth-century English law see Martin J. Wiener, *Men of Blood: Violence, Manliness, and Criminal Justice in Victorian England* (Cambridge University Press, 2004), 111–12. On the history of attempts to make rape a gender-neutral crime in India see Baxi, *Public Secrets*, 45–46.

marital rape was not a crime recognized by Indian law.[8] The sentence for rape was transportation for life or imprisonment (simple or rigorous) for up to ten years, plus a fine.[9] Over time, the most common sentence for men convicted of rape was three to five years' imprisonment for an "ordinary" case and seven years' rigorous imprisonment for a "very bad" one.[10] Convicted boys and teenagers were often sentenced to whipping rather than imprisonment because of their age.[11] Unlike in English law, where a boy under the age of fourteen could not be convicted of rape, under the Indian Penal Code (IPC) a boy could be found guilty of rape, or attempted rape, from the age of seven.[12] This reflected colonial notions of precocious sexual maturation associated with South Asians and tropical climates.[13]

The evidence in rape cases could be varied. If the woman or girl survived, her testimony typically constituted the evidential centerpiece. The First Information Report (FIR) created by police when the crime was first reported was usually the earliest written account of the crime. It did not constitute evidence in itself but was used to confirm or contradict the accuser's testimony.[14] Specifically, the timing of the FIR mattered: The longer the delay between the alleged crime and the accuser's reporting it to the police, the more courts doubted the veracity of her account.[15] Other kinds of evidence were assessed in relationship to the accuser's

---

On sexual violence against males in colonial India see Deana Heath, "Torture, the State, and Sexual Violence Against Men in Colonial India," *Radical History Review* 126 (2016): 122–33.

8. In 1891, the wife's minimum age (below which a husband would commit a crime by forcing her to have sex) was raised from ten to twelve (Act to amend the IPC, no. 10 of 1891, s.1). In 1925, this age was raised to thirteen (Act to further amend the IPC, no. 29 of 1925, s.2). On the history of child marriage and age-of-consent laws see Pande, *Sex*; and Ashwini Tambe, *Defining Girlhood in India: A Transnational History of Sexual Maturity Laws* (University of Illinois Press, 2019). Efforts to have marital rape recognized as a crime continue in India today. See Baxi, *Public Secrets*, 5, 21–23, 44–45; and Sneha Kadyan and N. Prabha Unnithan, "The Continuing Non-Criminalization of Marital Rape in India: A Critical Analysis," *Women and Criminal Justice*, 2023: 1–14.

9. IPC s.376 in Ranchhoddas and Thakore, *Indian Penal Code* (1926), 321.

10. *Emperor v. Mahadeo Tatya*, AIR Bom. 29 (1942): 122. For an example of a seven-year sentence of rigorous imprisonment see *Jantan v. Emperor*, MANU/LA/0665/1934.

11. For example see *King-Emperor v. Po Ba*, Lower Burma Rulings 8 (1915–16): 143–45; and *Mahraj Din v. Emperor*, MANU/LA/0262/1927. On whipping see Alastair McClure, "Archaic Sovereignty and Colonial Law: The Reintroduction of Corporal Punishment in Colonial India, 1864–1909," *MAS* 54, no. 5 (2020): 1712–47.

12. IPC ss.82–83, in Ranchhoddas and Thakore, *Indian Penal Code* (1926), 64–65. See *Emperor v. Paras Ram Dube*, AIR All. (1915): 134–35; and *Emperor v. Nga Tun Kaing*, AIR Lower Burma (1918): 96.

13. See Pande, *Sex*; and Tambe, *Defining Girlhood.*

14. A. C. Ganguly, *Practical Guide to Criminal Court Practice* (Calcutta: Eastern Law House, 1937), 40–43, 46–51, 596, 641.

15. The accuser's account was doubted in part because of delay in filing the FIR in *Abdul Rahman v. Emperor*, CrLJ 17 (1916): 150–51; and *Ram Kumar v. Emperor*, MANU/OU/0066/1936. Contrast

account, whether to confirm or contradict it. Witnesses to the sex act or to surrounding circumstances—often friends, relatives, or neighbors of the accuser or accused—sometimes provided testimony.

The physical examination of the accuser was also critical evidence. In case law of the 1850s and 1860s, Indian midwives sometimes examined the bodies of female accusers and testified in court.[16] Writing in Bengali in the 1870s, the medical jurisprudence treatise author Kanai Lal Dey noted that it was customary in India for "high-born women and girls to be examined by midwives in order to preserve their honor." Given the professional power struggle between allopathic physicians and midwives during this period, he predictably doubted the knowledge and competence of Indian midwives on matters of rape, warning readers to "be wary of their opinions."[17] From the last two decades of the nineteenth century on, it was more common to have a medical examination by a male civil surgeon or police surgeon, physicians who worked for the government in districts and larger cities, respectively.[18] The physician was looking for signs of sexual intercourse and injury that could have resulted from physical struggle. Rape did not require physical resistance under IPC s.375, but physical struggle indicated situations in which the act was clearly against the female's will or without her consent. Although physical injury could instantiate only some cases of rape, many lawyers, judges, and forensic experts were suspicious when there were no visible signs of struggle.[19]

Hymen analysis was also part of the physical examination of the accuser. Bombay police surgeon Arthur Powell complained in 1902 about the "romantic conceptions" that judges and juries sometimes entertained about the hymen: "They look on it as a mysterious snare set by a far-seeing Providence to trap the

---

with cases like *Soosalal Bania v. Emperor*, AIR Nag. 74 (1925): 76; and *Conroy v. Emp.*, 2. Unusually, a full FIR is reproduced in the case of *In re Karichiappa Goundan*, AIR Mad. 29 (1942): 285–87. On delay in reporting rape see also Kolsky, "'Body Evidencing the Crime,'" 119–20. On the FIR in twentieth-century South India see Radha Kumar, *Police Matters: The Everyday State and Caste Politics in South India, 1900–1975* (Cornell University Press, 2021), chap. 2. On the FIR in rape cases today in India see Baxi, *Public Secrets*, 349, 356, 358.

16. For instance see the 1853 case of *Chuttoo Goala and Musst. Jhoniah Goaleen and Govt v. Deoraj Singh Rajpoot*, Reports of Cases determined in the court of the Nizamut Adawlut, 1853–59, 669; and *Queen v. Banee Madhub Mookerjee*, Sutherland's Weekly Reporter 1 (1864): 29–31.

17. Kanai Lal Dey, *Medical Jurisprudence* (Calcutta, [1875]), 60 (Bengali).

18. On civil surgeons see "Civil Surgeons in India," *IMG* 3, no. 12 (1868): 284; and Patrick Hehir, *The Medical Profession in India* (London: Henry Frowde, 1923), 60–61.

19. For example see *Conroy v. Emp.* See also Kolsky, "'Body Evidencing the Crime,'" 120–22; and Mitra and Satish, "Testing Chastity," 54–55. For a notable exception in a treatise cited in India see John Glaister, *A Text-Book of Medical Jurisprudence and Toxicology* (Edinburgh: Livingstone, 1921), 498.

unwary ravisher. It is a seal which no weapon except the human penis is capable of breaking. The slightest touch of this magic wand, and Heigh presto! the whole structure completely disappears."[20] In fact, as Powell went on to say, hymen analysis was highly subjective. He had examined a girl thirty minutes after another surgeon, and their conclusions differed: Powell reported a hymen with two lacerations, while the other surgeon described the hymen as "*completely destroyed*." Powell blamed medical experts for their "slip-shod" descriptions.[21] The two-finger test, notorious in South Asia, emerged in this context.[22] It first appeared in the 1936 edition of J. P. Modi's medico-legal treatise, borrowed from a work on sexual crimes by the French forensic analyst Léon-Henri Thoinot.[23] In Modi's book, the test was a means of determining whether a female accuser with an intact hymen could have been raped. If the hymenal orifice was flexible enough to admit two fingers, for instance, then rape without damage to the hymen was possible.[24] However, the test shifted over time into a method for determining whether a female was habituated to sex.[25] As sociologist Pratiksha Baxi, historian Elizabeth Kolsky, and others have shown, the *habitué* was deemed more likely to have had sex willingly.[26]

In addition to analysis of the hymen, physicians physically examined accusers to look for signs of recent sexual intercourse (for instance, the absence of

---

20. Arthur Powell, "Medical Examination in Cases of Rape," *IMG* 37, no. 6 (1902): 232.

21. Powell, 232–33. Italics in original.

22. Pratiksha Baxi, Durba Mitra, and Mrinal Satish have documented the way the two-finger test has operated against women and girls reporting rape: Baxi, *Public Secrets*, 61–117, esp. 74–77; and Mitra and Satish, "Testing Chastity."

23. Léon-Henri Thoinot, *Attentat aux mœurs et perversions du sens génitals: Leçons professées à la Faculté de médecine* (Paris: Octave Doin, 1898), 31, 43. J. P. Modi probably used the English translation: Léon-Henri Thoinot, *Medicolegal Aspects of Moral Offences*, trans. Arthur W. Weysse (Philadelphia: F. A. Davis, 1911), 43, 55. On Thoinot see Cage, *Science of Proof*, 153, 160, 163–64.

24. "In cases where the hymen is intact and not lacerated, it is necessary to note the distensibility of the vaginal orifice. The possibility of sexual intercourse having taken place without rupturing the hymen may be inferred, if the vaginal orifice is big enough to admit easily the passage of two fingers." Jaising P. Modi, *A Textbook of Medical Jurisprudence and Toxicology*, 5th ed. (Calcutta: Butterworth, 1936), 337.

25. Writing on rape in India today, Mrinal Satish notes the two ways this test has been used—both to establish that a girl or woman with an intact hymen could have been raped (as laid out in Modi) *and* to determine whether a girl or woman has ever had sex. Mrinal Satish, *Discretion, Discrimination and the Rule of Law: Reforming Rape Sentencing in India* (Cambridge University Press, 2017), 46–48, 73–74.

26. Baxi, *Public Secrets*, 61–117; and, by Elizabeth Kolsky, "Rule of Colonial Indifference: Rape on Trial in Early Colonial India, 1805–57," *Journal of Asian Studies* 69, no. 4 (2010): 1109, and "'Body Evidencing the Crime,'" 114, 118–19.

smegma) and for injuries produced through physical struggle.[27] Here, too, judges criticized delay because it limited the kind of conclusions the physician could draw: The human body was constantly healing.[28]

Finally, there was evidence requiring lab analysis. Sometimes, this was to ascertain if a drug, intoxicant, or poison may have been involved.[29] More common in rape cases were suspect stains. These could be collected from the body or home of the accuser and accused, or from the crime scene. Clothing or bedding were the most common items sent for stain identification, but sometimes weapons and soil samples were also submitted.[30] These were supposed to be dried, packed, and sent to the nearest CE, and then sometimes forwarded for further analysis to the imperial serologist in Calcutta.[31] The CE would use procedures like the benzidine and spectroscopic tests to determine whether the stain was blood.[32] He would then send the stain to the imperial serologist, who would perform species-of-origin (precipitin) testing (chapter 2). For seminal stains, the CE did two types of analysis: one to test for semen, most often via the Florence test, and the other to identify sperm cells under the microscope. From the 1930s on, the imperial serologist also did precipitin testing on seminal stains.[33]

As it moved through the criminal legal system, a rape case could end at many points. Contrary to protocol, police sometimes refused to record a complaint, or they delayed or distorted an FIR, a phenomenon Pratiksha Baxi has

27. On the forensic significance of smegma see Powell, "Medical Examination," 231; and *Ram Kala v. Emp.*, AIR All. 33 (1946): 194.

28. See *Ram Kala v. Emp.*, 194; and *Angad and Others v. Emperor*, MANU/UP/0300/1946, para. 6.

29. For example see "Annual Report of the CE to the Governments of the United Provinces and of the Central Provinces for the Year 1928," 4 (IOR/V/24/416).

30. For instance see "Annual Report of the CE to Government, United Provinces and Central Provinces, for the Year 1940," 6–7 (IOR/V/24/417).

31. On the packing and sending of forensic materials see Uponita Mukherjee, "Colonial Detection: Crime, Evidence, and Inquiry in British India, 1790–1910" (PhD diss., Columbia University, 2022), 144–85.

32. The benzidine and confirmatory spectroscopic tests were the standard ones (performed together) at CE labs circa 1940. K. N. Bagchi, "Examination of Blood and Seminal Stains, and of Hair," in Jaising P. Modi, *A Textbook of Medical Jurisprudence*, 6th ed. (Bombay: Butterworth, 1940), 99. Earlier, the guaiac or guaiacum test was popular. W. D. Sutherland, *The Applicability to Medico-Legal Practice in India of the Biochemical Tests for the Origin of Blood-Stains* (Calcutta: Superintendent Government Printing, India, 1910), 16–24. On testing to identify the presence of blood see Sutherland, *Blood-Stains*, 11–47; Sutherland, "Blood-Stains," in Isidore Bernadotte Lyon, *Lyon's Medical Jurisprudence for India*, 7th ed., ed. L. A. Waddell (Calcutta: Thacker, Spink, 1921), 171–76; and Bagchi, "Examination," 89–99.

33. For instance see "Annual Report on the Working of the Imperial Serologist's Department, Calcutta for the Year 1938–39," 23–24, in "Report—Imperial Serologist's Dept. Calcutta, 1938–39," Education, Health and Lands: Health, file no. 33-5/39-H, 1939 (NAI).

documented in India even in recent decades.[34] In a 1933 case, a woman came to the police station to report being sexually assaulted—only to be raped there by police officers.[35] It was especially difficult for such custodial rape cases to proceed through the system, given the importance of police cooperation even in regular rape cases.[36] If test results raised doubts (for instance, suggesting planted animal blood), a case may have been dropped. Vestiges of these cases are visible in CE reports, although not in the reported case law—because they never reached the courtroom.[37]

If a case proceeded to court, a magistrate would commit the case to a Sessions Court for trial.[38] A magistrate did not have the power to try a rape case and was supposed to commit the case to trial only if he found that there was a prima facie case against the accused.[39] A Sessions Court rape trial often involved a jury.[40] After that, appeals went to the nearest High Court.[41] Sessions Court judges also had the power to send a case on reference to a High Court if they disagreed with a jury verdict, whether conviction or acquittal.[42] A High Court was usually the final stop. Although the Judicial Committee of the Privy Council was the apex court for the British empire, it accepted almost no criminal appeals (see appendix 2). Usually, only cases that reached a High Court appeared in the pages of the published law reports.

Some of these cases ended in a guilty verdict and sentencing for rape, followed by punishment, whether imprisonment, transportation, or a whipping. In other instances, female accusers were not believed, leading to the release of

34. See Baxi, *Public Secrets*, 320–21, 356, 358–59.

35. *Mir Mazaralli Mir Inayatalli Kureshi v. Emperor*, ILR Bom. 57 (1933): 400–412.

36. For custodial rape cases during the colonial period see *Queen v. Akbar Kazee*, Sutherland's Weekly Reporter (1864), 21–22; *Mir Moze Ali v. Emperor*, MANU/WB/0271/1919; "Alleged Police Outrage," *ABP*, May 27, 1920; *Sarat Chandra Chakravarty v. Emperor*, AIR Cal. (1937): 463–66; and *Emp. v. Mahadeo Tatya*. On custodial rape cases in independent India, including the infamous Mathura case that sparked a social movement for the reform of rape law, see Baxi, *Public Secrets*, 7, 11, 243–45. For the Indian Supreme Court decision in the Mathura case see *Tukaram and others v. State of Maharashtra*, MANU/SC/0190/1978.

37. Most short case descriptions in the CE reports noted results from lab tests but not any legal outcomes that may have followed.

38. CrPC s.206 in H. T. Prinsep, *The Code of Criminal Procedure Being Act V of 1898* (Calcutta: S. K. Lahiri, 1901), 204–5. See also Ganguly, *Practical Guide*, 144–48.

39. *Mir Moze Ali v. Emp.*, para. 6; and *In re Pattu Mudali*, MANU/TN/0551/1938, para. 1.

40. On Sessions Court trials see Ganguly, *Practical Guide*, 149–66. For cases without juries see Sutherland in *Lyon's Medical Jurisprudence* (1921), 203 (case 26) and 208–10 (case 55). These probably came from areas that did not employ juries for serious crimes. On the jury see appendix 2.

41. See CrPC 1898, s.417, in Prinsep, *Code of Criminal Procedure Being Act V of 1898*, 13th ed. (Calcutta: Thacker, Spink, 1901), 398–400; and Ganguly, *Practical Guide*, 243–51.

42. CrPC 1898, s.307, in Prinsep, *Code of Criminal Procedure*, 306–8.

the accused. Following some of these acquittals, the girl or woman herself then became the target of a new criminal prosecution—for giving false evidence (IPC s.191) or making false charges (IPC s.211). As the anticolonial newspaper *Amrita Bazar Patrika* asked sarcastically in 1886: "Is it possible that an Englishman, celebrated throughout the world for his chivalry, and an English Judge celebrated throughout the world for his rigid impartiality, should go down so low as to not only condone the offence [of rape], but to persecute the injured party?. . . This seems very hard to believe."[43]

One of the most egregious cases was an 1867 case in which a young British assistant magistrate and member of the Indian Civil Service was accused of raping a lower-caste woman in Bengal. She reported him, but instead of this leading to a criminal trial—of a judge, no less—the matter was "extra-judicially enquired into" by another district magistrate, who "hushed up" the case. The "poor woman" then found herself the defendant in a criminal trial for having brought a false charge against the magistrate. Her case seems to have attracted attention, and the barrister W. C. Bonnerjee (later a nationalist leader) represented her and secured an acquittal.[44]

Three cases from Burma offered variations on the theme of rape accusers being prosecuted for crimes of falsity. In 1906, a woman named Mi Dolabi was convicted of giving false evidence (perjury). She had testified in lower court that a man named Abdul Majid had raped her, but then she subsequently told an appellate court that he had not. This was a case of falsity produced by coercion: According to Mi Dolabi's later account, she denied her rape allegation on appeal because her uncle threatened to beat her if she did not. Abdul Majid had bribed her uncle to end the rape case.[45] In a 1935 case, a woman named Swee Ing reported that two men had raped her. The police and district magistrate of Rangoon dismissed the complaint as false. The two men then sued Swee Ing for criminal defamation. After an initial conviction, she was acquitted on appeal, but only because the charge was incorrect: The judge held that Swee Ing should have been prosecuted for making a false charge, not for defamation.[46] The most in-depth discussion of rape and false charges occurred in a 1937 case. A woman

43. "The Jorehat Coolie Rape Case," *ABP*, July 15, 1886. This article discussed several rape cases that ended in the prosecution of the female accuser. The newspaper often used sarcasm to avoid the colonial censors.

44. Unnamed case (1867) in Ram Gopal Sanyal, ed., *The Record of Criminal Cases as Between Europeans and Natives for the Last Hundred Years* (Calcutta, 1896), 29–30.

45. *Dolabi v. King-Emperor*, Lower Burma Rulings 3 (1905–6): 204–5. On coercion to accept a "compromise" or out-of-court settlement in rape cases in India today see Rupal Oza, *Semiotics of Rape: Sexual Subjectivity and Violation in Rural India* (Duke University Press, 2023), 36–103.

46. *Swee Ing v. Koon Han and Another*, AIR Rang. (1935): 163–65.

named Ma Ban Gyi reported to police that a man, Tun Gyaw, had raped her. Without providing details, the police decided that the accusation was false, and there was no trial for rape, but there was one for false charges. Justice Baguley of the Rangoon High Court used the occasion to develop the case law. The further the original case advanced through the system, the heavier the punishment would be for the person making the false charge (if convicted). Ma Ban Gyi's accusation had not moved very far—the police had prevented the case from reaching court—so her sentence was light.[47] While rape cases that turned into prosecutions of female accusers were rare, they highlight that a court's ruling on rape was not necessarily the end of the process. In some instances, the finding of falsity was secured not only through acquittal of the accused but also through conviction of the accuser in a subsequent trial.[48]

Dissimulation, Falsity, and Doubt in Rape Cases

Dissemblance about rape was unsurprisingly also associated with men and boys who used tactics of denial, avoidance, and interference to prevent formal rape cases from emerging. Police delay or refusal to file an FIR may have been the product of illicit influence or bribery, or of discriminatory values with regard to gender, caste, or other hierarchies. Radha Kumar shows that in the late colonial Madras Presidency there was a widespread belief that police fabricated FIRs.[49] At least one civil surgeon was investigated for taking bribes to produce expert opinions favorable to men or boys accused of rape (chapter 4).

British Burma was notorious for a high prevalence of rape cases and their suppression. Historian Jonathan Saha has documented numerous examples of subordinate officials there, especially police, township officers, and hospital assistants, "using their positions to sabotage or entirely suppress criminal accusations of rape and other forms of gendered violence."[50] Some high-profile cases from Burma attracted worldwide coverage. The most infamous was the 1899 daytime gang rape of a middle-aged Burmese woman named Ma Gun by a regiment of British soldiers in Rangoon. The woman lost her mind after the attack, and her

47. *The King v. Ma Ban Gyi*, Rangoon Law Reports (1938): 236–43.

48. For a fictionalized account of this phenomenon in a different setting see the Netflix show *Unbelievable* (2019).

49. Kumar is writing about all types of criminal cases, not only rape. See Kumar, *Police Matters*, chap. 2.

50. Jonathan Saha, "The Male State: Colonialism, Corruption and Rape Investigations in the Irrawaddy Delta c. 1900," *IESHR* 47 (2010): 368.

testimony was muddled and contradictory. The military closed ranks, refusing to share information with civil authorities about its own secret Court of Inquiry on the case. Not a single conviction resulted from a series of criminal trials.[51]

Also from Burma came the 1911 case of a British planter named McCormick, who was believed to have abducted and sexually assaulted an eleven-year-old Malay girl named Ainah. An investigation into the case started but then ended mysteriously. The case only came to light because G. P. Andrew, a deputy commissioner and district magistrate, sued a British journalist named Channing Arnold for criminal libel. Andrew had overseen the investigation of the case and had declined to commit McCormick for trial. The journalist accused Andrew of corruption for "burking," or burying, the case, contrary to "the fair play and judicial honor associated with the name of England."[52] We may assume that these cases were only a small sample of a much larger pool of sexual assaults that occurred with impunity. We may also assume that male dissimulation played a key role in keeping other, lesser-known cases out of public view.

In the primary sources, the possibility of female false claims of rape loomed larger than male false denials of rape. This was partly a reflection of the mistrust of women and girls that saturated the criminal legal system, a phenomenon documented at length by historians Elizabeth Kolsky and Durba Mitra, sociologist Pratiksha Baxi, and legal scholar Mrinal Satish, among others.[53] At times, though, anxiety over false charges was also a function of rule-of-law and due process–based principles in the adversarial courtroom, namely the burden of proof, standard of proof, and presumption of innocence. For all kinds of crime, doubt favored the accused. The criminal legal system was structured so that the prosecution, not the defense, had to prove its case beyond a reasonable doubt.[54] The difficulty of disentangling misogyny and due process concerns in historical rape trials should not be underestimated. The primary sources' focus on false

51. See Elizabeth Kolsky, *Colonial Justice in British India: White Violence and the Rule of Law* (Cambridge University Press, 2010), 199–203; and Jeremy Neill, "'This Is a Most Disgusting Case': Imperial Policy, Class and Gender in the 'Rangoon Outrage' of 1899," *Journal of Colonialism and Colonial History* 12, no. 1 (2011). Angered by the outcome of the case, Lord Curzon (the viceroy of India) punished the regiment by sending it to the undesirable post of Aden.

52. Channing Arnold, "A Mockery of British Justice," *Burma Critic*, April 28, 1912, described in the Privy Council decision in *Channing Arnold v. King-Emperor* (1914), United Kingdom Privy Council 28 (April 7, 1914) (Privy Council Appeal no. 26 of 1913), 1–2, 7–8. See also Jonathan Saha, "Whiteness, Masculinity and the Ambivalent Embodiment of 'British Justice' in Colonial Burma," *Cultural and Social History* 14, no. 4 (2017): 529–34.

53. See Kolsky, "Rule of Colonial Indifference"; Kolsky, "'Body Evidencing the Crime'"; Baxi, *Public Secrets*; and Mitra and Satish, "Testing Chastity."

54. See Ganguly, *Practical Guide*, 595, 629–32, 660.

rape accusations combined these two elements in ways that historians have not adequately acknowledged.

In the 1937 custodial rape case of *Sarat Chandra Chakravarty v. Emperor*, for example, an Indian police subinspector was acquitted of abducting and raping a young widow. The Calcutta High Court judges considered both sides' case to be false—in the prosecution's case, on the grounds of implausibility. (I will return shortly to the question of plausibility and how it reflected gender and caste bias.) A discussion ensued about what a court should do when it believed there was falsity on both sides. According to Justice Cunliffe, a shaky defense did not make the prosecution's story true: "It is a cardinal basis of our criminal law . . . that the true guide to the proving of guilt or innocence is whether the story of the prosecution is believed or not."[55] Justice Henderson concurred: If the jury "refused to believe the defense case it would in no way help in determining whether the prosecution was true or not. It sometimes happens that the prosecution story and the defense story are both false and such may possibly be the case here."[56] If in doubt about both sides, the court had to acquit because of the presumption of innocence.[57]

Signs of Falsity

To try to detect falsity, judges and lawyers looked for contradictions in the accuser's account. In many cases, they took inconsistencies to indicate native mendacity.[58] In some, though, these lapses were attributed to the accuser "feeling her position painfully" in court or to her young age.[59] Equally, judges and juries sometimes decided they were not convinced by accusers' testimony because it conflicted with other evidence they found compelling. This other evidence could be the civil surgeon's testimony on the medical examination or the CE's certificate.[60] Or other witnesses' accounts might contradict the accuser's. The court of

55. *Sarat Chandra Chakravarty v. Emperor*, AIR Cal. (1937): 465–66.

56. *Sarat Chandra Chakravarty v. Emp.*, 466.

57. Making the same point in the context of criminal breach of trust is *Gouri Narayan Barrua v. Tilbikram Chetri*, CWN 25 (1921): 838.

58. For example see *King-Emperor v. E. Maung and Six Others*, Lower Burma Rulings 3 (1905–6): 159; *Abdul Aziz Musalman v. Emperor*, MANU/NA/0001/1934, para. 5; and *In re Karichiappa Goundan*, 286.

59. Quotation from the early, pre-IPC case of *Musst. Arjoo v. Amiruddee*, Reports of cases determined in the court of Nizamut Adawlut 3 (1852): 290. For a similar IPC case see *Harendra Prosad Bagchi v. Emperor*, AIR Cal. 461 (1940): 464.

60. For example see *Empress v. Shankar*, ILR Bom. 5 (1881): 403–5.

first instance was the only one that observed the testimony firsthand. Subsequent courts only read the written record and occasionally deferred to the lower court because only that court had seen and heard the witnesses in person.[61] This deference was grounded in the belief that falsity in testimony could reveal itself through voice tone, speech patterns, eye movements, and other kinds of body language.

Judges in India also filtered accusers' accounts through the notion of plausibility, as legal historian Orna Alyagon Darr has shown their counterparts did in mandate Palestine in the 1930s and 1940s.[62] The more extreme the claim—and the more inconsistent with a judge's own personal experience—the more likely the judge would dismiss it as implausible. There were many such instances in the case law from India.[63] One of the most distressing was in the 1937 custodial rape case mentioned earlier: *Sarat Chandra Chakravarty v. Emperor*. The prosecution alleged that an upper-caste subinspector of police had brazenly abducted and sexually assaulted a lower-caste girl, a young widow named Madhumala.[64] Chakravarty (the subinspector) was accused of carrying the screaming girl away from her hut shortly after dusk. He allegedly raped her while holding her overnight on a police boat. In theory, the boldness and corruption of the policeman's actions should have made conviction likely, but for the Calcutta High Court, the extreme nature of the allegations only led the judges to doubt the accuser. In Cunliffe's words:

> I consider that this is a false case. I do not believe that [a] Brahmin Sub-Inspector of Police would openly carry off a Sudra girl widow in the presence of the whole village for the purpose of criminally assaulting her. I am not prepared to say that persons in this profession (I am referring to members of the police) do not surreptitiously at times indulge in connexion with village girls. I believe if such people wish to do that, it is not very difficult but it is not a course that they would ever pursue openly for very good reasons into which I need not enter.[65]

Cunliffe's colleague Henderson concurred. He found Madhumala's account implausible because he did not believe a police subinspector would carry out

---

61. For example see *Bishram Bahorik Satnami v. Emperor*, MANU/NA/0064/1944, para. 3.

62. Orna Alyagon Darr, *Plausible Crime Stories: The Legal History of Sexual Offences in Mandate Palestine* (Cambridge: Cambridge University Press, 2019).

63. For example see *Abdul Aziz Musalman v. Emperor*.

64. On caste and rape in India today see Baxi, *Public Secrets*, 174–339; and Oza, *Semiotics*, 2–4, 65–103.

65. *Sarat Chandra Chakravarty v. Emp.*, 464–65.

the abduction himself. Surely he would have delegated this task to his own constables. Or he would have had a local landlord procure the girl through that man's servants. For these judges, the brazen abduction and rape of a lower-caste woman by an upper-caste police officer was so bold that it must not have happened. Rather than accept that this was a criminal abuse of power, their logic led them to characterize Madhumala's account as a "concoction."[66]

Many judges and juries correlated virginity with truthfulness in unmarried girls. By this logic, an unmarried female who was sexually active was also probably a liar. In the 1933 case of *Surendra Nath Das v. Emperor*, a girl under the age of fourteen reported that she had been raped by the accused while his wife held the girl down.[67] In child rape cases, the accused often believed that his venereal disease (usually gonorrhea) would be cured by having sex with a virgin.[68] In this case, though, the medical examination showed that Das did not have a sexually transmitted disease, nor any signs of past affliction. The judges of the Calcutta High Court found the girl's account unconvincing for a number of reasons, including a doctor's opinion that she had first had sex at least three months before the alleged rape. (The court thought that she was making a false rape accusation to cover up consensual nonmarital sex with someone other than the accused.) Justice Lort-Williams's logic, which linked nonvirginity in an unmarried female to mendacity, is most relevant here. The jury should be satisfied, he ruled, "that she is a witness of truth, and if they find that she is a person of bad or loose character obviously they will be reluctant to accept her evidence."[69]

Legal historian Cynthia Farid has uncovered an extreme instance of this type of judicial reasoning in a case unrelated to sex crimes. In this 1888 case from Patna, a twelve-year-old girl named Budhia was a witness in a theft case. Some brass pots had been stolen from her relative's home, and she told the court

---

66. *Sarat Chandra Chakravarty v. Emp.*, 466.

67. *Surendra Nath Das v. Emperor*, AIR Cal. (1933): 833–35.

68. The belief that sex with a virgin cured sexually transmitted disease existed in other times and places, too. See Alfred Swaine Taylor, *The Principles and Practice of Medical Jurisprudence*, 4th ed., ed. Thomas Stevenson (London, 1894), 436; and Victoria Bates, "'So Far as I Can Define Without a Microscopical Examination': Venereal Disease Diagnosis in English Courts, 1850–1914," *Social History of Medicine* 26, no. 1 (2012): 39. For probable cases from colonial India see *Government v. Azeez-oo-Rahaman*, Reports of cases determined in the court of Nizamut Adawlut, 1851, 1:525; *Natha v. the Crown*, MANU/LA/0444/1923; *Emperor v. Asadali*, MANU/BH/0009/1927, para. 4; *Hanuman Sarma v. Emperor*, AIR Cal. (1932): 724; and *Sikandar Mian v. Emperor*, AIR Cal. (1937): 321. On timing and gonorrhea-based evidence see *Sikandar Mian v. Emp.*, 322–24, and Bates, "So Far," 48. For an unusual instance of a woman (*ayah*) allegedly infecting a ten-year-old boy with gonorrhea to cure herself see Powell, "Medical Examination," 231.

69. *Surendra Nath Das v. Emp.*, 835.

that she had seen the accused running away with them. To assess her credibility, Budhia was subjected to a virginity test, which caused a scandal. The judge, a Briton named Kirkwood, was disciplined for his action, deemed misconduct.[70] Still, the case illustrates the mentality that recurred in cases of rape alleged by unmarried girls. Hymen analysis and the question of whether an unmarried female was "habituated to sex" became an important part of the medical examination not only with reference to the facts of the alleged rape, but also as an apparent way to measure the accuser's credibility.

Delay in reporting a rape, which could occur for many reasons, was another reason why judges doubted some female accusers' accounts. The police may have caused delay through obfuscation. As Elizabeth Kolsky has shown, girls or women sometimes reported other accompanying crimes (like robbery) but not rape initially—out of shame. Later, they added rape, but this delay ran the risk of looking suspicious.[71] The thinking among many judges was that the greater the delay, the more time the accuser (and her side) might have to coordinate a false accusation and avoid a timely medical examination.

Judicial Explanations for Falsity

Within the pool of about seventy rape cases examined here, judges had two common explanations for cases they considered false. Before considering these explanatory narratives, it is important to say that the vast majority of cases assessed here were among South Asians; there were very few interracial rape cases.[72] The small number of interracial cases involved European men accused of raping South Asian women.[73] None involved the scenario in E. M. Forster's 1924 novel, *A Passage to India*, in which a South Asian man (Dr. Aziz) is accused of sexually violating a British woman (Adela Quested)—perhaps the most famous

70. Cynthia Farid, "Imperial Constitutionalism: Judicial Politics and Separation of Powers in Colonial India (1861–1935)" (SJD diss., University of Wisconsin Law School, 2020), 156–59.

71. In *Mussummaut Rookmun v. Ramsook* (1819), the court found the accused guilty of rape, despite the delay in adding this charge. Kolsky, "Rule of Colonial Indifference," 1102.

72. For an unusual interracial case involving two minors see Modi, *Textbook of Medical Jurisprudence* (1940), 335.

73. In addition to the Rangoon gang rape case (Ma Gun's case) and McCormick cases discussed earlier, these cases included *Empress v. Charles Webb* (1884), 107–16, and *Empress v. Keatinge, Wilson, and Brookes*, 117–18, both in Sanyal, *Record of Criminal Cases*, 117–18; as well as *Conroy v. Emp.* On the Webb case see also "The Jorehat Coolie Rape Case," *ABP*, July 15, 1886. In *Monga v. Burdis*, a Rajput woman was allegedly raped by a British soldier. He was acquitted by an all-white jury. See untitled, *ABP*, August 19, 1896.

false accusation of a sex crime in British Indian literature (in English). The reader is sympathetic to Dr. Aziz, but also to Adela Quested, the accuser, because the case was built up and pushed through the legal system by the racism of her fellow Britons in Chandrapore. Her doubts about what she remembered are dismissed by these other Britons, until she finally withdraws her allegation in court.[74] This version of rape—of white women by brown men—was also central to British depictions of the 1857 mutiny in visual culture and fiction during the later nineteenth century and early twentieth.[75]

In the case law surveyed here, judges often believed that the accuser and accused had been engaged in consensual but illicit sex. This first of two common judicial explanations applied in cases not involving children. The accused was not the accuser's husband, if she was married at all. When the couple was discovered, the female then falsely accused the male of rape, apparently to save her reputation.[76] For instance, in the 1927 case of *Siraj-ud-Din v. Emperor*, Justice Jai Lal of the Lahore High Court doubted the story of the accuser, a thirteen- or fourteen-year-old girl. She claimed to be taking tobacco to her father, who was working in the fields, when the eighteen-year-old Siraj-ud-Din grabbed her and carried her off to a nearby hut where he raped her. The hut was 150 paces from where the girl's father was working. He saw the abduction and came running, arriving by one account right after sex had occurred. The medical examination found that the girl's hymen had been ruptured, but not recently. Justice Lal found the accuser's account implausible and acquitted the accused. The judge thought the sex had been consensual.[77] The logic here was surprising: There were heavy reputational costs for a female to have illicit sex but also to be known as a rape victim. In fact, some judges and jurists regarded women and girls who reported rape as especially credible for this reason.[78] Given the reputational damage a person would suffer by alleging rape, this countervailing line

---

74. E. M. Forster, *A Passage to India* (Harcourt, Brace, 1924).

75. See Joanna de Groot, "Depicting Conflict in India in 1857–58: The Instabilities of Gender, Violence, and Colonialism," *Cultural and Social History* 14, no. 4 (2017): 473–75; and Clare Anderson, *Subaltern Lives: Biographies of Colonialism in the Indian Ocean World, 1790–1920* (Cambridge University Press, 2012), 124–56. On mutiny-related rape narratives and Forster's novel see Jenny Sharpe, "The Unspeakable Limits of Rape: Colonial Violence and Counter-Insurgency," *Genders* 10 (1991): 25–46.

76. See Powell, "Medical Examination," 231. This narrative persists in India today. See Oza, *Semiotics*, 20–21, 36–64.

77. *Siraj-ud-Din v. Emperor*, MANU/LA/0231/1927.

78. For example see *In re Harakchand Ghiwarmal Marwadi and Others*, MANU/NA/0117/1941, para. 6. In the postcolonial context see *Bhagwat Prakash v. the State*, MANU/UP/0012/1956, para. 5; and Ram Lal Gupta, *The Medico Legal Aspects of Sexual Offences* (Lucknow: Eastern Book, 1964), 1–2.

of reasoning acknowledged the powerful social *dis*incentives for reporting rape, including through a false accusation.[79]

The second explanation that judges used to explain allegedly false rape claims was the desire for revenge. As with the murder cases in chapter 2 involving planted animal blood and punitive self-harm, this proposed motive tapped into notions of retaliatory behavior. The revenge motive could apply to the individual or the family. Judges, treatise authors, and civil surgeons looked for signs that mothers (or other relatives) had inflicted injuries on little girls so they could be presented as rape victims.[80] For many judges and forensic analysts, not only bodily injury but also the testimony of the accuser and her associates could be part of a group effort to frame an innocent male for rape. Retaliation for a previous wrong was the most commonly proposed motive.

However, the female accuser herself was not necessarily the one seeking revenge in these alleged setups, nor was she necessarily acting voluntarily.[81] Some other party could have been the driving force behind the accusation. In a case set in the context of Sikh-Muslim communal conflict in late-1930s Lahore, a Muslim man named Fajja and a Sikh named Sohan Singh were convicted for abducting and raping a young woman named Aishan, age fifteen or sixteen. Singh was acquitted on appeal, when Justice Ram Lall of the Lahore High Court noted many odd aspects of the case. For one, Fajja had coached Aishan to implicate Singh when the police recorded the First Information Report. In addition, Singh had testified against Fajja and his cousins in a communal riot case shortly before and may also have owed Fajja money. The judge concluded that Fajja sought revenge against Singh by orchestrating a false rape accusation through the teenage girl that Fajja himself had captured and raped.[82]

In a second sex offense case, the coercion was even more clearly documented. This was a case from 1933 in the princely state of Dhenkanal (now in Odisha), governed by the Indian Penal Code and British-run criminal courts. Here, a woman named Ambika accused a state forest clerk named Nrushingh Charan Patanaik of a sexual offense that fell short of rape: trespass (in her house) with

79. For example see *Dattu Deoman v. Emperor*, MANU/NA/0157/1936, para. 3. For an extended postcolonial discussion see the Indian Supreme Court case of *Bharwada Bhoginbhai Hirjibhai v. State of Gujarat*, MANU/SC/0090/1983, para. 12.

80. Note that the suspicion that women (especially mothers) inflicted genital injuries on young girls existed outside of India, too. See, for example, Taylor, *Principles* (1894), 435–36; Stephen Robertson, "Signs, Marks, and Private Parts: Doctors, Legal Discourses, and Evidence of Rape in the United States, 1823–1930," *Journal of the History of Sexuality* 8, no. 3 (1998): 367–69; and Cage, *Science of Proof*, 145–46.

81. On coerced female accusers see *Dolabi v. King-Emperor*.

82. *Sohan Singh v. Emperor*, MANU/LA/0049/1938.

the intention to outrage her modesty. A British judge named N. A. J. Anderson convicted the clerk and sentenced him to six months' rigorous imprisonment. The superintendent of police for Dhenkanal State later reported that the allegation was false but that the woman had made it under threat of violence by at least one police officer. The officer later admitted that he had initiated a false case against Patanaik "under orders of the Ruler." He "was not aware why the Ruler wanted a false case to be instituted against Nrushingh. He only carried out the orders of the Ruler." False cases were commonly associated in judicial rhetoric with women (or their families) pursuing their own retaliatory ends. But the female accuser herself could have been acting under threat, caught in a web of intrigue spun by someone else.[83]

Judges searched for an "enmity context"—like the troubled relationship between Fajja and Sohan Singh—that might produce a false allegation. In *Sohan Singh*, the court was convinced by this idea, at least in relation to the rape charge against Sohan Singh. The argument also succeeded in the 1916 Punjab case of *Abdul Rahman v. Emperor.*[84] Abdul Rahman was a fifteen-year-old boy who was convicted of raping an eleven-year-old girl. The case was appealed to the Punjab Chief Court, where Justice Shadi Lal set aside the conviction. There was conflicting medical testimony; the FIR was not made immediately even though the girl's father was a police constable; and neither semen nor blood was found. The witnesses for the prosecution all claimed to have seen the sexual intercourse, but their testimony was contradictory. All were connected to the girl, so none was "disinterested." Most important for our purposes was the fact that the families of the girl and boy had been "at enmity for each other," including in court. The girl's father had won a civil suit against the boy's family in a dispute about field boundaries. The boy's father had sued the father of one of the girl's witnesses in a preemption suit decided two weeks before the alleged rape.[85] There were also multiple criminal cases between the families of the girl and boy. The enmity context, combined with the issues in the direct evidence, convinced the judge that he should give the boy the benefit of the doubt.

83. Criminal case no. 10/131, trial of 1932 in the Court of the S. D. O. Sadar, Dhenkanal State, Complainant: Ambika Stree of Dhenkanal town; versus: Nrushingh Charan Patnaik of Dhenkanal town, s.457 IPC, in "False Cases," 1944, unpaginated p. 12 (IOR/R/2/303/90).

84. *Abdul Rahman v. Emperor*, 150–51.

85. In late colonial India the law of preemption was a carryover from the Islamic law of property. When a landowner wanted to sell, certain interested parties (like particular relatives and neighbors) had the right of first refusal. See Syed Ameer Ali, *Mahommedan Law Compiled from Authorities in the Original Arabic*, vol. 1: *Gifts, Wakfs, Wills, Preemption and Bailment* (Calcutta: Thacker, Spink, 1904).

Perhaps because of cases like *Sohan Singh* and *Abdul Rahman*, the claim of an enmity context became a routine part of the defense in rape cases. But perhaps *because* the argument became so common, courts occasionally rejected it. In the 1930 Dinajpur case of *Sreehari Swarnakar*, a man was tried for the rape of an eight- or nine-year-old girl. She had been sent by her mother, a widow, to collect firewood in the forest with him. He suggested that the charges were fabricated because of an enmity context. The Calcutta High Court felt that the lower court judge had alerted the jury to the mother's admission that "since a certain salis [or *panchayat*] she did not allow the accused to come to her house." But this judge also wondered how strong the enmity could be, given that the mother had sent her daughter with the accused to collect firewood.[86] In *Dattu Deoman v. Emperor* (from Nagpur in 1936), the accused was a man in a village position of authority who had allegedly raped a teenage cotton picker. He argued that he had been framed and that the girl had been tutored to accuse him of rape because others resented him. The court was not convinced, ruling that the process by which Dattu Deoman became *kamdar patel* (a position of power in the village) had been properly carried out, and that no one resented his leadership role: "It is nothing but the usual custom" that others should have offered themselves as potential candidates. "The existence of factions in the village is not proved."[87] Where the defense claimed falsity, in other words, judges and juries also wondered if this argument itself was false. In short, allegations of falsity saturated the standard moves and countermoves in colonial rape trials. But despite the assumption of many colonial legal professionals that falsity was everywhere in these cases, simply alleging falsity did not mean it would be accepted in court.

Detecting Animal Blood in Rape Cases

Falsity was equally a focus at an earlier stage before the courtroom, in the lab. A competition between two forms of analysis—forensic serology and microscopy—unfolded in the labs of the CEs and imperial serologist during the first five decades of the twentieth century. The years from 1901 to 1921 were a particularly well-documented phase when precipitin testing produced crucial evidence for some defendants accused of rape. During the 1930s and 1940s, however, new sperm staining techniques did for accusers what precipitin testing had done for the accused.

86. *Sreehari Swarnakar v. Emperor*, AIR Cal. (1930): 132–34.
87. *Dattu Deoman v. Emperor*, para. 6.

As the first imperial serologist (chapter 2), W. D. Sutherland produced documents in 1915 and 1921 that included descriptions of cases revealed to be false (or partly false) through precipitin testing. In these cases, which must have occurred between 1901 and 1921, animal blood was identified among blood-stained evidence, and some of these were rape cases. Sutherland's case studies constitute the richest collection of rape cases deemed partly or wholly false due to the presence of animal blood.

Precipitin testing operated in favor of defendants because it was either neutral (if no animal blood was found) or strong evidence for falsity (if animal blood was found). Finding no animal blood did not necessarily make conviction likely—the mix of other evidence could lead the court either way—but a finding of animal blood could raise doubts about the prosecution's account, tilting the scales in favor of acquittal. Precipitin testing, then, could be good or neutral for the defense, and bad or neutral for the prosecution. Hence a man or boy accused of rape had much to gain and little to lose from this form of testing.

Sutherland's descriptions suggest that he thought some cases were completely false—and that rape or even sex had not occurred. These cases were characterized by the presence of animal blood paired with the absence of seminal stains. His views were based on lab findings alone, and his descriptions did not always include other types of evidence in the case (such as medical examinations and testimony of the accuser and witnesses). A case from a princely state in Kathiawar in western India included the petticoat of a woman who claimed to have been raped, along with the *dhoti* (loincloth) of the person she accused. Both pieces of clothing were found to be stained with sheep or goat's blood, and no seminal stains were mentioned.[88] In another case, a girl said that she had been gang raped by three men, each one having forced himself on her "with profuse ejaculation." However, no semen was found on her loincloth. It was stained with nonmammalian blood, so the charge of rape was "not pressed."[89] In a separate case, a girl or woman said that three young men had threatened her with weapons and taken her into the jungle, where they raped her. Her bodice, though, was stained with nonmammalian blood, and there was no mention of seminal stains. In court, it came out that the accuser's father had been put in custody for a day by the father, a magistrate, of one of the defendants. Another witness who had

88. "Note by Lieut.-Col. W. D. Sutherland, IMS, on the legal serological work carried out by him," May 29, 1915, 10 (case 10) in "Appointment of an imperial serologist for the whole of India," Bhopal Agency: General, Proc. no. 5, 1914 (NAI).

89. Sutherland in *Lyon's Medical Jurisprudence* (1921), 201 (case 9). This is probably the same case as in "Note by Sutherland," 10 (case 9).

given testimony confirming the accuser's account was involved in a dispute with this same magistrate over "money matters." The precipitin results plus the enmity context led to the discharge of the three youths.[90]

More ambiguous perhaps were cases with contradictory evidence that included animal blood. These sometimes led to acquittals. For example, a man between sixty and seventy years old, "his body covered with wrinkles," was alleged to have raped his eleven-year-old niece behind a bush while keeping her fourteen-year-old female friend standing by. No semen was found, and the blood on the niece's sari was from a sheep or goat. The medical examination noted a ruptured hymen and inflammation of the vulva. But the judge privileged the blood testing, pointing to the known hostility between the actors. The accused and the girl's parents, his relatives, had been fighting.[91]

False evidence did not necessarily mean a false case (chapter 2). Judges believed that a case could be bolstered: In an effort to strengthen the accuser's case, false evidence might be added as "embroidery."[92] Sutherland described cases where judges believed that a crime probably had been committed but that the evidence also had been embellished. In some of these cases, the falsity of some of the evidence led to acquittal. In one case from Jalpaiguri (today in West Bengal), the lab found that the sari of a woman who claimed to have been raped was stained with blood, but only from a nonmammal and a nonhuman mammal, and no seminal stains were found. Contrary to these lab findings, the medical examination of the woman (and perhaps the accused) was consistent with rape. The magistrate wrote that "the Medical Evidence makes it almost certain that the girl was raped, but the Chemical Examiner's report throws some doubt on it."[93] He acquitted the defendant. In a case of conflicting expert evidence like this, the relative status of the experts probably mattered. The medical exam would have been done by the local civil surgeon for the area, but the lab testing was done by the CE's lab for the whole of Bengal Presidency. And as discussed in chapters 4 and 5, the chemical examiner was usually not called to court for cross-examination, while the civil surgeon was. Civil surgeons' views could therefore be questioned more rigorously than CEs' findings.

In some cases with contradictory evidence, the judge thought that a lesser crime had been committed and the evidence had been bolstered to make a case

---

90. Sutherland in *Lyon's Medical Jurisprudence* (1921), 211–12 (case 63).

91. Sutherland in *Lyon's Medical Jurisprudence* (1921), 208 (case 53).

92. I borrow this language from the postcolonial Indian Supreme Court decision in *Gunnana Pentayya and Others v. State of A.P.*, MANU/SC/7955/2008, para. 15.

93. "Note by Sutherland," 11 (case 17). This is probably the same case as in Sutherland in *Lyon's Medical Jurisprudence* (1921), 203 (case 28).

for the more serious crime of rape. As in chapter 2, these were instances of justice being pursued (as the accusers saw it) not through truth but falsity. In one case, a cloth worn by a "little girl" was tested. It was supposed to be stained with her blood, due to rape. The girl claimed that a drunken man, the accused, had seized and dragged her into a walled enclosure, where he raped her. She produced two witnesses. One claimed to know nothing of the case. The other testified to having seen the girl leaving the enclosure, weeping and followed by the man, but this witness had not seen the sex act. The bloodstains were ox or buffalo blood, and no seminal stains were mentioned. The magistrate discharged the accused, finding that the case had been "got up" by the girl's parents, "who had stained her cloth merely to exaggerate matters, because she had been terrified by the drunken man."[94]

For some adjudicators, animal blood meant falsity and the failure of the prosecution's case. But others disregarded the false evidence if they found the rest to be compelling. Sutherland documented this patchwork in his case studies. From Dinajpur (today in Bangladesh), analysts received a cloth that a tribal or Indigenous Santhal woman claimed was stained with her blood during rape. The stains were nonmammalian alone, and no semen was found on the cloth. Nonetheless, the magistrate "found that the case was true." And yet he also found that there was insufficient evidence, without the cloth, to convict the two men accused.[95] This judge identified the false evidence and assessed the rest, although ultimately he felt there was not enough to convict.

Some similar cases with conflicting evidence resulted in convictions. A man of twenty was accused of raping a girl of eight. There were no seminal stains on her clothing, but there were bloodstains, which turned out to be sheep or goat. The judge admitted that this "cast grave doubts" on the other evidence. But he still convicted the defendant, a result Sutherland found problematic.[96]

Sutherland's most extensive account of a conviction despite conflicting evidence involved a fourteen-year-old girl named Bhagirthi from the Kumhar community (traditionally potters).[97] The girl was grazing her family's donkeys with her little brother, Haria, when the accused (probably a teenage boy) allegedly dragged her to an isolated spot and raped her. The little brother ran away and

94. Quoting Sutherland's account, not from the magistrate directly. Sutherland in *Lyon's Medical Jurisprudence* (1921), 208 (case 54).

95. Quoting Sutherland's account, not the magistrate directly. Sutherland in *Lyon's Medical Jurisprudence* (1921), 200 (case 6).

96. Quoting Sutherland's account, not the magistrate directly. Sutherland in *Lyon's Medical Jurisprudence* (1921), 203 (case 26).

97. Sutherland in *Lyon's Medical Jurisprudence* (1921), 208–10 (case 55).

told their grandmother, who reported the matter to the village authorities. This woman testified that she had found her granddaughter walking home, weeping with her *lehnga* (skirt) and legs wet with blood. Semen stains were identified on the clothing. But the blood was nonmammalian, and there was no trace of human blood. The civil surgeon reported that the girl's hymen had been torn several months before, and that there were scratch marks on her back.

The judge found the girl to be compelling and sincere in court: "The girl gave her evidence in a very simple, honest and unpretending manner, and I was very much impressed by her innocent demeanor." He also rejected the accused's attempt to set up an enmity context for the case. The accused claimed that he had driven away the girl's donkeys from his *juar* (millet) field earlier the same day, and that this had annoyed the Kumhars, who falsely accused him of rape as punishment. The judge found this account implausible because the triggering act was "too trivial." He also stressed the reputational price Bhagirthi, who was still unmarried, would pay for even alleging that she had been raped: "The imputation of rape is the [worst] kind of allegation against an unmarried girl's character, and it is inconceivable that a father would under any circumstances care to disgrace his daughter so openly in order to avenge himself for such a petty matter as the one asserted but not proved by the accused."[98]

The judge acknowledged that the evidence was contradictory. The absence of human blood was "inconsistent with the very strong evidence for the prosecution," for instance. He chose to privilege the girl's testimony and semen stains over the animal blood, finding the accused guilty. By contrast, the two assessors on the case found the accused not guilty, a verdict the judge called "altogether perverse and contrary to the positive and reliable evidence for the prosecution." The judge's guilty verdict won out, and the accused was sentenced to eighteen months' rigorous imprisonment on account of his young age.[99]

Sutherland disapproved of this outcome. It was better, he argued, to understand the case as a false rape allegation made to cover up premarital consensual sex (in this case, not with the accused). Sutherland focused on the medical examination's finding of a torn hymen some months earlier. The scratches on her back were probably also from this earlier consensual sex "amongst the bushes." The little brother may have seen consensual activity and run away to tell his grandmother. Bhagirthi realized it, and decided to claim she had been raped to protect

98. Quoting the unnamed judge in Sutherland in *Lyon's Medical Jurisprudence* (1921), 209.

99. Quoting the unnamed judge in Sutherland in *Lyon's Medical Jurisprudence* (1921), 209. Sutherland's account does not give the accused's age. On assessors see Mitra Sharafi, *Law and Identity in Colonial South Asia: Parsi Legal Culture, 1772–1947* (Cambridge University Press, 2014), 197–98.

her reputation, by Sutherland's logic. The grandmother "naturally tried to save her grandchild's reputation, being ignorant of the happenings of some months before." The nonmammalian blood must have been added, perhaps from a bird: "The point is that she was not so innocent as she might have been, and was not likely to receive injuries from coitus on the day in question, such as would cause profuse bleeding." The semen on the *lehnga* did not necessarily mean that the act was done "in an agitated and confused manner," as the judge had thought. Rather, Sutherland argued that the semen could have dripped out of the girl after sex. Sutherland's version of the story came down to this: "Had there been no little brother there that day it is likely that the young man would be still at liberty." For Sutherland and the assessors, this was a false case. For the judge, it was a genuine one, despite the animal blood.[100]

Privileging his own specialty of forensic serology in the cases of Bhagirthi and the eight-year-old girl, Sutherland favored a strict approach: The presence of fabricated evidence raised doubts about the prosecution's entire case and should lead automatically to acquittal. By contrast, judges who convicted in these two cases seemed to take the more pragmatic approach, perhaps believing that these were bolstered cases—at core, true cases, but with some false evidence added as a misguided effort at padding. These judges, who were magistrates without formal legal training, were willing to disregard the bloodstains and focus on the rest.[101]

Taking all these cases together, the point was that judges had a great deal of discretion when faced with contradictory evidence involving animal bloodstains. The case law was a patchwork of contrary results because judges took different views of the presence of animal blood. Sutherland favored the strict view in which animal blood meant acquittal. Unsurprisingly, this approach gave precipitin testing and the imperial serologist maximum influence. It also meant that the precipitin test aligned with patriarchal views, because the tests could only benefit, or at least could not hurt, the accused rapist. Sutherland's view that animal blood should mean acquittal would also have resonated with England-trained barristers who came to India at a relatively late age, whether as lawyers or to take up a position as High Court judges. It was often these figures, like J. Douglas Young (chapter 5), who saw themselves as champions of rule-of-law values, including the presumption of innocence. They were familiar with the *falsus in uno, falsus in omnibus* principle of English law (i.e., false in one thing, false in all)—that if

100. Sutherland in *Lyon's Medical Jurisprudence* (1921), 210.

101. On magistrates see Farid, "Imperial Constitutionalism," 50–51, 85–86, 168, 170–74, 180–91; and, for an earlier period, Brendon Gillis, "Conduits of Justice: Magistrates and the British Imperial State, 1732–1834" (PhD diss., Indiana University, 2015).

a witness testified falsely on one matter, they could not be deemed credible on another.[102] By contrast, adjudicators who were not trained as lawyers and often had been in India for longer (as Europeans) may have been more pragmatic and flexible in their approach to bolstered cases.[103] They may have been more willing to convict despite the presence of animal blood.

Detecting Semen and Sperm in Rape Cases

Forensic serology enjoyed the limelight in Indian sexual forensics during the first couple of decades of the twentieth century. But as Sutherland's rape cases showed, seminal stains mattered, too. Here there were two separate types of analysis: identifying semen through chemical reactions and looking for individual sperm cells under the microscope.[104] During the late colonial period, the rate of success in identifying sperm, in particular, rose significantly, and these improved techniques were quite valuable for accusers of rape. There were many reasons why semen or sperm might not be detected in India, particularly before 1936. As a result, some judges recognized that even by the standards of the day, analysts' failure to find semen or sperm did not necessarily mean that rape had not occurred.[105] A positive finding of semen or sperm, however, operated strongly in the accuser's favor. This was particularly true if she was a child. There was no legitimate explanation for the presence of semen or sperm on an unmarried female child's clothing, lending credence to her allegation of rape.[106] As a result, the identification of sperm, like that of gonorrhea bacilli (*gonococci*), provided especially powerful evidence for unmarried girls in rape cases.[107] For

---

102. Case law suggests that the *falsus in uno* rule did not clearly apply in India. See the 1929 case of *Sutar Jivraj Virji of Butawadar Under Dhrafa Thana v. King Emperor*, Western India States Agency Law Reports 5 (1929): 240. However, Young adhered to the rule in his decisions. See chapter 5.

103. When judges were mentioned at all in Sutherland's case studies, no names or ethnicities were included.

104. K. N. Bagchi, "Significance of Florence Test for Seminal Stains," *IMG* 72, no. 2 (1937): 91.

105. For instance see the 1936 decision in *Dattu Deoman v. Emp.*, para. 3. For a postcolonial case that cited the colonial-era treatise of *Lyon's Medical Jurisprudence*, 9th ed., ed. T. F. Owens (Calcutta: Thacker, Spink, 1935) see *Rajput Bhima Karasan v. the Kutch Government*, MANU/KU/0042/1949, para. 12.

106. For example see *Emperor v. Asadali*; *Jantan v. Emperor*; and "Annual Report of the CE to Government, Bengal, for the Year 1941," 14 (case 15) (IOR/V/24/424). The girls in these cases were between the ages of eight and thirteen. They seem to have been unmarried. On the history of child marriage in India see Pande, *Sex*; and Tambe, *Defining Girlhood*.

107. Gonorrhea in the girl was strong evidence against the accused if he also had it. See *Hanuman Sarma v. Emp.*, 723–27; and *Sikandar Mian v. Emp.*, 321–24. It was not clear how often gonorrhea was diagnosed through identification of *gonococci* in the early twentieth century, compared to diagnosis

rape accusers who were married, semen or sperm found on their clothing could belong to their spouse, rather than the accused.[108] This was before it was possible to connect a seminal stain to a particular man through lab testing.[109] And yet even in rape cases involving married girls and women, some judges took the presence of semen or sperm to corroborate the wife's account of rape.[110]

Semen and sperm analysis, then, were the mirror-image of precipitin testing: They were either neutral (nothing found) or favorable (semen or sperm found) for the accuser in rape cases, just as precipitin testing was neutral (no animal blood found) or favorable (animal blood found) for the accused. As F. N. Windsor, the CE for Burma, explained in 1906, "Although detection of spermatozoa is of value as evidence [for the accuser], a negative result of examination is valueless on the other side."[111]

The leading test used by CEs for the detection of semen during the early twentieth century was known as the Florence reaction. It was developed by a French physician, A. Florence of Lyon, in 1895–96.[112] All living cells contained a substance called choline, usually in a compound known as lecithin. Semen contained higher levels of choline than any other bodily substance. It could be as much as 0.514 percent choline, while brain tissue was 0.325 percent and blood 0.031 percent. Semen was the only bodily substance whose choline levels

via external symptoms only, but Bombay police surgeon Arthur Powell was identifying *gonococci* circa 1902. Powell, "Medical Examination," 231. It was possible for an infected person to have unprotected sex with an uninfected one and not communicate the disease. Thus, courts recognized that if the accused had gonorrhea but the girl did not, this did not necessarily mean that he had not raped her. See *Emp. v. Asadali*, para. 4. Because of no-touch toilets in India, there was little discussion in India (unlike in the US) of the theory that little girls could contract gonorrhea from infected toilet seats. See Powell, "Medical Examination," 231; and Lynn Sacco, "Sanitized for Your Protection: Medical Discourse and the Denial of Incest in the United States, 1890–1940," *Journal of Women's History* 14, no. 3 (2002): 80. For rare references to the toilet-seat theory of transmission in India see case no. 28 of 1938, "Parsi Chief Matrimonial Court Judge's Notebook, June 11, 1937–March 4, 1941," 3:53, 58 (courtroom 21, BHC).

108. *In re Karichiappa Goundan*, 286.

109. By the late 1930s, analysts realized that it was possible to identify "blood groups" in semen. For example see John C. Thomas, "The Examination of Blood and Seminal Stains," *Police Journal* 10 (1937): 503. If the husband and the accused had different blood groups, this type of testing could allow analysts to distinguish between semen of these two males. In 1941, though, some analysts in India felt that group testing was not as reliable for semen as for blood. S. D. S. Greval and S. N. Chandra, "Stains Other Than Blood-Stains as Medico-Legal Evidence," *IMG* 76, no. 12 (1941): 737, 739. For a postcolonial reference see Gupta, *Medico Legal Aspects*, 81.

110. For example see *Mir Moze Ali v. Emp.*, para. 6; and *In re Harakchand Ghiwarmal Marwadi*, para. 10.

111. "Report of the CE and Bacteriologist to the Government of Burma for the Year 1906," 1 (IOR/V/24/425).

112. A. Florence, "Du sperme et des taches de sperme en médecine légale," *Archives d'anthropologie criminelle et des sciences pénales* 10 (1895): 417–34, 520–43; and 11 (1896): 37–46, 146–63, 249–65.

produced dark brown microcrystals, visible under a microscope, when mixed with Florence's reagent.[113]

The Florence test's main competitor was the Barberios test. This reaction used picric acid, a favorite ingredient in Indian revolutionary bombs of the era.[114] The Barberios test had a variety of drawbacks: It took longer to perform and was less accurate. Another line of research during the 1930s—the use of ultraviolet light to detect seminal stains—was not yet effective on dark or soiled fabrics. UV light could not provide definitive evidence of semen, but it helped identify areas for further testing.[115]

The Florence test was the best available option, but it was not perfect. Factors such as prostate problems, the presence of blood, or bacterial action could produce false negatives.[116] Washing a semen-stained garment could also dilute the choline content.[117] As a consequence, a negative Florence reaction did not necessarily mean that an item contained no semen.

By contrast, a positive Florence reaction was a solid result. For K. N. Bagchi (the Bengal CE), it could only mean the presence of semen. He argued that there was no possibility of false positives.[118] However, the imperial serologist S. D. S. Greval and his first assistant S. N. Chandra (both also in Calcutta) took a more cautious approach. While there was a debate on whether a positive Florence reaction alone was enough to declare the presence of semen, their lab followed what they claimed was the majority approach—that it was not. At this lab, the first step was to do the Florence test to answer the question: Is this semen? If it was positive, the next step was to use microscopy to answer the question: Is there sperm? And in a development from the late 1930s, the final step was to conduct a version of the precipitin test, applied in this case to the seminal stain, not a

---

113. K. N. Bagchi, "Importance of Chemical Tests for Detection of Seminal Stains in Medico-Legal Investigations," *IMG* 74, no. 11 (1939): 683, 685. Florence's reagent contained iodine and potassium iodide. Greval and Chandra, "Stains," 737.

114. For example, picric acid was found among explosive substances associated with the Nasik conspiracy case (1910). "Report of the CA to Government, Bombay, for the Year 1910," 3 (IOR/V/24/406). It left telltale yellow stains on the hands and clothes of bomb makers, but was also used to treat burns. See "Report of the CA to Government, Bombay, for the Year 1930," 8 (case 22) (IOR/V/24/409). On the chief inspector of explosives see appendix 3.

115. "Report of the CE to Government, Madras, for the Year 1930," 5, in Annual Reports Government of Madras, box 1144.020000, G. O. no. 1175 (AAC, BL); Bagchi, "Examination," 109; and Greval and Chandra, "Stains," 737. The leading researcher on UV light for semen detection seems to have been Frank W. Martin at Glasgow University. See his article "Ultraviolet Rays and Seminal Stains," *BMJ* 1, no. 3809 (1934): 37–38; and Nicholas Edward Duvall, "Forensic Medicine in Scotland, 1914–39" (PhD diss., University of Manchester, 2013), 78, 85.

116. See, by Bagchi, "Importance," 683; "Significance," 91; and "Examination," 108.

117. Bagchi, "Significance," 90–91.

118. Bagchi, "Importance," 684–85; and Bagchi, "Significance," 91.

bloodstain. Despite preoccupation with the possibility of planted animal blood since the first decade of the twentieth century, testing for planted animal semen only seems to have begun in the late 1930s.[119]

The second mode of analysis was the search for sperm cells under the microscope (figure 8).[120] This did not necessarily compensate for the Florence test's weaknesses if the accused had few or no sperm cells, but if the accused had normal sperm counts, then the identification of sperm cells—arguably even one—could provide powerful evidence against him.[121] This would be particularly true if the Florence test had produced a false negative result for semen. It was standard practice, then, to do both Florence testing and to look for sperm in a seminal stain.

Sperm cells had a special weakness: They were delicate. Especially in a hot climate, their tails were fragile. They broke off or decomposed easily.[122] If police or medical officers folded or twisted a sperm-stained cloth, they could damage the flagella.[123] Once the cells were tailless, it was hard to tell the difference between the head of a sperm cell and other kinds of cells. And so while the identification of a single sperm cell could corroborate a rape accuser's testimony, for most of our period it was not easy to ascertain that a single spherical cell *was* the head of a spermatozoon. A sperm head could easily be mistaken for a yeast cell, bacterium, or fungal spore.[124]

This was why cell staining mattered. The right combination of coloring agents could make sperm cells visible, even without their tails. Sperm cell staining that was effective in a hot climate emerged out of the persistent tinkering of CEs across India and Burma, unlike the Florence test, which was imported from Europe. Like fingerprinting, this was one of British India's original

---

119. Research applying the precipitin test to semen began with the work of an American physician named Farnum in 1901. C. G. Farnum, "The Biologic Test for Semen," *Journal of the American Medical Association*, December 28, 1901: 1721. In Britain and India, precipitin testing was done on semen in the 1930s–40s. See Thomas, "Examination," 503; "Annual Report of the Imperial Serologist 1938–39," 23–24, 26; Bagchi, "Examination," 116; Greval and Chandra, "Stains," 737; and *In re Harakchand Ghiwarmal Marwadi and Others*, para. 10.

120. For a history of microscopy in colonial India see Projit B. Mukharji, *Doctoring Traditions: Ayurveda, Small Technologies, and Braided Sciences* (University of Chicago Press, 2016), 162–63.

121. On the prevalence of men with few or no sperm cells see, by Bagchi, "Importance," 685; "Significance," 91; and "Examination," 115–16.

122. "Appendix IX. Hankin's Test for Seminal Stains," in *Lyon's Medical Jurisprudence* (1921), 744; K. R. Ganguly, "Examination of Seminal Stains in Medico-Legal Cases," *IMG* 71, no. 7 (1936): 400; and Bagchi, "Examination," 115.

123. Bagchi, "Examination," 109.

124. Ganguly, "Examination," 400; and Bagchi, "Examination," 115.

FIGURE 8. / "Human spermatozoa x 900" under the microscope. *Lyon's Medical Jurisprudence for India*, 7th ed., ed. L. A. Waddell (Calcutta: Thacker, Spink, 1921), plate 5, facing p. 308.

contributions to forensic science.[125] Sperm cell staining techniques that were developed in South Asia were incorporated into textbooks across the English-speaking world.[126]

The South Asian sperm stain story began earlier, in British Burma, as historian Jonathan Saha discovered. During a misconduct investigation relating to a rape case in 1905, a deputy commissioner named H. C. Moore noticed that no seminal stain had been identified for several years in Burma. Rapid putrefaction was a challenge for the Florence test in hot climates. But while other CEs in India had annual semen detection rates as low as 17 percent for some of the same years, Rangoon's rate was 0 percent for several years in a row, despite a significant number of cases (161) submitted in 1901–3.[127] Unusually, hospital assistants had been allowed to do semen stain testing on behalf of the Burma CE since 1899, a move designed to reduce the CE's heavy workload. Moore doubted the wisdom of this practice.[128]

---

125. See Chandak Sengoopta, *Imprint of the Raj: How Fingerprinting Was Born in Colonial India* (Macmillan, 2003).

126. For example see John Glaister, *A Textbook of Medical Jurisprudence and Toxicology* (Edinburgh: E. and S. Livingstone, 1921), 509; and Abner Irving Weisman, *Spermatozoa and Sterility: A Clinical Manual* (New York: Paul H. Hoeber, 1941), 210.

127. Saha, "Male State," 370–72. In Burma, no semen was detected in any case in 1897, 1898, 1901, 1902, and 1903.

128. Saha, "'Uncivilized Practitioners,'" 439.

It was never determined whether misconduct or something else accounted for the poor record in Burma. Moore's call for an inquiry went unheeded. Saha speculates that because Moore, like his brother, had married a Burmese woman, he may have been marginalized within administrative circles.[129] Someone did listen, though. The Rangoon CE, M. Hunter, was replaced by F. N. Windsor, who produced more detailed and meticulous annual reports than his predecessor. By 1908, Windsor was devoting special energy to changing the way his lab dealt with potential seminal stains. Reforms to the lab's semen testing were not clearly identified in the annual reports, but during study leave in 1908, Windsor devised an improved sperm staining method. His lab's numbers rose—from identifying sperm in 5 out of 87 submissions in 1907 (5.7 percent) to 45 out of 150 (30 percent) in 1908.[130] As the inspector general of civil hospitals for Burma, W. G. King, wrote to the secretary to the Government of Burma, the contrast in results for sexual stains before and after Windsor's "personal efforts in perfecting tests" was striking. Windsor's "valuable technical advance" would be "of great utility" to Burma.[131] Windsor's method would be cited in American medical texts into the 1940s, so it had even greater reach than King predicted.[132]

From Rangoon, developments in sperm staining then shifted to Agra. From the early 1890s until 1922, the CE there was an unusual figure named E. H. Hankin.[133] He was a scientist, not a physician. He was not a member of the Indian Medical Service, and some attribute the conflict and criticism that occasionally flared during his Indian career to this outsider status.[134] Hankin obtained his doctorate while on leave around 1904, partway through his time as CE. He took

---

129. Saha, "Male State," 372. Similarly, see Chao Ren, "The Spectre of Ma Phyu? Loyalty, Competence, and the Spatial Dynamics of Imperial Administration in Colonial Burma," *MAS* 58, no. 2 (2024): 536–62.

130. "Report of the CE and Bacteriologist to Government, Burma, for the Year 1908," 1 (IOR/V/24/425). For a description of the new method see F. N. Windsor, "A Method of Examining Seminal Stains," June 14, 1909, Proceedings of the Home Dept., August 1909, no. 80 (IOR/P/8163).

131. Letter from W. G. King, inspector-general of civil hospitals, Burma, to the secretary to the government of Burma (Rangoon, March 12, 1909), 1, in CE Report for Burma 1908.

132. Weisman, *Spermatozoa*, 210.

133. For obituaries see "Dr. E. H. Hankin. Bacteriology in India," *TL*, April 3, 1939; and "Dr. E. H. Hankin," *Nature*, April 29, 1939, 711–12. See also Pratik Chakrabarti, *Bacteriology in British India: Laboratory Medicine and the Tropics* (University of Rochester Press, 2012), 33, 45, 48, 76, 145, 189, 211.

134. I thank Patricia Barton for this general observation (Madison, WI, October 18, 2019). For a specific example see exchange between Hankin and J. Cleghorn, director general, IMS, who characterized Hankin's work as irresponsible and untrustworthy: "Annual Report of the CE and Bacteriologist to the Governments of the Northwest Provinces and Oudh and of the Central Provinces" for 1895 and 1896 (IOR/V/24/414).

every opportunity to use his "Dr." title thereafter. Undoubtedly, this title mattered in the hierarchical world of the colonial military.

Hankin's true love was bacteriology, and he was the first CE designated "Chemical Examiner and Bacteriologist."[135] His annual reports were remarkable for their detailed and creative descriptions of his bacteriological projects. He did many experiments on cholera and water sources, observing that Brahmin caste purity rules aligned with bacteriology-informed best practices.[136] His method of "pinking" drinking water with permanganate of potash became widespread and continued until the introduction of chlorination.[137] Most memorable were his experiments on partly cremated, cholera-infected corpses in the Ganges and Jumna Rivers. Hankin was trying to understand why cholera was not transmitted through these waters.[138] In comparison to these bacteriological reports, his CE reports were brief and bland.

For most of Hankin's years heading the Agra lab, his bacteriology work and forensic work were distinct and separate. But in the one area of cell staining, the lab's forensic work benefited from Hankin's bacteriology. Just as cell staining techniques were important for sperm cell identification, they were also key to bacteriological research.[139] Hankin published his method of sperm cell staining in the *British Medical Journal* in 1906. He recommended boiling the suspected stain in a weak watery solution of tannin and sulfuric acid before soaking it in a solution of potassium cyanide, then washing, scraping, and teasing it on a glass slide, "dried, fixed by heat, and stained." By this technique, he had been able to identify sperm using an oil immersion lens even when they were "covered with masses of bacteria" or other substances like red ink and starch paste.[140] (These substances simulated blood and semen, respectively. Stiff semen-like

---

135. The only other CE to acquire the title of bacteriologist was in Burma from 1906, when the first title holder was F. N. Windsor. This was about a decade after the title was introduced in Agra for Hankin.

136. CE and Bacteriologist Report for the North-Western Provinces, Oudh, and the Central Provinces for 1894, 8–9.

137. "Dr. E. H. Hankin," *Nature*, 712.

138. CE and Bacteriologist Report for the NWP, Oudh, and the Central Provinces for 1895, 41–48.

139. For example see E. H. Hankin, *Some New Methods of Using the Aniline Dyes for Staining Bacteria* (London, 1887).

140. E. H. Hankin, "Improved Methods for Recognition of Blood and Seminal Stains," *BMJ* 2, no. 2393 (1906): 1261. See also "Annual Report of the CE and Bacteriologist to the Governments of the United Provinces of Agra and Oudh and of the Central Provinces for the Year 1906," 2 (IOR/V/24/414); and, for a later and very detailed version, appendix 9, "Hankin's Test for Seminal Stains," in *Lyon's Medical Jurisprudence* (1921), 741–44.

stains were sometimes found to be starch or egg white, for instance.)[141] By the 1920s, Hankin's method appeared in medical jurisprudence textbooks like Lyon's treatise using carbol fuchsin, a red dye common in bacterial staining.[142]

By 1936, Hankin had retired and returned to England. But the lab's momentum on cell staining continued, and the biggest advance in sperm cell staining came out of the Agra lab at this time, overtaking Hankin's own method. In 1936, K. R. Ganguly published an article on sperm staining in the *Indian Medical Gazette*. Ganguly was the third assistant to the Agra CE, D. N. Chatterji, and held an MSc degree. He had special training in Customs and Excise testing and was an active member of the lab's then-vibrant research culture.[143] He gave papers and published on everything from detecting arsenic in cremation ashes to the evaporation of alcohol in hot climates.[144] In his 1936 article, Ganguly critiqued Hankin's method of staining sperm cells as only suited to hot, dry climates and for its staining imprecision, which could yield both false negatives and false positives.[145]

Instead of using carbol fuchsin, Ganguly's new staining method used a double stain of erythrosine and malachite green, both dyes manufactured by the American company Merck. The result was that sperm heads were stained "beautifully red or pink, while the tails remained either green or blue." Any foreign debris remained either undyed or a light green. There was no need to use an oil immersion lens with this method. A regular dry microscope lens would do. Sperm cells took up the stain and stood out even when lying underneath inorganic material. And perhaps most importantly, sperm heads without flagella were readily identifiable.[146] Writing in 1938, S. N. Chakravarti (the Agra CE) and S. N. Roy called Ganguly's technique "superior to all other known methods of

141. Bagchi, "Significance," 91–92; Bagchi, "Examination," 109; and CE Report for Madras 1930, 5. For a Talmudic story of egg white being used to simulate semen see Sheila Jasanoff, *Science at the Bar: Law, Science, and Technology in America* (Harvard University Press, 1995), 42.

142. Although I was unable to locate an extant copy of the eighth edition of *Lyon's Medical Jurisprudence*, ed. Waddell (1928), Ganguly made reference to Hankin's method described there. Ganguly, "Examination," 400.

143. In 1934, Ganguly received special training at the Customs and Excise laboratory in Calcutta. "Annual Report of the CE to the Governments of the United Provinces and of the Central Provinces for the Year 1934," 2 (IOR/V/24/417).

144. Ganguly's paper on the evaporation of alcohol was on the 1936 Indian Science Congress program. "Annual Report of the CE to the Governments of the United Provinces and of the Central Provinces for the Year 1935," 2 (IOR/V/24/417). He coauthored the following: S. N. Chakravarti, M. Z. Faruqi, and K. R. Ganguly, "Detection of Arsenic in Burnt Human Bones and Ashes," *IMG* 76, no. 12 (1941): 722–24.

145. Ganguly, "Examination," 400.

146. Ganguly, 401.

detecting spermatozoa."[147] Two years later, Bengal CE Bagchi called it "the best method for staining spermatozoa, especially in India."[148]

Unsurprisingly, Agra lab members made the boldest claims for Ganguly's method, which was debated in the late 1930s and early 1940s. Chakravarti and Roy argued that finding sperm cells without tails would be enough to declare a positive finding of sperm. But the *Indian Medical Gazette* editor, L. Everard Napier, urged caution on that point.[149] Three years later in 1941, the imperial serologist S. D. S. Greval and his first assistant, S. N. Chandra, agreed, claiming that the majority position was still that entire cells—a spermatozoon with head, neck, and tail—were required to declare a positive result.[150]

Despite this disagreement among experts, the Agra lab forged ahead with its new method without objection from military superiors. Its sperm detection rates rose steeply. In 1935, the lab identified semen or sperm in 73.1 percent of suspected seminal stains. In 1936, using Ganguly's new method, this figure jumped to 90.6 percent. This figure combined sperm cell identification and positive Florence reactions, but the Agra CE S. N. Chakravarti noted that the "high degree of success achieved" with seminal stains was partly due to the lab's new staining method. It was now "often possible to detect spermatozoa clearly" even when the Florence test was negative.[151] The pattern continued in subsequent years, and with sperm-specific data. In 1937, the Agra lab identified sperm in 92.3 percent of sex offense cases.[152] Over the next decade, this success rate ranged between the low 90s and a high of 99.5 percent in 1946.[153] The search for sperm had changed drastically. Around 1900, Hankin noted that there were years when the Agra lab had not identified a single sperm cell, despite careful searching.[154]

---

147. S. N. Chakravarti and S. N. Roy, "Experiments on the Stability of Seminal Stains from a Medico-Legal Standpoint," *IMG* 73, no. 7 (1938): 413.

148. Bagchi considered Ganguly's staining method "too lengthy," although he could not propose an alternative. Bagchi, "Examination," 114.

149. Chakravarti and Roy, "Experiments," 413–14.

150. Greval and Chandra, "Stains," 737.

151. "Annual Report of the CE to Government, United Provinces and Central Provinces, for the Year 1936," 3 (IOR/V/24/417).

152. "Annual Report of the CE to Government, United Provinces and Central Provinces, for the Year 1937," 3 (IOR/V/24/417).

153. "Annual Report of the CE to Government, United Provinces, Agra, for the Year . . . 1946," 2 (IOR/V/24/417).

154. See "Annual Report of the CE and Bacteriologist of the Governments of the North-Western Provinces and Oudh and of the Central Provinces for the Year 1899," 3 (IOR/V/24/414); and "Annual Report of the CE and Bacteriologist to the Governments of the North-Western Provinces and Oudh and of the Central Provinces for the Year 1901," 1 (IOR/V/24/414). For similar earlier comments from the Punjab lab see "Report of the CE to Government, Punjab, for the Year 1879," 19 (IOR/V/24/418). For similar later comments from Hankin see appendix 9 in *Lyon's Medical Jurisprudence* (1921), 744.

Between 1900 and the late 1930s, in other words, innovations in staining moved the lab from zero to 99.5 percent identification rates.

But was such a high identification rate necessarily better? A very high detection rate could suggest the inclusion of false positives. One would not expect 100 percent of suspected seminal stains to contain semen or sperm, for instance.[155] On the logic of Greval and Chandra in Calcutta, one might note that the Agra lab's figures counted a single sperm cell head without a tail as a "hit," contrary to the dominant view (in 1941) that still required a connected head, neck, and tail. This could have inflated the Agra lab's sperm identification rate. There was also the possibility of planted human semen, particularly in the "enmity contexts" so often described in court. Could analysts tell if a man allied with an accuser planted his own semen on her clothing, for instance?[156] The application of blood-group testing to semen started in the late 1930s, but this could only reveal planted semen if the two men's blood groups were different, and some analysts felt that grouping was not as accurate for seminal stains as for blood. More broadly, this scenario exposes the limits of analysts' powers of detection—and of the historian's ability to distinguish between genuine success in the lab and a sperm detection rate that was probably too good to be true.

Aside from these limitations and scenarios, there was another reason why the Agra lab rates did not necessarily translate into a clear victory for women and girls who reported rape in the 1930s and 1940s. Stepping from the lab back into the courtroom, we notice that rape law was also changing at this time. As analysts' tool kits improved, the law of rape and its approach to this forensic science changed apace. It is to this parallel story about the corroboration rule for rape that I now turn.

The Corroboration Rule for Rape

The corroboration rule was understood as a means of countering false accusations. By the nineteenth century, it applied to a number of areas in common

155. I have been unable to find any studies establishing an average baseline detection rate for this period. However, if the poisoning context may be a guide, there were many cases of materials submitted for toxicological testing that turned out not to contain poison. See chapter 1.

156. A same-sex case from the US around the 1980s illustrated a similar scenario. Soon after forensic DNA testing became available, seminal material from what seemed like a same-sex male rape case was submitted to a forensic lab. The DNA test revealed that the semen belonged to the accuser himself. William J. Tilstone, Kathleen A. Savage, and Leigh A. Clark, eds., *Forensic Science: An Encyclopedia of History, Methods, and Techniques* (ABC Clio, 2006), 259–60.

law jurisdictions, including accomplices and sexual offenses.[157] The rationale was that for crimes that often had no witness other than the accuser and accused, the accuser's testimony had to be confirmed by independent evidence. A judge's explanation of corroboration for the jury came down to this: One should select a fact that, if true, would support the inference that the accused was guilty. Was there any evidence to support this fact, aside from the accuser's testimony?[158]

What counted as corroborating evidence was less clear. The leading English case of *R. v. Baskerville* (1916) was often cited in Indian courts.[159] According to this case, evidence in corroboration was "independent" evidence that connected the accused to the crime. "In other words, it must be evidence which implicates him, that is, which confirms in some material particular not only her evidence that the crime has been committed but also that the prisoner committed it." But what made evidence independent? The strict approach that developed in India required that this evidence be entirely separate from the accuser's verbal account. The accuser could not corroborate herself.[160] For instance, any of the following could count: another witness' description of relevant events (not reproducing statements from the accuser to the witness), a physician's medical examination of the accuser or accused, or stain testing results.[161] However, a more flexible approach also developed in the case law, allowing corroborating evidence to be connected to the accuser's account indirectly. For instance, a witness recounting what

157. Other areas included bribery, subornation of perjury, and knowing receipt of stolen goods. See J. H. Wigmore, *A Treatise on the Anglo-American System of Evidence in Trials at Common Law*, 2nd ed. (Little, Brown, 1923), 4:360, 368–78. On corroboration in various areas of Indian law see J. O'Kinealy, *The Indian Penal Code* (Calcutta: Thacker, Spink, 1869), 103; and Prinsep, *Code of Criminal Procedure*, 297–99. On the rule in English law see Ernest Cockle, *Cases and Statutes on the Law of Evidence* (London: Sweet & Maxwell, 1915), 141–47; C. S. Watson, *The Law of Evidence* (London: Stevens & Sons, 1917), 165; John H. Langbein, *The Origins of Adversary Criminal Trial* (Oxford University Press, 2005), 203–17; and Alyagon Darr, *Plausible Crime Stories*, 105–10. On the rule in other common law jurisdictions see Alyagon Darr, 110–21; T. W. Hughes, *An Illustrated Treatise on the Law of Evidence* (Chicago: Callaghan, 1907), 374–81; and Wigmore, *Treatise* (1923), 4:350–414. In jurisdictions with Roman law roots (including Scotland), corroboration was required for all crimes. See Wigmore, *Treatise* (1923), 4:291–308.

158. *Ali Hyder v. Emperor*, AIR Cal. (1938): 771 (paraphrasing Henderson J.).

159. For instance, *R. v. Baskerville* (1916), 2 KB 658, was cited in *Emp. v. Nur Ahmed*, AIR Cal. (1934): 9; and *Sikandar Mian v. Emp.*, 322.

160. *Emp. v. Nur Ahmed*, 9–10.

161. For example see *Soosalal Bania v. Emperor*, 74–77; *Emperor v. Asadali*, 1–3; and *Sohan Singh v. Emperor*, MANU/LA/0049/1938, para. 6.

the accuser told them about the crime was sometimes held to be corroborative, or partly so.[162]

Another feature of the rule mattered, for our purposes. The ability of a jury to sidestep the corroboration rule was curtailed during the 1930s and 1940s in a line of decisions initiated by the Calcutta High Court. Specifically, a group of three British judges whom we have already met—Justices Lort-Williams, Henderson, and Cunliffe—sat on various two-judge panels that purported simply to apply precedent, first from England and then from their own court's case law. But across a seven-year stretch, they changed Indian law by ending jurors' ability to opt out of the corroboration rule.

The most cited precedent in this line of cases was *Surendra Nath Das v. Emperor* (1933).[163] This was the case already noted in which a fourteen-year-old girl accused a man named Das of raping her while his wife held her down. Das was convicted in the lower court but acquitted by the Calcutta High Court, which ordered a retrial. The judges acquitted him in part because the lower court judge had failed to warn the jury about the importance of corroborative evidence. "In fact, he never used the word corroboration throughout the whole of his charge," observed Lort-Williams, who delivered the main opinion.[164] The deputy legal remembrancer, a lawyer named Khondkar, argued for the prosecution that Indian law did not require corroboration for rape, particularly when consent was a nonissue because the girl was a minor. Khondkar insisted that no warning about uncorroborated testimony had to be given to the jury.[165]

Lort-Williams was baffled. Unlike judges who came to the High Court bench through the Indian Civil Service, Lort-Williams was a barrister judge.[166] He had a prior career in the courts of England and had "taken silk," becoming a king's counsel (or senior barrister) there before coming to India quite late in his career, at the age of forty-five.[167] This background permeated his reaction to Khondkar's

162. For instance see *Naresh Chandra v. Emperor*, AIR Cal. (1938): 480; and *Harendra Prosad Bagchi v. Emp.*, 463.

163. Cited in *Sikandar Mian v. Emp.*, 323; *Harendra Prosad Bagchi v. Emp.*, 462, and *Emp. v. Mahadeo Tatya*, 123.

164. *Surendra Nath Das v. Emp.*, 834. Henderson J. gave a concurring opinion.

165. *Surendra Nath Das v. Emp.*, 833, 835.

166. On differences and tensions between barrister and ICS judges see Mitra Sharafi, "Judging Conversion to Zoroastrianism: Behind the Scenes of the Parsi Panchayat Case (1908)," in *Parsis in India and the Diaspora*, ed. John R. Hinnells and Alan Williams (Routledge, 2007), 161–63; Farid, "Imperial Constitutionalism," chap. 3; and Raymond Cocks, "'The Bengal Boiler': Legal Networks in Colonial Calcutta," *Networks and Connections in Legal History*, ed. Michael Lobban and Ian Williams (Cambridge University Press, 2020), 124–51.

167. "Sir John Lort-Williams," *TL*, June 13, 1966.

argument: "I confess that it is somewhat disconcerting to be so informed by the Deputy Legal Remembrancer about a rule which is so well recognized, and which has been a rule of practice familiar to me during the whole course of my professional life. There cannot be any doubt that recognized practice requires that such a warning should be given."[168]

Lort-Williams was thinking of his career in England, and he relied on English authorities. According to *Archibold's Criminal Pleadings*, "corroboration of the story of the prosecutrix is not essential, but it is the practice to warn the jury against the danger of acting upon her uncorroborated testimony, particularly where the issue is consent or no consent."[169] And in a 1925 English case on indecent assault, *R. v. Jones*, the chief justice presented the corroboration rule thus: "The proper direction in such a case is that it is not safe to convict upon the uncorroborated testimony of the prosecutrix, but that the jury, if they are satisfied of the truth of her evidence may, after paying attention to that warning, nevertheless convict."[170] The rule, as illustrated in these cases, had two parts: First, it was risky to convict based on the uncorroborated testimony of the accuser (part one). But, second, a jury *could still convict* if satisfied that the accuser's uncorroborated testimony was reliable on its own (part two).

In *Surendra Nath Das*, Lort-Williams imported the English version that gave parts one and two of the corroboration test equal weight. However, in the decisions that followed, the Calcutta High Court promoted part one and demoted part two. For instance, Lort-Williams (with Cunliffe concurring) produced this version of the test two years later in 1935, in *Chamuddin Sardar v. Emperor.* Here he stressed the exceptional and unusual nature of the rule's second part: "The Judge should point out to the jury that they are entitled, if they please, to convict the accused upon the uncorroborated testimony of the girl, but that it is dangerous to do so in cases dealing with sexual offense such as rape, abduction and similar cases, and that only in exceptional cases should they convict upon the uncorroborated testimony of the girl."[171] The assistant Sessions judge had failed to warn the jury about corroboration in *Chamuddin Sardar*, and the jury had convicted the men on the basis of the accuser's uncorroborated testimony. On appeal, these convictions were set aside because of the nondirection.

---

168. *Surendra Nath Das v. Emp.*, 835.

169. *Archibold's Criminal Pleadings*, 1047, cited in *Russell on Crimes*, 2138, in *Surendra Nath Das v. Emp.*, 835.

170. *R. v. Thomas James Jones*, Cr. App. Rep. 19 (1925): 41, cited in *Surendra Nath Das v. Emp.*, 835.

171. *Chamuddin Sardar and Another v. Emperor*, AIR Cal. (1936): 19.

One year later, in 1936, Cunliffe (this time with Henderson) continued the project in the police boat rape case, *Sarat Chandra Chakravarty v. Emperor.* Like Lort-Williams, Cunliffe was a barrister judge and thus probably came to South Asia later in his career.[172] Together, the two amplified the corroboration rule in Indian law as an English import. In Cunliffe's own words, the rule had "always been the practice and the procedure in the Courts sitting in London, and it has gradually become the practice and procedure here." Cunliffe criticized the Sessions judge in *Chakravarty* for failing to "warn the jury very gravely that when charges of a sexual criminal character are brought against an accused person in a criminal Court without corroborating evidence, then the jury must be told that whereas after due and careful consideration they are entitled to accept that uncorroborated evidence, it is rarely safe to do so and for the good reason which exists in all charges of this character made by women against men."[173] Like Lort-Williams in 1935, Cunliffe in 1936 emphasized just how rare and risky it would be for a jury to depart from the corroboration requirement. The lower judge's failure to say so to the jury was one reason the police subinspector's conviction was set aside.

The following year, in 1937, Cunliffe and Henderson decided another rape case. In *Sikandar Mian v. Emperor*, a man was tried for sexually assaulting a nine-year-old girl named Taramoni. He had occasionally helped her with her studies. Both she and he were diagnosed with gonorrhea, making this a case that probably involved the "virgin cleansing" myth. Cunliffe presented the corroboration rule again by emphasizing part one and deemphasizing part two. As in his pronouncement the year before, he stressed the lineage of the rule, making it seem set for a long time in England and increasingly in India. In fact, this rule was only the subject of extended discussion in South Asia's reported case law from 1933 in the Calcutta High Court.[174] Both in *Chakravarty* and *Sikandar Mian*, he also emphasized the gendered nature of rape allegations—females accusing males.

172. Cunliffe arrived in South Asia as a judge of the Rangoon High Court around 1925. Almost a decade later he was transferred to the Calcutta High Court (1934–37) at his own request after being passed over for promotion to chief justice in Rangoon. It thus seems that his career in South Asia lasted only twelve years (1925–37). On Cunliffe's career as a Rangoon High Court judge and his sympathies with the Burmese nationalist movement see Ba U, *My Burma: Autobiography of a President* (New York: Taplinger, 1959), 116–33.

173. *Sarat Chandra Chakravarty v. Emp.*, 465.

174. The corroboration rule was central in *Maung Ba Tin v. King-Emperor*; see *Burma Law Journal* 5 (1926): 112–13. However, the more common pattern was that corroboration was mentioned only briefly in pre-1933 rape decisions. For example see the following: *Musst. Chundeea v. Jhotee Roy*, Reports of cases determined in the court of Nizamut Adawlut, (1852): 3:28–29; *Mir Moze Ali v. Emp.*; *Soosalal Bania v. Emp.*, AIR Nag. (1925): 74–77; *Kala and Others v. Emperor*, MANU/LA/0150/1929; *Sreehari Swarnakar v. Emp.*, 132–34; and *Hanuman Sarma v. Emperor*, 723–27. Among the cases

This ignored the earlier gender-neutral framing of the rule, which also applied to same-sex cases under IPC s.377 ("carnal intercourse against the order of nature," including sodomy).[175] Cunliffe's framing in *Sikandar Mian* incorporated the figure of the mendacious female:

> As it has been pointed out both in England and in India, a rule has grown up that Judges when they charge juries in cases of this kind ought never to omit delivering a serious caution to the jury with regard to accepting the uncorroborated evidence of a woman to support a sexual charge against an accused person. . . . The way the rule has developed now is that the presiding Judge should tell the jury that they ought to scrutinize the uncorroborated evidence of a woman or girl with the greatest possible care, because it has been found by experience extending over many years that it is often dangerous that a man should be convicted on such uncorroborated testimony.[176]

He added part two almost as a postscript, noting that judges usually attached a rider that the jury still could accept the uncorroborated evidence of the accuser, after proper scrutiny and considering the judge's caution.[177]

The final move in this line of progression was simply to eliminate part two, only warning the jury of the dangers of convicting based on the accuser's uncorroborated testimony. This occurred in two Calcutta High Court decisions from 1938–40, this time by two other Calcutta High Court judges, Mahim Chandra Ghose and Charles Bartley.[178] In *Ebadi Khan v. Emperor* (1938), a young married woman named Lakmi Moni Dasi accused three men of abducting her from her parents' home and raping her in another house, returning her twenty-four hours later. The men were convicted of abduction, but not of rape, in the Sessions

surveyed here, the first Calcutta High Court judgment to extensively discuss corroboration for rape was *Nur Ahmed*; it was issued one month before *Surendra Nath Das.*

175. For s.377 sodomy cases involving corroboration see *Sardar Ahmad v. Emperor*, AIR Lah. (1914): 565–66; *Ganpat v. Emperor*, AIR Lah. (1918): 322–23; and especially the Calcutta case of *Bal Mukundo Singh v. Emperor*, MANU/WB/0262/1935. On antisodomy law in South Asian history see Anjali Arondekar, *For the Record: On Sexuality and the Colonial Archive in India* (Duke University Press, 2009), 67–96; Jessica Hinchy, *Governing Gender and Sexuality in Colonial India: The Hijra, c. 1850–1900* (Cambridge University Press, 2019); and Jyoti Puri, *Sexual States: Governance and the Struggle over the Antisodomy Law in India* (Duke University Press, 2016), 49–73. Relatedly, see Heath, "Torture."

176. *Sikandar Mian v. Emp.*, 321–22.

177. *Sikandar Mian v. Emp.*, 322.

178. Ghose was the second judge in *Emp. v. Nur Ahmed* (1933), alongside Lort-Williams. The discussion of corroboration in this case set the stage for *Surendra Nath Das v. Emp.*, which was decided soon after by Lort-Williams (with Henderson), also in the Calcutta High Court.

Court. This judge included part one of the corroboration rule in his instructions to the jury, but not part two. On appeal, Justice Ghose approved this version of the corroboration rule: "The learned Judge properly directed the jury that on the charge of rape there was no corroboration of the story of the young woman and that it is not prudent to convict an accused person of such an offence on the uncorroborated testimony of the woman. . . . We find no misdirection or material non-direction. The verdict of the jury must therefore stand."[179]

Bartley gave a two-word concurrence in *Ebadi Khan*, but two years later, in 1940, he delivered a full opinion in another rape case. *Harendra Prosad Bagchi v. Emperor* was a child rape case. A girl named Fudan Dasi, about nine years old, went to her neighbor's house to get some *alochal* (a kind of rice). On her way back, the shop owner defendant lured her into his store by promising her sweets. Fudan Dasi alleged that he shut the door, laid her on a *dhokra* (quilt), and sexually assaulted her.

A wealth of evidence confirmed the girl's account. Blood and sperm were found on the quilt.[180] The blood was presumably human. It was not clear whether Ganguly's sperm staining method from Agra was used on the sperm. The medical examination supported the claim of rape. There was witness testimony both about what the girl, once released by the shop owner, had told her mother and other villagers, and about the shop owner's attempt to beg the girl's family for forgiveness the next day. There was corroboration, in other words, and in child rape cases, consent was a nonissue.

The lower judge warned the jury about the danger of conviction based on uncorroborated testimony of the accuser (part one), but he failed to mention that the jury still could convict if it believed the accuser's testimony (part two). And, in any case, there *was* corroborating evidence, and the jury did convict. On appeal, Bagchi's lawyer tried to get the conviction thrown out because of the judge's failure to mention part two. Justices Bartley and Sen of the Calcutta High Court refused. Bartley found that the judge's failure to include part two in fact operated in Bagchi's favor—and even so, he was still convicted. Thus, the failure to include part two in a judge's instructions to the jury did not necessarily invalidate a conviction. A judge could validly warn of the risk of conviction on uncorroborated testimony *without telling the jury that it could make an exception.*

---

179. *Ebadi Khan and Others v. Emperor*, AIR Cal. (1938): 463.

180. The Sessions judge found that the blood and sperm were not corroborative evidence because the quilt belonged to the defendant, and the stains could have been deposited there through prior actions other than rape. However, on appeal, Justice Sen found that they were of corroborative value because the girl had mentioned a quilt specifically in her account, saying that she had been raped on it. *Harendra Prosad Bagchi v. Emperor*, 463.

Bartley seemed driven by the desire to uphold a conviction in a clear child rape case, but his opinion in *Bagchi* was also the final tightening of the corroboration rule.

Justice Sen, intriguingly, tried to rewind this line of Calcutta cases and return to *Surendra Nath Das*. He questioned his British colleagues' import of the English corroboration rule at all. Sen suggested that female mendacity was more of a problem in England than in India:

> The manners, customs and mode of life of women in this country are very different from those of women in England. A rule or practice which appropriately may be of general application there would not necessarily have the same utility or application here. If this be the English rule or practice I do not think that it is desirable in cases of this description to import it without qualification here. The Indian law of evidence nowhere suggests such an inflexible rule and conditions here do not, in my opinion, warrant the engrafting of such a rule on our system. . . . I do not think that any such inflexible rule was actually laid down in [*Surendra Nath Das*].[181]

In effect, Sen was siding with Khondkar, the legal remembrancer in *Surendra Nath Das* who tried to tell Lort-Williams that there was no corroboration rule for rape in Indian law. This was the initial "provocation" that set Lort-Williams on the path to cementing the corroboration rule in Indian law.

By this point, though, Sen's protest was too late. The Calcutta line of cases had steadily embedded the corroboration rule in Indian law and then closed off the workarounds. A year after *Bagchi*, the Bombay High Court picked up the thread and applied the stricter version of the corroboration rule in the police rape case of *Emperor v. Mahadeo Tatya* (1941). *Bagchi* had applied this version of the corroboration rule in a way that upheld a child rape conviction, one of the most extreme rape scenarios. By contrast, *Tatya* used the stricter rule to overturn the conviction of another of the most shocking types of cases: rape by a police officer.[182] *Mahadeo Tatya* took advantage of the opportunity created by *Bagchi*, in other words, and brought the Calcutta High Court's project to Bombay.

---

181. *Harendra Prosad Bagchi v. Emp.*, 464. For a postcolonial case on the corroboration rule asserting that Western women were more likely to lie about rape than Indian women see *Bharwada Bhoginbhai Hirjibhai v. State of Gujarat*, para. 9–12.

182. The trial and appellate judges in *Mahadeo Tatya* disagreed over the importance of the accused's status as a police officer. According to Chief Justice Beaumont of the Bombay High Court, the fact that the accused was a police constable was irrelevant because he was off duty at the time of the offense. *Emp. v. Mahadeo Tatya*, 122.

In *Mahadeo Tatya*, a married girl named Baloobai, age fifteen, was selling ghee near the seashore in Bombay. Tatya was a police constable who was on duty in the neighborhood. He wanted to buy some ghee and arranged for Baloobai to deliver it to his address at his sister's home in Kamathipura, Bombay's red light district.[183] Baloobai delivered it after Tatya had finished his shift. By her account, he trapped her inside and raped her, then sent her to the nearest railway station with the second defendant, who robbed her (with a weapon) of her jewelry, ghee pot, and scales.

Baloobai initially reported only the robbery to the police, but under questioning also divulged the rape. The medical exam by the police surgeon the next day showed no injuries to her private parts or other parts of her body, and no seminal stains were found on her skirt by the Bombay chemical analyser. Her testimony was thus uncorroborated, but the jury convicted Tatya of rape by eight to one. The judge sentenced Tatya to transportation for life.

On appeal, the Bombay chief justice, J. W. F. Beaumont, along with Justices N. J. Wadia and K. B. Wassoodew, overturned the rape conviction. They also found the sentence excessive, a seven-year sentence of rigorous imprisonment being the standard sentence for "very bad" rape cases. The conviction itself was problematic, in Beaumont's view, because the lower judge had given what seemed like the corroboration rule as presented in *Surendra Nath Das*: He had given equal weight to part one and part two. What Beaumont wanted, though, was the corroboration rule without any exit option—part one without part two:

> In our opinion, in a case such as this, the Judge is bound to tell the jury that *it is a rule of the Court, in cases of rape, not to act on the evidence of the complainant without some corroboration, and where there is no corroboration, as in this case, to direct them that their proper course is to return a verdict of not guilty. . . .* [The learned judge] referred to the rule which requires corroboration, and pointed out, accurately enough, that it is not a statutory rule and that the verdict of a jury based on the uncorroborated testimony of the complainant would not be bad in law. *But he certainly did not tell the jury that it was their duty not to act on the uncorroborated testimony of the complainant in view of the experience of the Courts that such evidence is not sufficiently reliable. That is the rule both in this country and in England.*[184]

183. On the history of the sex trade in Kamathipura see Ashwini Tambe, *Codes of Misconduct: Regulating Prostitution in Late Colonial Bombay* (Delhi: Zubaan, 2009).

184. *Emp. v. Mahadeo Tatya*, 4. Italics added.

From Lort-Williams's outburst in 1933 Calcutta (in *Surendra Nath Das*) to Beaumont's version of the test in 1941 Bombay (in *Mahadeo Tatya*), the English corroboration rule was given special prominence in Indian law during the 1930s–40s. It was then made stricter, removing the jury's ability to make an exception in favor of a female accuser's uncorroborated testimony.[185]

The Law-Science Nexus

The precipitin test could provide strong evidence for some males accused of rape, particularly from the 1900s and 1910s. New sperm staining methods could provide strong evidence for many female accusers of rape, particularly from the 1930s and 1940s. The contrary advantages with each test—one to the accused and the other to the accuser—suggest that contrary to scholarly assumptions, forensic science did not always work preferentially toward males. However, these advances in forensic lab science unfolded in dynamic relation to legal developments, which affected how stain analysis was interpreted and used.

Timing and geography do not suggest a direct causal link between advances in sperm cell staining and the adoption of a stricter version of the corroboration rule. The leading case of *Surendra Nath Das* was decided in 1933, but Ganguly published a description of his new method three years later, in 1936. *Das* was decided in Calcutta, but Ganguly's lab was across the subcontinent, in Agra. In Calcutta, the imperial serologist's lab was still cautious in 1941 about declaring that a single tailless sperm cell (using Ganguly's staining method) counted as a "hit."

Nevertheless, judges across India and Burma were part of larger knowledge networks on South Asian forensic science. They would have been aware of the wave of new state forensic institutions, especially during the 1890s through the 1910s, and they would have encountered a growing body of evidence in their courtrooms that was scientific or medical, whether in written form (such as CE

185. After independence, the Indian courts returned to the *Surendra Nath Das* version of the test that gave equal weight to parts one and two, although they did not go as far as Khondkar and Sen would have liked. For example, see Ratanlal Ranchhoddas and Dhirajlal Keshavlal Thakore, *The Indian Penal Code*, 19th ed. (Bombay Law Reporter Office, 1948), 294; *Shamsher Bahadur Saxena and Others v. State of Bihar*, MANU/BH/0099,1956, para. 23; and Baxi, *Public Secrets*, 29–33. The corroboration rule has been the target of social reform movements in postcolonial India, particularly after the Mathura case. See Kalpana Kannabiran, "A Ravished Justice: Half a Century of Judicial Discourse on Rape," in *De-Eroticizing Assault: Essays on Modesty, Honor and Power*, ed. K. Kannabiran and V. Kannabiran (Calcutta: Stree, 2002), 142–48.

certificates) or in person (such as the chief inspector of explosives).[186] The evidence from some of these experts, particularly when based on lab work, often determined the outcome of cases. (And as we will see in chapters 4 and 5, the CEs were insulated from cross-examination by Indian criminal procedure, which gave them tremendous power with little accountability.) In addition, every year judges read about the latest advances in South Asia's forensic labs through the annual CE reports. These reports were sold at authorized bookshops across India and Burma.[187] They were also routinely sent to the region's district magistrates, Sessions judges, High Court chief justices, and registrars of appellate courts "for the information of the judges."[188]

Appellate judges were sometimes dissatisfied with statements in CE certificates (chapters 4 and 5). An intriguing counterpoint, however, and a more significant one long term, is discernible in CE reports: These forensic analysts struggled in their reports to manage, and correct, the high and unrealistic expectations of police and the legal profession with respect to what science could do.[189] For instance, the Punjab CE William Center noted in 1879 that there was a popular misconception, even among magistrates, that bloodstain analysis could determine the species, body part, and sex of the creature from which the blood had come.[190] T. F. Owens, the CE of Burma, echoed this sentiment fifty years later when he wrote with an almost audible sigh, "The Chemical Examiner is not a magician."[191] And yet over time, it did indeed become possible to determine the species of origin of a bloodstain, as this chapter and the previous one have shown. By 1901 (and possibly before), CEs were identifying vaginal epithelial

186. See appendix 3.

187. For example see "List of Agents Authorized to Sell United Provinces Government Publications," in "Annual Report of the CE to Government, United Provinces and Central Provinces, for the Year 1939," back of title page (IOR/V/24/417).

188. For example see order by H. J. Maynard, judicial and general secretary to government, Punjab, in Proceedings of the Lieut.-Governor of Punjab, Home (Medical and Sanitary) Dept., no. 669 (May 15, 1899), 3, in "Report of the CE to Government, Punjab, for the Year 1898" (IOR/V/24/418); order by B. T. Gibson, financial secretary to government, Punjab, in Proceedings of Lieut.-Governor, Punjab, in the Home (Medical) Dept., no. 15828-M (May 11, 1920), n.p. in "Report of the CE to Government, Punjab, for the Year 1919" (IOR/V/24/418); and "Report of the CE to Government, Madras, for the Year 1909," 14 (which also lists the Crown prosecutor as a recipient) (IOR/P/8442).

189. Similar expectations existed among legal professionals in the US during the nineteenth century. See Jennifer L. Mnookin, "Idealizing Science and Demonizing Experts: An Intellectual History of Expert Evidence," *Villanova Law Review* 52, no. 4 (2007): 788–93.

190. CE Report for Punjab 1879, 18–19. From the 1850s see similarly Norman Chevers, *A Manual of Medical Jurisprudence for Bengal and the North-Western Provinces* (Calcutta: Bengal Military Orphan Press, 1856), 347.

191. "Report of the CE to Government, Burma, for the Year 1929," 2 (IOR/V/24/426). Owens was describing the message of his teaching lectures at the Criminal Investigation Department's training school.

cells in stain cases, which offered clues as to sex and body part when found in blood.[192] Advances in forensic science, then, only confirmed nonscientific actors' faith in science, even if the latter was sometimes unrealistic. Appellate judges' general faith in lab science was an important complement to their work on the corroboration rule.

The more forensic science developed, the more the legal system could lean on it—and it did. Forensic science offered a seductive new array of tools, and the corroboration rule tightened around them. Advances in forensic science did not necessarily cause the stricter version of the corroboration rule to be adopted, but arguably they did make it more palatable. Even the definition of "corroboration" became increasingly synonymous with scientific and medical evidence. Compare the 1852 case of *Musst. Chundeea v. Jhotee Roy*, which described any evidence supporting the accuser's account as "other corroborative *testimony*," with the 1941 *Mahadeo Tatya* case, which described corroborative evidence thus: "Where rape is denied, the sort of corroboration one looks for is *medical evidence* showing injury to the private parts of the complainant, injury to other parts of her body, which may have been occasioned in a struggle, seminal stains on her clothes or the clothes of the accused, or on the places where the offence is alleged to have been committed."[193]

Where did this interwoven history of stain testing and case law leave women and girls who reported rape? Those with scientific evidence to confirm their account—like an intact sperm cell—might have had a chance in the newly scientized courts of the 1930s–40s. But those who only had human testimony to confirm their claims found themselves worse off. By the 1940s the courts in South Asia wanted scientific or medical evidence, not the word of human witnesses.[194] This preference was part of a larger global trend favoring trace evidence over human testimony, driven in part by psychologists' findings since the late nineteenth century that human memory was malleable and unreliable.[195]

---

192. CE and Bacteriologist Report for North-West Province, Oudh and Central Provinces 1901, 3.

193. *Musst. Chundeea v. Jhotee Roy*, 28; and *Emp. v. Mahadeo Tatya*, 122–23 (also cited in *P. F. Conroy v. Emp.*, para. 7). Italics added to both quotations.

194. Historians of rape in other parts of the world have found a similar pattern during this period. For an exception see Lara Bergers, "A Culture of Testimony: The Importance of 'Speaking Witnesses' in Dutch Sexual Crimes Investigations and Trials, 1930–1960," in *Forensic Cultures in Modern Europe*, ed. Willemijn Ruberg et al. (Manchester University Press, 2023), 49–70.

195. The work of Hans Gross was particularly influential. See Heather Wolffram, *Forensic Psychology in Germany: Witnessing Crime, 1880–1939* (Palgrave Macmillan, 2018), 21–58, esp. at 44–45; and Ian Burney and Neil Pemberton, *Murder and the Making of English CSI* (Johns Hopkins University Press, 2016), 12, 14–15. On competing models that likened human memory to recording devices see Alison Winter, *Memory: Fragments of a Modern History* (University of Chicago Press, 2012).

As was true in other parts of the empire, British Indian courts leaned on forensic science to solve the perceived problems of native and female mendacity.[196] This point was perhaps clearest on sperm identification. Even though Ganguly's technique revealed the presence of sperm cells in many seminal stain cases, this did not cause courts to revise their earlier assumptions about female mendacity. Rather, the new method confirmed for judges the preeminent value of scientific evidence, particularly in a colonial context. In one dimension the contest between bloodstain and sperm analysis may read like a contest between tests that advantaged the male accused or the female accuser, respectively, but the larger story was that the courts' general awareness of advances in forensic science allowed them to insist on scientific and medical evidence in rape cases. This insistence was clear when they adopted a stricter version of the corroboration rule, requiring that "corroborative evidence" meant scientific or medical evidence (rather than the testimony of other witnesses) and preventing juries from making an exception to the rule.

And yet the belief that forensic science was the only truly reliable evidence and an antidote to dissimulation was misplaced: Falsity could be generated *from within* forensic systems, just as much as from without. Falsity may be the product of intentional acts such as expert corruption or the planting of animal blood to frame an enemy. But falsity may also emanate from less deliberate sources, including lax rules of criminal procedure and misalignment between legal and scientific "truth mechanics." It is this broader concept of falsity—both intentional and unintentional, flowing from structures and processes as much as individual decisions—that the second part of this book now explores.

196. For instance see Elizabeth Thornberry, *Colonizing Consent: Rape and Governance in South Africa's Eastern Cape* (Cambridge University Press, 2019), 253–54.

Part II

FALSITY FROM WITHIN

4

EXPERT MISCONDUCT

The chemical examiners' annual reports create an astonishing archive of records on toxicology, serology, bacteriology, and explosives from the 1870s until 1947 (figure 9). Among them, the 1879 report for Punjab stands out.[1] In a classic act of colonial summary, the Punjab CE, a Scottish physician named William Center, provided a detailed overview of how medico-legal systems worked in British India. He noted that CEs and civil surgeons in India did not function like experts in the imperial metropole. For poison murder trials in England, "all the scientific witnesses, medical and chemical, give their evidence personally as to the facts they have observed and state the opinions they have formed from them, with their reasons. All these can be cross-examined, and the opinions of other experts may be called in."[2]

The South Asian model of the scientific expert was different. First, CEs did not have to appear in court to be cross-examined under oath on their written certificates, which constituted evidence in and of themselves (CrPC s.510).[3] Usually, they did

1. "Report of the CE to Government, Punjab, for the Year 1879," 17–18 (IOR/V/24/418).

2. CE Report for Punjab 1879, 13.

3. For most of the late colonial period, the relevant provision was s.510 of the CrPC (1882, replicated in 1898): "Any document purporting to be a report under the hand of the Chemical Examiner or Assistant Chemical Examiner to Government, upon any matter or thing duly submitted to him for examination or analysis and report in the course of any proceeding under this Code, may be used as evidence in any inquiry, trial or other proceeding under this Code." "Act No. X of 1882: An Act to consolidate and amend the law relating to Criminal Procedure" (IOR/V/8/54). Earlier versions of this provision were s.370 of CrPC (1861) and s.325 of CrPC (1872), the latter applying during William Center's time.

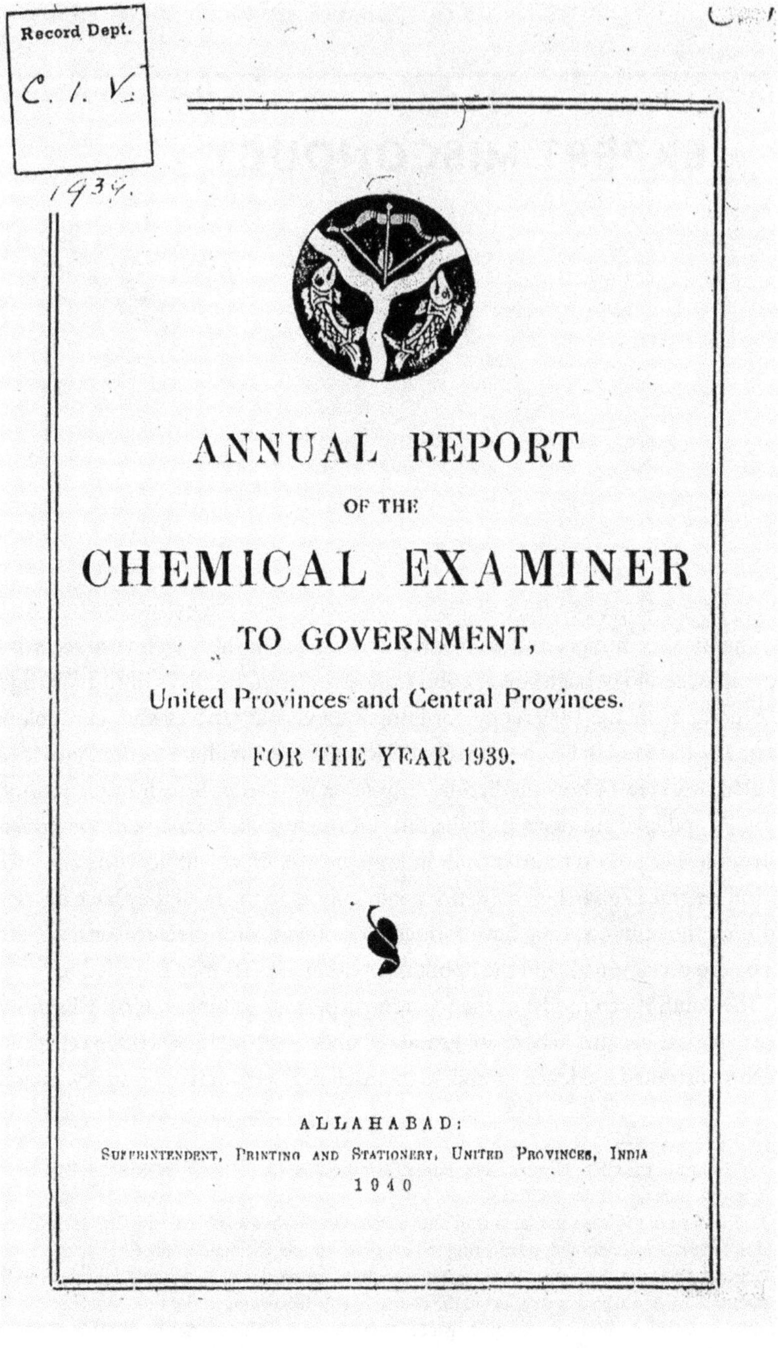

ANNUAL REPORT

OF THE

CHEMICAL EXAMINER

TO GOVERNMENT,

United Provinces and Central Provinces.

FOR THE YEAR 1939.

ALLAHABAD:
SUPERINTENDENT, PRINTING AND STATIONERY, UNITED PROVINCES, INDIA
1940

FIGURE 9. / Title page of a CE report, "Annual Report of the Chemical Examiner to Government, United Provinces and Central Provinces, for 1939." From the British Library Collection (IOR/V/24/417).

not come to court. Second, medical experts who were cross-examined in court, like civil surgeons (under CrPC s.509), normally did not face off against another expert in the same field who could contradict them.[4] Essentially, CEs and civil surgeons acted like court-appointed experts (whether in writing or in person), a model that Center likened more to the German medical "referee" than to anything in English law. Like others in Anglophone scientific circles before World War I, Center felt the German model of the single, authoritative, court-appointed expert was superior to the messy English courtroom tussle between partisan experts.[5]

The Indian criminal trial did not embody the adversarial principle for scientific experts, and Center approved of this: "Scientific men" doubted that the adversarial method was appropriate for science. The Indian (and German) model avoided the paralysis and frustration so frequent in common law "battle of the experts" scenarios that left judge and jury, as scientific laypeople, confused (see chapter 5). Center failed to mention that the Indian model also concentrated power in state lab experts, giving cover to carelessness and corruption.

This chapter explores misconduct among forensic experts as a type of behavior, whether negligent or corrupt, that produced false evidence. It begins by considering the significance of careless or corrupt British experts vis-à-vis foundational colonial beliefs about British rule in India. More specifically, it reveals how, on the one hand, these dissimulating or careless figures posed a threat to race- and class-based narratives about corruption in India, and on the other hand, how their existence undermined the new forensic science for India, which presented itself as a solution to another kind of perceived falsity—the problem of native mendacity. Entrenched colonial fears of native mendacity led colonizers to give resources and status to forensic science, as we have seen, and in some respects forensic science developed, innovated, and flourished more in India than elsewhere, as did an early iteration of the innocence movement—energized by racialized and gendered fears of native dissimulation. In this way the colonial context mattered a great deal to the evolution of the field. But in the spiral of colonial rule, this meant that any *expert* falsity, broadly defined to include carelessness and incompetence as well as deliberate falsification and corruption, threatened not only the prestige of the science itself but British justifications for rule and its antidotes to "native mendacity" as well.

---

4. CE Report for Punjab 1879, 13. For an exception see the child rape case involving Drs. Falvey and Bhargava in this chapter. For most of the late colonial period, s.509 of CrPC (1882, replicated in 1898) was the relevant provision for civil surgeons. See H. T. Prinsep, *Code of Criminal Procedure Being Act V of 1898*, 13th ed. (Calcutta: Thacker, Spink, 1901), 497–99.

5. CE Report for Punjab 1879, 13–14.

The chapter focuses on allegations against two European and two South Asian forensic experts accused of misconduct. The cases of W. S. Newman (1893) and C. V. Falvey (1939) exposed the risks of the Indian model that put strong reliance on forensic experts' evidence with few opportunities to challenge or check their work. Both individuals were dealt with quietly by the colonial state. Allegations of corruption were processed differently when the experts were South Asian, however—a contrast visible in the proceedings against Indian physicians J. K. Banerji (1933) and K. D. Mehta (1940). The reduced accountability of experts in South Asia facilitated misconduct—and falsity—*from within* forensic systems. In turn, misconduct cases enacted racialized double standards and anxieties about the fragility of truth mechanics under colonial conditions.

Discourses of Corruption and Forensic Science

The possibility that European experts might be corrupt threatened a number of foundational assumptions of the Raj. First and foremost, it destabilized race- and class-based representations of corruption. As historians of corruption and colonialism have shown, the corrupt colonized subject was a common stereotype, and the colonizer used an anticorruption ethic to justify European rule.[6] These stereotypes also promulgated class-related elements. A long-standing discourse about "Oriental despots" portrayed Indian rulers as decadent, cruel, capricious, and corrupt.[7] This stereotype about elite corruption informed British decisions

---

6. See, by Jonathan Saha, "'Uncivilized Practitioners': Medical Subordinates, Medico-Legal Evidence, and Misconduct in Colonial Burma, 1875–1907," *South East Asia Research* 20, no. 3 (2012): 423–43; *Law, Disorder and the Colonial State: Corruption in Burma c.1900* (Palgrave Macmillan, 2013); and "'Devious Documents': Corruption and Paperwork in Colonial Burma, Circa 1900," in *Subverting Empire: Deviance and Disorder in the British Colonial World*, ed. Will Jackson and Emily J. Manktelow (Palgrave Macmillan, 2015); along with Jens Ivo Engels and Frédéric Monier, "Colonial and Corruption History: Conclusions and Future Research Perspectives," in *Corruption, Empire, and Colonialism in the Modern Era: A Global Perspective*, ed. Ronald Kroeze, Pol Dalmau, and Frédéric Monier (Palgrave Macmillan, 2021), 344–46. See also Robert Travers, *Ideology and Empire in Eighteenth-Century India* (Cambridge University Press, 2007), 194, 199; and T. C. A. Achintya, "Practitioners of the Law: Legal Professionals in British South Asia 1770–1870" (PhD diss., University of Virginia, 2025).

7. For example see Francis Buchanan, *A Journey from Madras Through the Countries of Mysore, Canara, and Malabar* (London, 1807), 2:551, noted in Santhosh Abraham, "The Making of Colonial Law, Discipline and Corruption in British India," *Journal of Indian Law and Society* 1, no. 2 (2010): 80. See also James Jaffe, *Ironies of Colonial Governance: Law, Custom and Justice in Colonial India* (Cambridge University Press, 2015), 9–10.

to intervene in the internal affairs of princely states.[8] In the medico-legal world, though, it was the lower-ranked official who by convention was deemed untrustworthy. Race, class, and caste often converged in the figure of the low-level South Asian functionary who accepted bribes or interfered with public processes for private gain. Above all, British colonizers associated rank-and-file Indian policemen with corruption. Both popular depictions and occasional inquiries into low-level police corruption abounded during the Raj.[9]

Fear of low-level corruption by Indian state actors influenced the design of medico-legal processes. In particular, this anxiety figured prominently in methods used for the collection and transportation of forensic evidence from the crime scene to the regional CE's lab (see map 1). Each lab did testing for a physical territory and population often two to three times the size of England. Human and animal viscera had to be transported over long distances, which raised chain-of-custody concerns. Given the large volume of material flowing into each lab, these samples had to travel unescorted and without illegitimate interference from employees of the civil surgeon, police, postal service, railways, or CE.

Between 1880 and 1908, colonial officials debated how best to send forensic samples to CE labs by post and rail. Occasionally, a packet of human or animal body parts burst open en route, spilling its rotten, stinking contents and causing a health risk to postal and railway workers.[10] "Nearly every day bottles of putrid viscera are arriving," complained Bengal CE L. A. Waddell, noting that the "overpowering stench" that emanated from such packets made it hard for anyone to stay in the lab and constituted "a grave danger to the health of everyone" employed there.[11] These episodes prompted officials to reassess their preservation and transportation methods. Historian Uponita Mukherjee has illuminated a debate from the 1890s on whether saline, alcohol, or formalin was the best preservative fluid (chapter 1). Opponents of saline argued that using a salt solution

---

8. For example see Mark Knights and Zak Leonard, "Bribery in Baroda: The Politics of Corruption in Nineteenth-Century India," in *Corruption, Empire, and Colonialism in the Modern Era: A Global Perspective*, ed. Ronald Kroeze, Pol Dalmau, and Frédéric Monier (Palgrave Macmillan, 2021).

9. See William Gould, *Bureaucracy, Community and Influence in India: Society and the State, 1930s–1960s* (Routledge, 2011); and Radha Kumar, *Police Matters: The Everyday State and Caste Politics in South India, 1900–1975* (Cornell University Press, 2021).

10. For example see "Issue of instructions for the careful packing of human and other viscera sent through the Post Office or by rail to the Chemical Examiner for analysis," Home: Judicial, Proc. no. 157–68, December 1897, part A (NAI).

11. "No. R/1121. From Surgeon-Major L. A. Waddell, Chemical Examiner to Government of Bengal. To the Inspector-General of Civil Hospitals, Bengal. Calcutta, 29 Oct. 1896," 4, in "Preservative Medicine (common salt) to be used in packing viscera in certain cases," Home: Medical, Proc. no. 157, May 1897 (NAI).

heightened the risk of corruption (namely the mixing of poison into saline preservative to frame a rival) by the local civil surgeon's low-level staff, always South Asian. Distrust of menial staff also accounted for the rule that the local civil surgeon, and not his subordinates, should send the parcels through the post office and be held personally responsible for the evidence sent.[12]

Colonial administrators also worried that workers in the postal service and railroads might tamper with evidence as it passed through their hands.[13] Officials agreed, for instance, that no description of the contents should be given on the outside of these parcels, even though this meant that packets could not be insured.[14] This position was striking for its disregard of religious sensitivities: Many Indian workers objected to handling dead matter, which was ritually polluting. It was best not to let them know what was inside, agreed British officials.[15] They seemed oblivious to the lessons of the 1857 rebellion. It began with rumors that Indian soldiers were being exposed surreptitiously to polluting substances, namely beef and pork fat in rifle cartridges that they had to tear open with their teeth.

Packing and sealing procedures also aimed to prevent postal and railway workers from tampering with evidence in transit. Around 1900, samples were put into special glass bottles with stoppers, both of which bore etched serial numbers. The lip of the bottle was sealed with bee's or candle wax, then the stopper was tied down "with bladder or leather" and sealed again with the same wax. A seal was stamped at multiple points on all wax. All stamps had to be identical and made by the same device. "The device must in no case be that of a current coin or merely a series of straight, curved, or crossed lines" or consist of "undecipherable vernacular impressions." After sealing, the jar would be turned upside down and left for a few minutes to ensure that there were no leaks. It was then packed into an unmarked tin or wooden box stuffed with raw cotton. By 1908, only the civil surgeon at the point of origin and the CE at the destination point had a key to these boxes.[16] Once at the CE's lab, the bottles were kept under lock

12. "Rules for preserving and packing human and other viscera for transmission to the CEs for analysis," 29, in "Revised rules for the preservation and transmission of human and other viscera to the CEs for analysis," Home: Medical, Proc. no. 64–78, August 1898 (NAI).

13. For instance see untitled, *ABP*, July 8, 1886.

14. General correspondence (July 1898), 5, in "Revised rules for the preservation and transmission of human and other viscera."

15. "Note No. 7152," 4, in "Transmission by post of packages containing human or other viscera to the Chemical Examiner for analysis," Home: Judicial, Proc. no. 263–72, January 1880 (NAI).

16. "Rules for preserving and packing human and other viscera for transmission to the CEs for analysis," 29; and "No. 514–422, from P. W. Monie, under secretary to the government of India, to chief secretary to the government of Madras and others. Simla, 14 May 1908," 13–14, in "Reports

and key, using padlocks sent directly from England and not unpacked in India "before coming into use in this office." The keys were stored in a special iron key box. The key to this box was always in the possession of the CE. The doors and windows of the lab were also lined with iron bars.[17]

In short, all measures were taken to ensure that no one interfered with the evidence between when it was sent and when it was received by the CE—but none of these safeguards mattered if the civil surgeon or CE *himself* acted improperly. The possibility that senior British experts could be corrupt inverted racial and caste-based stereotypes, making a mockery of the focus on low-status South Asian workers.

High-level expert misconduct upended another narrative, too. These cases corroded the credibility of India's new forensic science, and its status. As Waddell and Lyon's treatise put it in 1921, forensic science mattered in India because "expert medical testimony, important in every country, is especially so in the East, where it is often the only trustworthy evidence on which hangs the liberty or the life of a human being."[18] And yet, as high-level expert misdeeds revealed, falsity could also come from within the system—through acts of misconduct, including negligence and corruption. When European experts tampered with evidence or gave suspicious expert witness testimony out of carelessness or for bribes, to secure convictions or acquittals, or to avoid prosecution themselves, they undermined the promise that forensic science would solve the problem of deception in the courtroom and subverted the trope of native mendacity.

Alcohol and Bloodstains in South India

William Samuel Newman had been the assistant CE of Madras for fifteen years when he was dismissed in 1893 for misconduct. Newman had no medical qualifications and was not a member of the Indian Medical Service (IMS), a status that made him more expendable than IMS member Civil Surgeon C. V. Falvey (to whom I return below). There were two types of allegations against Newman, one

of the CEs for 1907, Provision of special bottles and boxes for transmission of viscera to the CE for examination," Home: Medical, Proc. no. 114–23, July 1908, part A (NAI).

17. "No. 514–422, from P. W. Monie (14 May 1908)," 14. For corruption-related concerns when a CE left an *almirah* (or cabinet) unlocked at the lab see statement to the chief secretary to government from T. H. Pope, acting CE (Madras, December 7, 1891), no. 1032, 10, in "Memorial from Mr. W. S. Newman, late Assistant CE, Madras, appealing against his dismissal" [hereafter "Memorial from Newman"], April 7, 1893 (IOR/L/PJ/6/346, file 879).

18. Isidore Bernadotte Lyon, *Lyon's Medical Jurisprudence for India*, 7th ed., ed. L. A. Waddell (Calcutta: Thacker, Spink, 1921), 2.

more comical than the other. The first concerned alcohol. CEs tested substances not only for criminal courts, but also for Customs and Excise. Particularly in port cities like Madras and Calcutta, these labs strained under the enormous volume of testing required for tax purposes.[19] When alcohol was sent in, CEs tested both for alcohol content and adulteration, performing both a tax and a public health service. The volume of alcohol submitted was larger than what was required for testing, and the remaining quantity was supposed to be returned to Customs authorities. In Madras, though, the volume sent back to Customs dwindled during the early 1890s.[20] When the collector of sea customs inquired, an Indian colleague of Newman's named Rungaswami Iyengar (himself a nondrinker) reported that he had seen Newman skim off extra alcohol from the samples. Iyengar had observed Newman instruct servants to pack it in his tiffin box for later. He had also seen Newman drink the extra alcohol in the lab.[21] Iyengar said he cordially asked Newman to stop and repeated this request to a servant. But Newman persisted. K. Dowlet Roy, a servant at the lab, said he had seen Newman take away spirits fifty or sixty times.[22] Three other lab servants said that Newman brought an empty bottle from home and took it home filled with alcohol.[23]

Newman's response was twofold. On the one hand, he claimed that his two "inveterate enemies," two Indians at the lab named Goolab Roy and Cunniah Naidoo, had been scheming against him since 1884 because they wanted his job. Newman claimed he had also caught Cunniah Naidoo stealing something out of his locked office drawer, having opened it with keys extracted from Newman's coat pocket.[24] After Newman's dismissal, Goolab Roy had indeed stepped into Newman's post, although he was no more than "a mere manipulist in the Laboratory without even pretension to chemical science," in Newman's

19. For example see cover letter from inspector general of civil hospitals, Bengal (February 22 1904), 1, in "Report of the CE to Government, Bengal for the Year 1903" (IOR/V/24/422).

20. Letter from W. P. Austin, collector of sea customs to Madras CE (Madras, December 3, 1891), 7, in "Memorial from Newman."

21. Letter from T. [Rungaswami Iyengar] ([Madras], November 30, 1891), 7, and "Statement made by Mr. Rungaswami Iyengar B.A. in continuation of his report dated November 30, 1891," 8, both in "Memorial from Newman."

22. "Statement made by K. Dowlet Roy, Lascar employed under Mr Rungaswamy Iyengar in the spirits obscuration tests," 8 (translated from Hindustani, undated), in "Memorial from Newman."

23. "Statement made by C. Moonooswamy, Gas lascar in the CE's Office on the subject of Mr. Newman's appropriating spirits sent from the Sea Customs to his own use," 9 (translated from Tamil, undated); and untitled statement by T. H. Pope on lascars Govinden and Ragavelo (translated from Tamil, undated), in "Memorial from Newman."

24. "Memorial of the Ex-Assistant Chemical Examiner Mr. W. S. Newman clearing him of the charges by reference to enclosures, and seeking redress for his summary dismissal from the Public Service," from W. S. Newman to Governor, Madras (August 1892), 4–5, in "Memorial from Newman."

words. (In contrast, Newman's boss called Roy "an intelligent chemist" who was careful, as "able and practical" as Newman, and "thoroughly versed in medico-legal testing.")[25] Cunniah Naidoo was "an illiterate man" who had entered the CE's office as "a mere laboratory attendant or lascar" and had also been promoted as a result of Newman's dismissal.[26] At a time when Indians were rising through the ranks in many professions across India, the competitive racial dynamics here were hard to miss—as was Newman's gesture toward the "native mendacity" stereotype. But at the same time, Newman admitted that he had been drinking the extra alcohol. Intriguingly, he turned to the idea of corruption as culture, a longtime explanation favored by Britons to explain South Asian corruption.[27] If Newman was guilty of misappropriation of spirits, "it would equally involve every single individual in the Chemical Examiner's office, except Mr. Rungaswamy Iyengar, from the Chemical Examiner himself downwards, it being a well-known fact that from the custom of the office, long prior to my entertainment, samples of articles sent to be tested and retained for obvious reasons were used for the private purposes of the establishment."[28] In other words, Newman drank the alcohol because he thought it was allowed by the culture of the lab.

Unsurprisingly, his superiors disagreed with his broad definition of "private purposes of the establishment." Many forensic labs used extraneous materials from one process for another kind of testing. Several decades after Newman's case, for instance, the imperial serologist's department in Calcutta needed human blood to make antihuman serum for precipitin testing. Human blood was not a commodity that could be purchased, but the lab was able to use the extra blood left over from its Wassermann testing of private individuals for syphilis.[29] So forensic labs did use leftover materials for their own "private purposes." But satisfying one's own need to drink was different. If the concept underpinning

25. Letter from W. S. Newman to T. H. Pope, acting CE to government, Madras (Madras, December 2, 1891), 13; and letter from T. H. Pope, acting CE, to chief secretary to government (Madras, December 7, 1891), 10; both in "Memorial from Newman."

26. "Memorial of the Ex-Assistant CE Mr. W. S. Newman" (August 1892), 5, in "Memorial from Newman."

27. See Vinod Pavarala, "Cultures of Corruption and the Corruption of Culture: The East India Company and the Hastings Impeachment," in *Corrupt Histories*, ed. Emmanuel Kreike and William Chester Jordan (University of Rochester Press, 2004), 291.

28. Letter to T. H. Pope, acting CE, Madras, from W. S. Newman (Madras, February 11, 1892), 3, in "Memorial from Newman."

29. Statement by J. W. D. Megaw (April 1, 1933), 15, in "Transfer of the Imperial Serologist's Department to the direct control of the Government of India and revision of the emoluments of the Imperial Serologist," Finance: Expenditure-I, 1933, Proc. no. 83-Exl, 1933 (NAI). See also chapter 2.

corruption was the use of public goods for private gain, then Newman was guilty by his own admission.[30]

The second allegation was more consequential. Newman was accused of improper bloodstain analysis in the Triplicane murder case. On the night of June 15, 1891, two people were killed in Kistnampett, a neighborhood adjacent to the Triplicane area of Madras City. The accused, a mendicant named Ramcharan Doss, was convicted "on purely circumstantial evidence" and sentenced to death.[31] Here it was unclear whether Newman had in fact done anything corrupt.[32] For some, his case fell in the gray zone between corruption and negligence. For others, his case turned on a fundamental disagreement over the proper role of the forensic expert. Either way, as I will now tell, a distinctively colonial and controversial feature of Indian criminal procedure enabled Newman's dubious work to become evidence in a death penalty case.

Two and a half weeks after the Triplicane murders, the Madras police had sent a sealed packet to the Madras CE's lab. It contained a bloodstained iron chopper (a short-handled cleaver) and two pieces of cloth worn by the murder suspect when he was arrested three days after the killings. The chopper was the suspected murder weapon. Three days after the murders, it was found in a sewage drain not far from the scene of the crime. The police note asked whether any of these items bore stains of mammalian blood.[33]

In 1891, the precipitin test that would be able to identify the species of origin was still a decade or two away (see chapter 2). However, the Madras CE lab had other ways of answering the police's question. Newman first ran the guaiacum test to establish that the stains on the chopper blade were in fact blood.[34] With positive results, Newman then conducted microscopic analysis of the bloodstains, comparing the size of the red blood cells or corpuscles on the blade with those

30. For discussions of definitions of corruption see Diego Gambetta, "Corruption: An Analytical Map," in Kreike and Jordan, *Corrupt Histories*, 3–28; and Janine R. Wedel, "Rethinking Corruption in an Age of Ambiguity," *Annual Review of Law and Social Science* 8 (2012): 453–98.

31. "The Triplicane Double Murder," *TI*, August 15, 1891; and "The Memorial of the Ex-Assistant Chemical Examiner Mr. W. S. Newman," 10, in "Memorial from Newman."

32. On bribery and CE labs see cover letter (April 28, 1891), 1, to "Report of the CE to Government, Punjab, for the Year 1890" (IOR/V/24/418); "Report of the CE and Bacteriologist to Government, United Provinces of Agra and Oudh, and Central Provinces, for the Year 1915," 2 (IOR/V/24/415); and "Report of the CE and Bacteriologist to Government, United Provinces of Agra and Oudh, and Central Provinces, for the Year 1917," 2–3 (IOR/V/24/415).

33. Note from T. Weldon, Commissioner of Police, Madras, to the CE (Madras, July 2, 1891), 6, in "Paper from Col. T. Weldon, Commissioner of Police, Madras, to the Chief Secretary to Government (Madras, Sept. 10, 1891), No. 65," in "Memorial from Newman."

34. On the guaiacum test see *Lyon's Medical Jurisprudence*, 3rd ed., ed. L. A. Waddell (Calcutta: Thacker, Spink, 1904), 94–95.

of mammals. Newman found that here, too, the chopper blood was within the normal range of mammalian corpuscles.[35] Newman did not perform a further test that would be recommended by the Calcutta CE in hindsight: the spectroscopic test for oxyhemoglobin.[36] Once under suspicion for misconduct, though, Newman frantically wrote to experts elsewhere in India for confirmation that spectroscopic analysis would have been unlikely to detect mammalian blood. By Newman's account, the blade had been "subjected to the action of sewage matter by being thrown in and allowed to remain three or four days, the action of the filthy water and gases from decomposing filth tending to decompose the blood rendering its presence beyond detection by [a] test."[37] The Bengal CE agreed that the spectroscopic test would be unlikely to work, given the chopper's time in the sewer.[38]

But as with the alcohol issue, Newman's self-defense was focused on the wrong thing. In his written certificate, Newman had reported his finding of mammalian blood on the chopper's edge. He claimed that the rest of the blade was covered in thick mud on both sides.[39] Newman did not analyze the rest of the blade because he did not believe any of his tests could detect blood through mud (and sewage residue), a view questioned later by the Madras CE.[40] Rather than saying this in his certificate, though, Newman suggested that no mammalian blood was found elsewhere on the blade, implying that the rest of the blade *had* in fact been tested.[41]

This sloppiness mattered because the chopper had apparently been recovered from the sewer and used "for domestic purposes" before it was recovered by police.[42] Although he did not say so in his certificate, Newman thought the blood on the edge was fresh. It could be explained if the person who found the

---

35. On the microscopic analysis of bloodstains see *Lyon's Medical Jurisprudence* (1904), 95–97; and chapter 2.

36. On spectroscopic analysis see *Lyon's Medical Jurisprudence* (1904), 98–100.

37. Letter from W. S. Newman to the CE, Calcutta (Madras, July 7, 1892), 18 (item 18), in "Memorial from Newman."

38. Letter from John T. W. Leslie, CE, Calcutta, to W. S. Newman (Calcutta, July 22, 1892), 18 (item 19), in "Memorial from Newman."

39. The acting CE had examined the chopper with Newman, and disagreed. He reported that "a filmy layer of rust and mud" appeared on the blade, but with patches of metal exposed. Statement from T. H. Pope, acting CE, Madras, to the chief secretary to government (Madras, November 17, 1891), 2, in "Memorial from Newman."

40. Statement from T. H. Pope (November 17, 1891), 2, in "Memorial from Newman."

41. For the best summary of the mud issue see "Order (Jan. 23, 1892), No. 56, Public," 14–15, in "Memorial from Newman."

42. Memo from Judicial Department, Government of Madras, no. 2068 (October 8, 1891), 2, in "Memorial from Newman."

tool had cut red meat with it, for instance.[43] Any blood under the mud, though, could have belonged to the murder victims. What mattered was what lay beneath the mud, and this area had not been tested, although Newman's certificate stated that he had "examined the iron chopper."[44]

At first glance, Newman's misleading report might seem to favor the defendant. But Ramcharan Doss was convicted, so if Newman's certificate helped Doss, it apparently did not help him enough. In fact, the prosecution argued that the chopper was not the murder weapon, advancing instead an alternative theory for Doss's guilt. For some reason, as Newman saw it, the fact that any blood at all was found on the chopper undermined the prosecution's case.[45] Still, his certificate did report blood—and Doss was convicted all the same. Whether or not better information would have saved a man's life in the Triplicane case, officials as far up as the governor of Madras Presidency insisted that the criminal courts get information of the highest quality. This was particularly important in death penalty cases.

As mentioned, the CE submitted a certificate of his findings but did not have to be cross-examined under oath to explain them (CrPC s.510). From thc 1920s, most of the key forensic officials in India tried to get the same kind of exemption from court appearances. The imperial serologist (IS), the chief inspector of explosives, the government examiner of documents, fingerprint experts, and anatomists (who analyzed bones) wanted to be deemed CEs for the purposes of s.510.[46] Only the IS was successful before 1947, although others were later.[47] The larger point was that the exemption from mandatory cross-examination under oath was not a small exception created for a minor category of experts. It was an exception made for all of the state toxicology labs in British India, and then it was extended to others (see introduction).

---

43. The cutting of mammalian (nonhuman) meat was a common alternative explanation in murder cases involving bloodstains. See W. D. Sutherland, "Blood-Stains," in *Lyon's Medical Jurisprudence* (1921), 203–8 (case studies 23, 36, 44, 46, 52); and chapter 2.

44. W. S. Gantz, "The Triplicane Murder Case," *Madras Mail*, August 24, 1891.

45. "Memorial of the Ex-Assistant CE Mr. W. S. Newman" (August 1892), 12, in "Memorial from Newman."

46. For instance see "Proposal to amend s.510 of the CrPC so as to include Anatomist, negative," Home: Judicial, 1922, Proc. no. 1336; "Proposed inclusion of the Chief Inspector of Explosives in s.510 of CrPC so as to enable his reports on bombs to be used as evidence in trials under the Code," Industries and Labor: Explosives, 1924, file no. M-830–31; and "Summoning of the Chief Inspector of Explosives to give evidence in Criminal Courts," Home: Judicial, 1928, Proc. no. 738 (all at NAI).

47. The colonial state regarded anatomy and the analysis of questioned documents as more interpretive than fields like forensic toxicology and serology. H. Tonkinson (October 7, 1922), 4, in "Proposal to amend s.510 CrPC so as to include Anatomist, negatived." By 1973, the CIE, director of the Finger Print Bureau, and several other experts were granted this privilege (CrPC 1973, s.293).

Newman's case illustrated the dangers of the s.510 exception. Had he (or his CE) been cross-examined in court, it was likely that his misleading written statement would have been corrected. As the Madras commissioner of police, T. Weldon, observed, "One result of this case is to make it imperative to accept with caution bare reports of this nature by the Chemical Examiner and that when possible this officer should, like any other expert, be subject to personal examination and cross-examination."[48] Weldon said he would insist on cross-examination in future, and others noted that this had been the custom in Madras Presidency in murder cases, too. But it did not happen in the Triplicane murder case, and excusing CEs (and assistant CEs) from appearing in court only became more common across South Asia in the decades to come (see chapter 5).

Newman's immediate superior was the Madras CE, A. E. Grant. Grant tried to reframe the case as a disagreement over the proper role of the expert. In his view, the job of the CE was to answer the question put by the police, and nothing more. If further explanation was needed, it was the job of those in court to call in the CE. Had this been done in the Triplicane murder case, Grant had no doubt that valuable and "extremely important" evidence could have been given by Newman about the relative distribution of the mud and the apparently fresh stains. But as this had not been done, responsibility lay with the legal professionals in court, and not the CE's lab. According to Grant, offering such explanations lay "quite outside the duties of the chemical examiner in such a matter til requested to do so."[49]

Higher-ups disagreed. The chief secretary to the Madras government, J. F. Price, rejected Grant's restricted model of the expert. "It is impossible for such an officer to anticipate what discoveries will be made by the Chemical Examiner and to frame his questions accordingly," Price insisted. The "interests of justice" demanded that the CE "shall state fully in his report all that he has discovered or can discover." Failing to communicate all of the lab's findings was "a grave error."[50] Newman's case revealed conflicting ideas about how the needs of courts and labs should intersect. And it illuminated the potentially grave consequences of allowing lab experts to sidestep a key feature of colonial truth mechanics in law: cross-examination under oath.

48. Paper from T. Weldon (September 10, 1891), 3, in "Memorial from Newman."

49. Paper from A. E. Grant, acting CE, Madras, to the Chief Secretary to Government (Madras, September 21, 1891), 6, in "Memorial from Newman."

50. "Order (Oct. 8, 1891). No. 2068, Judicial" from J. F. Price, chief secretary, 7, in "Memorial from Newman."

Sex Crimes and Age Determination in North India

Almost half a century later in north India, another set of corruption-related allegations emerged against a different European expert. Major Cornelius Vincent Falvey was an Irish physician with a "not very brilliant" academic record who joined the IMS in 1922 and was superintendent of a jail and a leper hospital, among other postings, mainly in north India.[51] Sometime in the early 1930s, he was posted to Bareilly, a district not far from Delhi in the United Provinces. There, he was a civil surgeon tasked with conducting medical examinations of people targeted by and accused of crime in his locale.[52] Falvey had been practicing in the IMS for seventeen years when allegations of corruption surfaced against him. His unidentified accusers claimed that Falvey had taken bribes from criminal defendants and altered his medical findings in their favor.[53]

The accusations against Falvey related to a series of cases, including two sex crimes. In the first, a six-year-old girl named Phulmati had allegedly been raped by a sixteen-year-old boy named Dalel Jat in June 1937. The girl's injuries were serious. Falvey examined thc child and noted in his report that her vagina was "badly ruptured and torn half way through to the anus." Another tear in the "fourchetta" was "septic" or putrefying. The medical officer at Sardhana (a town adjacent to the city of Meerut), Dr. Bhargava, initially examined the teenage boy. He reported that the boy had three abrasions on his body and that he was capable of committing rape. Dr. Bhargava took the view that "a man may have no mark of injury whatsoever even immediately after, or two days after, the rape on his penis."[54]

---

51. Note by [AM], 3, in "Request from C. V. Falvey, IMS for the appointment of 2nd Resident Surgeon, Presidency General Hospital, Calcutta," DGIMS: IMS, Progs. no. 703, 1931 (NAI); entry for Cornelius Vincent Falvey in Indian Army Records of Service 1900–47 (IOR/L/MIL/14/68670) and in *Thacker's Indian Directory 1933* (Thacker's Press and Directories, 1933), 123. On the disproportionate presence of physicians from the "Celtic fringe" (Ireland and Scotland) in the IMS see Mark Harrison, *Public Health in British India: Anglo-Indian Preventive Medicine, 1859–1914* (Cambridge University Press, 1994), 26, 30–31, 35.

52. See Patrick Hehir, *The Medical Profession in India* (London: Henry Frowde, 1923), 60–61.

53. The authorities did not reveal the identity of the original accusers, despite requests from Falvey's lawyer for names and addresses "so that we may seek the redress to which we think [Falvey] is entitled." Letter from Hampsons, Bedford House, 33 Henrietta Street, Strand, London to the Under Secretary of State for India, Military Dept., India Office, London (July 26, 1939), 17 [hereafter "letter from Hampsons"]. See also confidential letter no. 1921/V-1 (35) from the Government of the United Provinces (June 10, 1939), 4 [hereafter "letter from UP Government"]. Both sources appear in "Charges of corruption and bribery against Major C. V. Falvey, IMS (Civil Surgeon, United Provinces)," DGIMS, Proc. no. 79-1/39-P (NAI).

54. "Charge No. 2" in letter from UP Government.

Falvey initially examined Phulmati and told the police, ambiguously, that injury could have been caused by rape "or otherwise," without offering any alternatives. The complaint against Falvey claimed that the boy's relatives had visited Falvey at his home, and that Falvey had offered to produce an opinion in the defendant's favor for 115 rupees. Allegedly, Falvey instructed them to apply through their vakil (lawyer) for Falvey to examine the boy. Falvey did the exam and agreed with Dr. Bhargava that the boy's penis showed no signs of injury, but he disagreed with Bhargava on what this fact meant. As Falvey testified in court, "From the nature of the injuries I cannot say definitely that the injuries were due to rape. The injuries caused by a penis or any other hard substance like a stick would be similar. If a boy of the accused's age commits rape with a child of 6 years I do not think it likely that his penis will escape injury. . . . If the penis penetrated to the extent found in Mst. Pulmati's case I would expect it to be injured." Falvey was charged with taking a bribe from three relatives and friends of the accused, and with falsely certifying in the young man's favor.[55]

The second sex-related crime was a sodomy case. In July 1937, Falvey examined a fifteen-year-old boy named Mahabir Prasad. Mahabir was probably sexually assaulted, but in colonial India, the rape of a man or boy was governed by the antisodomy section of the IPC (s.377) rather than by the rape provision (s.375), which only applied to male-female sex (see chapter 3). Falvey examined the boy three times over the course of July and August 1937. His statements became increasingly detailed and pro-defendant over time. Falvey allegedly received bribes twice from a friend of Nem Chandra, the accused, during this time. Falvey's initial certificate (issued soon after July 10) read: "Abrasion triangular, lower right side of anus." On July 21, he added on a further police report that the injury could have been caused by sodomy but that the boy was not accustomed to sodomy, meaning that the boy did not have regular anal intercourse. Falvey's next report (July 31) stated that "I do not consider it possible to commit sodomy with this boy his sphincter anus is so tight." And finally, on August 21 during cross-examination in court, Falvey testified, "I believe that the sodomy was not committed. It is impossible to commit sodomy with this boy as his anus was so tight. The anus would not become tight if a man is examined several days after the sodomy."[56] When defending himself later in a letter to his superiors, Falvey explained that he had been unable to insert a speculum into the boy's anus

55. "Charge No. 2."
56. "Charge No. 3."

due to "the spasmodic contraction of his sphincter muscle."[57] In the subsequent disciplinary process, Falvey was charged with issuing false and contradictory certificates in this case for payment.[58]

A second group of cases involved the determination of age. Falvey was accused in these cases of inflating his estimate of girls' ages in order to place them in the adult category. For the purposes of the crimes at issue here, this meant declaring them to be over eighteen. As the work of historian Ishita Pande shows, determining age was not always a straightforward exercise in a society in which many people's births were not recorded and where age and time were measured in different ways.[59] Pande examines forensic methods for determining age in the context of child marriage, including the examination of teeth, physical signs of puberty, and extent of ossification (using X-rays).[60] The determination of age was relevant to a number of other areas of criminal law, too, including child abduction and child prostitution.

In a 1937 case, a defendant named Maqbool was tried for abducting a girl named Bhagwani, who had been freed by the time of the trial. Her age mattered because the abduction of a female minor was its own separate crime under the IPC (s.366A). This provision was added to the IPC in 1923 to operationalize the International Convention for the Suppression of Traffic in Women and Children. It carried a maximum ten-year sentence (as opposed to seven years under s.363, the more generic abduction provision) and aimed to punish the sex trafficking of girls.[61] Falvey was accused of progressively moving his estimate of the girl's age upward because he had taken a bribe from the defendant. When he first examined her in July 1937, Falvey counted the girl's teeth and certified that she was about fourteen years old. Three months later, in October 1937, though, Falvey testified in court that the girl in front of him was eighteen or nineteen. When confronted with the contradictory claims of his earlier certificate, he claimed, "I never saw this girl before today" and "I do not think this girl appeared before me for examination," implying that an impersonator had been sent to him earlier. However, the Finger Print Bureau reported that the thumbprint of the girl he

57. "Letter from Major C. V. Falvey, IMS, 106 Sketty Road, Swansea, Glamorgan to the Under-Secretary of State for India, Military Department, India Office, SW1, London. July 26, 1939," 4 [hereafter "letter from Falvey"], in "Charges of corruption and bribery against Major C. V. Falvey."

58. "Charge No. 3" in letter from UP Government.

59. Some communities calculated age from conception (not birth) and used local, religious, and lunar calendars (not the Gregorian). See Ishita Pande, *Sex, Law, and the Politics of Age: Child Marriage in India, 1891–1937* (Cambridge University Press, 2020), 15, 150.

60. Pande, 109–15.

61. Ratanlal Ranchhoddas and Dhirajlal Keshavlal Thakore, *The Indian Penal Code*, 11th ed. (Bombay: Law Reporter Office, 1926), 312–14.

examined in July 1937 was the same as the one in October. Falvey was charged with having changed his evidence in the interests of the accused, who had paid him thirty-two rupees.[62]

Age determination was also at the heart of ten cases that all fell under the Naik Girls Protection Act of 1929.[63] Between 1935 and 1938, Falvey had allegedly issued false certificates of majority to ten girls from the Naik community. (By the 1930s colonial legislators, including many Indians, effectively viewed the sex trade as the hereditary profession of Naik women.) All these girls were subject to a statutory regime aimed at preventing them from becoming child prostitutes. This list was perhaps the crowning charge against Falvey because his actions were so well documented. Falvey's accusers took advantage of the recordkeeping practices of the colonial state. They contrasted Falvey's claims that the girls were over eighteen with state records, including birth registers and vaccination records (which presumably included an estimated age).[64] For instance, one entry from this long and repetitive list read, "Mst. Basanti, born on 16.10.25 and vaccinated on 17.10.26, obtained a certificate from you on 2.1.38 to the effect that she was 18 years old, when according to the date of her birth in the register she was only 12 years, 2 months and 16 days old. You were paid Rs.32/–for this certificate."[65] Falvey had first learned of the complaints against him during a visit from Mr. Ballah, an investigating officer of the Anticorruption Committee in July 1938. The racial dynamics of that interview must have not been lost on Falvey, whose London-based lawyer subsequently wrote with confidence that Ballah had no evidence of any kind.[66] By June 1939, though, the charges were issued in precise, written form.

Falvey rebutted them by deploying the colonial stereotype of native mendacity. He claimed to be "very familiar with the atrocities that can occur in India," suggesting that he was the victim of false accusations.[67] The charges against him in the abduction case included notes of court proceedings that claimed Falvey had counted the teeth of the girl present in court. "No such count took place," he wrote, and the notes were "recorded in Babu English which is certainly not

62. "Charge No. 1" in letter from UP Government.

63. For discussion among legislators of the working of the Act see *Proceedings of the Legislative Council of the United Provinces* (Allahabad: Superintendent, Government Press, United Provinces, 1931), 51, no. 3: 229–45 (July 22, 1931); and (Allahabad: Superintendent, Printing and Stationery, United Provinces, 1934), 64, no. 1: 12–13, 99, 127 (October 29, 1934).

64. See relatedly Pande, *Sex*, 116–17.

65. "Charge No. 5" in letter from UP Government.

66. Letter from Hampsons, [2].

67. Letter from Falvey, [4].

my manner of expression"—again, suggesting that they were false.[68] In the Naik cases, Falvey claimed that the girls always came to see him with at least one other female, and that this other person may have undergone the examination while the "real" girl in question gave her fingerprints.[69] He also suggested that the age certificates he allegedly issued had in fact been fabricated. The gap in years between these girls' actual age and his alleged certificates made their falsity seem likely: "It is always possible to make a mistake of a year or two or even three but I cannot believe that it would be possible for any skilled medical man to certify a child of 11 years 7 months as being of the age of 18."[70]

Falvey's lawyer expressed outrage at the suggestion that an expert witness might be biased "in favor of those by whom he is called rather than that he should give his expert views with impartiality for the assistance of the Court and the administration of justice."[71] The "battle of the experts" problem was a more common phenomenon in the civil courtroom than the criminal, both in India and England, and India had taken a turn away from the English model, narrowing opportunities for competing experts to be produced in criminal cases. As the Punjab CE in 1879 noted of the civil surgeon: "There is no possibility, as a rule, of opposing medical evidence or opinion being brought against his to allow of the judge and his assessors choosing between the two."[72] The civil surgeon in India did not enjoy the privilege of the CE and was cross-examined in court. But normally, a civil surgeon did not have to worry about being contradicted by another expert.

The existence of a second opinion in Falvey's child rape case was unusual. It may have been a result of the defendant living outside of Falvey's district.[73] The Punjab CE asserted in 1879 that there was usually no competing expert, but Indian criminal procedure did allow defendants to call their own expert witnesses—if the funds for the witnesses' reasonable expenses, including professional fees, had been deposited with the court in advance.[74] Most defendants probably did not call their own experts because of the expense. However it came to be, the existence of a competing expert was important. It was Bhargava's

68. Letter from Falvey, [2].

69. Letter from Falvey, [3] and [7].

70. Letter from Falvey, [7].

71. Letter from Hampsons, [3].

72. CE Report for Punjab 1879, 13.

73. Bhargava was identified as the "Medical Officer, Sardhana" in Meerut district. "Charge No. 2" in letter from UP Government. Falvey was civil surgeon in the nearby district of Bareilly.

74. See CrPC (1872) ss.200, 358–59 in *The Code of Indian Criminal Procedure: Being Act No. X of 1872* (London, 1872); and CrPC (1898) ss.216 and 257, in Prinsep, *Code of Criminal Procedure*, 216–17, 257–58.

contrary opinion—that a male could commit child rape without visible injury to the penis—that allowed Falvey's accusers to cast doubt on Falvey's insistence on visible injury.

Processing Corruption Charges

As an "uncovenanted" civil servant, Newman was terminated more swiftly and easily than Falvey, who enjoyed added protections as a member of the IMS. Newman admitted he had been drinking the leftover alcohol samples, and in that way confirmed the charges of corruption against him. His analysis of the Triplicane bloodstains also constituted misconduct, but whether his superiors regarded it as careless or corrupt was less clear. In any case, despite multiple pleas by Newman for further information, he was dismissed without any kind of subsistence allowance.[75]

As for Falvey, his health deteriorated under the stress of the charges made against him, and a medical board certified that he was unfit for further service. "Invaliding recommended," read the telegram to the viceroy.[76] Falvey then returned to Britain despite the ongoing investigations in India. His superior, R. N. Dey, commented that Falvey had "failed to rebut most of the extremely serious charges of corruption against him," some of which were "*prima facie* well established."[77] It is worth noting that Falvey had been struggling financially for years. In a string of letters to his superiors in the 1920s and '30s, he begged them for a more lucrative post, claiming that his salary could not cover his family's schooling and medical expenses.[78] Insufficient pay in the IMS was an issue communicated to the highest levels from the 1920s on, and not just by Falvey.[79]

75. Letter from T. H. Pope, acting CE to W. S. Newman, Mylapore (February 15, 1892), 3, in "Memorial from Newman."

76. Telegram from secretary of state for India, London, to viceroy (Education, Health and Lands dept.), no. 2864, sent on November 11, 1939, in "Charges of corruption and bribery against Major C. V. Falvey."

77. Letter from R. N. Dey, secretary to government, United Provinces, Medical department, to secretary to government of India, Education, Health and Labor dept., no. 3992 (Lucknow, January 13, 1940), [1], in "Charges of corruption and bribery against Major C. V. Falvey."

78. For example see "Application from Captain C. V. Falvey for a permanent commission in the IMS," DGIMS: IMS, 1926, Proc. no. 691; "Request from C. V. Falvey, IMS for the appointment of 2nd Resident Surgeon, Presidency General Hospital, Calcutta," DGIMS: IMS, 1931, Proc. no. 703/31; "Application for civil employment from Capt. C. V. Falvey, IMS," DGIMS: Personal section, 1938, F. no-17-85/38 (all at NAI).

79. Pratik Chakrabarti, "'Signs of the Times': Medicine and Nationhood in British India," *Osiris* 24 (2009): 188–90.

Falvey's departure from India halted the entire disciplinary process. Dey noted that ordinarily the case would have been handled through one of three processes: criminal prosecution, a departmental inquiry, or an inquiry under the Public Servants (Inquiries) Act. In Falvey's case, though, the authorities had decided not to proceed with the charges "in view of the fact that this would involve his return to India which owing to his state of health and for other reasons is out of the question."[80] The file gives no clue about these "other reasons," nor does it explain why the IMS could not hold an inquiry from its London office, collecting evidence and conducting cross-examination in India.[81] Apparently, the fact that Falvey would be retiring prematurely on an annual pension of 4,180 rupees was "in itself a punishment."[82] In short, Falvey's case was handled with remarkable leniency. Early retirement and a return to Britain buried the corruption charges, allowing both the individual and the state to keep the suspected misconduct out of public view. These were not unusual outcomes for British officials who came under suspicion in India.[83]

While the cases of Newman and Falvey were resolved quietly and out of the public eye, with almost no mention of either case in the press, this approach was not necessarily followed when the expert was Indian.[84] In 1933, allegations of corruption emerged against Captain Jitendra Kumar Banerji. Like Newman, Banerji was an assistant CE, although in Bengal, not Madras. Unlike Newman, Banerji was a member of the IMS. The allegations against Banerji were processed

---

80. Letter from Dey (January 13, 1940), [1].

81. In litigation, the taking of testimony and cross-examination in other cities and countries was carried out regularly by setting up a "commission" in these other places. See introduction. One wonders why no such process was available for IMS disciplinary proceedings.

82. Letter from Dey, [2]. Falvey retired from the service on December 6, 1939. "Question of the Transfer to the U.P. Civil Medical Dept. of a British officer of the IMS, [. . .] Major C. V. Falvey, IMS," DGIMS: IMS, 1939, file no-39–12/39 (NAI). However, his period of military service continued after his return to England, when he was about forty-one, until 1948, when he would have been about fifty. C. V. Falvey entry, Indian Army Records of Service 1900–47. Presumably, Britain's wartime needs trumped everything else. Falvey died in 1968 at the age of seventy. Entry for Cornelius V. Falvey, England & Wales Deaths 1837–2007: Birth, Marriage, Death & Parish Records—Civil Deaths and Burials, vol. 7A, 498 (Kingsbridge, Devon, England), accessed via FindMyPast.co.uk on February 20, 2025.

83. For instance see Ram Gopal Sanyal, ed., *The Record of Criminal Cases as Between Europeans and Natives for the Last Hundred Years* (Calcutta, 1896), 58–60; and "The Real Issue," *TI*, December 3, 1918. For an unusual case that involved a criminal prosecution (by court-martial) but little press coverage (1943) see Aditya Balasubramanian, "Anticorruption, Development, and the Indian State: A History of Decolonization," *Journal of Asian Studies* 83, no. 1 (2024): 91.

84. The exception was Gantz, "Triplicane Murder Case." This was a letter to the editor written by the defendant's lawyer in the Triplicane case. This was not press coverage of a case once it was moving through disciplinary channels, but rather led to allegations of misconduct being made against Newman. On the differential treatment of British versus Indian officials accused of corruption see "European and Native Bribe-Takers," *ABP*, August 5, 1895.

through a Court of Inquiry established under the Public Servants (Inquiries) Act. Presiding over this court was a judge named T. J. Y. Roxburgh and an IMS forensic toxicologist, Lieutenant Colonel R. N. Chopra.[85] Captain Banerji was accused of either submitting a "deliberately false report" or committing an act of "gross and culpable negligence" in his analysis of bloodstains. A man named Hiralal Ahir had been tried and acquitted of murder in connection with the death of one Sheikh Idu during Calcutta's city elections. Banerji issued a certificate stating that the stains on Ahir's clothing were not blood. After the Ahir trial, though, the clothing was sent to the imperial serologist. He found that the stains were indeed human blood. Another expert, the Bengal surgeon general, obtained the same result.[86]

Press coverage stressed the severity of the charges. The report of the CE or his assistant was "vested with a sanctity peculiar to itself," a reference to CrPC s.510. "The law rested upon the assumption that such a report would never lie," said the deputy legal remembrancer, M. A. Khondkar. A false CE's certificate therefore threatened to erode "one of the foundations of the judicial system in this country."[87] Comments like these acknowledged the tremendous power of experts in the criminal legal system. And yet no such public pronouncements appeared in the Newman or Falvey case—although officials were saying the very same things to each other. Furthermore, while the cases of Newman and Falvey played out in the privacy of upper officialdom, Banerji's disciplinary process was reported by newspapers, not only in India but also elsewhere.[88] He was ultimately dismissed for misconduct, although the records do not specify whether for gross negligence or corruption.[89]

In 1940 another Indian medical officer, a physician named K. D. Mehta, was dismissed from the subordinate medical service of the province of Bombay and

85. R. N. Chopra was the author of the classic work *Indigenous Drugs of India* and a leading forensic toxicologist. He was surgeon general for the government of Bengal in the 1930s and led the Indigenous Drugs Inquiry in the 1940s. See "Report of the work done by the Indigenous Drugs Inquiry under Col. Sir R. N. Chopra, Kt., CIE, IMS (R) at the Drug Research Laboratory, Jammu . . . up to the end of September 1946," 1–5, in "Reports on the work done on various enquiries" (MSS Eur. F709/3). For his bio see *Indigenous Drugs of India* title page; and David Arnold, "Colonial Medicine in the Transition: Medical Research in India, 1910–47," *South Asia Research* 14, no. 1 (1994): 28.

86. "Alleged False Report. Bloodstains. Officer Charge in Bengal," *TI*, August 18, 1933; and "Bengal Official Charged. Accused of Making False Report on Murder Case," *Scotsman*, August 17, 1933. Neither newspaper account identifies the procedural mechanism used to obtain additional expert opinions in this case, which were both post-conviction.

87. "Alleged False Report."

88. For example see "Sequel to Murder Trial. Doctor Accused of Making False Report," *Straits Times*, September 9, 1933.

89. "Report of the CE to Government, Bengal, for the Year 1933," 14 (IOR/V/24/424).

convicted in a criminal trial for corruption. He had accepted 210 rupees as "illegal gratification" in return for medically examining and recommending two men for false "certificates of fitness." Newspaper accounts are not clear about how they intended to use these certificates, but this was a case in which the IPC's extensive provisions on false documents were applied to a state physician. Falvey's superiors noted that a criminal trial was one of three possible ways to deal with allegations of corruption in a medical officer, although they did not elaborate on the rationale for pursuing the criminal avenue. Mehta himself was the target of a police sting: Two men, F. D'Souza and I. Khwaja, had been given marked bills by the police and sent to set up Mehta.[90] It may have been, then, that Mehta was given a criminal trial because the police were involved in his case from the start. Indeed, they created it. It may equally have been that Indians accused of misconduct could be slotted comfortably into racialized narratives of native mendacity and corruption, and explained as instances where Western education had failed. The cases of Banerji and Mehta may have been discursively useful to these narratives, reinforcing colonial worldviews, in one dimension, when each case became public, even if they simultaneously introduced the troubling possibility of misconduct in forensic systems. By contrast, the existence of potentially corrupt British officials threatened to unravel these narratives. Consequently, Indian men of science like Banerji and Mehta may have been more likely to be processed through public venues than their British counterparts, Newman and Falvey, who were discreetly dismissed or allowed to flee to Britain. These cases suggested that there were racialized differences in the way allegations of corruption were handled in forensic systems.

More broadly, these four misconduct cases suggest that the system designed and enshrined to combat falsity was about combating *native* falsity. When the goal of combating falsity generally clashed with the goal of justifying imperial rule as a campaign against falsity and corruption, the imperial goal prevailed. In short, forensic expertise was profoundly contoured by the social hierarchies and agendas around it, including protection of the narrative of European anticorruption against putative native mendacity.

In 1933, the Allahabad High Court overturned the conviction of a man named Happu in a death penalty case alleging murder by arsenic. The author of the leading opinion, Justice J. Douglas Young, was troubled by the power that CrPC s.510

90. "Bombay High Court: Taking Illegal Gratification. Sentence on Medical Office Upheld," *TI*, October 3, 1940.

gave CEs. He worried that CEs could be careless or corrupt. And although they *could* be called to court under s.510, "in practice they never are in this province." In short, allowing experts merely to submit a written report denied due process protections for the accused.[91] As Young delivered his judgment, J. K. Banerji was being investigated for misconduct relating to the CE certificate in Bengal. And by chance, Happu's case came from Bareilly, the same district where Falvey would be accused of taking bribes six years later.

Young's *Happu* decision was rejected the following year in a sequel case (chapter 5). His opinion, however, stood as the high-water mark of a stream of criticism that ran through the case law. These judges warned that the heightened power and reduced accountability of experts undermined defendants' rights.[92] Whether the product of gross negligence or corruption, dubious expert opinion in India was more likely to go undetected because CEs (or assistant CEs like Newman) were allowed to submit written opinions without being cross-examined under oath. The bloodstain analysis of Newman and Banerji highlighted the fact that it was not always easy to distinguish between carelessness and corruption.[93] Misbehaving experts presented a special challenge: The identification of an expert opinion as suspect could be difficult if one was not an expert oneself.[94]

When the expert was Indian, any misconduct could be understood by Britons as the failure of Western education to counteract native mendacity. But misbehaving European experts threatened to erode the narrative of the incorruptible white official. Newman and Falvey were dealt with discreetly, while allegations against Indian physicians like Banerji and Mehta were processed in very public ways. Protecting British racial prestige mattered (see chapter 5). This was true even to the extent that cases of Indian official misconduct that tacitly undermined the vying prestige of "objective" forensic science were nonetheless publicized. Colonial stereotypes associated corruption with Indians, and an anti-corruption ethic was a pillar of the "civilizing mission" in India. As a result, falsity

91. *Emp. v. Happu*, ILR All. 56 (1934): 233; see also chapter 5. For an exception from Madras where a CE was called to court, see the 1886 case of Venkatasawmi Achari (alias Chinnasawmi Achari), in K. Jagannatha Aiyar, ed., *Weir's Criminal Rulings (Madras)*, 2:661–62.

92. See "Proposed amendment of the form used by CEs in recording results of analyses of the contents of human viscera," Home: Judicial, Proc. no. 241–2, June 1905, 1 (NAI). For postcolonial criticism see Law Commission of India, *Twenty-Fifth Report (Report on Evidence of Officers About Forged Stamps, Currency Notes, etc.)* (Delhi: Ministry of Law, Government of India, 1963), 12–13 (appendix 4).

93. Similarly, see Saha, "'Uncivilized Practitioners,'" 439.

94. See Gambetta, "Corruption," 24.

from within the system—especially by white experts—posed a special threat not only in particular criminal cases, but also ideologically. The forensic expert was supposed to reveal truth in a neutral and reliable manner, sidestepping the problems of perjury and forgery in the courtroom. But enabled by criminal procedure, the expert himself could become an insidious source of falsity.

5

ADVERSARIALISM, INQUISITORIALISM, AND EXPERTS

Experts' vision of themselves as neutral truth-seeking figures was misaligned with the adversarial approach of lawyers in the colonial courtroom. Agra CE E. H. Hankin wondered whether it was worthwhile "to bring an expert to court to play tricks on him," as lawyers so often did.[1] Bengal CE L. A. Waddell insisted that "the medical witness should remember that he is not, and should not be, a partisan on either side. He has come to tell the truth, what he *knows* about the case, and not to clench the case against the prisoner."[2] Waddell, whom we met in chapter 1, may have expected scientific experts to be treated like objective authorities not only because he was a man of science, but also because it was what he knew from Scots law (which with its Roman law roots was related to continental law), as opposed to English law.[3]

The writings of Hankin and Waddell referred to two competing visions of scientific expertise in the colonial courtroom. For many men of science, the

1. E. H. Hankin, *The Mental Limitations of the Expert* (Calcutta: Butterworth, 1920), 72.

2. Isidore Bernadotte Lyon, *Lyon's Medical Jurisprudence for India*, 3rd ed., ed L. A. Waddell (Calcutta: Thacker, Spink, 1904), 12. Italics in original. The same passage appears in the 7th ed., ed. Waddell (1921), 15.

3. Waddell characterized Indian law as based on English *and* Roman law, and it is likely that in the forensic domain especially, Indian law was disproportionately influenced by Roman law through the Scottish presence. See *Lyon's Medical Jurisprudence* (1921), 2 at note 2, 3.

adversarial model (typical in jurisdictions modeled on English law) interfered with the pure and noble quest for truth. From this perspective, which preferred the inquisitorial model of continental European systems (and Scotland), it was easy to regard experts in adversarial systems as partisan hucksters willing to sell their opinion to the highest bidder. By contrast, defenders of adversarialism saw the courtroom as a place where players in the free marketplace of ideas fought it out. With its competing experts cross-examined rigorously, the adversarial model was a rough and messy one—and one that was arguably skeptical about the possibility of discovering the full truth at all.[4] Then as now, the battle of the experts in the adversarial courtroom often led to paralysis by bewildered judge and jury, who were usually scientific laypeople.[5] However, the adversarial model also made visible something that was harder to see in its inquisitorial counterpart: difference of opinion within a specialized field of knowledge.

In Victorian England, a heated debate developed between advocates of the adversarial and inquisitorial trial. The question was whether the rise of partisan experts through the "adversarial revolution" represented a cheapening of the honorable "man of science" ideal with its belief in universal truth and impartiality—or whether a tumble of competing views wrestling it out in the courtroom was actually the best way to identify the most plausible account.[6] By historian of science Chris Hamlin's account, proponents of adversarialism regarded expert disagreement as "a normal, rather than a pathological, phenomenon." The adversarial model acknowledged that "rigorous examination of uncertainty and careful articulation of assumptions and deductions" could be "enormously useful."[7] By contrast, historian of science Tal Golan describes the scientific community as being in a state of crisis following a series of compromising battle-of-the-expert scenes in high profile Victorian lawsuits. By the mid-nineteenth century, putting men of science in the English courtroom had resulted in a "growing public mistrust of scientific knowledge." The adversarial courtroom damaged the public image of the Victorian scientific community, which was working hard to achieve professional status and to expand its influence with government and industry.[8]

4. For this view see S. C. Sarkar, *Hints on Modern Advocacy and Cross-Examination*, 2nd ed. (Calcutta: M. C. Sarkar & Sons, 1931), 454–59.

5. On a battle of the experts over the efficacy of illicit oral abortifacients in 1920s Bombay see Mitra Sharafi, "Abortion in South Asia, 1860–1947: A Medico-Legal History," *MAS* 55, no. 2 (2021): 381–83.

6. On plausibility see Orna Alyagon Darr, *Plausible Crime Stories: The Legal History of Sexual Offences in Mandate Palestine* (Cambridge University Press, 2019).

7. Christopher Hamlin, "Scientific Method and Expert Witnessing: Victorian Perspectives on a Modern Problem," *Social Studies of Science* 16, no. 3 (1986): 485, 506.

8. Tal Golan, *Laws of Men and Laws of Nature: The History of Scientific Expert Testimony in England and America* (Harvard University Press, 2004), 106.

The adversarial-inquisitorial debate that had long raged in Anglo-American and European settings took on new shape in colonial South Asia. Here, adversarialism was locked in a struggle with the more inquisitorial model of the single court-appointed expert, but with a colonial extension: CEs were not required to come to court for questioning. When the debate was dominated by British figures like the physician William Center in the 1870s and the judge J. Douglas Young in the 1930s, both sides reiterated colonial stereotypes consistent with the perceived imperatives of British rule. The inquisitorial model promoted by men of science like Center projected a coherent view of truth that maintained the prestige of Western science and British rule in the face of native mendacity. Adversarialists such as Young worried about the rights of the accused, given the CEs' exemption from cross-examination, precisely *because* they adhered to views of native mendacity affecting evidence. However, when South Asians like treatise author J. P. Modi rose through the forensic ranks during the twentieth century, ideas about truth, justice, science, and legal process shifted again, shedding their colonial undercoat.

Belief in native mendacity created fears of falsity and spurred an innocence discourse grounded in racial bias (chapter 1). But when we read against the grain of the colonizers' sources, we can see an alternative conception of justice—punitive self-harm—in what they perceived merely as falsity (chapter 2). Whatever the case, the result of this concern was to embolden CEs and forensic science—which ironically created more opportunities for falsity (including through corruption) within the very truth mechanics of forensic science originally envisioned as an antidote to native mendacity (chapter 4). Here, in chapter 5, we see a shift as India moved into a late colonial moment with men of law and science engaged in the debate over adversarial or inquisitorial forms of the criminal trial. British participants in this debate, regardless of their side, still promulgated colonial notions of native mendacity to argue their case, but the rise of South Asians in the forensic professions in tandem with the nationalist movement made that belief obsolete.

Adversarialism vs. Inquisitorialism

A long-standing debate compares the merits of adversarial and inquisitorial trial, originally in the criminal context.[9] These are ideal types, as legal

9. For contrasting descriptions of the adversarial and inquisitorial models see Stephan Landsman, "A Brief Survey on the Development of the Adversary System," *Ohio State Law Journal* 44

historian Amalia Kessler notes; few legal systems (past or present) follow either model completely.[10] By the nineteenth century, the adversarial trial judge (sitting with a jury) played a neutral and passive role, assessing the evidence and arguments presented by each side. His job (these judges were male) was to select the most convincing case put to him, not to produce his own independent theory. Lawyers gathered evidence and had a duty of zealous advocacy on behalf of their clients.[11] They were also bound by a code of ethics. Expert witnesses could be produced by either side and cross-examined under oath by lawyers on both sides.[12] The dominant mode of adversarial interaction was public and oral.

In the inquisitorial trial, the judge (without a jury) or judge-like investigator would oversee the collection of evidence and compilation of a written dossier.[13] At trial, the judge would examine the witnesses. Lawyers for each side might recommend certain lines of inquiry, but they would not control the process. Inquisitorial proceedings made great use of written sources and took place behind closed doors. Although there were opportunities for the defense to call its own expert, these were restricted or controlled by the judge and were sometimes at the defendant's own expense.[14] The dominant model was the court-appointed expert. If the judge, prosecution, or defense was dissatisfied on a point of expert opinion, the question would be sent to progressively larger and more prestigious professional bodies for resolution.[15] In late nineteenth-century Prussia, for instance, there were four stages of medico-legal expert consultation. First, a court-appointed expert would be consulted and questioned

(1983): 713–39; Mirjan A. Damaška, *Evidence Law Adrift* (Yale University Press, 1995), 74–124; John H. Langbein, *The Origins of Adversary Criminal Trial* (Oxford University Press, 2005), 1–9; Fabien Gélinas et al., *Foundations of Civil Justice: Toward a Value-Based Framework for Reform* (Springer, 2015), 65–67; and Amalia Kessler, *Inventing American Exceptionalism: The Origins of American Adversarial Legal Culture, 1800–1877* (Yale University Press, 2017), 2–4.

10. Kessler, *Inventing American Exceptionalism*, 2.

11. See generally Christopher Whelan, *The Bodyguard of Lies: Lawyers' Power and Professional Responsibility* (Hart, 2022).

12. On the rise of the adversarial expert witness in seventeenth-to-nineteenth-century England see Golan, *Laws of Men*, 5–51.

13. On dossier compilation in the French system see P. N. Ramaswami, "Criminal Procedure—Accusatorial and Inquisitorial," *Criminal Law Journal of India* (1955): 37–45; and E. Claire Cage, *The Science of Proof: Forensic Medicine in Modern France* (Cambridge University Press, 2022), 174–75.

14. See Charles Greene Cumston, *The Law and Medical Experts, with Particular Reference to the Codes of Criminal Procedure of European Countries* (D. C. Heath, 1908), 15–17; and Cage, *Science of Proof*, 130.

15. See Cumston, *Law and Medical Experts*, 15–17; and José Ramón Bertomeu-Sánchez, "Managing Uncertainty in the Academy and the Courtroom: Normal Arsenic and Nineteenth-Century Toxicology," *Isis* 104, no. 2 (2013): 208–9.

by the judge in a case. If the prosecution or defense was dissatisfied, the evidence and expert's report would be forwarded to a Medical Court of Appeal for the province, consisting of four to six members. If this second decision was challenged, an appeal would be made to a scientific deputation, composed of experts of national reputation. Finally, the scientific point of dispute could be sent to the minister of medical affairs, who presided over a medico-legal organization as head of the department of state medicine.[16] By the nineteenth century, academics in forensic medicine noted that inquisitorial (or quasi-inquisitorial) jurisdictions from Germany to Scotland had more sophisticated traditions of medical jurisprudence than did the more adversarial jurisdictions of England and the United States.[17]

For legal historian John Langbein (an anti-adversarialist), the inquisitorial judge was truth-seeking, while the adversarial model "presupposed that truth would somehow emerge when no one was in charge of seeking it."[18] Anti-inquisitorialists saw the adversarial model as more open to new rights claims, less elitist (through the jury), more publicly accountable, and more closely linked to notions of due process and the rule of law. The adversarial model aligned with market-based capitalism and mistrust of state bureaucracy and officialdom. Its proponents also showed Protestant bias, associating inquisitorialism not only with canon and Roman law but also with the hierarchical power structures of the Catholic Church, the Inquisition, and despotism generally.[19] There was an Anglocentric self-aggrandizing politics to the debate between adversarial and inquisitorial, in other words.[20] This view persisted despite traditions of inquisitorialism in long-standing Anglo institutions like the courts of equity and coroners' inquests.[21]

---

16. Stanford E. Chaillé, *Origin and Progress of Medical Jurisprudence, 1776–1876. A Centennial Address* (Philadelphia, 1876), 26.

17. See Chaillé, *Origin*; Douglas Maclagan, "Address in Forensic Medicine, Delivered at the Forty-Sixth Annual Meeting of the British Medical Association, Held in Bath, August 6–9, 1878," *British Medical Journal* 2, no. 920 (1878), 233–39; and Christopher Hamlin and Ian Burney, "History of Forensic Science," in *Encyclopedia of Forensic Sciences*, vol. 3, ed. Max M. Houck (Elsevier, 2023), 172–73.

18. Langbein, *Origins*, 333.

19. An important part of the longer history of this debate was the permitted use of judicial torture to extract confessions in European continental law. See Langbein, *Origins*.

20. For instance see Blackstone's history of civil (Roman) and canon law in England: William Blackstone, *Commentaries on the Laws of England: In Four Books* (London, 1862), 1: 9–17, 65–67.

21. On the quasi-inquisitorialism of the courts of equity in US legal history see, by Kessler, *Inventing American Exceptionalism*, and "Our Inquisitorial Tradition: Equity Procedure, Due Process, and the Search for an Alternative to the Adversarial," *Cornell Law Review* 90, no. 5 (2005): 1181–1276.

William Center, the Protected Expert, and Inquisitorial Approaches

Punjab CE William Center, a Scot, was the clearest opponent of adversarialism. He described the courtroom role of the scientific expert in his 1879 annual report. As a court of first instance, the Indian criminal court generally consisted of a magistrate sitting alone or with three "native assessors" whose views were not binding on the judge.[22] Without professional scientific training, Center wrote, none of these actors could properly interpret the significance of peculiar symptoms in live bodies or postmortem signs in dead ones. In England, the approach was to have "a variety of medical opinion . . . called in on both sides," and "in the conflict of opinion the jury decides on the more trustworthy." Under this adversarial model (what Center called "the legal method"), "it is undoubtedly found the best means of evolving the truth that one side should state all possible arguments in favor of one side, and another those on the opposite, each finding every possible fault with the other's arguments." Center, however, considered adversarialism to be fundamentally incompatible with the scientific quest for truth: "*It is doubted by scientific men whether . . . the spirit of this method should be followed.* It is considered that *the position of the scientific evidence ought to be judicial and truth-seeking and not partisan*."[23]

In many parts of Germany, Center noted, courts used a system of court-appointed experts. Medical men or chemists working for the state acted as "referees" to judges. The court-appointed expert's opinion typically determined the outcome of the case. And in fact, Indian courts operated more like this German model than like the full-blown English adversarial one. In many criminal trials involving medical issues, Center noted, the only expert was the local civil surgeon: "He is a paid official of Government, engaged in the same way as the police in ascertaining facts" and practically performs a similar function to a German referee.[24] "There is *no possibility*, as a rule, *of opposing medical evidence or opinion being brought against his to allow of the judge and his assessors choosing between the two*."[25] Center seemed untroubled by reliance on a single expert's

---

22. On the use of assessors in Indian courts see Mitra Sharafi, *Law and Identity in Colonial South Asia: Parsi Legal Culture, 1772–1947* (Cambridge University Press, 2014), 197–98.

23. "Report of the CE to Government, Punjab, for the Year 1879," 13 (IOR/V/24/418). Italics added.

24. On civil surgeons more broadly see CE Report for Punjab 1879, 3, 8–14.

25. CE Report for Punjab 1879, 13. Italics added. See chapter 4 for an unusual exception (competing experts in a child rape case).

view because the magistrate could question this expert using a series of prompts provided by upper court circulars.

Center might have made the same observation for his own role as chemical examiner. CEs were the quintessential court-appointed experts in South Asia, typically unopposed by competing experts. CEs submitted written findings and were not required to appear in court, which made them even more powerful than the civil surgeons described by Center. And in the South Asian system, unlike the Prussian, there was no progression of expert bodies that could be activated if there was dissatisfaction with the CE's findings.

The justification, to recall, for CrPC s.510 (s.325 of CrPC 1872 in Center's time) related to distance, logistics, and experts' convenience: CEs were originally exempted from court appearances because it was difficult for them—and disruptive to their lab work—to travel long distances in order to reach courts in rural areas. Interestingly, though, the exemption applied to appearances in *all* courts, not just those that were far from CE labs (see introduction and map 1).

Another theory explaining this rule of criminal procedure is more speculative. The confrontation of an expert witness, along with the appearance of multiple expert witnesses, produced a complicated portrait of Western science. Expert adversarialism led to a confusing, contradictory, and discrediting version of Western science for an audience of colonized subjects. Put bluntly, adversarial experts being questioned in court undermined the credibility of Western science. From this perspective, a more strategic approach was to offer one written expert opinion, allowing Western science—or one version of it—to present itself as clear, coherent, and definitive.

The suppression of disagreement shaped other legal institutions in the empire. The most striking example was the "no dissents" rule of the Judicial Committee of the Privy Council (JCPC), the final court of appeal for the British empire.[26] Sitting in London, the judges of this court were almost the same individuals who sat as Law Lords.[27] The Law Lords manned what was then the final court of appeal for Britain itself: the House of Lords sitting in its judicial capacity.[28] When hearing British cases, these judges issued dissenting and concurring opinions—in

26. See Viscount Haldane of Cloan, "The Work for the Empire of the Judicial Committee of the Privy Council," *Cambridge Law Journal* 1 (1923): 145.

27. The key difference was that from 1909, an Indian judge joined the Privy Council judges for JCPC appeals coming from India. A similar practice developed with judges and appeals from Canada, South Africa, Australia, and New Zealand. The majority of the JCPC's cases were Indian appeals before the JCPC's Indian jurisdiction ended in 1949. See Haldane, "Work," 148; Sharafi, *Law and Identity*, 55–56; and Rohit De, "'A Peripatetic World Court': Cosmopolitan Courts, Nationalist Judges and the Indian Appeal to the Privy Council," *Law and History Review* 32, no. 4 (2014): 821–51.

28. The House of Lords' judicial role was replaced by the UK Supreme Court in 2006.

the former a judge disagreed with the majority on the bench, and in the latter a judge agreed with the majority's conclusion, but for different reasons. Dissenting and concurring judgments allowed judges to seed jurisprudence with alternative logics for the future.[29]

Unlike the Law Lords, however, between 1878 and 1966, judges of the Privy Council could only issue a single, collective opinion. They were not permitted to issue dissents (or concurring judgments).[30] In the words of Lord Haldane, a Privy Council judge who spoke to a group of law students in 1921: "The Judges do not give any judgment; *one of them speaks, after they have been in consultation, on behalf of the whole body of five, and there is no dissent.* It is a most solemn part of the oath not to reveal what has passed in deliberation. If any Judge were to say that he had not agreed with his colleagues, the sword of the [unwritten] Constitution would descend on him. It never happens."[31]

According to Oliver Jones, the "no dissents" rule emerged out of a controversy over the JCPC's ecclesiastical jurisdiction in the 1870s.[32] I would suggest, though, that the rule may also have aligned with larger, more political concerns. At a time when the Indian nationalist movement was gaining force, the "no dissents" rule may have met the perceived need to project uniformity, clarity, and certainty from the metropole—and to avoid complexity and contradiction. In jurisdictions like civilian continental ones that only permitted unanimous judgments, the justification was to foster the public perception that law was stable and secure.[33] Likewise, the Privy Council's "no dissents" rule may have stuck in part because it projected a coherent, consistent, and singular image of British authority to an imperial audience. How could British rule maintain itself, particularly in nonsettler colonies, if the judges of the highest court in the empire could not agree on the outcome of important cases?[34]

---

29. On this and other arguments in favor of the dissent as a device see Ruth Bader Ginsburg, "The Role of Dissenting Opinions," *Minnesota Law Review* 95, no. 1 (2010): 1–8; and Joe McIntyre, "In Defence of Judicial Dissent," *Adelaide Law Review* 37, no. 2 (2016): 438–41.

30. See Oliver Jones, "*Public Prosecutor v. Oie Hee Koi* (1968): Not So Humbly Advising? Sir Garfield Barwick and the Introduction of Dissenting Reasons to the Judicial Committee of the Privy Council," in *Great Australian Dissents*, ed. Andrew Lynch (Cambridge University Press, 2016), 119–26; P. A. Howell, *The Judicial Committee of the Privy Council, 1833–1876* (Cambridge University Press, 1979), 201–4, 221–22; and Yogesh Pratap Singh, *Judicial Dissent and the Indian Supreme Court* (Delhi: Thomson Reuters, 2018), 36–37, 64.

31. Haldane, "Work," 145. Italics added.

32. Jones, "*Public Prosecutor*," 119–26.

33. Ginsburg, "Role," 3.

34. For a similar argument made against dissents generally see Henry Wollman, "Evils of Dissenting Opinions," *Albany Law Journal* 57 (1898): 74–75.

The same reasoning may have applied to science in the Indian courtroom. How could British rule, propped up rhetorically by the rule of law and Western science, command respect if its forensic science was unsettled? From this perspective, the structural suppression of disagreement among experts and adjudicators reflected the idea that like political "children" stuck in the "waiting room of history," colonized peoples required a clear and simple message.[35] If contradictory experts produced "humiliation to science" even in England (in the words of an exasperated chief justice in 1820), then adversarialism may have been deemed even more intolerable in South Asia.[36] After all, fear of racial embarrassment or the desire to protect British prestige shaped everything from the demand for racially segregated prisons to the deportation of elite white lunatics from the colony back to Britain.[37]

"Shooting an Elephant," the (perhaps fictionalized) autobiographical essay by George Orwell (Eric Blair), published in 1936, captures this sentiment. Like Blair himself in the 1920s, the narrator is a British police officer in Burma. He shoots an elephant that has escaped from its *mahout* or handler, although he is convinced that the animal is no longer a danger to the public. The narrator kills the elephant because he feels he has no choice: He cannot look weak in front of the large crowd of Burmese onlookers. "A white man mustn't be frightened in front of 'natives'; and so, in general, he isn't frightened," observes the narrator, who has developed a deep hatred of the imperialism that he is administering. "And my whole life, every white man's life in the East, was one long struggle not to be laughed at."[38]

In the case of CrPC s.510 and the Privy Council's "no dissents" rule, what resulted was a stripped-down and impoverished version of forensic science and imperial jurisprudence. Or at least this was how Anglo adversarialists might have seen it. As for CrPC s.510, the primary sources do not reveal that legislators

35. Uday Singh Mehta, *Liberalism and Empire: A Study in Nineteenth-Century British Liberal Thought* (Chicago University Press, 1999), 31–33; and Dipesh Chakrabarty, *Provincializing Europe: Postcolonial Thought and Historical Difference* (Princeton University Press, 2000), 8–10.

36. Chief Justice Dallas in *Severn, King and Co. v. Imperial Insurance Company* (1820), quoted in Golan, *Laws of Men*, 62.

37. For instance see Arthur Templeton, "Memorial to His Excellency the Viceroy and Governor General of India" (December 18, 1897), 16, in "Hyderabad Abortion Case (1899): *Empress v. Templeton*" (IOR/R/1/1/1273); and Jonathan Saha, "Madness and the Making of a Colonial Order in Burma," *MAS* 47, no. 2 (2013): 425–34. See also Elizabeth Kolsky, *Colonial Justice in British India: White Violence and the Rule of Law* (Cambridge University Press, 2010); and Satoshi Mizutani, *The Meaning of White: Race, Class, and the "Domiciled Community" in British India 1858–1930* (Oxford University Press, 2011).

38. George Orwell, "Shooting an Elephant," in *The Collected Essays, Journalism, and Letters of George Orwell*, ed. Sonia Orwell and Ian Angus (Harcourt, Brace, 1968), 1:239–40.

intended to make science seem simple when they excused CEs from cross-examination. But this was the rule's effect. This aspect of the South Asian system went unmentioned in Center's critique of the adversarial approach to experts.

J. Douglas Young and the Expert Exposed

Against this alignment of inquisitorialism and the perceived imperatives of colonial rule with "men of science" like William Center was a cluster of judges who pushed for adversarialism and defendants' due process rights. These values meant a messier path to justice—and suggested skepticism toward the possibility of gaining access to the full truth at all. These judges' beliefs were at odds not only with state forensic experts and inquisitorial ideals but also with schools of officialdom like the Punjab school of public administration that wanted to rule the colony *without law*.[39] Historians of South Asia often treat the rule of law as the handmaiden of colonialism, but debates over adversarialism revealed that colonialism and the rule-of-law agenda (the latter as a set of ideals, not practices) were distinct projects that at times came into direct conflict with each other.[40]

The most vocal of the adversarialists was John Douglas Young, a judge of the Allahabad High Court and chief justice of the Lahore High Court during the 1930s.[41] His decision in the 1933 Allahabad case of *Emperor v. Happu* became the most explicit judicial critique of s.510. In *Happu*, the lower-caste defendant had been convicted and sentenced to death for fatally poisoning Babu Singh with arsenic.[42] The lower court had convicted Happu on the basis of the CE's written certificate. These test results were positive for arsenic. However, the certificate failed to state *how much* arsenic had been found. The CE was not cross-examined in court because of s.510, which in Young's words enabled a "dangerous practice" that was contrary to "the accumulated experience of centuries of what is necessary for the protection of accused persons." "It has undoubtedly been the practice in India to rely upon such a report, even where there is no quantitative analysis, to prove death by arsenic poison," and on this basis many people

39. On the Punjab school see Mitra Sharafi, "Indian Constitutionalism, the Rule of Law, and Parsi Legal Culture," *Indian Law Review* 7, no. 3 (2023): 8.

40. For an elaboration of this argument see Sharafi, "Indian Constitutionalism," 8–10.

41. For an earlier critique of CrPC s.510 by Allahabad High Court Chief Justice John Edge see untitled, *ABP*, July 8, 1886.

42. Happu was identified as being of "caste Nat." *Emp. v. Happu*, ILR All. 56 (1934): 229. See W. Crooke, *The North-Western Provinces of India: Their History, Ethnology, and Administration* (London, 1897), 213.

had been convicted—and executed.[43] Young noted that arsenic was contained in a wide variety of everyday foods and substances, from beer to aphrodisiacs to Indian and European medicines.[44] Young described the process for carrying out the Marsh-Berzelius test for arsenic a "delicate operation" in which the CE, "being human," could err.[45] Young did not suggest that the CE in *Happu* had behaved improperly, but it was always possible that such a "privileged person" might be "half blind, incompetent, or even corrupt." No person therefore "ought to be put in peril of capital, or any, punishment on a written report not given on oath and untested by cross-examination." To accept such a report as proof of arsenic poisoning was for Young "an impossible proposition in law."[46] Unusually, Indian law permitted appellate judges to take new evidence if they thought it necessary.[47] Young used this power often. In *Happu*, he ordered a quantitative analysis during the appeal. This time, the CE's report found only "0'182 of a grain of arsenic"—less than the fatal dose of two grains.[48]

As if in rebuttal to William Center half a century earlier, Young compared the Indian rule with the English, but disapprovingly. In arsenic trials in England, even the most eminent chemists were called to prove that at least two grains of arsenic had been given. They were "subjected to the severest cross-examination" before their evidence was adopted. Young wanted to ensure due process for defendants in India as in England. He tried to do it in this case by claiming that while s.510 made the cross-examination of a CE merely optional, it said nothing of the *weight* of an expert's written report by itself. For Young, the report had no weight without cross-examination under oath.[49] Thus while he followed the statute in principle, he gutted it in practice.

Within less than a year, *Happu* was undermined by two High Court rulings, including one by a fellow Allahabad judge named Collister, who had concurred

43. *Emp. v. Happu*, 233.

44. *Emp. v. Happu*, 231. For a similar discussion see *Gajrani v. Emp.*, AIR All. (1933): 398.

45. *Emp. v. Happu*, 234. On the history of the Marsh test see José Ramón Bertomeu-Sánchez, "Managing Uncertainty in the Academy and the Courtroom: Normal Arsenic and Nineteenth-Century Toxicology," *Isis* 104, no. 2 (2013): 197–225; and Katherine D. Watson, "Criminal Poisoning in England and the Origins of the Marsh Test for Arsenic," 183–207 in *Chemistry, Medicine, and Crime: Mateu J. B. Orfila (1787–1853) and His Times*, ed. José Ramón Bertomeu-Sánchez and Agustí Nieto-Galan (Science History Publications, 2006). See also chapter 1.

46. *Emp. v. Happu*, 234.

47. CrPC s.428. See H. T. Prinsep, *The Code of Criminal Procedure Being Act V of 1898* (Calcutta: Thacker, Spink), 1901, 418–19.

48. *Emp. v. Happu*, 231. As a unit, one grain was the equivalent of 64.8 milligrams.

49. *Emp. v. Happu*, 229, 233–35.

with Young in *Happu*.[50] *Happu* was only briefly a clear precedent, but it did articulate an important line of critique in legal history. Young was joined by other sympathetic judges, both British and South Asian, who worried that written expert evidence—neither questioned nor under oath—could be itself a dangerous source of falsity.[51] Intriguingly, *Happu* was cited in forensic science treatises for decades to come, unlike the subsequent cases that curtailed it.[52] This suggested that prominent treatise authors also sympathized with the judges' critique of s.510.

It is important not to mistake Young for a racially progressive champion of Indian defendants against predominantly European experts. Young espoused colonial stereotypes about South Asians. Like the CEs described in chapter 1, he worried about the rights of the accused precisely *because* he held a deep-seated belief in native mendacity. Like most British judges and lawyers in late colonial India, Young believed that South Asians lied and dissembled habitually, and that perjury and forgery were the rule rather than the exception. When he moved from Allahabad in north-central India to the Lahore High Court in its northwest (today Pakistan), he shared his views in a speech to the Lahore bar. The new chief justice of Lahore had been informed by longtime litigators when he first arrived in India "that evidence in this country was almost wholly unreliable, and that perjury was the curse of the administration of justice in India." His own experience as a judge in Allahabad confirmed these warnings. He had no doubt that the sentiment behind the Hindustani (now Hindi) expression "such bolo, adalat mein nahin ho"—*tell the truth, you are not in court*—was a common one across India. "In the estimation of prominent Indian lawyers a large proportion of witnesses in the Courts of this country are prepared to swear falsely."[53]

Young was also convinced that corruption was all around him. In his speeches across north India, he decried the prevalence of corruption—that "filthy thing"—among Indians in the legal profession, police, and general population.[54]

50. *Emperor v. Bachcha*, ILR All. 57 (1935): 256–60; and *Aishan Bibi v. Emperor*, AIR Lah. (1934): 150–53. Collister J., who had concurred with Young in *Happu*, asserted in *Bachcha* that the CE should be called in arsenic murder cases but not necessarily in all cases involving chemical analysis.

51. In addition to *Gajrani v. Emp.* and *K. E. v. Mst. Gaya Kunwar* (discussed in this chapter) see *Queen-Empress v. Autal Muchi* in chapter 1.

52. See Jaising P. Modi, *A Textbook of Medical Jurisprudence*, 6th ed. (Bombay: Butterworth, 1940), 18; and Ram Lal Gupta, *Law of Identification* (Lucknow: Eastern Book, 1963), 149.

53. "Welcome at Lahore" (Lahore, May 7, 1934), in Shri Ram and V. M. Kulkarni, eds., *For Necessary Action: Speeches and Judgments of Sir Douglas Young, Chief Justice, High Court of Judicature at Lahore* (Lahore: Indian Cases, 1941), 6–7.

54. "Speech at Khalsa College" (Amritsar, 1938), in Ram and Kulkarni, 66/3. In the same volume see also these speeches by Young: "Address to Punjab Judiciary" ([Lahore,] 1934), 16–18; "Corruption

His rather bizarre solution was the Boy Scouts. Joining the scouts would instill in Indian males a sense of character, discipline, self-control, and public spiritedness that would rid the new India (with independence looming) of corruption, communalism, and crime.[55] Young also worried about the risk of corrupt forensic experts—another reason why he objected to certain lab experts' exemption from coming to court. In *Happu*, he took judicial notice of the 1933 inquiry into an alleged false report by the Bengal assistant CE, J. K. Banerji (see chapter 4).

Young's belief in native mendacity and corruption heightened his awareness of the risk of wrongful convictions. In the majority of his criminal suits (cases among South Asians), he worried that false allegations and fabricated evidence would end in the conviction of innocent people. "Anyone procuring false evidence runs the risk of imprisonment and degradation from office," he fumed at the end of a case in which police may have fabricated evidence, "and what is still more serious, [he] may have the burden on his soul of sending an innocent man to the gallows."[56]

Young's concern with falsity was particularly clear in a series of riot cases from the 1930s. Some were alleged riots between Hindus and Muslims. Others were between caste communities. They usually ended with Young acquitting many defendants because he thought the accusations were false. In the 1933 Raiya riot case, for instance, one Shukul Pandey was convicted of murder in the lower court, having been found to be the ringleader in an anti-Muslim attack that left four people dead. The communal violence was triggered by the alleged killing of a cow by a Muslim.[57] Seventeen witnesses testified against the defendant. They said he had wielded at different times a gun, an ax, and a sword, and that he had bounded across rooftops, armed. Given the evidence, Young expected Pandey to be "a man of powerful physique, untiring energy, exceptional endurance, possessed of the strength and prowess of an athlete and the agility of an acrobat." But when Pandey was brought into court, Young realized that he was "a wizened old man of about 70 years of age," "in the last stages of senility and physical decrepitude." Young ordered the man to be examined by the Allahabad civil surgeon, who confirmed that he was a "weak, done old man," "unable to run," who could

and Communalism" (Lahore, 1935), 28–31; "Advice to New Law Graduates" (Lahore, 1936), 47–48; and "Address at Punjab Civil Service Association Dinner" ([Lahore,] 1937), 56–57.

55. In Ram and Kulkarni see Douglas Young, "Importance of Scouting in India" (Sargodha, 1936), 45; and cartoon of Young in a Boy Scout uniform, plate opposite 40.

56. "An Answer to Prayer: *Ashiq Mahomed and Others v. Emperor*," in Ram and Kulkarni, 180.

57. Cow-killing had (and still has) complex interreligious and intercaste valences in India. See chapter 1 on caste. On Muslim butchers in Indian legal history see Rohit De, *A People's Constitution: The Everyday Life of Law in the Indian Republic* (Princeton University Press, 2018), 123–68.

perhaps "hobble along" for two or three miles but that this "would take him the better part of the day." He also had extra bones in one foot that caused him pain. Shukul Pandey had been in this pitiful state for the past several years.[58] It was thus impossible for him to have led the killings. Young acquitted him and vacated his death sentence.

Young had harsh words for both lower courts that had convicted Pandey. Had either the magistrate or Sessions Court judge seen the man they were condemning to death, they would have realized that the "evidence against him was false from beginning to end."[59] More unusually, Young declared that the seventeen witnesses against Pandey had committed perjury. He insisted that perjury cases should not be shelved simply because the courts were backlogged. (In addition to the chronic problem of arrears in the courts, perjury prosecutions were relatively rare because of the view that one should not convict of perjury a person who had shifted from falsity to truth, but only from truth to falsity.)[60] He also applied the *falsus in uno* principle that was standard in the courts of England, where he had been a practicing barrister until coming to India at the age of forty-six: If *any part* of a witness' testimony was deemed unreliable, *none* of the testimony could be used. By contrast, the standard approach in India was usually to excise the tainted part and use the rest (see chapter 3). Young repeatedly followed the stricter English approach.[61] The idea was to communicate to the colonized population that any whiff of falsity would discredit a witness completely, leading to acquittal of the defendant and even to prosecution of the witness for perjury.

Young saw the pursuit of truth as the aim of the criminal legal system.[62] But he also recognized that the ability to unearth truth was limited and imperfect, particularly in a colonial setting. If there was sufficient doubt about the defendant's role and the truth seemed impossible to ascertain, then one had to acquit. If there was any hope, though, of knowing the truth, it would be through science. In another riot case, Young acquitted one "fairly old man" and another "old man

58. "Raiya Riot Case: *Shukul and Others v. King-Emperor*," in Ram and Kulkarni, *For Necessary Action*, 74–75.

59. "Raiya Riot Case," 77.

60. The idea was that the law of perjury should not create a disincentive that would prevent people from correcting their own false testimony. This approach was meant to reduce the risk of wrongful convictions. See three judgments by Aston J. in 1890s Burma: *Mi Me Ma v. Queen-Empress*, Printed Judgments Lower Burma (1893–1900): 91–93; *Queen-Empress v. Nga Po Nyun*, Moyle's Criminal Rulings and Judgments, Criminal (Lower Burma) 3 (1893–94): 47–50; and *Murvena Madoo v. Queen-Empress*, Burma Law Reports 3 (1897): 28–30.

61. For example see "Raiya Riot Case," 82–83; and "Nothing can be multiplied or corroborated. *Asmatullah and Others v. Emperor*," in Ram and Kulkarni, *For Necessary Action*, 95–98.

62. For instance see "Raiya Riot Case," 79–80.

of 60" who was nearly blind. The second man, Bisheshar, had signs of injury on his body, but these could have been produced as he tried to protect himself against attackers. The first man, Baldeo Koeri, had allegedly attacked and killed an experienced wrestler and *lathi* fighter.[63] A spear had been found at Baldeo's house, but suspiciously, it was not sent to the CE or imperial serologist for testing. Without scientific evidence of the presence of blood, Young concluded that this weapon, which was allegedly used to kill one man and injure another, had been planted. He acquitted both men, and upheld the convictions of others whose physical injuries were consistent with having been attackers. In a case like this where the evidence was "entirely conflicting," where both sides had produced "perjured evidence," and where the real motives could never be known, or whose *lathi* struck whom, the one thing a judge could rely on were the marks of injury (presumably as interpreted by the civil surgeon)—that is, the court could turn to science.[64]

And yet for Young, the science had to show and prove itself. The expert had to leave his lab and explain himself in court in terms accessible and persuasive to legal laypeople, particularly the judge (or jury, if there was one; see appendix 2). By Young's vision, it was the judge who decided the case, not the expert. Young had to see things for himself, a point made clear when he made a field trip of over five hundred miles to inspect the dirt floor of a hut. He observed that the dirt floor had not been dug up, that the prosecution's evidence was thus false, and that the allegations were "a fabrication from start to finish."[65]

For Young, "sequestered science" (as it would later be called) was unacceptable science.[66] In *Happu*, Young refused to give weight to an expert's nonquantitative test results on the presence of arsenic. In a 1936 case from Lahore, Young acquitted two men sentenced to death for the murder and gang rape of a young woman because he was convinced the case was false. He was not even sure that there had been a murder (or rape). A bundle of bones had been found with the woman's clothing, and an "approver" (cooperating with the police) gave a detailed account of how the woman's body had been dismembered by the men in

63. A *lathi* is a heavy wooden stick bound with iron and used as a weapon.

64. *Emp. v. Ram Adhin Singh*, AIR All. (1931): 440–43.

65. "Answer to Prayer," 179. The defendants, who were members of the Ahmadi religious minority, considered the judges' five-hundred-mile journey "an answer" to their community's prayers. "Answer to Prayer," 181.

66. See special issue on "Sequestered Science: The Consequences of Undisclosed Knowledge," *Law and Contemporary Problems* 69, no. 3 (2006), including David Michaels, "Foreword: Sarbanes-Oxley for Science," 1–19; and Sheila Jasanoff, "Transparency in Public Science: Purposes, Reasons, Limits," 21–45.

the group as they prepared to hide her body.[67] But "dead bones speak"—in this case, through science in the form of the civil surgeon. This physician revealed that the bones had never been separated in the ways described: "The head was never severed from the body. The skull, the cervical vertebrae and two dorsal vertebrae were all in one piece. The arm which, according to the approver, he had severed from the body was intact; the right scapula, humerus, radius and ulna were all in one piece, which proves that the approver is lying when he says that he cut off the right arm."[68]

The report by the civil surgeon, Bhagwan Das, was meticulous and compelling. Young was "so impressed by this report" that he summoned Das to court for questioning and also directed that the bones should be disinterred and reexamined. Suspiciously, the woman's husband could not remember where he had buried his wife's bones. This was "another astonishing circumstance of the case" that made Young suspect that the case had been concocted by the woman's husband and father, along with the approver.[69] Even when handed an excellent written report, Young wanted the expert and bones checked again.

The judge again made clear his reservations toward the protected expert in a 1938 case, *Ujagar Singh v. Crown*, in which three Sikh men appealed their convictions for the murder of another Sikh man.[70] They had been sentenced to penal transportation for life.[71] Against them, the advocate general of the Punjab Government asked the court to enhance their sentences—from transportation to the death penalty. As in the bones case, there was an approver, and he described the alleged crime as exceedingly violent. However, expert opinion contradicted the approver's testimony and some of the evidence, notably a spearhead that the imperial serologist confirmed was smeared with human blood. Unusually, the assistant surgeon who gave his opinion on the wounds had to face off against an expert for the defense: the civil surgeon of Gurdaspur, Colonel D'Arcy. The existence of competing experts here may have reflected the defendants' access to good counsel and the money needed to pay an expert (see chapter 4). D'Arcy convinced Young that a spear could not have been used in the murder, given the dead man's injuries: "All the 28 injuries are incised. There is not one punctured

67. Under the corroboration rule, accomplice testimony had to be consistent with other evidence. Langbein, *Origins*, 203–17. See chapter 3.

68. "Dead Bones Speak: *Nikka and Another v. Crown*," in Ram and Kulkarni, *For Necessary Action*, 217.

69. "Dead Bones Speak," 217.

70. See *Ujagar Singh and Others v. Crown*, ILR Lah. 20 (1939): 206–15.

71. In the 1930s, most convicts sentenced to transportation would have been sent to the penal colony in the Andaman Islands. Clare Anderson, "The British Indian Empire, 1789–1939," in *A Global History of Convicts and Penal Colonies*, ed. Clare Anderson (Bloomsbury, 2018), 215, 229–30.

wound."[72] Young concluded that the spearhead coated in human blood had been planted.

Other evidence included defendants' fingernail clippings, taken roughly twenty-seven days after the alleged crime. These specimens were sent to the CE and then the imperial serologist. As in the arsenic case of *Happu*, the CrPC s.510 treatment of the protected lab expert applied. The imperial serologist sent a written certificate, stating that human blood was indeed found on the nail parings. The lower court judge had convicted on the basis of this evidence especially. But hearing the appeal, Young was not convinced. "One of us" on the bench had recently come across an article on the hazards of using bloody nail parings as evidence. Young then called the CE for Punjab, D. R. Thomas, to be cross-examined on the topic.[73]

Thomas confirmed that when trimming nails to collect parings, it was easy enough to cut some live tissue, and cause bleeding. Equally, "if you scratch a pimple you will naturally draw blood and this will remain on the nail."[74] It was also unlikely that the perpetrators' fingernails would still bear traces of blood from a murder committed twenty-seven days earlier. As Sikh men, the defendants would have been expected to wash their hands at least three times a day.[75] It was permitted but not typical for the CE to be called to court, given s.510 (see introduction and chapter 4). Just as unusually, Young reproduced in his opinion the CE's full testimony, including the following:

Q. (By Court). Therefore it appears to follow that if any of us here had our nails pared today, there is a grave possibility that they would be stained with human blood?

A. That is quite correct, and that of course applies to any human being. It will apply more strongly to persons who do not look after their nails.

Q. (By Court) Therefore if a person innocent of murder had his nails pared, the nail parings might show human blood normally?

A. Quite so, there is absolutely no medico-legal value whatsoever.

Q. (By Court) Then the evidence which is frequently produced in the Courts of this Province of blood-stains on nail parings is of no value?

A. That is true.[76]

---

72. Quoting Young (not D'Arcy) in *Ujagar Singh v. Crown*, 211.
73. *Ujagar Singh v. Crown*, 212.
74. Quoting Thomas in *Ujagar Singh v. Crown*, 213.
75. *Ujagar Singh v. Crown*, 212–13.
76. *Ujagar Singh v. Crown*, 214.

Because—and only because—Young had called the expert to court were the risks involved in bloody nail parings properly recognized. The judge set aside the three convictions. Had "this dangerous practice" of using bloody nail parings been exposed earlier, people accused of murder, "perhaps innocent . . . might not have been convicted on this useless and deceptive evidence."[77] Although Young's active role did not necessarily comport with the idea of the passive adversarial judge, the net result here—that multiple forensic experts and their findings were challenged and prodded in open court—embodied an adversarial approach to scientific expertise.

Young's time on the bench in India included a bizarre twist. The chief justice who was so concerned about corruption among experts resigned over a corruption scandal himself. A Lahore barrister named K. L. Gauba accused Young of protecting a contact, Nazir Ahmed, from exposure over shady property dealings. Gauba (who was also a bestselling author) privately published a book about it, which was promptly banned by the Punjab government.[78] When Gauba continued to share copies, the chief justice convicted Gauba of contempt of court, giving him the maximum six-month prison sentence. Gauba served his time, but the book reached the viceroy, who forced Young to resign.[79] Young and Gauba met shortly before Young left Lahore, and Young conceded defeat "like a gallant gentleman." He asked Gauba to "say something nice about me" if "you ever write again of these things." Gauba did. In his autobiography published three decades later, Gauba spent several chapters on his conflict with the judge. But in praise of Young, he noted that the chief justice had been preeminent in criminal matters: "Many an accused got the benefit of [the] doubt that no other judge would have given him, and the police and other officials who abused their powers were mortally afraid of him and he spared no one by reason of office or quality in such matters."[80] Young's refusal to let experts do shoddy work made Gauba's point.

---

77. *Ujagar Singh v. Crown*, 215. The debate over bloody nail parings that began with *Ujagar Singh* continued in the pages of the *IMG*. D. P. Lambert conducted experiments to test the views of Thomas (and Young). His preliminary findings suggested that they were wrong, and that it was not easy to accidentally contaminate nail clippings with one's own blood. D. P. Lambert, "A Preliminary Report on the Medico-Legal Value of the Finding of Blood on Nail Parings," *IMG* 74, no. 12 (1939): 744–45.

78. K. L. Gauba, *The New Magna Carta: A Tale of Judicial Tyranny. The Curious Case of Khwaja Nazir Ahmed* (Delhi: Law and Justice Publishing, 2022).

79. K. L. Gauba, *Friends and Foes: An Autobiography* (Delhi: Indian Book, 1974), 157–202. Gauba used his time in prison to write two more books; see p. 199.

80. Gauba, *Friends and* Foes, 202.

J. P. Modi and the Rejection of Native Mendacity

For its British participants, racial stereotypes and the perceived imperatives of colonial rule colored both sides of the adversarial-inquisitorial debate in late colonial India. On the inquisitorial side the protected status of lab experts may have dovetailed with the desire to make Western science seem coherent, authoritative, and simple for a colonial audience. This colonial agenda would have meshed nicely with the views of Center, who in the 1870s insisted that adversarialism was incompatible with the truth-seeking mission of Western science. On the adversarialist side were proponents like J. Douglas Young in the 1930s. This High Court judge resisted the spirit of s.510 as best he could and pressed scientific experts to explain themselves in the courtroom. By prodding the science, Young aimed to expose false charges rooted in native mendacity and corruption, both phenomena he considered widespread in India.

A great deal had changed between the 1870s and 1930s, however. South Asians were rising in the forensic professions on both the scientific-medical and the legal side (chapter 1), and the adversarial-inquisitorial debate changed as South Asian professionals added their voices. Indian lawyers, judges, CEs, and other forensic experts contributed to the wave of treatises on forensic science that appeared in the late nineteenth and early twentieth centuries. Among these, the preeminent Indian textbook author was Jaising Prabhudas Modi. The first edition of his *Textbook of Medical Jurisprudence and Toxicology* came out in 1920. In its twelfth edition by 1955, the book had become a leading authority in India's courts.[81]

J. P. Modi (figure 10) was a Gujarati physician who began his medical education in Bombay and then obtained the medical "triple diploma" in Scotland.[82] He joined government service on his return to India. Modi was based in the United Provinces (now Uttar Pradesh) in north India, including in Lucknow, where he worked as a hospital administrator and taught courses in medical jurisprudence, chemistry, physics, and hygiene. Modi's textbook was his most significant contribution to forensic science, but he also served as medico-legal expert to government and examiner on state medical boards. Modi was seventy-two when British

81. New editions of Modi's textbook continue to be published today. For a list of editions from 1920 to 2011 see J. P. Modi, *A Textbook of Medical Jurisprudence and Toxicology*, 24th ed., ed. K. Kannan and K. Mathiharan (Nagpur: LexisNexis Butterworths Wadhwa, 2011), page facing title page.

82. Edinburgh University's "triple diploma" bestowed medical licentiates (Licentiate of the Royal College of Physicians and Surgeons) from both Edinburgh and Glasgow. See Douglas Guthrie, *The Medical School of Edinburgh* (Edinburgh [1959]), 19.

FIGURE 10. / Passport photo of J. P. Modi. From the British Library Collection: "Duplicate passport," Passport no. 12816, Rai Bahadur Jaising Prabhudas Modi, 1934, p. 2 (IOR/L/PJ/11/3/2939).

rule ended in 1947. The government of independent India continued to consult him on forensic matters until his death in 1954 at the age of seventy-nine.[83]

Like British "men of science" of his era, Modi believed that the scientific expert's role in court should be nonpartisan and truth-seeking. "The medical practitioner" called to court "must remember that *he is there to tell the truth . . .* and should, therefore, give his evidence irrespective of whether it is likely to lead to conviction or acquittal of the accused." The expert witness should "use plain and simple language" and avoid technical jargon, "as the bench and the bar are not expected to be familiar with medical terms."[84] Modi did not think of lawyers as tricksters to the degree that Agra CE Hankin did. Modi seemed to have a reasonably productive relationship with "men of law" and worked to facilitate clear communication between the professional cultures of law, science, and medicine. While Modi advised the expert to be succinct in his explanations, for instance, he also recommended something rather unusual by the standards of these treatises: He suggested that medical men volunteer to give an extended statement to the court, to prevent omission of any relevant scientific aspects of the case. This idea came out of a conversation Modi once had with a judge of the Judicial Commissioner's Court of Oudh in north India. Since then, he had made it his practice to offer such statements, which magistrates and lawyers appreciated.[85] In this respect Modi endorsed some version of the inquisitorial model of the court-appointed expert.

At the same time, Modi was sympathetic to the adversarial critique of CrPC s.510. In his 1940 edition, Modi included a reference to a 1933 case from the Oudh Chief Commissioner's Court that followed Young's decision in *Happu*.[86] Both cases were arsenic murder trials, and the judges in both had harsh words for the s.510 exemption. In the Oudh case, Chief Justice Sir Syed Wazir Hasan and Justice B. N. Srivastava warned that while s.510 allowed cross-examination of a CE at the court's discretion, the practice that had developed in Oudh was not to call the expert to court. "It is to be expected that whenever a Magistrate or a Court of Sessions finds that the report of the CE is inadequate, they should not admit it in evidence unless the officer concerned submits a full and satisfactory

83. C. B. Singh, "Jaising P. Modi," in *A Textbook of Medical Jurisprudence and Toxicology*, by J. P. Modi, 12th ed., ed. N. J. Modi (Bombay: N. M. Tripathi, 1955), v–vi; and "Dr. J. P. Mody dead. Master of Medical Jurisprudence," *TI*, June 20, 1954, 10. See also biographical information on title page of Modi, *Medical Jurisprudence* (1940).

84. Modi, *Medical Jurisprudence* (1940), 19. Italics added.

85. J. P. Modi, *A Textbook of Medical Jurisprudence and Toxicology*, 10th ed. (Bombay: N. M. Tripathi, 1949), 16.

86. *Mt. Gaya Kunwar v. Emperor*, AIR Oudh (1934): 62, in Modi, *Medical Jurisprudence* (1940), 18.

report or he has been examined in support of it."[87] Modi cited this case in the main text and put *Happu* in a footnote, prioritizing South Asian judges over a British judge from the more prominent Allahabad High Court.[88] His failure to mention the High Court cases that subsequently undermined *Happu* suggests that he favored the critics of s.510.[89] Modi was open to tempering one aspect of inquisitorialism—the court-appointed expert—with a feature of adversarialism, namely cross-examination under oath by lawyers. This distinguished him from most other "men of science" treatise authors, who were more antiadversarial.

Modi also diverged from other treatise authors in another way. Medical jurisprudence treatises for India classically opened with a section, sometimes a chapter long, on native mendacity.[90] These early passages established the special need for forensic science, before launching into its inner workings, as a truth technology in India. Modi's book addressed the danger of fabricated evidence and false charges at various points. But Modi did not use native mendacity as his book's starting point, nor did he slide from particular false cases into generalizations about South Asian dishonesty.[91] Like Chunilal Bose on poisoning (chapter 1), Modi did not treat dissimulation in India as a cultural or racialized problem, but as a general problem one might find in any society. With Modi's textbook, the racialized stereotype that animated colonial forensic science faded away. Forensic science and the criminal legal system needed to prevent wrongful convictions, but not because of some South Asian propensity toward dissimulation. With this interpretation and approach Modi contributed to and continued a longer tradition of South Asian critiques of the native mendacity narrative (see introduction). His reconceptualization, coupled with his use of Indianized hypotheticals, catapulted Modi's treatise over its colonial-era competitors to become the leading medico-legal treatise in the postcolonial age. Rather than writing about Dick and Harry having a drunken brawl, for instance, Modi had Ramu and Kalua fighting over their cattle. "Only we, of the profession, can understand the difference," an Indian surgery professor wrote appreciatively of

87. Modi, *Medical Jurisprudence* (1940), 18.

88. Justice Syed Wazir Hasan or B. N. Srivastava may have been the judge who gave Modi the idea of offering extended statements.

89. *Emperor v. Bachcha* and *Aishan Bibi v. Emperor*, noted earlier in this chapter.

90. For instance see Norman Chevers, *A Manual of Medical Jurisprudence for Bengal and the North-Western Provinces* (Calcutta, 1856), 5–14; Patrick Hehir and J. D. B. Gribble, *Outlines of Medical Jurisprudence for India* (Madras: Higginbotham, 1908), 28–35; and *Lyon's Medical Jurisprudence* (1921), 22–24. See also chapter 1.

91. For example see Modi, *Medical Jurisprudence* (1940), 6–9.

Modi's contribution.[92] "Modi's Juris," as it is still called today, was forensic science reframed for the new India.[93]

However, like J. Douglas Young, J. P. Modi was a complicated figure. His timely rejection of the native mendacity narrative—as nationalists were forging a mass movement—did not mean that he rejected other "hierarchies of credibility."[94] For instance, Modi said this about women alleging rape: "In the majority of rape cases on adult women the charge is made with the object of blackmail, or the act is done with the consent of the woman, but when discovered, to get herself out of the trouble, she does not scruple to accuse the man of rape. If the complaint in these cases is made a day or two after the act, the case is probably one of concoction."[95]

Modi described many cases of women inflicting injuries on themselves in order to make false accusations of rape or other violence.[96] As with injuries self-inflicted by men, the telltale signs included cuts on the front of the body and reachable parts of the back side; multiple superficial parallel cuts; cuts on the left side of the body if right-handed or on the right if left-handed; and the use of chemical irritants like marking nut, sulfuric acid, or a hot rupee coin to simulate bruises or burns.[97] Modi's image early in this book of a woman with alleged strangulation marks on her neck (figure 2) showed fake bruises created by marking nut. Unlike some other works in the field, Modi's treatise did not suggest associations between Muslims and mendacity.[98] But Modi, who was from a middling Vaishya community, may have associated dissimulation with the lower castes.[99] Here let us return to the photo from Modi's treatise with which this

---

92. C. B. Singh, "Jaising P. Modi," v, in *Modi's Textbook of Medical Jurisprudence and Toxicology*, by J. P. Modi, 12th ed., ed. N. J. Modi (Bombay: N. M. Tripathi, 1955). See also Durba Mitra and Mrinal Satish, "Testing Chastity, Evidencing Rape: Impact of Medical Jurisprudence on Rape Adjudication in India," *Economic & Political Weekly* 49, no. 41 (2014): 52.

93. Singh, "Jaising P. Modi," v–vi.

94. I borrow this phrase from Jonathan Saha, who was not describing Modi. Saha, "'Devious Documents': Corruption and Paperwork in Colonial Burma, Circa 1900," in *Subverting Empire: Deviance and Disorder in the British Colonial World*, ed. Will Jackson and Emily J. Manktelow (Palgrave Macmillan, 2015), 175.

95. Modi, *Medical Jurisprudence* (1940), 341. This passage was the same in Modi's first edition (1920).

96. For example see Modi, *Medical Jurisprudence* (1940), 208, 220–21, 242, 262, 336. For a similar case in a more recent edition of Modi see Flavia Agnes, "To Whom Do Experts Testify? Ideological Challenges of Feminist Jurisprudence," *Economic & Political Weekly* 40, no. 18 (2005): 1864.

97. Modi, *Medical Jurisprudence* (1940), 219–21, 262–63.

98. For a forensic treatise in Bengali with pronounced anti-Muslim views see Kanai Lal Dey, *Medical Jurisprudence* (Calcutta, [1875]), 42, 265, 302.

99. Modi's caste was listed as "Vaisha (Hindu)" in "Duplicate passport," no. 12816, Rai Bahadur Jaisingh Parbhudas [*sic*] Modi, issued April 18, 1934 (IOR/L/PJ/11/2/2939). See figure 10.

book began (figure 1). A rolled-up sleeve revealed seven horizontal cuts down a dark-skinned upper forearm. The man told Modi that "he was struck with a razor by his opponent." The parallel slashes were each between one and four inches long but only one-eighth to one-sixth of an inch deep. They were "directed from within outwards." Because of their orientation and superficiality, Modi believed that these wounds were self-inflicted.[100] Modi's description of the man as a sweeper, along with almost a full-page photo, highlighted the man's Dalit status. Modi also complained about misinformation submitted by local police (many of whom would have been from lower castes) when they found a dead body.[101] Modi seemed to consider these reports careless, not deliberately false.[102]

In short, Modi positioned himself as the premier forensic treatise author when India was shaking off British rule. In doing so, he rejected the concept of native mendacity, while retaining other stereotypical views about falsity and dissimulation. Taking a position between the antiadversarial view of William Center and the anti-inquisitorial view of J. Douglas Young, J. P. Modi took a constructive stance on India's mixed criminal procedure: He wanted court-appointed lab experts to provide detailed written reports, and to be cross-examined under oath often.

As the adversarial-inquisitorial debate traveled to South Asia, it brought into focus the divide between men of science and men of law, and between supporters of Anglo adversarial legal systems and those in the Scots and German continental inquisitorial mode. Against this backdrop, the forensic lab expert's exemption from court appearances in India polarized figures with views like CE William Center's in the 1870s and Judge J. Douglas Young's in the 1930s. Although Young was Scottish, he was trained as a barrister in England, and his insistence on the rigorous adversarial treatment of experts reflected this. He had been a middleweight boxing champion at Cambridge, and in a verbal sense, boxing was what he wanted in the courtroom, as well.[103] Center's view aligned the scientific quest for truth with inquisitorialism, and arguably with the perceived imperatives of colonial rule. In between, J. P. Modi mixed and matched, shedding earlier English, Protestant, and colonial associations around how truth should be

100. Modi, *Medical Jurisprudence* (1940), 263.

101. See Deana Heath, *Colonial Terror: Torture and State Violence in Colonial India* (Oxford University Press, 2021), 161–62, 173. On caste and colonial policing in South India see Radha Kumar, *Police Matters: The Everyday State and Caste Politics in South India, 1900–1975* (Cornell University Press, 2021).

102. Modi, *Medical Jurisprudence* (1940), 4–5.

103. Ram and Kulkarni, *For Necessary Action*, 11.

pursued when law, science, and medicine met. All sides worried about the risk of falsity and wrongful convictions but disagreed over the source of the danger—whether competing partisan experts, the unaccountable solo lab expert, native mendacity, or some combination of these factors. At issue were questions about the mechanics of the search for truth. The question was not whether all sides were truth-seeking (they were), but rather, what the best *method* for discovering truth might be. The answer looked different not only between professionalized fields of knowledge but also within them.[104] And as Indian independence loomed, Modi's intervention in the debate changed the underlying assumption about why workable truth mechanics were so necessary—for justice, as in any society, and not because "the natives lied."

104. The incompatibility between professional cultures is a common theme in the history of forensic science and medicine. See Catherine Kelly and Imogen Goold, "Introduction: Lawyers' Medicine: The Interaction of the Medical Profession and the Law, 1760–2000," in *Lawyers' Medicine: The Legislature, the Courts and Medical Practice, 1760–2000*, ed. Imogen Goold and Catherine Kelly (Hart, 2009), 6–7; and Alison Adam, *A History of Forensic Science: British Beginnings in the Twentieth Century* (Routledge, 2016), 39–40.

CONCLUSION / Truth, Justice, and Testing

In 1871, three linked murder cases came before the Bombay High Court. Alibhai Mitha and his family were "on terms of enmity" with Umar Vali and his family. Both groups were part of the Bohra community of Shia Muslims in Broach (today, Bharuch in Gujarat). As the judge, James Gibbs, described it, "murders have been committed on each side—not, as would be naturally expected, by members of one faction on a member of the other, but by members of one faction on a helpless female of their own, *so as to throw either the guilt of blood or the blame of the crime on the other party*."[1] This book has featured other extreme cases of punitive self-harm reconfigured as false accusations of murder. Like those cases, the Broach cases were deeply gendered: Everyone who died for the sake of the family stratagem was female. What set the Broach cases apart and made them, in the judge's view, stranger than fiction, were their many reciprocal rounds of falsity.

In the first case, Alibhai Mitha was convicted of murdering his mother. The two families had a physical altercation, and Gori, the mother, was slightly wounded on the head. Alibhai confessed that his side had inflicted this injury—allegedly with his mother's consent—after a member of the other side was hit. Gori was admitted to hospital, and she died three days later. But the head injury did not kill her. Alibhai confessed that he initially planned to accuse Umar and his friends of simple assault. Then, though, "at the instigation of his own comrades he poisoned his mother and charged Umar and his friends with murder."

1. *Reg. v. Alibhai Mitha*, BHC Reports 8 (1871): 110. Italics added.

Alibhai brought his mother a meal laced with arsenic. She vomited so violently after eating it that she ruptured her spleen. According to the postmortem examination and chemical analysis, it was this organ injury, rather than the poisoning itself, that killed her.[2]

Meanwhile in the other family, Muhammad Vali was convicted of murdering his sister, Fatta, with an ax. This was the second case. Witnesses heard the woman scream, "Why do you kill me for other people?" Muhammad then "dashed his own head against the wall, wounding it severely" before riding off on his pony. He reported that his sister had been killed by the rival family during a scuffle over the construction of a wall. Soon, he was blamed for the murder himself. He claimed (without evidence) that he had been framed by Kavasha, a police inspector being investigated for taking bribes.[3]

The third case was the only one that did not end in a murder conviction. As a "set-off against the girl Fatta's death," another Muhammad—this time from Alibhai Mitha's side—said he wanted to kill himself. But his elderly mother begged "that she might be the victim instead." Muhammad or his relatives agreed and then assaulted her. The police found the mother wounded and "senseless on a cot," and her son with a chest wound. The old woman spent fifteen days in hospital, returned home, and then died six days later. The civil surgeon of Broach, Dr. Glen, certified that "these wounds did not bring about the death of the woman: she died of old age."[4] Any false accusation of murder against the other side did not make it into the record. But presumably the plan here, too, was to blame this death on the other side.

The Broach cases exemplify a key pattern from part 1 of this book, namely gendered instances of punitive self-harm repackaged as false accusations of murder. This form of disputing was not grounded in religion. In fact, it was often contrary to religious tenets (see chapter 2). A small number of people, both Hindu and Muslim, were willing to commit extreme violence to further disputes. When not committed on the individual self, this violence usually targeted vulnerable females in the larger clan. Reminiscent of *sati*, the narrative was often that the woman volunteered; she was typically elderly.

The Broach cases also illustrate falsity produced by forensic experts. Dr. Glen performed poorly in the Broach cases and was harshly rebuked by

2. *Reg. v. Alibhai Mitha*, 103–4; and *Reg. v. Muhammad Amanji and Hosan Amanji* (1871), in *Reg. v. Alibhai Mitha*, 111. Presumably, the chemical analysis detected only subfatal amounts of arsenic in Gori's body. On toxicological challenges relating to quantity see chapter 1.

3. *Reg. v. Muhammad Valli* (1871), in *R. v. Alibhai Mitha*, 109–10; and *Reg. v. Muhammad Amanji and Hosan Amanji*, in *R. v. Alibhai Mitha*, 111.

4. *Reg. v. Muhammad Amanji and Hosan Amanji*, in *Reg. v. Alibhai Mitha*, 112.

Justice Gibbs. In the first case (involving poison), Glen forwarded the contents of the stomach and vomit for analysis with "great delay and carelessness," although the results did lead to a conviction. In the third case, the court found his "death by old age" conclusion to be "unsatisfactory." Here there was no conviction, in part because of Glen's testimony. Gibbs criticized "the imperfect manner" in which Glen appeared to examine the bodies in these two cases. Although the judge did not say whether he thought corruption played a role, he did plan to recommend that the government remove Glen from his post. But then the doctor set sail for England and died on the way.[5]

The Broach cases also invite contemplation of larger questions that emerge out of this study. What was the relationship between truth and justice, and how was it shaped by the colonial context? In most times and places, we assume that we need truth to reach justice. To be sure, there are truth-based processes that do not promise justice, or at least that do not result in formal punishment other than public shaming—for example, truth-and-reconciliation processes from South Africa to Canada.[6] But examples of justice that do not involve extensive truth-determination processes are limited to a relatively small number of no-fault contexts. Think, for instance, of the Tokyo tuna court or strict liability regimes that apply to ultrahazardous activities.[7] Most legal systems aim to establish truth—or, for adversarialists, to get as close to it as possible—in order to provide justice through punishment or compensation for loss.

The Broach cases challenge the assumption that truth is a necessary precondition for justice. For some colonized subjects, fabricated accusations were attempts to obtain justice not through truth, but through falsity. In the Broach killings, actors tried to shoehorn one form of disputing (punitive self-harm) into another (colonial criminal law). They were trying to obtain justice for genuine wrongs through fabricated ones. Had the families of Alibhai Mitha and Umar Vali succeeded, three wrongful convictions would have delivered their idea of justice. These convictions effectively would have used the colonial legal system to perpetuate the opposite of that system's declared aims: the conviction of the wrong men for murder, where "wrong" was defined by a common law definition of causation and individual responsibility (chapter 2). Further, one could

5. *Reg. v. Muhammad Amanji and Hosan Amanji*, in *Reg. v. Alibhai Mitha*, 112. Glen and his wife left India on the P&O steamship *Khedive* in August 1871. "Homeward Mail," *TI*, August 15, 1871.

6. See Onur Bakiner, "Truth Commission Impact on Policy, Courts, and Society," *Annual Review of Law and Social Science* 17 (2021): 73–91.

7. See Eric A. Feldman, "The Tuna Court: Law and Norms in the World's Premier Fish Market," *California Law Review* 94 (2006): 313–69; and Cristina Carmody Tilley, "Just Strict Liability," *Cardozo Law Review* 43 (2022): 2317–35.

imagine that Alibhai Mitha and the two Muhammads might have understood their false accusations as anticolonial acts. The study of legal pluralism examines relationships between systems of norms, including the imitation or destruction of one legal order by another.[8] The Broach trio reveals another form of legal pluralism—namely, attempts by a noncolonial form of disputing to harness and subvert the colonial legal system. Like the Nadars of chapter 2, these Bohra defendants failed in their falsity. This is how we know about them. But others who are invisible in the archives of false cases must have succeeded, having thereby weakened the truth-justice connection intended by most legal systems. Cases like these show what we can see if we simultaneously remain open to the possibility that some accusations were false while rejecting the colonial sources' "native mendacity" explanations. Specifically, this approach makes visible legal pluralist interactions that were possibly anticolonial.

If we shift perspective from users of colonial law to those running the system itself, truth *was* necessary for justice. But what were the mechanics of truth determination, and how did the colonial context shape them? The Broach cases also speak to these questions, from part 2. The Broach judge's criticism of the civil surgeon reveals trouble in the relationship between law, science, and medicine. The colonial courts could promise neither truth nor justice if figures like Dr. Glen provided substandard scientific and medical analysis. Falsity could be the product just as much of incompetence as of trickery.

Much of this book, particularly part 1, has related to the history of forensic lab tests, including serological and toxicological testing. Science and technology studies (STS) scholars such as Trevor Pinch have generated a rich body of work on the role of scientific testing, identifying three types: prospective testing of a new technology, current testing of a technology that is already in use, and retrospective testing to figure out what went wrong after an accident or malfunction.[9] Forensic tests described here were of the third type, applied to a potential crime scene rather than a piece of technology. The question was always: What happened?

The testing framework is also useful for law. To conduct a legal analysis, one must determine whether a situation contains the necessary ingredients to make a particular "cause of action" (like breach of contract or the tort of fraud) or crime

8. See William Twining, "Normative and Legal Pluralism: A Global Perspective," *Duke Journal of Comparative and International Law* 20 (2010): 489.

9. See, by Trevor Pinch, "'Testing—One, Two, Three . . . Testing!': Toward a Sociology of Testing," *Science, Technology, and Human Values* 10, no. 1 (1993): 27, and "Coda: Testing and Why It Matters," in *Testing Hearing: The Making of Modern Aurality*, ed. Viktoria Tkaczyk, Mara Mills, and Alexandra Hui (Oxford University Press, 2020).

(like murder or rape). This recipe or list of relevant features is what lawyers call a test. The test is usually inherited within one's jurisdiction through precedent or laid out in legislation. In interdisciplinary legal studies, a common critique of this process of "doctrinal distillation" (to borrow Risa Goluboff's phrase) is that stripping away other contextual features of a case is a deliberate and demeaning act of erasure.[10] However, the exclusive focus on features that are relevant to the test reflects the process of legal analysis in a system that aims for precedent-based fairness, aspiring at least to treat like cases alike.[11] Deciding what makes two cases similar requires a comparison of the features identified by the test.[12] Without it, one has arbitration, not (state) law: fully contextualized, case-by-case dispute resolution with inconsistent outcomes.[13] Scientific tests help establish scientific facts, and legal tests determine guilt or liability. Each type of test seeks to approach truth in its own domain by focusing on particular features of a case, to the exclusion of others.

At times, scientific and legal testing interact with each other. The best known examples across common law jurisdictions are the American *Frye* and *Daubert* tests of the twentieth century.[14] These tests determined the admissibility of scientific findings, particularly for new or controversial methods and techniques.[15] *Frye v. US* (1923) established a test that gave decision-making power to the scientific community.[16] The legal test was whether a scientific test or method was generally accepted within the relevant scientific community. Since *Daubert v. Merrell Dow Pharmaceuticals* (1993), control has shifted back to the judiciary. Under

10. Risa Goluboff, *The Lost Promise of Civil Rights* (Harvard University Press, 2007), 238. For example, Dylan Penningroth makes this argument with reference to the omission of Black litigants' race in many US contract law cases. See Dylan C. Penningroth, "Race in Contract Law," *University of Pennsylvania Law Review* 170 (2022): 1199–1301.

11. See Nina Varsava, "Precedent, Reliance, and *Dobbs*," *Harvard Law Review* 136, no. 7 (2023): 1848–57.

12. Trevor Pinch's work on similarity analysis in scientific testing is useful for the legal context (particularly the precedent system). See Pinch, "'Testing,'" 30–35.

13. On the many problematic aspects of arbitration in the US context see Erik Encarnacion, "Boilerplate Indignity," *Indiana Law Journal* 94, no. 4 (2019): 1305–50; and Judith Resnik, "Diffusing Disputes: The Public in the Private of Arbitration, the Private in Courts, and the Erasure of Rights," *Yale Law Journal* 124, no. 8 (2015): 2804–2939. Arbitration has been restricted in the Indian context: Karan Gulati and Renuka Sane, "Consumer Disputes in the Financial Sector—Grievance Redress by Courts," *Indian Law Review* 6, no. 3 (2022): 417.

14. The Indian Supreme Court has cited and discussed *Frye* and *Daubert*. For instance see *Dharam Deo Yadav v. State of U.P.*, MANU/SC/0298/2014; and *Selvi and Others v. State of Karnataka*, MANU/SC/0325/2010.

15. See Jennifer L. Mnookin, "Idealizing Science and Demonizing Experts: An Intellectual History of Expert Evidence," *Villanova Law Review* 52, no. 4 (2007): 764–66; and Sheila Jasanoff, *Science at the Bar: Law, Science, and Technology in America* (Harvard University Press, 1995), 61–65.

16. *Frye v. US*, 293 F. 1013 (1923).

this test, the judge must weigh a series of criteria, of which general acceptability in the scientific community is but one.[17] These kinds of legal tests are meant to check scientific ones, blocking findings that fall short of legal standards despite meeting some scientific ones.[18]

In some instances, however, the layering of legal upon scientific tests produces a less, not more, rigorous result. For instance, historian of science Angela Creager has shown that in the US, the Toxic Substances Control Act of 1976 created disincentives for manufacturers to test the carcinogenicity of chemicals in their products.[19] In other words, the law may not improve, but instead worsen, the quality of work done by scientific testing for the public.

Something similar happened in colonial South Asia. The law in England applied a check on scientific testing: cross-examination of experts under oath. But in India and Burma, lab analysts deemed CEs did not have to come to court for questioning on their written findings, and they usually did not. Because of this rule (CrPC s.510), courts accepted misleading reports by careless or corrupt experts like Newman (chapter 4) without the benefit of clarification or explanation. The protected lab expert owed this special treatment to the colonial context, initially because travel to remote courts was disruptive to lab work. But then the rule persisted, even when logistical conditions improved (see introduction and chapters 4–5). The civil surgeon Glen from the Broach cases was not a CE, and he did have to undergo cross-examination. Even with cross-examination under oath, there were issues with substandard medical opinions, but at least criminal procedure for civil surgeons meant that their weaknesses were more easily exposed.

This book has shown that fear of false evidence in South Asia led to advances that contributed to forensic knowledge worldwide. The ability to detect venom in cattle rags and the fine-tuning of the precipitin test for bloodstains are cases in point. But although fear of the false was a catalyst for scientific innovation, its mirror image—increased reliance on and trust in forensic lab testing—produced law like CrPC s.510 that allowed lab experts to be careless at best and corrupt at worst. Like the Toxic Substances Control Act in the US, India's

---

17. Under the *Daubert* test, the factors to be weighed are (1) whether the technique can be and has been tested; (2) whether it has been subjected to peer review and publication; (3) its known or potential error rate; (4) the existence and maintenance of standards controlling its operation; and (5) whether it is generally accepted within the relevant scientific community. *Daubert v. Merrell Dow Pharmaceuticals*, 113 S. Ct. 2790 (1993).

18. It is worth acknowledging the counterargument that the *Frye* test, in particular, harmed the public by preventing new, cutting-edge science from being used in the courtroom.

19. Angela N. H. Creager, "To Test or Not to Test: Tools, Rules, and Corporate Data in US Chemicals Regulation," *Science, Technology, and Human Values* 46, no. 5 (2021): 975–97.

Criminal Procedure Code disincentivized rigorous testing in the lab. Colonial conditions eroded the intended bond between truth and justice, then, by allowing falsity to assert itself as truth through inadequate lab reports admitted as evidence. The colonial context may have produced better *tests* in particular areas of forensic science, but it also produced worse *testing* in general.

This book has also shown that falsity thrived through the interaction of systems of norms and knowledge. Contact between noncolonial disputing modes and criminal law could produce fabricated cases. Falsity also emerged from the interplay between legal tests and scientific ones—criminal procedure made lax for the convenience of colonial lab analysts. Of course, interaction between modes of disputing and knowledge systems such as science and law was (and still is) inevitable. But in the colonial context, these relationships could become distinctive engines of falsity. The result was the manipulation of colonial law, whether by the colonized trickster or corrupt expert, to produce a creative anticolonial concoction, a sinister miscarriage of justice, or both at the same time. The craft of the historian of the false lies in handling, and not avoiding, the connection between falsity, on the one hand, and diversity of knowledge or value systems, on the other.

Finally, the relationship between fear of falsity and concern over wrongful convictions has taken various forms over the past century and a half. In a setting like the US today, the innocence movement is powered by a modern version of fear of the false—that is, fear of false evidence generated by legal systems permeated by racial and class bias. In India and Burma a century ago, by contrast, concern over wrongful convictions flowed from fear of native and female mendacity, while colonial officials failed to recognize the role of procedural shortcuts and legal pluralism in the creation of false evidence. The shortcut for chemical examiners remains a feature of criminal procedure across South Asia—and one now being applied to a growing number of experts. And in India today, fear of the false has morphed from a predominantly racialized and gendered anxiety in the colonial era into one directed at ethno-religious minorities, those at the bottom of the caste hierarchy, and women (still).[20] Fear of the false and the risk of wrongful convictions did not evaporate when colonialism ended in South Asia; they just reconfigured themselves.

20. For instance see Manisha Sethi, *Kafkaland: Prejudice, Law and Counterterrorism in India* (Gurgaon: Three Essays Collective, 2014); and Mayur R. Suresh, *Terror Trials: Life and Law in Delhi's Courts* (Fordham University Press, 2023).

ACKNOWLEDGMENTS

This book has been in the works for over a decade against the backdrop of a global pandemic and a ransomware cyberattack on the British Library. I am grateful to many people and institutions for helping the project reach this point.

Working with the Corpus Juris book series and Cornell University Press has been an absolute pleasure. I thank Elizabeth Anker, Mahinder Kingra, and Jennifer Savran Kelly, along with everyone else at the press, for their good judgment and professionalism at every step of the publishing process. Comments from Susanna Blumenthal and the second reviewer, along with Pamela Haag, made this a better book. Thanks are also due to Lisa DeBoer for creating the index, Glenn Novak for copyediting, and Michelle Moran for proofreading.

I received generous external funding for this project. The Andrew W. Mellon Foundation Fellowship for Assistant Professors allowed me to pursue this research at the School of Historical Studies, Institute for Advanced Study (IAS) in Princeton, New Jersey (2011–12), as did a Shelby Cullom Davis Center Fellowship at the History Department, Princeton University (fall 2018). I received a National Endowment for the Humanities (NEH) summer stipend (2018). Any views, findings, conclusions, or recommendations expressed in this publication do not necessarily reflect those of the NEH. I was also the recipient of a Frederick Burkhardt Fellowship for Recently Tenured Scholars (F'18) from the American Council of Learned Societies, made possible by the Andrew W. Mellon Foundation. This fellowship was virtual at the National Humanities Center (NHC) in 2020–21. I thank everyone at these programs (both organizers and fellows) who made my time there so valuable, especially Marian Zelazny at the IAS, Matthew Booker and the librarians at the NHC, and Angela Creager at the Davis Center.

At the University of Wisconsin–Madison, I received significant support for this project (2010–25). I was the recipient of a UW Institute for Research in the Humanities Resident Fellowship (with thanks to the UW Law School), and of research funding from the Office of the Vice Chancellor for Research over many years. I am grateful for a Vilas Life Cycle Professorship and a Center for South Asia travel grant. This project also benefited from an H. I. Romnes Faculty Fellowship, consisting of research funds provided by the UW–Madison Office for the Vice Chancellor for Research and Graduate Education with funding from the Wisconsin Alumni Research Foundation.

The UW Law School has supported this project in more ways than I can mention here (2010–25). I received annual research funds, a summer seed grant, and regular summer salary support for work on this project. I must single out two units that provided crucial infrastructure for this research: the UW Law librarians and our IT department. I thank in particular Victoria Coulter, Petcy Lawrence-Wehrle, Sunil Rao, Bonnie Shucha, Jay Tucker, and Kristopher Turner at the Law Library, along with Darryl Berney, Eric Giefer, and Patrick Long at IT.

Many people worked on various aspects of this project while they were students at UW–Madison (2010–25): Aislinn Bailie, Ben Cramer, Alexandra Fleagle, Thomas Gordon, Sarah Kuelbs, Josslyne Kunz, Anwesha Maity, Shatrunjay Mall, Maddie Pollack, Mehak Qureshi, Sydney Schwantes, Hannah Schwartz, Nikhita Singam, and Lesley Skousen. They brought talents and training from many different fields, including comparative literature, geography, history, and law. Anwesha Maity translated Bengali sources. Ben Cramer designed the maps through the UW Cartography Lab. Shatrunjay Mall created the bibliography.

I would also like to thank the students in my undergraduate History of Forensic Science course and the experts specializing in canine detection of explosives, crime scene investigation, forensic pathology, and wood forensics who visited our class (2014–25). I was lucky to tour the Wisconsin State Crime Lab (Madison) and to observe an autopsy performed by Dr. Jamie E. Kallan. These experiences gave me a better understanding of forensics today and helped me historicize the themes of this book.

I gave talks and papers from this project at many scholarly institutions (2011–25). I thank everyone who organized these visits and shared their thoughts at the following: the American Bar Foundation (Chicago); the Baldy Center, University at Buffalo School of Law (SUNY); the Shelby Cullom Davis Center at the Department of History, Princeton University; Drexel University; the Emory University School of Law; the Indiana University Bloomington Arts and Humanities Festival; the School of Historical Studies, Institute for Advanced Study (Princeton, NJ); the Centre for the Study of Law and Governance, Jawaharlal Nehru University; the Center for South Asian Studies, University of Michigan; the University of Minnesota Law School; the Department of the History and Sociology of Science, University of Pennsylvania; the Department of History, Queen's University (Kingston, ON); Rutgers University; the Center for Law and History, Stanford University; the Department of History, Syracuse University; the University of California, Irvine Law School; the Department of History, Washington University in St. Louis; and Yale Law School.

Since the pandemic, we have seen a flowering of online academic events. I thank everyone who hosted and provided feedback at virtual events when I presented this work (2020–22) via the Jawaharlal Nehru University and O. P. Jindal Global University LASSnet webinar; the Global Forensic Histories workshop; the International Symposium on Crime Studies, Centre for Criminology and Forensic Studies, O. P. Jindal Global University; the Max Planck Institute for Legal History–Tel Aviv University Law's Transnational Legal History Workshop; the National Humanities Center; New York University's South Asia talk series; and the Department of History and British Studies Center, Rutgers University.

I also presented this research at many conferences and workshops (2012–25), including the American Association for the History of Medicine conference (Minneapolis); the American Society for Legal History conference (Toronto); the Annual Conference on South Asia (Madison, WI); the Asian Legal History conferences (Hong Kong and Hue, Vietnam); the "Contours of Legal History in India" workshop (National Law School of India University, Bengaluru, cosponsored by the Max Planck Institute for Legal History and Legal Theory); the History of Science Society meeting (Atlanta); the Law and Social Sciences Research Network (LASSnet) conference (Delhi); the Law and Society Association meetings (Mexico City, Minneapolis, New Orleans); the "Locating Forensic Science and Medicine" conference (London); and the Legal Histories of Empire conferences (Barbados and Maynooth, Ireland). The questions and comments I received at these meetings greatly enriched the project.

At my home institution of UW–Madison, I presented this work at the Center for the Humanities; the Center for South Asia; the Department of History; the History of Science, Medicine, and Technology program; the Institute for Research in the Humanities; and at South Asia Legal Studies Working Group sessions and Wednesday Workshops at the UW Law School.

It is one of the great pleasures of my life to interact with so many intellectually curious and learned people. My sincere thanks to the following scholars, lawyers, and others for so generously sharing their thoughts in person or by e-mail: Flavia Agnes, Andrew Amstutz, George Aumoithe, Danna Agmon, Orna Alyagon Darr, Kunal Ambasta, Saloni Ambastha, Aparna Balachandran, Aditya Balasubramanian, Swethaa S. Ballakrishnen, Patricia Barton, Pratiksha Baxi, Yael Berda, Poulomi Bhadra, Debjani Bhattacharyya, Deborah Blum, Susanna Blumenthal, Ian Burney, Christian Burset, E. Claire Cage, Pratik Chakrabarti, Yug Mohit Chaudhry, Raymond Cocks, Donal Coffey, Jonathan Connolly, Fara Dabhoiwala, Donald R. Davis Jr., Manpreet Dhillon, Catherine Evans, Khaled Fahmy, Anwesha Ghosh, Ruth Ginio, Ryan Greenwood, Daniel Grey, Sumit Guha,

Menaka Guruswamy, Christopher Hamlin, Rivi Handler-Spitz, Will Hanley, Samantha Kahn Herrick, Isabel Huacuja Alonso, Neha Jain, Jeffrey Jentzen, Tom Johnson, Aparna Kapadia, Manav Kapur, Vikramaditya Khanna, Rahela Khorakiwala, Elizabeth Kolsky, Riyad Sadiq Koya, Jayanth Krishnan, Harshan Kumarasingham, Kiran Kumbhar, Jack Jin Gary Lee, Janny Leung, Elizabeth Lhost, Assaf Likhovski, Sida Liu, Jinee Lokaneeta, Chandra Mallampalli, Serena Mayeri, Michael W. McCann, Alastair McClure, Paul G. McHugh, John E. McLeod, Mary X. Mitchell, Uponita Mukherjee, Ishita Pande, Dinyar Patel, Trais (Quentin) Pearson, Bianca Premo, Helmut Puff, Mrinalini Rajagopalan, Jothie Rajah, Bhavani Raman, Kalyani Ramnath, Reeju Ray, Jeff Redding, Tamara Relis, Chao Ren, Alison Dundes Renteln, Christopher Roberts, Cassia Roth, Jonathan Saha, Priyasha Saksena, Mrinal Satish, Benjamin Schonthal, David Schorr, Abhinav Sekhri, Franziska Seraphim, Madhavi Shukla, Charu Singh, Radhika Singha, Matthew Sommer, Julia Stephens, Rachel Sturman, Anup Surendranath, Kara W. Swanson, Anisha Thomas, Elizabeth Thornberry, Helen Tilley, Robert Travers, Sylvia Vatuk, Neha Vermani, Stefan Vogenauer, Rachel Watson, Keren Weitzberg, Barbara Welke, Natasha Wheatley, Mike Widener, Heather Wolffram, Dominik Wujastyk, and Nurfadzilah Yahaya. I apologize to anyone I may have left out inadvertently. Special thanks for their friendship and insights on this project are due to Binyamin Blum, Rohit De, and Projit Bihari Mukharji.

I thank all of the scholars I interacted with via #twitterstorians during that platform's heyday (2014–24), including Rohan Deb Roy, Sanchia deSouza, and Rakesh Sengupta. I have also enjoyed communications sparked by my South Asian Legal History Resources website. Working with Sujata Massey (author of the Perveen Mistry novels) and Rose Eveleth (host of the Flash Forward podcast), along with Shrishti Malhotra and Anahita Sachdev (of *The Swaddle*), were among the most rewarding of these connections. I thank them for making my research more accessible to nonacademic audiences.

At UW–Madison, many colleagues (past and present) gave me excellent feedback on parts of this project over the years. For this I thank BJ Ard, Nate Atkinson, Joshua Braver, Tonya Brito, Thomas H. Broman, Susannah Camic Tahk, Emily Cauble, Anthony Cerulli, Anuj Desai, Torey Dolan, Howard S. Erlanger, Keith A. Findley, Nyamagaga Gondwe, Florence C. Hsia, Richard C. Keller, Devin Kennedy, Cecelia M. Klingele, Heinz Klug, Christopher Lau, Gwendolyn Leachman, Susan E. Lederer, B. Venkat Mani, Ion Meyn, Nicole C. Nelson, Lynn K. Nyhart, Renagh O'Leary, Sunil Rao, Margaret Raymond, David S. Schwartz, Steph Tai, Dan Tokaji, Nina Varsava, Lisa Washington, and Louise Young. I am especially grateful to Sumudu Atapattu, Mou Banerjee, Alexandra Huneeus, and James A. Jaffe (and Lucy) for their thoughts and friendship. In addition, we were lucky to have Cynthia Farid and Maryam Khan as SJD candidates at the UW Law School: Their time in Madison was a golden age for South Asian legal studies at UW. Nicole Nelson's graduate History of Science proseminar, which I audited, was excellent preparation for this project.

Also in Madison, I thank the Game Night gang: Saverio, Elena, and Carina Spagnolie; Madison Thompson, Oliver Levine, and Cashew; Brian Street, Hui Wang, and Summer; Chris Rycroft, Marta Gaglia, and Leo; Stephen Wright and Jim Luedtke—and of course Jean-Luc Thiffeault. Our Friday-night dinners made the past eight years so much better.

Further away, I thank my grad school friends, the Princeton Family: Kutlu Akalin, Ryan Jordan, Volker Menze, Mark Meulenbeld, Clara Oberle, Ishita Pande, and Klaus Veigel. We are now spread across so many time zones that we have to alternate zoom calls when those of us in Hong Kong or California can join. I am also grateful to these friends around the world: Lalita du Perron in the Bay area; Debra Shushan in Virginia; Farzin Vejdani and Hengameh Saberi in Toronto; Rachel Berger in Montréal; Aditi Khanna and Biliana Draganova in London; Eleanor Newbigin in Cambridge/London; Tushna Thapliyal in Mumbai; and Devika Bordia, Arudra Burra, Kaveri Gill, and Dinesh Singh in Delhi. And I cherish the friendship of my former teachers John Hannah and D. B. J. Snyder in Penticton; Elizabeth Elbourne and Faith Wallis in Montréal; and Dirk Hartog in Princeton.

I thank my family, particularly my sister, Pari Sharafi, and nieces, Sunniva and Stella Sharafi-Listhaug, to whom this book is dedicated. They have shown remarkable strength and courage over the past decade, while this book was being written. I hope that my elderly father, Mohammad Ali Ghaed Sharafi, will still be with us when this book is published. His life and love of books are an inspiration to me and many of our relatives in Canada, the US, Norway, Germany, and Iran.

At home in Madison, I am grateful for my two boys. Our chihuahua mix Feni (AKA Tiny) was by my side most of the time while I was working on this book, whether on our front porch or wrapped in a blanket in his daybed by my desk. He is my ur-dog and the ideal writing coach. Most of all, I thank my husband Jean-Luc Thiffeault—for making me laugh so much and for our life together.

An earlier version of chapter 2 was published as "The Imperial Serologist and Punitive Self-Harm: Bloodstains and Legal Pluralism in British India," in Ian Burney and Christopher Hamlin, eds., *Global Forensic Cultures: Making Fact and Justice in the Modern Era*, pp. 60–85. © 2019 Johns Hopkins University Press. Reprinted with permission of Johns Hopkins University Press.

APPENDIX 1

THE LAW OF CRIME

The law governing crime in late colonial South Asia was the product of intensive legislating by the Indian Law Commissions, four successive bodies set up between 1834 and 1879.[1] The centerpiece of substantive criminal law was the Indian Penal Code (IPC) of 1860, a colossus that took several decades to complete.[2] It was unlike anything in English criminal law at the time, which consisted mainly of case law.[3] Another key statute was the Criminal Procedure Code (CrPC) of 1861, which covered police, prosecution, court, and penal processes, including search and seizure, arrest, detention, charging, bail, trial, appeals, and penalties.[4] And there was the Indian Evidence Act of 1872, which governed the admissibility of evidence across civil and criminal domains.[5] These three foundational statutes were revised many times. During the colonial era, key amendments to the CrPC were passed in 1872, 1882, and 1898, and included changes to the use of the jury and bail.[6] In 1883–84, the highly volatile Ilbert Bill controversy erupted over whether the CrPC should permit South Asian judges to try European criminal

1. M. P. Jain, *Outlines of Indian Legal and Constitutional History* (Gurgaon: LexisNexis Butterworths Wadhwa Nagpur, 2006), 427–62.

2. Jain, 463–70. See also David Skuy, "Macaulay and the Indian Penal Code of 1862: The Myth of the Inherent Superiority and Modernity of the English Legal System Compared to India's Legal System in the Nineteenth Century," *MAS* 32, no. 3 (1998): 513–57; Barry Wright, "Macaulay's Indian Penal Code: Historical Context and Originating Principles," in *Codification, Macaulay and the Indian Penal Code: The Legacies and Modern Challenges of Criminal Law Reform*, ed. Wing-Cheong Chan et al. (Ashgate, 2011); and Arushi Garg, "Thomas Macaulay, the Indian Penal Code (1837)," in *Leading Works in Criminal Law*, ed. Chloë Kennedy and Lindsay Farmer (Routledge, 2024), 14–39.

3. One notable exception in English criminal law was the Offences Against the Person Act of 1861.

4. Jain, *Outlines*, 485–86. See also Elizabeth Kolsky, "Codification and the Rule of Colonial Difference: Criminal Procedure in British India," *Law and History Review* 23, no. 3 (2005): 631–83.

5. Jain, *Outlines*, 483–85. See also H. S. Cunningham, *The Indian Evidence Act, No. I of 1872*, ed. H. H. Shephard (Madras: Higginbotham, 1908), i–lxxi; and Kunal Ambasta, "One Hundred (and Fifty) Years of Solitude: The Indian Evidence Act 1872 as a Lost Project of Law Reform," *Indian Law Review* 8, no. 1 (2024): 1–19.

6. After independence, there were further amendments to the CrPC in India, Pakistan, and Bangladesh. These included versions of 1955 and 1973 for India; 1958 for East and West Pakistan; 1993, 2011, and 2022 for Pakistan; and 1992 and 2009 for Bangladesh.

defendants (the outcome was to allow it but with a majority-white jury).[7] All three statutes (the CrPC, IPC, and Indian Evidence Act) would be exported to many other parts of the British empire, from Sudan to the Straits Settlements.[8]

A vast case law built up around these statutes. These precedents were made visible and accessible for future use through the rise of published law reports, including publications with regional series like the official *Indian Law Reports* and the *All India Reporter*.[9] In addition, a universe of colonial law journals like the *Criminal Law Journal of India* sprang up around the turn of the twentieth century.[10] Many journals published both recent judgments and articles for practitioners in South Asia, along with reprinted articles from across the common law world.[11]

7. See Partha Chatterjee, *The Nation and Its Fragments: Colonial and Postcolonial Histories* (Princeton University Press, 1993), 20–22; Mrinalini Sinha, *Colonial Masculinity: The "Manly Englishman" and the "Effeminate Bengali" in Late Nineteenth Century India* (Manchester University Press, 1995), 33–68; Kolsky, "Codification," 680–82; and Cynthia Farid, "Perceiving Law Without Colonialism: Revisiting Courts and Constitutionalism in South Asia," *International Journal of Law in Context* 19, no. 3 (2023): 287–88.

8. See W. F. Craies, "Soudan Criminal Law," *Journal of the Society of Comparative Legislation* 2, no. 1 (1900): 137–40; and Walter J. Napier, "Eastern Colonies: Straits Settlements," *Journal of the Society of Comparative Legislation* 3, no. 2 (1901): 323–25.

9. See Jain, *Outlines*, 659–64, especially on the Indian Law Reports Act of 1875. For a list of citation abbreviations for law reports from colonial South Asia see South Asian Legal History Resources, https://salh.law.wisc.edu/about-me/citation-abbreviations-explained/, last modified April 19, 2023.

10. See Jain, *Outlines*, 662–63. The earliest law journal in this wave of publications was the *Madras Law Journal*, which began in 1891. The *Criminal Law Journal of India* started in 1904.

11. For a list of articles in seven leading law journals from colonial South Asia see South Asian Legal History Resources, https://salh.law.wisc.edu/article-listings-for-colonial-south-asian-law-journals/, last modified on March 3, 2020.

APPENDIX 2

CRIMINAL COURTS AND JURIES

At the bottom of the pyramid of criminal courts was a tiered series of magistrates' courts. Magistrates were not generally trained as lawyers but were lay judges. They handled crimes deemed minor or involving small sums of money.[1] The highest ranking—district magistrates—were members of the Indian Civil Service (ICS).[2] In major cities like Bombay, Calcutta, and Madras, magistrates' courts were called Police Courts (although they were institutionally separate from the police).

One level above magistrates' courts were the Sessions Courts, which drew its judges from the legal profession and the ICS.[3] These courts handled more serious criminal cases, along with appeals and references on points of law from magistrates' courts.[4]

Above the Sessions Courts were the regional High Courts, which were the highest courts in South Asia itself for most of the colonial period (see map 2).[5] In addition to exercising appellate jurisdiction over cases from the Sessions Courts, the High Courts had original jurisdiction over some cases coming from within their respective cities. Most High Court judges came from the ICS or were

1. On the many subtypes of magistrates see A. C. Ganguly, *Practical Guide to Criminal Court Practice* (Calcutta: Eastern Law House, 1937), 30–33.

2. ICS training did involve some study of law, but it was brief and oriented toward statutes, not case law. See Cynthia Farid, "Imperial Constitutionalism: Judicial Politics and Separation of Powers in Colonial India (1861–1935)" (SJD diss., University of Wisconsin Law School, 2020), 122–39; and James A. Jaffe, "'Grim Presents': ICS Judges and Trial by Jury," in *Trial by Jury in India: A History, 1862–1973* (in progress).

3. For a sample of District and Sessions judges who were pleaders, vakils, barristers, or ICS members see V. Ramanjulu Naidu, ed., *Indian Year-Book and Annual, 1912* (Nayudupeta: Indian Year Book and Annual Office, 1912), 279 (S. Gopala Chari), 281 (B. L. Gupta), 306 (Muhammad Rafik), and 340 (C. K. Srinivasa Row).

4. The District Court was the highest court for each district on the civil side. The phrase "District and Sessions Court" referred to the combined civil and criminal apex court for each district.

5. See Alastair McClure, *Trials of Sovereignty: Mercy, Violence, and the Making of Criminal Law in British India, 1857–1922* (Cambridge University Press, 2024), 150–54; and Rahela Khorakiwala, *From the Colonial to the Contemporary: Images, Iconography, Memories, and Performances of Law in India's High Courts* (Hart, 2019).

trained as barristers at the Inns of Court in London.[6] If a Sessions Court issued a death sentence, it had to be confirmed by the relevant High Court.[7]

Technically, South Asian cases could be appealed from the High Courts to the Judicial Committee of the Privy Council (JCPC) in London, which was the British empire's apex court. However, the JCPC took very few criminal appeals. It did not regard itself as a criminal court of appeal, as it only accepted criminal cases in extreme cases where there was "a disregard of the forms of legal process," "some violation of the principles of natural justice," or similar serious issue that caused "substantial and grave injustice."[8] The principle at work was a distinctly colonial one: The JCPC seemed to understand how much colonial rule was held in place by criminal law, and refused to interfere.[9] During the last decade of the colonial era (1938–47), a court called the Federal Court became the first India-based single apex court for South Asia. But its criminal jurisdiction was limited—to appeals that involved "a substantial question of law as to the interpretation" of the Government of India Act of 1935—and its caseload was small.[10] In short, the High Courts were the final courts of appeal for most criminal cases from South Asia.

Some Courts of Session used juries.[11] The use of juries was highly variable across British India and Burma. Local governments could extend the right to

---

6. See M. P. Jain, *Outlines of Indian Legal and Constitutional History* (Gurgaon: LexisNexis Butterworths Wadhwa Nagpur, 2006), 258–70. On ICS and barrister-judges in colonial India see Farid, "Imperial Constitutionalism." On the Inns see Mitra Sharafi, "South Asians at the Inns of Court: Empire, Expulsion, and Redemption Circa 1900," in *In Between and Across: Legal History Without Boundaries*, ed. Kenneth W. Mack and Jacob Katz Cogan (Oxford University Press, 2024), 179–201. Some early South Asian judges were vakils (rather than barristers or ICS members) before their elevation to the High Court bench. See T. C. A. Achintya, "Practitioners of the Law: Legal Professionals in British South Asia 1770–1870" (PhD diss., University of Virginia, 2025), 246–47.

7. Ganguly, *Practical Guide*, 34.

8. *In re Abraham Mallory Dillett*, Law Reports, Appeal Cases 12 (1887): 459, 467; and *Clifford and Others v. The King-Emperor*, CWN 18 (1913–14): 376. See also "Indian Murder Appeal," *ABP*, April 16, 1917.

9. See *In re Abraham Mallory Dillett*, 466; the 1862 case of *Queen v. Joykissen Mookerjee*, Moore NS 1, 295–98, reprinted in English Reports (full reprint) 15 (1809–65): 712–13; and the 1863 case of *The Falkland Islands Company v. the Queen*, Moore NS 1, 312–13, reprinted in English Reports (full reprint) 15 (1809–65): 718–19.

10. Rohit De, "Emasculating the Executive: The Federal Court and Civil Liberties in Late Colonial India: 1942–1944," in *Fates of Political Liberalism in the British Post-Colony: The Politics of the Legal Complex*, ed. Terence C. Halliday et al. (Cambridge University Press, 2012), 67–68.

11. On the jury in South Asian legal history see Manmatha N. Mukerji, *Trial by Jury and Misdirection* (Calcutta: Eastern Law House, 1937). Also see, by James A. Jaffe, "Custom, Identity, and the Jury in India, 1800–1832," *Historical Journal* 57, no. 1 (2014): 131–55, "After Nanavati," *Economic and Political Weekly* 53, no. 32 (2017): 18–20, and *Trial by Jury in India* (in progress); McClure, *Trials of Sovereignty*, 137–43; Elizabeth Kolsky, *Colonial Justice in British India: White Violence and the Rule of Law* (Cambridge University Press, 2010), esp. 217–21; Mitra Sharafi, *Law and Identity in Colonial*

jury trial to any type of criminal case by district.[12] As a result, some districts used it, while others did not. Some used the jury only for serious violent crimes, while others used it only for property crimes. There was also the "special jury" (rather than the "common jury"), which was used in death penalty cases, at a judge's discretion in presidency towns, or when the local government had designated its use for certain offenses. Special jurors were deemed to have "superior qualifications in respect of property, character or education." In practice, the pool of special jurors was more heavily European than the regular pool of jurors. Often, the outcome of a case was determined by the decision to use a special jury, as opposed to a regular one.[13]

In general, jurors' racial loyalties dominated in colonial India and Burma. White jurors in interracial criminal cases tended to acquit white defendants, even when the evidence supported conviction.[14] Despite this dynamic, the colonial state attempted to dilute the power of juries by enabling judges to refer jury verdicts to the upper courts for potential reversal.[15] In turn, preservation of the jury became a key aim of the rising nationalist movement in the early twentieth century.[16] In postcolonial India, the jury was ultimately eliminated in criminal trials. Contrary to popular belief, the jury was abolished not as a result of the infamous Nanavati case of 1959, but quietly in the CrPC 1973 owing to misgivings among politico-legal elites over caste, class, and jury nullification.[17]

South Asia: Parsi Legal Culture, 1772–1947 (Cambridge University Press, 2014), 198–210; and Kalyani Ramnath, "The Colonial Difference Between Law and Fact: Notes on the Criminal Jury in India," *IESHR* 50, no. 3 (2013): 341–63.

12. CrPC (1898), s.269 in H. T. Prinsep, *The Code of Criminal Procedure Being Act V of 1898* (Calcutta: Thacker, Spink, 1901), 270–72.

13. On the special jury see CrPC (1898), ss.269, 276, 312–14, 325, and 330 in Prinsep, 270–72, 277–80, 311–12, 316, and 318. See also Sharafi, *Law and Identity*, 199, at note 33, 253.

14. Kolsky, *Colonial Justice*, 219–21.

15. Sharafi, *Law and Identity*, 205.

16. Sharafi, 200–205.

17. Jaffe, "After Nanavati." This change was not regarded favorably by judges of the Calcutta High Court. See James A. Jaffe, "Calcutta and the 'Real' Last Jury Trial in India," NLSIR Online, October 19, 2022 (on file with author).

APPENDIX 3

FORENSIC INSTITUTIONS

Two forensic institutions were well established in British India and Burma before the twentieth century. The first was the chemical examiners (CEs). The first CE, W. B. O'Shaughnessy, was appointed in 1840 in Calcutta, but it was only in the 1870s that the CEs became well known as a network of military physicians whose labs tested chemical samples for the state.[1] The CEs processed an extraordinary number of submissions for many different parts of the state, including food products checked for adulteration and a vast flow of everything from alcohol to explosives for Customs and Excise (particularly at port cities).[2] In cases of suspected poisoning, they produced written certificates for the criminal courts.[3] This network of labs grew around the turn of the twentieth century. New regional CE labs emerged during these decades, sometimes as an offshoot from another lab like Sind from Bombay and the North-West Frontier Province from Punjab.[4] By 1908, there were eight regional labs covering Bengal, Bombay, Burma, Madras, the North-West Frontier Province, Punjab, Sind, and the United and Central Provinces (shown a few decades later in map 1).[5] Each lab produced

1. See David Arnold, *Toxic Histories: Poison and Pollution in Modern India* (Cambridge University Press, 2016), 50–54, 111–17; and Patricia Barton, "Innovative Knowledge in Traditional Settings: The Bengal Chemical Examiners' Laboratory and the Medico-Legal Understanding of Cocaine, 1880s–1920s" (talk presented at the 50th Annual Conference on South Asia, Madison, WI, October 22, 2022). On the early history of the CEs see "Report of the CE to Government, Punjab, for the Year 1879" (IOR/V/24/418).

2. CEs based in port cities regularly complained of the heavy flow of submissions coming from Customs and Excise. For example see "The Bombay Chemical Analyser's Report for 1895," *IMCR* 4, no. 5 (1896): 235–36. On adulteration see Rachel Berger, "Clarified Commodities: Managing Ghee in Interwar India," *Technology and Culture* 60, no. 4 (2019): 1004–26.

3. I have been unable to find a single CE's certificate preserved in the archives.

4. See Reports of the Bombay Chemical Analyser to Government for the years 1891–1935 (IOR/V/24/406–409), which includes the early reports for Sind; and Reports of the CE to the Government of the North-West Frontier Province, 1922–31 (IOR/V/24/429).

5. The title "chemical analyser" was distinctive to Bombay and Sind, but the position appears to have been identical to a CE. The full title of the CE for Burma (1906–15) and the United and Central Provinces ([1894?]–1917) was "CE and Bacteriologist." Until 1901, the CE for the United and Central Provinces was known as the CE for the North-Western Provinces and Oudh, and for the Central Provinces. On the creation of the Burma CE lab see Jonathan Saha, "'Uncivilized Practitioners':

an annual report, creating by 1947 a formidable archive of quantitative and qualitative accounts of suspected poisoning.[6]

The second forensic institution that had an early start in colonial India was the coroner's inquest. Outside of the colonial context, death investigation in much of South Asia was handled by *panchayat*, a group of senior male members of the village, caste, or religious community. Many communities prohibited the handling of their dead by outsiders.[7] During the colonial period, *panchayats* ceded power over death investigation to the coroner's system, particularly in cases like poisoning where the cause of death was not obvious to the naked eye.[8] The coroner's system was a medieval English institution that came to South Asia with the East India Company.[9] Coroners oversaw the inquest, which determined cause of death and used a jury.[10] The coroner's jury consisted of an odd number of five to fifteen people from the local community who issued a verdict of accident, suicide, homicide, or natural cause.[11] The coroner and jury would typically visit the site of death and view the body. The coroner could call witnesses and order an autopsy by a physician, whether a "police surgeon" (in large urban centers) or civil surgeon (a physician representing the state in a district).[12] During the late

Medical Subordinates, Medico-Legal Evidence, and Misconduct in Colonial Burma, 1875–1907," *South East Asia Research* 20, no. 3 (2012): 439.

6. See CE Reports from across South Asia (IOR/V/24/404–31). For Madras CE reports see the IOR/P series and Annual Reports, Government of Madras, box 1144.020000 (AAC, BL). Summaries of annual CE reports were occasionally published in periodicals like *The Analyst* and *The Indian Medico-Chirurgical Review*.

7. For example see "Notes of a lecture delivered at the Detective Training School, Howrah by Colonel Sutherland, Government Serologist" [1918], no. 1, 2 (unpaginated), in Papers of Ormandy Ballantine Fane Sewell, MSS Eur F419.

8. For instance see Mitra Sharafi, *Law and Identity in Colonial South Asia: Parsi Legal Culture, 1772–1947* (Cambridge University Press, 2014), 52. It is important to note, however, that *panchayats* have continued to play a role in state-run death investigation processes. For example see Devika Bordia, "The Politics of Custom: Blood Money, Disputes, and Tribal Leadership in Western India," *Diogenes* 60, no. 3–4 (2015): 156–58; and Radha Kumar, "Witnessing Violence, Witnessing as Violence: Police Torture and Power in Twentieth-Century India," *Law & Social Inquiry* 47, no. 3 (2022): 953.

9. On the coroner's system during the East India Company era see the papers of Robert Kitson, Bombay Civil Service (1775–83) (IOR/H/732); and Elizabeth Kolsky, *Colonial Justice in British India: White Violence and the Rule of Law* (Cambridge University Press, 2010), 123–24, which refers to *John C. Marshman, The Darogah's Manual, Comprising Also the Duties of Landholders in Connection with the Police* ([Serampore,] 1850), 42–47.

10. See generally Jeffrey M. Jentzen, "Death and Empire: Medicolegal Investigations and Practice Across the British Empire," in *Global Forensic Cultures: Making Fact and Justice in the Modern Era*, ed. Ian Burney and Christopher Hamlin (Johns Hopkins University Press, 2019), 149–62.

11. Coroners' juries in colonial India do not seem to have issued "undetermined" verdicts.

12. The police surgeon was originally a Scottish institution. See Brenda White, "Training Medical Policemen: Forensic Medicine and Public Health in Nineteenth-Century Scotland," in *Legal Medicine in History*, ed. Michael Clark and Catherine Crawford (Cambridge University Press, 1994), 155–58;

nineteenth century, the Coroners' Act of 1871, the Prisons Act of 1894, and various versions of the CrPC further developed the inquest system. Coroners' inquests continued in Calcutta and Bombay.[13] But both in such cities and outside of them, the alternative was a police inquest, which was overseen by a police officer and used "two or more respectable inhabitants of the neighborhood" instead of a jury.[14] In addition, there were special processes for the investigation of deaths in police custody and those involving railway accidents.[15] If these various types of inquest produced a verdict of homicide—and if there was a suspect—the case could proceed to a murder trial in the criminal courts.

Aside from the CEs and coroners, most other forensic institutions sprang up in the 1890s to the 1910s. The forensic use of fingerprinting emerged out of colonial India, adapting the centuries-old Asian practice of using fingerprints as signatures.[16] The world's first fingerprint bureau opened in Calcutta in 1897, and the appointment of regional fingerprint experts followed.[17] Some police

---

and K. A. Couzens, "The Police Surgeon, Medico-Legal Networks and Criminal Investigation in Victorian Scotland," in *Crime and the Construction of Forensic Objectivity from 1850*, ed. Alison Adam (Palgrave Macmillan, 2020), 125–59.

13. See the Coroners' Act (no. 4 of 1871) (IOR/L/PJ/6/1997, file 925).

14. CrPC, 1898, s.174 in H. T. Prinsep, *The Code of Criminal Procedure Being Act V of 1898* (Calcutta: Lahiri & Co., 1901), 153. See also CrPC, 1898, ss.175–76 in Prinsep, 156–57; CrPC, 1872, ss.21, 135 in [William Griffith], *The Code of Indian Criminal Procedure: Being Act No. X of 1872* (London, 1872), 7, 37; and CrPC, 1882 (Act 10 of 1882), ss.176, 529 (IOR/V/8/54). On the police inquest see A. C. Ganguly, *Practical Guide to Criminal Court Practice* (Calcutta: Eastern Law House, 1937), 59–60. There were criticisms and calls to abolish the coroner's inquest in the colonial period. For example see "The Coroner's Court," *TI*, January 15, 1925. However, as the police inquest became dominant, there have been calls in postcolonial India to replace it with the coroner's inquest. For example see Law Commission of India, "Report No. 206: Proposal for Enactment of New Coroners Act Applied to the Whole of India" (Delhi: Law Commission of India, 2008). On death investigation in India today see Fabien Provost, *Les mots de la morgue: La médicine légale en Inde du Nord* (Éditions Mimésis, 2021).

15. On railway accidents see s.174 of CrPC, 1898, in Prinsep, *Code of Criminal Procedure*, 155–56. For deaths in custody, a magistrate held an inquiry into the cause of death. In other situations, this decision was left to the magistrate's discretion. See s.176 of CrPC, 1898 in Prinsep, 157, and the Prisons Act (9 of 1894), ss.15, 17 in H. A. B. Rattigan, *The Bengal Regulations, the Acts of the Governor-General in Council, the Acts of the Lieutenant-Governor of the Punjab in Council, and the Frontier Regulations. . . .* 5th ed. (Lahore, 1899), 3:2790–91.

16. See Radhika Singha, "Settle, Mobilize, Verify: Identification Practices in Colonial India," *Studies in History* 16, no. 2 (2000): 151–98; Chandak Sengoopta, *Imprint of the Raj: How Fingerprinting Was Born in Colonial India* (Macmillan, 2003); and Simon Cole, *Suspect Identities: A History of Fingerprinting and Criminal Identification* (Harvard University Press, 2001), 60–96.

17. R. K. Tewari and K. V. Ravikumar, "History and Development of Forensic Science in India," *Journal of Postgraduate Medicine* 46, no. 4 (2000): 303–8. For references to regional fingerprint experts see "Summoning of the Chief Inspector of Explosives to give evidence in Criminal Courts," 18, Home: Judicial, Proc. no. 738, 1928 (NAI) and "Plan for the Forensic Science Laboratory, United Provinces, Being the Proposals Formulated by the Forensic Science Laboratory Committee and a

departments also had their own fingerprint analysts.[18] Palm print analysis was accepted as an extension of the study of fingerprints.[19] There was also some use of footprint analysis, although government efforts were more sustained in Ceylon than in India.[20]

The post of chief inspector of explosives (CIE) was created in 1898. This figure was based in northern India or Calcutta, and extra inspectors were added elsewhere.[21] These inspectors, who were initially British but also South Asian by the 1920s, traveled along regional "circles" for much of the year to inspect sites and testify in court.[22] Their original purpose was to reduce accidents caused by the manufacture, storage, and transportation of petroleum and other industrial explosives. However, they soon became crucial experts in political bomb cases associated with anarchists and nationalist revolutionaries.[23]

The post of government examiner of questioned documents (GEQD) was created in 1904. Until this time, witnesses on the authenticity of handwriting were usually bank clerks or people who knew the individual in question.[24] The

---

Sub-Committee of Specialists, 1945–46" (hereafter "Plan for the Forensic Science Laboratory"), 4, in Papers of Harold Charles Mitchell, Indian Police, United Provinces, 1920–47 (MSS Eur F255/9).

18. For example see *Emperor v. Babulal Behari and Others*, AIR Bom. (1928): 158; and *Emp. v. Abdul Hamid*, ILR Cal. 32 (1905): 759, esp. at 764.

19. See *Emp. v. Babulal Behari*, 158–59; and "Millhand Murder Mystery: Palm Print as Clue," *TI*, April 19, 1937.

20. P. Ramanatha Aiyer and N. S. Ranganatha Aiyer, *The Detection of Forgery or A Study in Handwriting* (Trichonopoly: Dodson, 1927), 215; Tewari and Ravikumar, "History," 304; and Binyamin Blum, "Forensic Empire: How Colonialism Shaped the Forensic Sciences," paper presented at the Global Forensic Histories workshop, virtual, March 26, 2021. Footprint analysis appeared often in Bengali detective fiction. For example see Priyanath Mukhopadhyay, "Ubhay Sankat" (story no. 160) in his *Darogar Daptar* (Kolkata: Punashcha, 2004) (Bengali).

21. A smaller experiment hiring explosives inspectors in 1892 preceded the creation of the CIE in 1898: "The Inspection of Explosives," *TI*, April 27, 1897. When not traveling, the main CIE was based in Calcutta during the 1920s. See letter from N. L. Sheldon, CIE (Department of Explosives, Calcutta, April 15, 1924), 1–2 in "Proposed inclusion of the CIE in s.510 of CrPC so as to enable his reports on bombs to be used as evidence in trials under the Code," Industries and Labor: Explosives, 1924, file no. M-830-1 (NAI). By the 1940s, the CIE was based at the Ordnance Laboratory in Lahore. "Plan for the Forensic Science Laboratory," 4.

22. For references to inspectors A. K. Sen, M. K. Maitra, and B. N. Pal, as well as South, North-East, and Calcutta Circles, see "Untitled chart listing court appearances of Chief Inspector and Inspectors of Explosives, 1929–31," Home: Judicial, 1932, Progs. no. 332 (NAI).

23. For example see "Another Bomb Outrage," *TI*, March 16, 1909; "Explosives Department: Twenty Years' Work in India," *TI*, July 12, 1918; "Summoning of the Chief Inspector of Explosives to give evidence in Criminal Courts," Home: Judicial, 1928, Progs. no. 738 (NAI); and "Untitled chart listing court appearances." On antinationalist surveillance and forensics see Saumitra Basu, *The History of Forensic Science in India* (Routledge, 2021), 182–84.

24. For example see the 1875 case of *Baboo Gunga Persad and Another v. Baboo Inderjit Singh and Another*, in *Sutherland's Indian Appeal Cases* 3 (1871–80): 133–34. For an example from a princely

GEQD analyzed handwriting, and at times typewriting, too.[25] This analyst and the explosives inspectors worked closely with the CE on the chemical analysis of paper, ink, and bombs. Based in the Himalayan hill station of Simla from 1906, the GEQD's office began rotating in the 1930s, like so many other parts of the government of India, between Simla during "the hot weather" and Delhi during the cold.[26] By the 1940s, the GEQD was based in the Intelligence Bureau within the Home department in Delhi.[27] There were also handwriting experts within police departments, including the Criminal Investigation Department of the Calcutta Police.[28]

The office of the imperial serologist (IS) grew out of the Calcutta CE's department and in 1914–16 became its own separate office in charge of testing bloodstains. This expert's work focused on precipitin testing, which determined the species of origin of a bloodstain. Precipitin testing was used to establish whether animal blood had been planted in murder, assault, and rape cases. The IS also did blood-group testing, which could be relevant in paternity, maternity, assault, and murder cases (see chapters 2 and 3).

Other kinds of forensic experts fell short of having their own state-sponsored department. Anatomists, for instance, were lecturers and professors of anatomy at medical schools who produced written opinions on bones sent by the police. They determined whether the bones were human or animal, and if human, what the age and sex of the individual may have been.[29]

---

state see *Amthabhai Punjabhai v. Pranabhai Mithabhai, Baroda Law Reports* 1 (1891–92): 237–38. See generally Aiyer and Aiyer, *Detection*, 1–2, 156–59.

25. On handwriting see works published by members of the Hardless family of handwriting analysts in the 1910s–30s: Projit Bihari Mukharji, "Handwriting Analysis as a Dynamic Artisanal Science: The Hardless Detective Dynasty and the Forensic Cultures of the British Raj," in Burney and Hamlin, *Global Forensic Cultures*; and Mitra Sharafi, "Forensic Experts in Colonial South Asia: Handwriting Analysis as a Suspect Science" (in progress). On typewriting see "Inquest on a Parsi. Verdict of Accidental Death," *TI*, November 5, 1915; "Government of Madras: Report of the CE for the Year 1932," *Analyst* 59, no. 694 (1934): 39; Frank Brewester, "The Identification of Typewritten Documents," CrLJ 15 (1914): 29–37; Frank Brewester, *Contested Documents and Forgeries* (Calcutta: Book, 1932), 271–93; Aiyer and Aiyer, *Detection*, 200–207; and Blum, "Forensic Empire."

26. "Move to Delhi for the winter season 1930–31 of the office of the Government Examiner of Questioned Documents," Home: Police, 1930, Prog. no. 128/II (NAI); Tewari and Ravikumar, "History," 304.

27. "Plan for the Forensic Science Laboratory," 4.

28. For instance see Partha Chatterjee, *A Princely Impostor? The Strange and Universal History of the Kumar of Bhawal* (Princeton University Press, 2002), 186–87.

29. From 1917 in Bombay Presidency, questions of sex and age (at death) for human bones were referred to the anatomy professor at Bombay's Grant Medical College or to lecturers in anatomy at the medical schools in Ahmedabad, Hyderabad, or Poona. No. 1877-A, from G. Wiles, deputy secretary to the government of Bombay, Home dept., to secretary to government of India, Home dept. (Bombay, August 19, 1922), in "Proposal to amend s.510 of the Criminal Procedure Code so as to

Medical experts assessed bullet wounds, but ballistics as a nonmedical field was in its nascent phase in South Asia during the colonial era.[30] Guns and bombs often came up in nationalist revolutionary cases involving assassinations and other planned attacks. But while the CIE offered expertise on explosives, he had no official counterpart for ballistics. Instead, early ballistics experts in the Indian courts were gun sellers, police inspectors, and, in a high-profile political trial like the Lahore conspiracy case (1928–30), England's top ballistics analyst.[31] In the 1930s, the government of India tried to assign firearms-related analysis to the CIE and the GEQD—the latter probably because he had high-quality photographic equipment for the analysis of handwriting that could be useful for ballistics.[32] However, the knowledge of guns was closely tied to military expertise, particularly given the large number of unauthorized firearms from around the world that entered India during and after the two world wars.[33] Police had used military men who ran ammunition depots for ballistics expertise, and resisted the switch to civilian experts.[34] In practice, the ammunitions factory at Kirkee

---

include the Anatomist, negatived," Home: Judicial, Proc. no. 1366, 1922 (NAI). See also *Imperator v. Ahila Manaji*, AIR Bom. (1923): 185.

30. See "Plan for the Forensic Science Laboratory," 11. Medical experts assessed bullet wounds during the colonial period. For example see *Abdul Ghani v. Emp.*, CrLJ 28 (1927): 117; and Jaising P. Modi, *A Textbook of Medical Jurisprudence and Toxicology*, 6th ed. (Bombay: Butterworth, 1940), 228–38. Ballistics as a nonmedical field would establish itself in India by the 1960s. See R. L. Gupta, *Ballistic Firearms and Jurisprudence* (Allahabad: Law Book, 1964).

31. For example see *Emp. v. Ali Cassim Ariff*, CrLJ 12 (1911): 339, 344; *Manghan Khan v. Emp.*, CrLJ 38 (1937): 489; and "Shells of Cast Iron: Bomb Case Hearing Explosives Inspector Examined," *TI*, September 17, 1927. On Robert Churchill, expert in the Lahore conspiracy case, see "Lahore Conspiracy Trial: Gun Expert's Evidence," *TI*, June 30, 1930; F. R. Stockwell, "Report on Scientific Investigations in the Metropolitan Police," June 24, 1945, 1, in "Plan for the Forensic Science Laboratory"; Macdonald Hastings, *The Other Mr. Churchill: A Lifetime of Shooting and Murder* (London: Four Square Book, 1966), 154–62; and Alison Adam, *A History of Forensic Science: British Beginnings in the Twentieth Century* (Routledge, 2016), 35–37, 73. On the Lahore conspiracy case see K. L. Gauba, *Famous and Historic Trials* (Lahore: Lion, 1946), 133–62; Durba Ghosh, *Gentlemanly Terrorists: Political Violence and the Colonial State in India, 1919–1947* (Cambridge University Press, 2017), 94–95; and Satvinder Singh Juss, *The Execution of Bhagat Singh: Legal Heresies of the Raj* (Stroud, UK: Amberley, 2020).

32. See Robert Churchill, "The Forensic Examination of Firearms and Projectiles," *Police Journal* 2, no. 3 (1929): 373–79; and Christopher Hamlin and Ian Burney, "History of Forensic Science," in *Encyclopedia of Forensic Sciences*, ed. Max M. Houck (Elsevier, 2023), 3:175.

33. For instance see letter from N. M. Kamte, deputy inspector general of police, CID, Bombay province, to inspector general of police, Bombay province, Poona, on the identification of arms, ammunition, and explosives on behalf of provincial police by the technical development establishment, Kirkee (Poona, July 31, 1947), 8, in "Crime and Criminology. Arms, Ammunition and Explosives—Identification of—for the Provincial Police by the Expert of the Technical Development Establishment, Kirkee, Poona," Home: Police, file no. 35/5/47-Police, 1947 (NAI).

34. For example see "Bengal Anarchists. Another Bomb Outrage," *TI*, November 27, 1908. In favor of the forensic work done by military ballistics experts at Kirkee in the 1930s–40s see "Crime and Criminology. Arms, Ammunition and Explosives . . . Kirkee, Poona."

unofficially monopolized ballistics analysis in the 1930–40s because of its collection of firearms from around the world.[35] There were more local efforts within some police departments, too. In 1930, for instance, the Calcutta police set up a small ballistics laboratory with its own arms expert.[36]

There were new detective training schools, like the one at Howrah that opened around 1918 and the school planned for Bihar in the mid-1940s.[37] And there were early hints of fields that would come into their own postindependence. These included forensic entomology, which used the presence of insects (particularly maggots) in a corpse to estimate the time or location of death, and forensic linguistics, which analyzed speech patterns.[38] The same was true for the analysis of hair, textile fibers, and blood spatter marks, along with the assessment of bite-mark evidence using forensic odontology.[39]

How was forensic analysis done in the princely states? First, codes of criminal law and procedure looked very similar in princely and British India, and British precedent was also cited in princely courts.[40] For scientific analysis, princely states often sent evidence from crime scenes to the CEs and IS in British India.[41] However, the fact that princely states also sent forensic experts to CE labs for training suggests that they had some degree of forensic infrastructure at home.[42]

---

35. A reference collection of firearms was essential for ballistics analysis. The analyst had to shoot guns of various models in order to produce striations he could compare to the evidence. See "Crime and Criminology. Arms, Ammunition and Explosives . . . Kirkee, Poona."

36. Tewari and Ravikumar, "History," 304.

37. "Notes of a lecture delivered at the Detective Training School, Howrah"; and [B. S. L. TenBroeke], "Note on the Scientific detection of crime," [1945], 1, in "Plan for the Forensic Science Laboratory." On detectives in colonial India see Uponita Mukherjee, "Colonial Detection: Crime, Evidence and Inquiry in British India, 1790–1910" (PhD diss., Columbia University, 2022).

38. For example, "Notes of a lecture delivered at the Detective Training School, Howrah," 1, 3. Although French analysts used forensic entomology in criminal trials from 1850, the technique seems not to have been used in British India until much later. On the French context see E. Claire Cage, *The Science of Proof: Forensic Medicine in Modern France* (Cambridge University Press, 2022), 125.

39. See Jaising P. Modi, *A Textbook of Medical Jurisprudence* (Calcutta: Butterworth, 1920), 67, 80–82; and Modi, *Medical Jurisprudence* (1940), 222, 340. On the history of blood spatter analysis in the 1950s–60s elsewhere see Ian Burney, "Spatters and Lies: Contrasting Forensic Cultures in the Trials of Sam Sheppard, 1954–66," in Burney and Hamlin, *Global Forensic Cultures*, 112–46.

40. For example see cases listed in the *Baroda Law Reports* 2 (1892): 11, 20–22; and *Govt. v. M. H. Sakur, Baroda Law Reports* 12 supp. (1902–3): 67–71.

41. For instance, princely state samples constituted almost 20 percent of annual testing done at one CE lab in 1932. "Report of the CE to Government, United Provinces and Central Provinces, for the Year 1932," 1 (IOR/V/24/417). See also "Report of the CE and Bacteriologist to Government, North-Western Provinces and Oudh, and Central Provinces, for the Year 1897," 1 (IOR/V/24/414); and "Report of the CE to Government, Bengal, for the Year 1917," 6 (IOR/V/24/422).

42. For example see "Report of the CA to Government, Bombay, for the Year 1911," 4 (IOR/V/24/407); and "Report of the CE to Government, Bengal, for the Year 1915," 7 (IOR/V/24/422).

Centralized forensic labs were first contemplated for British India in the late colonial period. A combined lab was created in Lahore in 1933.[43] One with chemical, physics, and pathology sections was proposed for the United Provinces in 1945–46.[44] By the mid-1940s, scientists rather than physicians were expected to be in charge of forensic labs in India, reflecting a shift across the English-speaking world.[45] Other centralized labs were created in independent India during the 1950s and '60s.[46] The early independence period, like the turn of the twentieth century, was an era of forensic institution-building for India.[47]

43. Tewari and Ravikumar, "History," 305.

44. How independent the lab would be from the police was a subject of debate. One proposal put a police official at the head of the lab, but another recommended that the lab be manned by non-police under the control of the Home department. See "Plan for the Forensic Science Laboratory." CE labs had been under the control of the inspector general of hospitals, not the police. See introduction.

45. See "Plan for the Forensic Science Laboratory," 8. For an early critique of MDs (without special training in chemistry) becoming CEs see untitled editorial in the *Medical Reporter*, July 16, 1895, 48–49. On the twentieth-century shift from physicians to scientists in Scottish forensics see M. Anne Crowther and Brenda White, *On Soul and Conscience: The Medical Expert and Crime; 150 Years of Forensic Medicine in Glasgow* (Aberdeen University Press, 1988), 98, 113.

46. Central forensic science labs were established in Calcutta (1957) and Hyderabad (1965). Tewari and Ravikumar, "History," 305.

47. Among others, the following entities were created during the 1950s–60s: the central forensic science advisory committee and central medico-legal advisory committee (both 1959), central detective training schools in Calcutta (1956) and Hyderabad (1964), and the Indian Academy of Forensic Sciences in Calcutta (1960). See Tewari and Ravikumar, "History," 305–6; and B. B. Nanda and R. K. Tewari, *Forensic Science in India: A Vision for the Twenty-First Century* (Delhi: Select, 2001), 35–43.

BIBLIOGRAPHY

PRIMARY SOURCES

Archives and Collections

Bombay High Court (Courtroom 21), Mumbai
Parsi Chief Matrimonial Court Notebooks (1893–1947)

British Library, Asia and Africa Collections, London

India Office Records
IOR/H: Home Miscellaneous records
IOR/L/MIL: Military Department records
IOR/L/PJ: Public and Judicial Department records
IOR/P: Proceedings and Consultations of the Government of India and of the Presidencies and Provinces
IOR/R/1/1: Records transferred later through official channels—Internal branch
IOR/V/8: Official Publications—Acts and Codes
IOR/V/24: Official Publications—Departmental Annual Reports (including chemical analyser and chemical examiner reports, 1873–1947)

Private Papers (formerly European manuscripts)
MSS Eur C336: Memoirs and articles by Sir Torick Ameer Ali (1891–1975), Calcutta High Court
MSS Eur F161: Indian Police Collection (1765–1961)
MSS Eur F255: Papers of Harold Charles Mitchell, Indian Police, United Provinces (1920–47)
MSS Eur F419: Papers of Ormandy Ballantine Fane Sewell, Indian Police (1902–23)

Inner Temple Archives, London
Records of Disciplinary Cases, Honourable Society of the Inner Temple. DIS/1/K2: S. Krishnavarma (1909)

National Archives of India, Delhi
Baghelkhand Political Agency: English Files
Bhopal Agency: General
Director General, Indian Medical Services including Personal section
Education, Health and Lands: Health branch

Finance
Home: Judicial
Home: Medical
Home: Police
Industries and Labor: Explosives

University of Chicago's Hannah Holborn Gray Special Collections Research Center
Bernard Cohn Papers (1942–2000)

University of Glasgow Archives and Special Collections
MS Gen 1691: Papers of Laurence Austine Waddell (1834–1938)

Periodicals, Including Law Reports and Newspapers

Albany Law Journal
All India Reporter: Allahabad, Bombay, Calcutta, Lahore, Lower Burma, Madras series
Amrita Bazar Patrika (Bengali then English)
Analyst
Baroda Law Reports (Gujarati with some English)
Bioscope
Bombay High Court Reports
Bombay Law Journal
Bombay Law Reporter
Bombay Times and Standard
British Medical Journal
Burma Law Reports
Calcutta Review
Calcutta Weekly Notes
Canadian Law Review
Ceylon Observer
Civil & Military Gazette
Criminal Law Journal of India
Eastern Daily Mail and Straits Morning Advertiser
English Review
Indian Daily News
Indian Journal of Medicine
Indian Law Reports: Bombay, Calcutta, Madras series
Indian Listener
Indian Medical Gazette
Indian Medico-Chirurgical Review
Indian Police Gazette & Annual
Indian Sociologist
Journal of the American Medical Association
Journal of Experimental Medicine
Journal of Hygiene
Journal of the Society of Comparative Legislation

Kaiser-i-Hind (Gujarati with some English)
Lancet
Leader
Lower Burma Rulings
Madras Law Journal
Madras Mail
Medical Reporter
National Medical Journal of India
Nature
Pearson's Weekly
Police Journal
Rangoon Law Reports
Rhodesia Herald
Scotsman
Solicitors' Journal
Straits Times
Sutherland's Indian Appeal Cases
Sutherland's Weekly Reporter
Times of India
Times of London
Western India States Agency Law Reports

Other Published Primary Sources

Adam, H. L. *Oriental Crime*. London: T. Werner Laurie, [1908–9].

Aiyer, P. Ramanatha, and N. S. Ranganatha Aiyer. *The Detection of Forgery or A Study in Handwriting*. Trichonopoly: Dodson, 1927.

Ameer Ali, Syed. *Mahommedan Law Compiled from Authorities in the Original Arabic*. Vol. 1, *Gifts, Wakfs, Wills, Pre-Emption and Bailment*. Calcutta: Thacker, Spink, 1904.

Banerjee, B. N. *Aids to the Investigation of Professional Crime*. Calcutta: Sanskrit Press, 1920.

Bell, Clark. "Medical Jurisprudence in America in the Nineteenth Century." *Texas Medical Journal* 16, no. 5 (1900): 201–8.

Billington, Mary Frances. *Woman in India*. London, 1895.

Blackstone, William. *Commentaries on the Laws of England: In Four Books*. London, 1862.

Borchard, Edwin M. *Convicting the Innocent: Sixty-Five Actual Errors of Criminal Justice*. Garden City Publishing, 1932.

Borchard, Edwin M. *State Indemnity for Errors of Criminal Justice*. Washington, DC: Government Printing Office, 1912.

Bose, Bejoy Krishna. *The Alipore Bomb Trial*. Calcutta: Butterworth, 1922.

Bose, J. P., ed. *The Scientific and Other Papers of Rai Chunilal Bose Bahadur*. Calcutta, 1924.

Brewester, Frank. *Contested Documents and Forgeries*. Calcutta: Book, 1932.

Buchanan, Francis. *A Journey from Madras Through the Countries of Mysore, Canara, and Malabar*. London, 1807.

Buchanan, W. J. "A Chapter on Medical Jurisprudence in India." In Taylor, *Principles and Practice of Medical Jurisprudence*, 5th ed. (1905), 852–82.

Carswell, Donald. *Trial of Ronald True*. Edinburgh: William Hodge, 1925.

Chaillé, Stanford E. *Origin and Progress of Medical Jurisprudence, 1776–1876. A Centennial Address*. Philadelphia, 1876.

Chevers, Norman. *A Manual of Medical Jurisprudence for Bengal and the North-Western Provinces*. Calcutta, 1856.

Chopra, R. N. *Indigenous Drugs of India: Their Medicinal and Economic Aspects*. Calcutta: Art, 1933.

The Code of Indian Criminal Procedure: Being Act No. X of 1872. London, 1872.

Commission for the Investigation of Snake-Poisoning (India). *Report on the Effects of Artificial Respiration, Intravenous Injection of Ammonia, and Administration of Various Drugs, &c. in Indian and Australian Snake-Poisoning, and the Physiological, Chemical, and Microscopical Nature of Snake-Poisons*. Calcutta, 1874.

Crawford, D. G. *A History of the Indian Medical Service, 1600–1913*. London: Thacker, 1914.

Crooke, W. *The North-Western Provinces of India: Their History, Ethnology, and Administration*. London, 1897.

Cumston, Charles Greene. *The Law and Medical Experts, with Particular Reference to the Codes of Criminal Procedure of European Countries*. Boston: D. C. Heath, 1908.

Cunningham, H. S. *The Indian Evidence Act, No. I of 1872*. Edited by H. H. Shephard. Madras: Higginbotham, 1908.

Deshmukh, Moreshvar Gopal. *The Evils of the Military Medical Service Monopoly*. Bombay, 1893.

Dey, Kanai Lal (or Kanny Lall). *Medical Jurisprudence*. Calcutta, [1875]. (Bengali)

Dey, Kanny Lall (or Kanai Lal). *The Indigenous Drugs of India*. Calcutta, 1867.

Doyle, Arthur Conan. *The Case of Oscar Slater*. New York: Hodder & Stoughton, 1912.

Doyle, Arthur Conan. *The Story of Mr. George Edalji*. Edited by Richard Whittington-Egan and Molly Whittington-Egan. London: Grey House Books, 1985.

Dymock, William, C. J. H. Warden, and David Hooper. *Pharmacographia Indica: A History of the Principal Drugs of Vegetable Origin, Met with in British India*. Calcutta, 1890.

Fayrer, Joseph. *The Thanatophidia of India: Being a Description of the Venomous Snakes of the Indian Peninsula, with an Account of the Influence of Their Poison on Life and a Series of Experiments*. London, 1872.

Florence, A. "Du sperme et des taches de sperme en médecine légale." *Archives d'anthropologie criminelle et des sciences pénales* 10 (1895): 417–34.

Forbes, Alexander Kinloch. *Ras-Mala: Hindu Annals of Western India with Particular Reference to Gujarat*. Delhi: Heritage, 1973. Originally published in 1878.

Ganguly, A. C. *Practical Guide to Criminal Court Practice*. Calcutta: Eastern Law House, 1937.

Gauba, K. L. *Famous and Historic Trials*. Lahore: Lion, 1946.

Gauba, K. L. *Friends and Foes: An Autobiography*. Delhi: Indian Book, 1974.

Gauba, K. L. *The New Magna Carta: A Tale of Judicial Tyranny. The Curious Case of Khwaja Nazir Ahmed*. Delhi: Law and Justice Publishing, 2022.

Glaister, John. *A Text-Book of Medical Jurisprudence and Toxicology*. Edinburgh: E. & S. Livingstone, 1921.

Grady, Standish Grove, ed. *Institutes of Hindu Law; or, The Ordinances of Menu*. Translated by William Jones. London, 1869.

Gupta, Ram Lal. *Ballistic Firearms and Jurisprudence*. Allahabad: Law Book, 1964.

Gupta, Ram Lal. *Law of Identification*. Lucknow: Eastern Book, 1963.

Gupta, Ram Lal. *The Medico Legal Aspects of Sexual Offences*. Lucknow: Eastern Book, 1964.

Guthrie, Douglas. *The Medical School of Edinburgh*. Edinburgh, [1959].

Haldane, Viscount of Cloan. "The Work for the Empire of the Judicial Committee of the Privy Council." *Cambridge Law Journal* 1 (1923): 143–55.

Hankin, E. H. *The Mental Limitations of the Expert*. Calcutta: Butterworth, 1920.

Hankin, E. H. *Some New Methods of Using the Aniline Dyes for Staining Bacteria*. London, 1887.

Hastings, Macdonald. *The Other Mr. Churchill: A Lifetime of Shooting and Murder*. London: Four Square Book, 1966.

Hehir, Patrick. *The Medical Profession in India*. London: Henry Frowde, 1923.

Hehir, Patrick, and J. D. B. Gribble, eds. *Outlines of Medical Jurisprudence for India*. Madras: Higginbotham. Multiple editions:
2nd ed. 1891.
5th ed. 1908.

Howard, Pendleton. "The English Court of Criminal Appeal." *American Bar Association Journal* 17, no. 3 (1931): 149–52.

Irving, H. B. *Trial of Mrs. Maybrick*. New York: John Day, 1927.

Karbhari, Bhagu F. *A New Pocket Gujarati-English Dictionary*. Bombay: N. M. Tripathi, 1912.

Keedy, Edwin R. "Criminal Procedure in Scotland. A Report Presented to the American Institute of Criminal Law and Criminology." *Journal of Criminal Law and Criminology* 11 (1913): 1–47.

Kemp, Stanley. *Catalogue of the Scientific Serial Publications in the Principal Libraries of Calcutta*. Calcutta: Asiatic Society of Bengal, 1918.

Khan, Raheem. *A Manual of Medical Jurisprudence in Urdu*. Lahore: Anjuman-i-Punjab, 1881.

Kirtikar, K. R., and B. D. Basu. *Indian Medicinal Plants*. Allahabad: S. N. Basu, 1918.

Lambert, D. P. *The Medico-Legal Post-Mortem in India*. London: J. & A. Churchill, 1937.

Lyon, Isidore Bernadotte. *Lyon's Medical Jurisprudence for India*. Calcutta: Thacker, Spink. Multiple editions:
2nd ed. 1889. Titled *A Text Book of Medical Jurisprudence for India*.
3rd ed. Edited by L. A. Waddell. 1904.
5th ed. Edited by L. A. Waddell. 1914.
7th ed. Edited by L. A. Waddell. 1921.
9th ed. Edited by T. F. Owens. 1935.
10th ed. Edited by S. D. S. Greval. 1953.

Marshman, John C. *The Darogah's Manual, Comprising Also the Duties of Landholders in Connection with the Police*. [Serampore], 1850.

Maybrick, Florence Elizabeth. *My Fifteen Lost Years*. London: Funk & Wagnalls, 1905.

Mistry, A. J. C. *Forty Years Reminiscences of the High Court of Judicature at Bombay*. Bombay: published by the author, 1925.

Mistry, A. J. C. *Reminiscences of the Office of Messrs Wadia Ghandy & Co.* Bombay: published by the author, [1911].

Modi, Jaising P. *A Textbook of Medical Jurisprudence and Toxicology.* Multiple editions:
1st ed. Calcutta: Butterworth, 1920.
4th ed. Calcutta: Butterworth, 1932.
5th ed. Calcutta: Butterworth, 1936.
6th ed. Bombay: Butterworth, 1940.
10th ed. Bombay: N. M. Tripathi, 1949.
12th ed. Edited by N. J. Modi. Bombay: N. M. Tripathi, 1955.
24th ed. Edited by K. Kannan and K. Mathiharan. Nagpur: LexisNexis Butterworths Wadhwa, 2011.

Mukerji, Manmatha N. *Trial by Jury and Misdirection.* Calcutta: Eastern Law House, 1937.

Naidu, M. Pauparao. *The History of Professional Poisoners and Coiners of India.* Madras: Higginbotham, 1912.

Naidu, V. Ramanjulu, ed. *Indian Year-Book and Annual, 1912.* Nayudupeta: Indian Year Book & Annual Office, 1912.

Naoroji, Dadabhai. "The European and Asiatic Races." In *The Grand Little Man of India: Dadabhai Naoroji Speeches and Writings*, edited by A. M. Zaidi. Delhi: S. Chand, 1984.

Nichols, Beverley. *Verdict on India.* London: Jonathan Cape, 1944.

Nuttall, George H. F. *Blood Immunity and Blood Relationship: A Demonstration of Certain Blood-Relationships amongst Animals by Means of the Precipitin Test for Blood.* Cambridge University Press, 1904.

O'Kinealy, J. *The Indian Penal Code.* Calcutta: Thacker, Spink, 1869.

Oppé, A. S. *Wharton's Law Lexicon . . . with Selected Titles Relating to the Civil, Scots, and Indian Law.* London: Sweet and Maxwell, 1938.

Orwell, George. "Shooting an Elephant." In *The Collected Essays, Journalism, and Letters of George Orwell*, edited by Sonia Orwell and Ian Angus. Harcourt, Brace, and World, 1968.

Overbury, Thomas, and Joseph Strutt. *An Account of Two Remarkable Trials for Murder, in the Counties of Gloucester and Essex.* London, 1806.

Park, William. *The Truth About Oscar Slater.* London: Psychic, [1927].

Pillai, K. Subrahmania. *Principles of Criminology.* Madras, 1924.

Prinsep, H. T. *The Code of Criminal Procedure Being Act V of 1898.* 13th ed. Calcutta: Thacker, Spink, 1901.

Raina, B. L. *Official History of the Indian Armed Forces in the Second World War 1939–45: Medical Services. Administration.* Delhi: Combined Inter Services Historical Section, India & Pakistan, 1953.

Ram, Shri, and V. M. Kulkarni, eds. *For Necessary Action: Speeches and Judgments of Sir Douglas Young, Chief Justice, High Court of Judicature at Lahore.* Lahore: Indian Cases, 1941.

Ranchhoddas, Ratanlal, and Dhirajlal Keshavlal Thakore. *The Indian Penal Code.* Bombay: Bombay Law Reporter Office. Multiple editions:
11th ed. 1926.
19th ed. 1948.

Rattigan, H. A. B. *The Bengal Regulations, the Acts of the Governor-General in Council, the Acts of the Lieutenant-Governor of the Punjab in Council, and the Frontier Regulations*. Vol. 3. 5th ed. Lahore, 1899.

Richards, Vincent. *The Land-Marks of Snake-Poison Literature, Being a Review of the More Important Researches into the Nature of Snake-Poisons*. Calcutta, 1885.

Roughead, William. *Trial of Oscar Slater*. Edinburgh: William Hodge, 1915.

Sanyal, Ram Gopal, ed. *The Record of Criminal Cases as Between Europeans and Natives for the Last Hundred Years*. Calcutta, 1896.

Sarkar, S. C. *Hints on Modern Advocacy and Cross-Examination*. 2nd ed. Calcutta: M. C. Sarkar & Sons, 1931.

Sarkar, S. C. *The Notable Indian Trials*. Calcutta: M. C. Sarkar & Sons, [1940–49].

Sengupta, Srish Chandra. *Bhaishajya Bichar or a Handbook of Medical Jurisprudence in Bengali*. Dacca, 1894.

Sims, George R. *Two King's Pardons: The Martyrdom of Adolf Beck*. London: Daily Mail, [1905].

Sleeman, W. H. *Ramblings and Recollections of an Indian Official*. Karachi: Oxford University Press, 1915. Originally published in 1844.

Sorabji, Cornelia. *The Purdahnashin*. Calcutta: Thacker, Spink, 1917.

Statistical Abstract Relating to British India from 1894–95 to 1903–4. London: H.M.S.O., 1905.

Sutherland, W. D. *The Applicability to Medico-Legal Practice in India of the Biochemical Tests for the Origin of Blood-Stains*. Calcutta: Superintendent Government Printing, India, 1910.

Sutherland, W. D. *Blood-Stains: Their Detection, and the Determination of Their Source*. London: Ballière, Tindall and Cox, 1907.

Taylor, Alfred Swaine. *Principles and Practice of Medical Jurisprudence*. London: J. & A. Churchill. Originally published as *A Manual of Medical Jurisprudence*. London, 1844. Multiple editions:
4th ed. Edited by Thomas Stevenson. 1894.
5th ed. Edited by Fred J. Smith. 1905.
7th ed. Edited by Fred J. Smith. 1920.
8th ed. Edited by Sydney Smith and W. G. H. Cook. 1928.

Taylor, George P. *The Student's Gujarati Grammar*. Bombay: Thacker, 1908.

Thoinot, Léon-Henri. *Attentat aux mœurs et perversions du sens génitals: Leçons professées à la Faculté de médecine*. Paris: Octave Doin, 1898.

Thoinot, Léon-Henri. *Medicolegal Aspects of Moral Offences*. Translated by Arthur W. Weysse. Philadelphia: F. A. Davis, 1911.

Thurston, Edgar, and K. Rangachari. *Castes and Tribes of Southern India*. Madras: Government Press, 1909.

The Tichborne Trial: The Summing-Up by the Lord Chief Justice of England, Together with the Addresses to the Judges, the Verdict, and the Sentence; The Whole Accompanied by a History of the Case and Copious Alphabetical Index. London, 1874.

Tyabji, Husain B. *Badruddin Tyabji: A Biography*. Bombay: Thacker, 1952.

U, Ba. *My Burma: Autobiography of a President*. New York: Taplinger, 1959.

Waddell, L. A. *Are Venomous Snakes Auto-Toxic? An Inquiry into the Effect of Serpent Venom upon the Serpents Themselves*. Calcutta, 1889.

Walsh, Cecil. *Crime in India with an Introduction on Forensic Difficulties and Peculiarities*. London: Ernest Benn, 1930.

Walsh, Cecil. *Indian Village Crimes with an Introduction on Police Investigation and Confessions*. London: Ernest Benn, 1929.

Watson, Eric R. *Adolf Beck (1877–1904)*. Edinburgh: William Hodge, [1924].

Watson, C. S. *The Law of Evidence*. London: Stevens & Sons, 1917.

Watt, George. *A Dictionary of the Economic Products of India*. Calcutta, 1889.

Weisman, Abner Irving. *Spermatozoa and Sterility: A Clinical Manual*. New York: Paul H. Hoeber, 1941.

Wigmore, John Henry. *A Treatise on the System of Evidence in Trials at Common Law*. Little, Brown, 1904. Later edition titled *A Treatise on the Anglo-American System of Evidence in Trials at Common Law*. 2nd ed. Boston: Little, Brown, 1923.

Yule, Henry. *Hobson-Jobson: A Glossary of Colloquial Anglo-Indian Words and Phrases*. Edited by William Crooke. London: J. Murray, 1903.

Online Primary Sources and Platforms

FindMyPast.co.uk. Accessed March 9, 2025. https://www.findmypast.co.uk/.

"James Baldwin Discusses Racism. The Dick Cavett Show." Aired May 16, 1969. Accessed March 10, 2025. https://www.youtube.com/watch?v=WWwOi17WHpE.

Law Library Microform Consortium Digital. Accessed March 10, 2025. https://llmc.com/.

Manupatra. Accessed March 9, 2025. https://www.manupatrafast.com/?t=desktop.

SECONDARY SOURCES

Published Works

Abraham, Santhosh. "The Making of Colonial Law, Discipline and Corruption in British India." *Journal of Indian Law and Society* 1, no. 2 (2010): 64–82.

Adam, Alison. *A History of Forensic Science: British Beginnings in the Twentieth Century*. Routledge, 2016.

Agnes, Flavia. "To Whom Do Experts Testify? Ideological Challenges of Feminist Jurisprudence." *Economic and Political Weekly* 40, no. 18 (2005): 1859–66.

Alonso, Isabel Huacuja. *Radio for the Millions: Hindi-Urdu Broadcasting Across Borders*. Columbia University Press, 2023.

Alyagon Darr, Orna. *Plausible Crime Stories: The Legal History of Sexual Offences in Mandate Palestine*. Cambridge University Press, 2019.

Ambasta, Kunal. "One Hundred (and Fifty) Years of Solitude: The Indian Evidence Act 1872 as a Lost Project of Law Reform." *Indian Law Review* 8, no. 1 (2024): 1–19.

Anderson, Clare. "The British Indian Empire, 1789–1939." In *A Global History of Convicts and Penal Colonies*, edited by Clare Anderson. Bloomsbury, 2018.

Anderson, Clare. *Subaltern Lives: Biographies of Colonialism in the Indian Ocean World, 1790–1920*. Cambridge University Press, 2012.

Arnold, David. "Colonial Medicine in Transition: Medical Research in India, 1910–47." *South Asia Research* 14, no. 1 (1994): 10–35.

Arnold, David. *Colonizing the Body: State Medicine and Epidemic Disease in Nineteenth-Century India*. University of California Press, 1993.

Arnold, David. *Toxic Histories: Poison and Pollution in Modern India*. Cambridge University Press, 2016.

Arondekar, Anjali. *For the Record: On Sexuality and the Colonial Archive in India*. Duke University Press, 2009.

Asen, Daniel. *Death in Beijing: Murder and Forensic Science in Republican China*. Cambridge University Press, 2016.

Babcock-Abrahams, Barbara. "'A Tolerated Margin of Mess': The Trickster and His Tales Reconsidered." *Journal of the Folklore Institute* 11, no. 3 (1975): 147–86.

Badassy, Prinisha. "Stewed Plums, Baked Porridge and Flavoured Tea: Poisoning by Indian Domestic Servants in Colonial Natal." In *Beyond Indenture: Agency and Resistance in the Colonial South Asian Diaspora*, edited by Crispin Bates. Cambridge University Press, 2024.

Bailkin, Jordanna. "The Boot and the Spleen: When Was Murder Possible in British India?" *Comparative Studies in Society and History* 48, no. 2 (2006): 462–93.

Bakiner, Onur. "Truth Commission Impact on Policy, Courts, and Society." *Annual Review of Law and Social Science* 17 (2021): 73–91.

Balasubramanian, Aditya. "Anticorruption, Development, and the Indian State: A History of Decolonization." *Journal of Asian Studies* 83, no. 1 (2024): 88–115.

Balleisen, E. J. *Fraud: An American History from Barnum to Madoff*. Princeton University Press, 2017.

Bandopadhyay, Arun. "The Origin of a Social Conflict in South India: The Sivakasi Riots of 1899." *Studies in People's History* 1, no. 1 (2014): 69–80.

Banerjee, Mou. *The Disinherited: The Politics of Christian Conversion in Colonial India*. Harvard University Press, 2025.

Banerjee-Dube, Ishita. *A History of Modern India*. Cambridge University Press, 2015.

Barman, Debayan Deb, ed. *Critical Essays on English and Bengali Detective Fiction*. Lexington Books, 2022.

Barton, Patricia. "Innovative Knowledge in Traditional Settings: The Bengal Chemical Examiners' Laboratory and the Medico-Legal Understanding of Cocaine, 1880s–1920s." Talk presented at the 50th Annual Conference on South Asia, Madison, WI, October 22, 2022.

Basu, Saumitra. *The History of Forensic Science in India*. Routledge, 2021.

Bates, Victoria. *Sexual Forensics in Victorian and Edwardian England: Age, Crime and Consent in the Courts*. Palgrave Macmillan, 2016.

Bates, Victoria. "'So Far as I Can Define Without a Microscopical Examination': Venereal Disease Diagnosis in English Courts, 1850–1914." *Social History of Medicine* 26, no. 1 (2012): 38–55.

Baxi, Pratiksha. *Public Secrets of Law: Rape Trials in India*. Oxford University Press, 2014.

Berger, Rachel. "Clarified Commodities: Managing Ghee in Interwar India." *Technology and Culture* 60, no. 4 (2019): 1004–26.

Bergers, Lara. "A Culture of Testimony: The Importance of 'Speaking Witnesses' in Dutch Sexual Crimes Investigations and Trials, 1930–1960." In *Forensic Cultures in Modern Europe*, edited by Willemijn Ruberg, Lara Bergers, Pauline Dirven, and Sara Serrano Martínez. Manchester University Press, 2023.

Berman, Paul Schiff. *Global Legal Pluralism: A Jurisprudence of Law Beyond Borders.* Cambridge University Press, 2012.

Bertomeu-Sánchez, José Ramón. "Chemistry, Microscopy and Smell: Bloodstains and Nineteenth-Century Legal Medicine." *Annals of Science* 72, no. 4 (2015): 490–516.

Bertomeu-Sánchez, José Ramón. "Managing Uncertainty in the Academy and the Courtroom: Normal Arsenic and Nineteenth-Century Toxicology." *Isis* 104, no. 2 (2013): 197–225.

Bhabha, Homi K. *The Location of Culture.* Routledge, 1994.

Blum, Binyamin. "Forensic Empire: How Colonialism Shaped the Forensic Sciences." Paper presented at the Global Forensic Histories workshop, cosponsored by the American Society for Legal History, UC Law San Francisco and the University of Wisconsin Law School, virtual, March 26, 2021.

Blum, Binyamin. "From Bedouin Trackers to Doberman Pinschers: The Rise of Dog Tracking as Forensic Evidence in Palestine." In Burney and Hamlin, *Global Forensic Cultures*, 205–34.

Blum, Binyamin. "The Hounds of Empire: Forensic Dog Tracking in Britain and Its Colonies, 1888–1953." *Law and History Review* 35, no. 3 (2017): 621–65.

Blumenthal, Susanna. "Humbug: Toward a Legal History." *Buffalo Law Review* 64 (2016): 161–92

Bordia, Devika. "The Politics of Custom: Blood Money, Disputes, and Tribal Leadership in Western India." *Diogenes* 60, no. 3–4 (2015): 153–65.

Borrows, John. *Recovering Canada: The Resurgence of Indigenous Law.* University of Toronto Press, 2002.

Bose, Sugata, and Ayesha Jalal. *Modern South Asia: History, Culture, Political Economy.* Routledge, 2018.

Brown, Mark. "The Birth of Criminology in Colonial South Asia: 1765–1947." In *Crime, Criminal Justice, and the Evolving Science of Criminology in South Asia: India, Pakistan, and Bangladesh*, edited by Shahid M. Shahidullah. Palgrave Macmillan, 2017.

Burney, Ian. *Poison, Detection and the Victorian Imagination.* Manchester University Press, 2006.

Burney, Ian. "Spatters and Lies: Contrasting Forensic Cultures in the Trials of Sam Sheppard, 1954–66." In Burney and Hamlin, *Global Forensic Cultures.*

Burney, Ian. "Testing Testimony: Toxicology and the Law of Evidence in Early Nineteenth-Century England." *Studies in History and Philosophy of Science* 33 (2002): 289–314.

Burney, Ian, and Christopher Hamlin, eds. *Global Forensic Cultures: Making Fact and Justice in the Modern Era.* Johns Hopkins University Press, 2019.

Burney, Ian, David A. Kirby, and Neil Pemberton, eds. "Forensic Cultures." Special issue, *Studies in History and Philosophy of Biological and Biomedical Sciences* 44 (2013).

Burney, Ian, and Neil Pemberton. *Murder and the Making of English CSI.* Johns Hopkins University Press, 2016.

Burton, Antoinette. "S Is for Scorpion." In *Animalia: An Anti-Imperial Bestiary for Our Times*, edited by Antoinette Burton and Renisa Mawani. Duke University Press, 2020.

Cage, E. Claire. *The Science of Proof: Forensic Medicine in Modern France*. Cambridge University Press, 2022.

Chakrabarti, Pratik. *Bacteriology in British India: Laboratory Medicine and the Tropics*. University of Rochester Press, 2012.

Chakrabarti, Pratik. *Medicine & Empire 1600–1960*. Palgrave Macmillan, 2014.

Chakrabarti, Pratik. " 'Signs of the Times': Medicine and Nationhood in British India." *Osiris* 24 (2009): 188–211.

Chakrabarty, Dipesh. *Provincializing Europe: Postcolonial Thought and Historical Difference*. Princeton University Press, 2000.

Chakraborti, Dipankar, et al. "Groundwater Arsenic Contamination in Bangladesh—21 Years of Research." *Journal of Trace Elements in Medicine and Biology* 31 (2015): 237–48.

Chakraborty (or Chakrabarti), Pratik. "Science, Nationalism, and Colonial Contestations: P. C. Ray and His *Hindu Chemistry*." *Indian Economic and Social History Review* 37, no. 2 (2000): 185–213.

Chan, Shelly, Yoav Di-Capua, Catherine Cymone Fourshey, Joshua L. Reid, and Wendy Warren, eds. "Histories of Resilience." Special issue, *American Historical Review* 129, no. 4 (2024).

Chatterjee, Partha. *The Nation and Its Fragments: Colonial and Postcolonial Histories*. Princeton University Press, 1993.

Chatterjee, Partha. *A Princely Impostor? The Strange and Universal History of the Kumar of Bhawal*. Princeton University Press, 2002.

Cocks, Raymond. " 'The Bengal Boiler': Legal Networks in Colonial Calcutta." In *Networks and Connections in Legal History*, edited by Michael Lobban and Ian Williams. Cambridge University Press, 2020.

Cohn, Samuel K., Jr. "The Black Death and the Burning of Jews." *Past & Present* 196 (2007): 3–36.

Cole, Simon A. "Afterword: A Tale of Two Cities? Locating the History of Forensic Science and Medicine in Contemporary Forensic Reform Discourse." In Burney and Hamlin, *Global Forensic Cultures*.

Cole, Simon A. "Forensic Culture as Epistemic Culture: The Sociology of Forensic Science." *Studies in History and Philosophy of Biological and Biomedical Sciences* 44 (2013): 36–46.

Cole, Simon A. *Suspect Identities: A History of Fingerprinting and Criminal Identification*. Harvard University Press, 2001.

Cook, Karoline P. *Forbidden Passages: Muslims and Moriscos in Colonial Spanish America*. University of Pennsylvania Press, 2016.

Couzens, K. A. "The Police Surgeon, Medico-Legal Networks and Criminal Investigation in Victorian Scotland." In *Crime and the Construction of Forensic Objectivity from 1850*, edited by Alison Adam. Palgrave Macmillan, 2020.

Creager, Angela N. H. "To Test or Not to Test: Tools, Rules, and Corporate Data in US Chemicals Regulation." *Science, Technology, and Human Values* 46, no. 5 (2021): 975–97.

Crowther, M. Anne, and Brenda White. *On Soul and Conscience: The Medical Expert and Crime; 150 Years of Forensic Medicine in Glasgow*. Aberdeen University Press, 1988.

Daly, Sam Fury Childs. *A History of the Republic of Biafra: Law, Crime, and the Nigerian Civil War*. Cambridge University Press, 2020.

Damaška, Mirjan A. *Evidence Law Adrift*. Yale University Press, 1995.

Davis, Angela J., ed. *Policing the Black Man: Arrest, Prosecution, and Imprisonment*. Pantheon Books, 2017.

Davis, Donald R., Jr. *The Boundaries of Hindu Law: Tradition, Custom and Politics in Medieval Kerala*. Turin: CESMEO, 2004.

Davis, Donald R., Jr., and John Nemec. "Legal Consciousness in Medieval Indian Narratives." *Law, Culture and the Humanities* 12, no. 1 (2016): 106–31.

Davis, Natalie Zemon. *The Return of Martin Guerre*. Harvard University Press, 1983.

De, Rohit. "Emasculating the Executive: The Federal Court and Civil Liberties in Late Colonial India: 1942–1944." In *Fates of Political Liberalism in the British Post-Colony: The Politics of the Legal Complex*, edited by Terence C. Halliday, Lucien Karpik, and Malcolm M. Feeley. Cambridge University Press, 2012.

De, Rohit. *A People's Constitution: The Everyday Life of Law in the Indian Republic*. Princeton University Press, 2018.

De, Rohit. "'A Peripatetic World Court': Cosmopolitan Courts, Nationalist Judges and the Indian Appeal to the Privy Council." *Law and History Review* 32, no. 4 (2014): 821–51.

Deitsch, Adam. "An Inconvenient Tooth: Forensic Odontology Is an Inadmissible Junk Science When It Is Used to 'Match' Teeth to Bitemarks in Skin." *Wisconsin Law Review* 2009, no. 5: 1205–36.

Derrett, J. Duncan M. *Religion, Law, and the State in India*. Oxford University Press, 1999.

Devine, T. M. *Scotland's Empire 1600–1815*. Allen Lane, 2003.

Dietz, Simone. "White and Prosocial Lies." In the *Oxford Handbook of Lying*, edited by Joerg Meibauer. Oxford: Oxford University Press, 2019.

Encarnacion, Erik. "Boilerplate Indignity." *Indiana Law Journal* 94, no. 4 (2019): 1305–50.

Erdoes, Richard, and Alfonso Ortiz, eds. *American Indian Trickster Tales*. Viking, 1998.

Ernst, Waltraud. "The Indianization of Colonial Medicine: The Case of Psychiatry in Early Twentieth-Century British India." *Naturwissenschaften, Technik und Medizin* 20 (2012): 61–89.

Evans, Catherine. *Unsound Empire: Civilization and Madness in Late-Victorian Law*. Yale University Press, 2021.

Farid, Cynthia. "Perceiving Law Without Colonialism: Revisiting Courts and Constitutionalism in South Asia." *International Journal of Law in Context* 19, no. 3 (2023): 278–95.

Farmer, Lindsay. "Arthur and Oscar (and Sherlock): The Reconstructive Trial and the 'Hermeneutics of Suspicion.'" *International Commentary on Evidence* 5, no. 1 (2007): 1–17.

Feldman, Eric A. "The Tuna Court: Law and Norms in the World's Premier Fish Market." *California Law Review* 94 (2006): 313–69.

Findley, Keith A. "Innocence Found: The New Revolution in American Criminal Justice." In *Controversies in Innocence Cases in America*, edited by Sarah Lucy Cooper. Ashgate, 2014.

Findley, Keith A., Cyrille Rossant, Kana Sasakura, Leila Schneps, Waney Squier, and Knut Wester, eds. *Shaken Baby Syndrome: Investigating the Abusive Head Trauma Controversy*. Cambridge University Press, 2023.

Fisch, Jorg. *Cheap Lives and Dear Limbs: The British Transformation of the Bengal Criminal Law, 1769–1817*. Wiesbaden: F. Steiner, 1983.

Fischer-Tiné, Harald, ed. *Anxieties, Fear and Panic in Colonial Settings: Empires on the Verge of a Nervous Breakdown*. Palgrave Macmillan, 2016.

Fisher, Michael H. *Indirect Rule in India: Residents and the Residency System, 1764–1858*. Oxford University Press, 1991.

Forbes, Geraldine. *Women in Modern India: The New Cambridge History of India*. Cambridge University Press, 1996.

Fox, Margalit. *Conan Doyle for the Defense: The True Story of a Sensational British Murder, a Quest for Justice, and the World's Most Famous Detective Writer*. Random House, 2018.

Gambetta, Diego. "Corruption: An Analytical Map." In Kreike and Jordan, *Corrupt Histories*.

Gaonkar, Dilip Parameshwar. "On Alternative Modernities." In *Alternative Modernities*, edited by Dilip Parameshwar Gaonkar. Duke University Press, 2001.

Garg, Arushi. "Thomas Macaulay, the Indian Penal Code (1837)." In *Leading Works in Criminal Law*, edited by Chloë Kennedy and Lindsay Farmer. Routledge, 2024.

Garrett, Brandon. *Convicting the Innocent: Where Criminal Prosecutions Go Wrong*. Harvard University Press, 2011.

Gélinas, Fabien, Clément Camion, Karine Bates, et al. *Foundations of Civil Justice: Toward a Value-Based Framework for Reform*. Springer, 2015.

Ghosh, Durba. "Gandhi and the Terrorists: Revolutionary Challenges from Bengal and Engagements with Non-Violent Political Protest." *South Asia: Journal of South Asian Studies* 39, no. 3 (2016): 560–76.

Ghosh, Durba. *Gentlemanly Terrorists: Political Violence and the Colonial State in India, 1919–1947*. Cambridge University Press, 2017.

Ginsburg, Ruth Bader. "The Role of Dissenting Opinions." *Minnesota Law Review* 95, no. 1 (2010): 1–8.

Golan, Tal. *Laws of Men and Laws of Nature: The History of Scientific Expert Testimony in England and America*. Harvard University Press, 2004.

Goluboff, Risa. *The Lost Promise of Civil Rights*. Harvard University Press, 2007.

Gould, William. *Bureaucracy, Community and Influence in India: Society and the State, 1930s–1960s*. Routledge, 2011.

Grafton, Anthony. *Forgers and Critics: Creativity and Duplicity in Western Scholarship*. Princeton University Press, 1990.

Greif, Avner. "Impersonal Exchange Without Impartial Law: The Community Responsibility System." *Chicago Journal of International Law* 109 (2004–5): 109–38.

Groot, Joanna de. "Depicting Conflict in India in 1857–8: The Instabilities of Gender, Violence, and Colonialism." *Cultural and Social History* 14, no. 4 (2017): 463–82.

Groves, Matthew. "Law, Religion and Public Order in Colonial India: Contextualising the 1887 Allahabad High Court Case on 'Sacred' Cows." *South Asia: Journal of South Asian Studies* 33, no. 1 (2010): 87–121.

Guha, Ranajit. *Dominance Without Hegemony: History and Power in Colonial India*. Harvard University Press, 1997.

Guha, Ranajit. *Elementary Aspects of Peasant Insurgency in Colonial India*. Duke University Press, 1999.

Gulati, Karan, and Renuka Sane. "Consumer Disputes in the Financial Sector—Grievance Redress by Courts." *Indian Law Review* 6, no. 3 (2022): 409–33.

Hamlin, Christopher. "Forensic Facts, the Guts of Rights." In Burney and Hamlin, *Global Forensic Cultures*.

Hamlin, Christopher. "Scientific Method and Expert Witnessing: Victorian Perspectives on a Modern Problem." *Social Studies of Science* 16 (1986): 485–513.

Hamlin, Christopher, and Ian Burney, "History of Forensic Science." In *Encyclopedia of Forensic Sciences*, vol. 3, edited by Max M. Houck. Elsevier, 2023.

Harrison, Mark. *Public Health in British India: Anglo-Indian Preventive Medicine, 1859–1914*. Cambridge University Press, 1994.

Harvey, L. P. "The Political, Social and Cultural History of the Moriscos." In *The Legacy of Muslim Spain*, edited by Salma Khadra Jayyusi. Brill, 1992.

Heath, Deana. *Colonial Terror: Torture and State Violence in Colonial India*. Oxford University Press, 2021.

Heath, Deana. "Torture, the State, and Sexual Violence Against Men in Colonial India." *Radical History Review* 126 (2016): 122–33.

Hinchy, Jessica. "Conjugality, Colonialism and the 'Criminal Tribes' in North India." *Studies in History* 36, no. 1 (2020): 20–46.

Hinchy, Jessica. "Gender, Family, and the Policing of the 'Criminal Tribes' in Nineteenth-Century North India." *Modern Asian Studies* 54, no. 5 (2020): 1669–1711.

Hinchy, Jessica. *Governing Gender and Sexuality in Colonial India: The Hijra, c. 1850–1900*. Cambridge University Press, 2019.

Hobbins, Peter. *Venomous Encounters: Snakes, Vivisection and Scientific Medicine in Colonial Australia*. Manchester University Press, 2017.

Hofmeyr, Isabel. *Gandhi's Printing Press: Experiments in Slow Reading*. Harvard University Press, 2013.

Houlbrook, Matt. *Prince of Tricksters: The Incredible True Story of Netley Lucas, Gentleman Crook*. University of Chicago Press, 2016.

Howell, P. A. *The Judicial Committee of the Privy Council, 1833–1876*. Cambridge University Press, 1979.

Ingram, Kevin, ed. *The Conversos and Moriscos in Late Medieval Spain and Beyond*. Vol. 1, *Departures and Change*. Brill, 2009.

Jaffe, James A. "After Nanavati." *Economic and Political Weekly* 53, no. 32 (2017): 18–20.

Jaffe, James A. "Custom, Identity, and the Jury in India, 1800–1832." *Historical Journal* 57, no. 1 (2014): 131–55.

Jaffe, James A. *Ironies of Colonial Governance: Law, Custom and Justice in Colonial India*. Cambridge University Press, 2015.

Jain, M. P. *Outlines of Indian Legal and Constitutional History*. Gurgaon: LexisNexis Butterworths Wadhwa, Nagpur, 2006.

Jasanoff, Sheila. *Science at the Bar: Law, Science, and Technology in America*. Harvard University Press, 1995.

Jentzen, Jeffrey M. "Death and Empire: Medicolegal Investigations and Practice Across the British Empire." In Burney and Hamlin, *Global Forensic Cultures*.

Jentzen, Jeffrey M. *Death Investigation in America: Coroners, Medical Examiners, and the Pursuit of Medical Certainty*. Harvard University Press, 2009.

Jones, Oliver. "*Public Prosecutor v. Oie Hee Koi* (1968): Not So Humbly Advising? Sir Garfield Barwick and the Introduction of Dissenting Reasons to the Judicial

Committee of the Privy Council." In *Great Australian Dissents*, edited by Andrew Lynch. Cambridge University Press, 2016.

Juss, Satvinder Singh. *The Execution of Bhagat Singh: Legal Heresies of the Raj*. Stroud, UK: Amberley, 2020.

Kadyan, Sneha, and N. Prabha Unnithan. "The Continuing Non-Criminalization of Marital Rape in India: A Critical Analysis." *Women & Criminal Justice* (2023): 1–14.

Kalathil, Suramya Thekke, and Santhosh Abraham. "Regulation and Resistance: Defactorisation in the Beedi Industry of Colonial Malabar, 1937–1942." *Labor History* 61, no. 5–6 (2020): 658–76.

Kannabiran, Kalpana. "A Ravished Justice: Half a Century of Judicial Discourse on Rape." In *De-Eroticizing Assault: Essays on Modesty, Honor and Power*, edited by K. Kannabiran and V. Kannabiran. Calcutta: Stree, 2002.

Kapila, Shruti. "Gandhi Before Mahatma: The Foundations of Political Truth." *Public Culture* 23, no. 2 (2011): 431–48.

Kelly, Catherine, and Imogen Goold. "Introduction: Lawyers' Medicine: The Interaction of the Medical Profession and the Law, 1760–2000." In *Lawyers' Medicine: The Legislature, the Courts and Medical Practice, 1760–2000*, edited by Imogen Goold and Catherine Kelly. Hart, 2009.

Kessler, Amalia D. *Inventing American Exceptionalism: The Origins of American Adversarial Legal Culture, 1800–1877*. Yale University Press, 2017.

Kessler, Amalia D. "Our Inquisitorial Tradition: Equity Procedure, Due Process, and the Search for an Alternative to the Adversarial." *Cornell Law Review* 90, no. 5 (2005): 1181–1275.

Khorakiwala, Rahela. *From the Colonial to the Contemporary: Images, Iconography, Memories, and Performances of Law in India's High Courts*. Hart, 2019.

Knights, Mark, and Zak Leonard. "Bribery in Baroda: The Politics of Corruption in Nineteenth-Century India." In *Corruption, Empire, and Colonialism in the Modern Era: A Global Perspective*, edited by Ronald Kroeze, Pol Dalmau, and Frédéric Monier. Palgrave Macmillan, 2021.

Kohlberg, Etan. "*Taqiyya* in Shi'i Theology and Religion." In *Secrecy and Concealment: Studies in the History of Mediterranean and Near Eastern Religions*, edited by Hans G. Kippenberg and Guy G. Stroumsa. Brill, 1995.

Kolsky, Elizabeth. "'The Body Evidencing the Crime': Rape on Trial in Colonial India, 1860–1947." *Gender & History* 22, no. 1 (2010): 109–30.

Kolsky, Elizabeth. "Codification and the Rule of Colonial Difference: Criminal Procedure in British India." *Law and History Review* 23, no. 3 (2005): 631–83.

Kolsky, Elizabeth. *Colonial Justice in British India: White Violence and the Rule of Law*. Cambridge University Press, 2010.

Kolsky, Elizabeth. "Rule of Colonial Indifference: Rape on Trial in Early Colonial India, 1805–57." *Journal of Asian Studies* 69, no. 4 (2010): 1093–1117.

Kreike, Emmanuel, and William Chester Jordan, eds. *Corrupt Histories*. University of Rochester Press, 2004.

Kumar, Radha. *Police Matters: The Everyday State and Caste Politics in South India, 1900–1975*. Cornell University Press, 2021.

Kumar, Radha. "Witnessing Violence, Witnessing as Violence: Police Torture and Power in Twentieth-Century India." *Law & Social Inquiry* 47, no. 3 (2022): 946–70.

Lahiri, Simanti. *Suicide Protest in South Asia: Consumed by Commitment*. Routledge, 2014.

Lal, Vinay. "Everyday Crime, Native Mendacity and the Cultural Psychology of Justice in Colonial India." *Studies in History* 15 (1999): 145–66.

Landsman, Stephan. "A Brief Survey on the Development of the Adversary System." *Ohio State Law Journal* 44 (1983): 713–39.

Langbein, John H. *The Origins of Adversary Criminal Trial*. Oxford University Press, 2005.

Lhost, Elizabeth. *Everyday Islamic Law and the Making of Modern South Asia*. University of North Carolina Press, 2022.

Lokaneeta, Jinee. *The Truth Machines: Policing, Violence, and Scientific Interrogations in India*. University of Michigan Press, 2020.

MacKenzie, John M., and T. M. Devine, eds. *Scotland and the British Empire*. Oxford University Press, 2011.

Macklin, Graham. "The Two Lives of John Hooper Harvey." *Patterns of Prejudice* 42, no. 2 (2008): 167–90.

Manmadhan, Ullattil. "Doyle and the Edalji Case." *National Medical Journal of India* 29, no. 5 (2016): n.p.

Maxwell, Clarence V. H. " 'The Horrid Villainy': Sarah Bassett and the Poisoning Conspiracies in Bermuda, 1727–30." *Slavery and Abolition* 21, no. 3 (2000): 48–74.

Mays, Devi. *Forging Ties, Forging Passports: Migration and the Modern Sephardi Diaspora*. Stanford University Press, 2020.

McClure, Alastair. "Archaic Sovereignty and Colonial Law: The Reintroduction of Corporal Punishment in Colonial India, 1864–1909." *Modern Asian Studies* 54, no. 5 (2020): 1712–47.

McClure, Alastair. "Killing in the Name Of? Capital Punishment in Colonial and Postcolonial India." *Law and History Review* 41 (2023): 365–85.

McClure, Alastair. *Trials of Sovereignty: Mercy, Violence, and the Making of Criminal Law in British India, 1857–1922*. Cambridge University Press, 2024.

McIntyre, Joe. "In Defence of Judicial Dissent." *Adelaide Law Review* 37, no. 2 (2016): 431–59.

McMurtie, Jacqueline. "The Innocence Network: From Beginning to Branding." In *Controversies in Innocence Cases in America*, edited by Sarah Lucy Cooper. Ashgate, 2014.

McNicholas, Mark. *Forgery and Impersonation in Imperial China: Popular Deceptions and the High Qing State*. University of Washington Press, 2016.

Medwed, Daniel S. *Wrongful Convictions and the DNA Revolution: Twenty-Five Years of Freeing the Innocent*. Cambridge University Press, 2017.

Meharg, Andrew A. *Venomous Earth: How Arsenic Caused the World's Worst Mass Poisoning*. Macmillan, 2005.

Mehta, Uday Singh. *Liberalism and Empire: A Study in Nineteenth-Century British Liberal Thought*. University of Chicago Press, 1999.

Merry, Sally Engle. "Legal Pluralism." *Law & Society Review* 22, no. 5 (1988): 869–96.

Michaels, David, and Neil Vidmar, eds. "Sequestered Science: The Consequences of Undisclosed Knowledge." Special issue, *Law and Contemporary Problems* 69, no. 3 (2006).

Mihm, Stephen. *A Nation of Counterfeiters: Capitalists, Con Men, and the Making of the United States*. Harvard University Press, 2007.

Mishra, Saurabh. *Beastly Encounters of the Raj: Livelihoods, Livestock, and Veterinary Health in North India, 1790–1920*. University of Manchester Press, 2015.

Mitchell, Peter. *Imperial Nostalgia: How the British Conquered Themselves*. University of Manchester Press, 2021.

Mitra, Durba. *Indian Sex Life: Sexuality and the Colonial Origins of Modern Social Thought*. Princeton University Press, 2020.

Mitra, Durba, and Mrinal Satish. "Testing Chastity, Evidencing Rape: Impact of Medical Jurisprudence on Rape Adjudication in India." *Economic & Political Weekly* 49, no. 41 (2014): 51–58.

Mizutani, Satoshi. *The Meaning of White: Race, Class, and the "Domiciled Community" in British India 1858–1930*. Oxford University Press, 2011.

Mnookin, Jennifer. "Idealizing Science and Demonizing Experts: An Intellectual History of Expert Evidence." *Villanova Law Review* 52, no. 4 (2007): 763–801.

Mohr, James C. *Doctors and the Law: Medical Jurisprudence in Nineteenth-Century America*. Johns Hopkins University Press, 1993.

Morgan, Winifred. *The Trickster Figure in American Literature*. Palgrave Macmillan, 2013.

Mossman, Mary Jane. "Gender and Professionalism in Law: The Challenge of (Women's) Biography." *Windsor Yearbook of Access to Justice* 27, no. 1 (2009): 19–34.

Mukharji, Projit Bihari. *Brown Skins, White Coats: Race Science in India, 1920–66*. University of Chicago Press, 2022.

Mukharji, Projit Bihari. *Doctoring Traditions: Ayurveda, Small Technologies, and Braided Sciences*. University of Chicago Press, 2016.

Mukharji, Projit Bihari. "From Serosocial to Sanguinary Identities: Caste, Transnational Race Science and the Shifting Metonymies of Blood Group B, India c. 1918–1960." *Indian Economic and Social History Review* 51, no. 2 (2014): 143–76.

Mukharji, Projit Bihari. "Gariahat Whisky: Bootlegged Cosmopolitanism and the Making of the Nationalistic State, Calcutta, c. 1923–1935." In *Alcohol Flows Across Cultures: Drinking Cultures in Transnational and Comparative Perspective*, edited by Waltraud Ernst. Routledge, 2020.

Mukharji, Projit Bihari. "Handwriting Analysis as a Dynamic Artisanal Science: The Hardless Detective Dynasty and the Forensic Cultures of the British Raj." In Burney and Hamlin, *Global Forensic Cultures*.

Mukharji, Projit Bihari. "Sero-Tropicality: Blood and the Reinvention of Tropical Medicine, 1930–50." Talk presented at the University of Wisconsin–Madison, March 20, 2015.

Mukherjee, Debashree. *Bombay Hustle: Making Movies in a Colonial City*. Columbia University Press, 2020.

Mukherjee, Sujata. *Gender, Medicine, and Society in Colonial India: Women's Health Care in Nineteenth- and Early Twentieth-Century Bengal*. Oxford University Press, 2017.

Nanda, B. B., and R. K. Tewari. *Forensic Science in India: A Vision for the Twenty-First Century*. Delhi: Select, 2001.

Neill, Jeremy. " 'This Is a Most Disgusting Case': Imperial Policy, Class and Gender in the 'Rangoon Outrage' of 1899." *Journal of Colonialism and Colonial History* 12, no. 1 (2011): [1–23].

Newton, Melanie J. "The King v. Robert James, a Slave, for Rape: Inequality, Gender, and British Slave Amelioration, 1823–1834." *Comparative Studies in Society and History* 47, no. 3 (2005): 583–610.

Orsini, Francesca. "Detective Novels: A Commercial Genre in Nineteenth-Century North India." In *India's Literary History: Essays on the Nineteenth Century*, edited by Stuart Blackburn and Vasudha Dalmia. Delhi: Permanent Black, 2004.

Oza, Rupal. *Semiotics of Rape: Sexual Subjectivity and Violation in Rural India*. Duke University Press, 2023.

Pande, Ishita. *Sex, Law, and the Politics of Age: Child Marriage in India, 1891–1937*. Cambridge University Press, 2020.

Pavarala, Vinod. "Cultures of Corruption and the Corruption of Culture: The East India Company and the Hastings Impeachment." In Kreike and Jordan, *Corrupt Histories*.

Pearson, Trais. *Sovereign Necropolis: The Politics of Death in Semi-Colonial Siam*. Cornell University Press, 2020.

Penningroth, Dylan C. "Race in Contract Law." *University of Pennsylvania Law Review* 170 (2022): 1199–1301.

Pernau, Margrit. *Emotions and Modernity in Colonial India: From Balance to Fervor*. Oxford University Press, 2020.

Pinch, Trevor. "Coda: Testing and Why It Matters." In *Testing Hearing: The Making of Modern Aurality*, edited by Viktoria Tkaczyk, Mara Mills, and Alexandra Hui. Oxford University Press, 2020.

Pinch, Trevor. "'Testing—One, Two, Three . . . Testing!': Toward a Sociology of Testing." *Science, Technology, and Human Values* 10, no. 1 (1993): 25–41.

Prakash, Gyan. *Another Reason: Science and the Imagination of Modern India*. Princeton University Press, 1999.

Provost, Fabien. *Les mots de la morgue: La médicine légale en Inde du Nord*. Éditions Mimésis, 2021.

Puri, Jyoti. *Sexual States: Governance and the Struggle over the Antisodomy Law in India*. Duke University Press, 2016.

Radin, Joanna. *Life on Ice: A History of New Uses for Cold Blood*. University of Chicago Press, 2017.

Raman, Bhavani. *Document Raj: Writing and Scribes in Early Colonial South India*. University of Chicago Press, 2012.

Ramanna, Mridula. "Women Physicians as Vital Intermediaries in Colonial Bombay." *Economic and Political Weekly* 43, nos. 12–13 (2008): 71–78.

Ramnath, Kalyani. "The Colonial Difference Between Law and Fact: Notes on the Criminal Jury in India." *Indian Economic and Social History Review* 50, no. 3 (2013): 341–63.

Randall, Marilynn. "Imperial Plagiarism." In *Perspectives on Plagiarism and Intellectual Property in a Postmodern World*, edited by Lisa Buranen and Alice M. Roy. State University of New York Press, 1999.

Rawat, Ramnarayan S. *Reconsidering Untouchability: Chamars and Dalit History in North India*. Indiana University Press, 2011.

Ray, Sharmita. "Women Doctors' Masterful Maneuverings: Colonial Bengal, Late Nineteenth and Early Twentieth Centuries." *Social Scientist* 42, nos. 3–4 (2014): 59–76.

Reitz, Caroline. *Detecting the Nation: Fictions of Detection and the Imperial Venture*. Ohio State University Press, 2004.

Ren, Chao. "The Spectre of Ma Phyu? Loyalty, Competence, and the Spatial Dynamics of Imperial Administration in Colonial Burma." *Modern Asian Studies* 58, no. 2 (2024): 536–62.

Resnik, Judith. "Diffusing Disputes: The Public in the Private of Arbitration, the Private in Courts, and the Erasure of Rights." *Yale Law Journal* 124, no. 8 (2015): 2804–2939.

Risinger, D. Michael. "Boxes in Boxes: Julian Barnes, Conan Doyle, Sherlock Holmes, and the Edalji Case." *International Commentary on Evidence* 4, no. 2 (2006): 1–90.

Roach, Levi. *Forgery and Memory at the End of the First Millennium*. Princeton University Press, 2021.

Robb, Megan Eaton. *Print and the Urdu Public: Muslims, Newspapers, and Urban Life in Colonial India*. Oxford University Press, 2020.

Robertson, Stephen. "Signs, Marks, and Private Parts: Doctors, Legal Discourses, and Evidence of Rape in the United States, 1823–1930." *Journal of the History of Sexuality* 8, no. 3 (1998): 345–88.

Rosenfeld, Sophie. *Democracy and Truth: A Short History*. University of Pennsylvania Press, 2019.

Roy, Shampa. *Gender and Criminality in Bangla Crime Narratives*. Palgrave Macmillan, 2017.

Roy Chaudhury, Shrimoy. "Toxic Matters: Medical Jurisprudence and the Making of the Indian Poisons Act (1904)." *Crime, History & Societies* 22, no. 1 (2018): 81–105.

Saha, Jonathan. "'Devious Documents': Corruption and Paperwork in Colonial Burma, Circa 1900." In *Subverting Empire: Deviance and Disorder in the British Colonial World*, edited by Will Jackson and Emily J. Manktelow. Palgrave Macmillan, 2015.

Saha, Jonathan. *Law, Disorder and the Colonial State: Corruption in Burma c. 1900*. Palgrave Macmillan, 2013.

Saha, Jonathan. "Madness and the Making of a Colonial Order in Burma." *Modern Asian Studies* 47, no. 2 (2013): 406–35.

Saha, Jonathan. "The Male State: Colonialism, Corruption and Rape Investigations in the Irrawaddy Delta c. 1900." *Indian Economic & Social History Review* 47 (2010): 343–76.

Saha, Jonathan. "Paperwork as Commodity, Corruption as Accumulation: Land Records and Licenses in Colonial Myanmar, c. 1900." In *Corruption, Empire and Colonialism in the Modern Era: A Global Perspective*, edited by Ronald Kroeze, Pol Dalmau, and Frédéric Monier. Palgrave Macmillan, 2021.

Saha, Jonathan. "'Uncivilized Practitioners': Medical Subordinates, Medico-Legal Evidence, and Misconduct in Colonial Burma, 1875–1907." *South East Asia Research* 20, no. 3 (2012): 423–43.

Saha, Jonathan. "Whiteness, Masculinity and the Ambivalent Embodiment of 'British Justice' in Colonial Burma." *Cultural and Social History* 14, no. 4 (2017): 527–42.

Said, Edward. *Orientalism*. Vintage, 2003.

Sanyal, Indranil. "Dr. Chunilal Bose: A Forgotten Scientist and a Science Communicator." *Indian Journal of History of Science* 57 (2022): 151–69.

Satish, Mrinal. *Discretion, Discrimination and the Rule of Law: Reforming Rape Sentencing in India*. Cambridge University Press, 2017.

Schickore, Jutte. *About Method: Experimenters, Snake Venom, and the History of Writing Scientifically*. University of Chicago Press, 2017.

Schneider, Wendie Ellen. *Engines of Truth: Producing Veracity in the Victorian Classroom*. Yale University Press, 2015.

Scott, James C. *Weapons of the Weak: Everyday Forms of Peasant Resistance*. Yale University Press, 1985.

Sehrawat, Samiksha. "Feminising Empire: The Association of Medical Women in India and the Campaign to Found a Women's Medical Service." *Social Scientist* 41, nos. 5–6 (2013): 65–81.

Seidman Diamond, Shari, and Richard O. Lempert, eds. "Science and the Legal System." Special issue, *Daedalus* 147, no. 4 (2018).

Sengoopta, Chandak. *Imprint of the Raj: How Fingerprinting Was Born in Colonial India*. Macmillan, 2003.

Sethi, Manisha. *Kafkaland: Prejudice, Law and Counterterrorism in India*. Gurgaon: Three Essays Collective, 2014.

Sharafi, Mitra. "Abortion in South Asia, 1860–1947: A Medico-Legal History." *Modern Asian Studies* 55, no. 2 (2021): 371–428.

Sharafi, Mitra. "Indian Constitutionalism, the Rule of Law, and Parsi Legal Culture." *Indian Law Review* 7, no. 3 (2023): 259–80.

Sharafi, Mitra. "Judging Conversion to Zoroastrianism: Behind the Scenes of the Parsi Panchayat Case (1908)." In *Parsis in India and the Diaspora*, edited by John R. Hinnells and Alan Williams. Routledge, 2007.

Sharafi, Mitra. *Law and Identity in Colonial South Asia: Parsi Legal Culture, 1772–1947*. Cambridge University Press, 2014.

Sharafi, Mitra. "Parsi Life Writing: Memoirs and Family Histories of Modern Zoroastrians." In *Holy Wealth: Accounting for This World and the Next in Religious Belief and Practice; Festschrift for John R. Hinnells*, edited by Almut Hintze and Alan Williams. Wiesbaden: Harrassowitz, 2017.

Sharafi, Mitra. "South Asians at the Inns of Court: Empire, Expulsion, and Redemption Circa 1900." In *In Between and Across: Legal History Without Boundaries*, edited by Kenneth Mack and Jacob Cogan. Oxford University Press, 2024.

Sharpe, Jenny. "The Unspeakable Limits of Rape: Colonial Violence and Counter-Insurgency." *Genders* 10 (1991): 25–46.

Shmuely, Shira. *The Bureaucracy of Empathy: Law, Vivisection, and Animal Pain in Late Nineteenth-Century Britain*. Cornell University Press, 2023.

Shmuely, Shira. "Law and the Laboratory: The British Vivisection Inspectorate in the 1890s." *Law & Social Inquiry* 46, no. 4 (2021): 933–63.

Singh, Charu. "Science in the Vernacular? Translation, Terminology and Lexicography in the *Hindi Scientific Glossary* (1906)." *South Asian History and Culture* 13, no. 1 (2022): 63–86.

Singh, Charu. "The Shastri and the Air-Pump: Experimental Fictions and Fictions of Experiment for Hindi Readers in Colonial North India." *History of Science* 60, no. 2 (2022): 232–54.

Singh, Gagan Preet. "Forensics, Body and State Power in South Asia: Recent Interventions and Their Importance." *History Compass* 19, no. 11 (2021): 1–11.

Singh, Yogesh Pratap. *Judicial Dissent and the Indian Supreme Court*. Delhi: Thomson Reuters, 2018.

Singha, Radhika. *The Coolie's Great War: Indian Labor in a Global Conflict, 1914–1932*. Oxford University Press, 2020.

Singha, Radhika. *A Despotism of Law: Crime and Justice in Early Colonial India*. Oxford University Press, 1998.

Singha, Radhika. "Punished by Surveillance: Policing 'Dangerousness' in Colonial India, 1872–1918." *Modern Asian Studies* 48, no. 1 (2014): 1–29.

Singha, Radhika. "Settle, Mobilize, Verify: Identification Practices in Colonial India." *Studies in History* 16, no. 2 (2000): 151–98.

Sinha, Mrinalini. *Colonial Masculinity: The "Manly Englishman" and the "Effeminate Bengali" in Late Nineteenth-Century India*. Manchester University Press, 1995.

Skuy, David. "Macaulay and the Indian Penal Code of 1862: The Myth of the Inherent Superiority and Modernity of the English Legal System Compared to India's Legal System in the Nineteenth Century." *Modern Asian Studies* 32, no. 3 (1998): 513–57.

Sriraman, Tarangini. *In Pursuit of Proof: A History of Identification Documents in India*. Oxford University Press, 2018.

Suresh, Mayur. *Terror Trials: Life and Law in Delhi's Courts*. Fordham University Press, 2023.

Tambe, Ashwini. *Codes of Misconduct: Regulating Prostitution in Late Colonial Bombay*. Delhi: Zubaan, 2009.

Tambe, Ashwini. *Defining Girlhood in India: A Transnational History of Sexual Maturity Laws*. University of Illinois Press, 2019.

Terkourafi, Marina. "Lying and Politeness." In *The Oxford Handbook of Lying*, edited by Joerg Meibauer. Oxford University Press, 2019.

Tewari, R. K., and K. V. Ravikumar. "History and Development of Forensic Science in India." *Journal of Postgraduate Medicine* 46, no. 4 (2000): 303–8.

Thomas, Ronald R. *Detective Fiction and the Rise of Forensic Science*. Cambridge University Press, 1999.

Thompson, Edward, and G. T. Garratt. *Rise and Fulfilment of British Rule in India*. Allahabad: Central Book Depot, 1962.

Thornberry, Elizabeth. *Colonizing Consent: Rape and Governance in South Africa's Eastern Cape*. Cambridge University Press, 2019.

Tilley, Cristina Carmody. "Just Strict Liability." *Cardozo Law Review* 43 (2022): 2317–84.

Tilstone, William J., Kathleen A. Savage, and Leigh A. Clark, eds. *Forensic Science: An Encyclopedia of History, Methods, and Techniques*. ABC Clio, 2006.

Travers, Robert. *Ideology and Empire in Eighteenth-Century India*. Cambridge University Press, 2007.

Tuerkheimer, Deborah. *Flawed Convictions: "Shaken Baby Syndrome" and the Inertia of Injustice*. Oxford University Press, 2014.

Twining, William. "Normative and Legal Pluralism: A Global Perspective." *Duke Journal of Comparative and International Law* 20 (2010): 473–517.

Virani, Shafique N. "*Taqiyya* and Identity in a South Asian Community." *Journal of Asian Studies* 70, no. 1 (2011): 99–139.

Wagner, Kim A. *Thuggee: Banditry and the British in Early Nineteenth-Century India*. Palgrave Macmillan, 2007.

Watson, Katherine D. "Criminal Poisoning in England and the Origins of the Marsh Test for Arsenic." In *Chemistry, Medicine, and Crime: Mateu J. B. Orfila (1787–1853) and His Times*, edited by José Ramón Bertomeu-Sánchez and Agustí Nieto-Galan. Science History Publications, 2006.

Watson, Katherine D. *Forensic Medicine in Western Society: A History*. Routledge, 2011.

Wedel, Janine R. "Rethinking Corruption in an Age of Ambiguity." *Annual Review of Law and Social Science* 8 (2012): 453–98.

Whelan, Christopher. *The Bodyguard of Lies: Lawyers' Power and Professional Responsibility*. Hart, 2022.

White, Brenda. "Training Medical Policemen: Forensic Medicine and Public Health in Nineteenth-Century Scotland." In *Legal Medicine in History*, edited by Michael Clark and Catherine Crawford. Cambridge University, 1994.

Wiener, Martin J. *Men of Blood: Violence, Manliness, and Criminal Justice in Victorian England*. Cambridge University Press, 2004.

Winter, Alison. *Memory: Fragments of a Modern History*. University of Chicago Press, 2012.

Wolffram, Heather. *Forensic Psychology in Germany: Witnessing Crime, 1880–1939*. Palgrave Macmillan, 2018.

Wood, Laurie M. "Recovering the Debris of Fortunes Between France and Its Colonies in the 18th Century." *Journal of Social History* 51, no. 4 (2018): 808–36.

Woods, Rebecca J. H. "Nature and the Refrigerating Machine: The Politics and Production of Cold in the Nineteenth Century." In *Cryopolitics: Frozen Life in a Melting World*, edited by Joanna Radin and Emma Kowal. MIT Press, 2017.

Wright, Barry. "Macaulay's Indian Penal Code: Historical Context and Originating Principles." In *Codification, Macaulay and the Indian Penal Code: The Legacies and Modern Challenges of Criminal Law Reform*, edited by Wing-Cheong Chan, Barry Wright, and Stanley Yeo. Ashgate, 2011.

Zagorin, Perez. *Ways of Lying: Dissimulation, Persecution, and Conformity in Early Modern Europe*. Harvard University Press, 1990.

Unpublished Doctoral Dissertations

Achintya, T. C. A. "Practitioners of the Law: Legal Professionals in British South Asia 1770–1870." PhD diss., University of Virginia, 2025.

Duvall, Nicholas Edward. "Forensic Medicine in Scotland, 1914–39." PhD diss., University of Manchester, 2013.

Farid, Cynthia. "Imperial Constitutionalism: Judicial Politics and Separation of Powers in Colonial India (1861–1935)." SJD diss., University of Wisconsin–Madison, 2020.

Maity, Anwesha. "Imaginary Science and Cultural Signs: Mapping Postcolonial Bangla (Bengali) Science Fiction." PhD diss., University of Wisconsin–Madison, 2019.

McClure, Alastair. "Violence, Sovereignty, and the Making of Colonial Criminal Law in India, 1857–1914." PhD diss., University of Cambridge, 2017.

Mukherjee, Uponita. "Colonial Detection: Crime, Evidence, and Inquiry in British India, 1790–1910." PhD diss., Columbia University, 2022.

Rabitoy, Neil. "Sovereignty, Profits, and Social Change: The Development of British Administration in Western India, 1800–1820." PhD diss., University of Pennsylvania, 1972.

Sharafi, Mitra. "Bella's Case: Parsi Identity and the Law in Colonial Rangoon, Bombay and London, 1887–1925." PhD diss., Princeton University, 2006.

Secondary Sources Accessed Online

Beeman, William. "*Ta'arof.*" In *Encyclopedia Iranica*, online ed., 2017. https://www.iranicaonline.org/articles/taarof.

Jaffe, James A. "Calcutta and the 'Real' Last Jury Trial in India." *NSLIReview Online*, October 19, 2022. On file with author.

Sharafi, Mitra. "The History of Poison and Stereotypical Narratives." *Madras Courier*, November 12, 2018. https://madrascourier.com/opinion/the-history-of-poison-stereotypical-narratives/.

FICTION

Doyle, Arthur Conan. *The Adventures of Sherlock Holmes*. Doubleday, [1930].

Forster, E. M. *A Passage to India*. Harcourt, Brace, 1924.

Gupta, Nihar Ranjan. *Kiriti Omnibus*. Kolkata: Amar, 1972. (Bengali)

Mukhopadhyay, Priyanath. *Darogar Daptar*. Kolkata: Punashcha, 2004. (Bengali)

Ray, Hemendra Kumar. *Bimal-Kumar Adventure Samagra (Akhanda Sangskaran)*. N.p., n.d. (Bengali)

Ray, Hemendra Kumar. *Jayanta-Manik Samagra (Akhanda Sangskaran)*. N.p., n.d. (Bengali)

Smith, Zadie. *The Fraud: A Novel*. Penguin, 2023.

INDEX

Note: Page numbers in *italics* refer to illustrations.

www.ingramcontent.com/pod-product-compliance
Lightning Source LLC
Chambersburg PA
CBHW020844270326
41928CB00006B/544
9781501785986

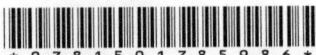